Computing:
fundamentals
and applications

Computing:
fundamentals and applications

TAYLOR L. BOOTH

YI-TZUU CHIEN

Computer Science Group
Department of Electrical Engineering and Computer Science
University of Connecticut

HAMILTON PUBLISHING COMPANY
Santa Barbara, California

Copyright © 1974, by John Wiley & Sons, Inc.

Published by **Hamilton Publishing Company**
a Division of John Wiley & Sons, Inc.

Library of Congress Cataloging in Publication Data:

Booth, Taylor L.

Computing: fundamentals and applications.

Includes bibliographies.

1. Electronic digital computers—Programming.

2. Algorithms. I. Chien, Yi-tzuu, joint author.

II. Title.

QA76.6.B65   001.6′42   73-20157

ISBN 0-471-08847-1

Printed in the United States of America

10 9 8 7 6 5 4 3 2

To Aline, Michael, Shari, and Laurine Booth

and Janet, Mark, Deborah, and Roger Chien

preface

When computers first became available for general use on college campuses there was a demand for one or more introductory programming courses designed to teach a student how to write programs (in a particular language) for execution on the local computer system. The early pressure for these courses came from the scientific areas where there was a considerable need to carry out massive calculations.

This emphasis upon the mechanics of programming occurred because most of the initial computational tasks involved performing fairly standard mathematical calculations. As the capabilities of a computer became better understood it was soon evident that the computer was a general information processing device. The point has now been reached where the information processing power of a computer is being applied to almost every possible academic discipline.

As computers have become more commonplace it has been realized that the methods used to solve a problem by hand are not necessarily the best ones to use if the problem is to be solved by the use of a computer. Many of the hand solution techniques were found to be too cumbersome to program or to rely heavily upon the intuition of the problem solver. It soon became evident that the effective use of a computer as a problem solving aid requires more than the simple ability to write a program in a particular programming language.

The introductory programming courses have now evolved into introductory computing courses where the methods of carrying out computations receive equal, and often more, attention than the techniques of writing a program in a particular programming language. This book has been developed for such a course.

A typical computer user will probably have the need to learn a number of different programming languages. This is easily accomplished if the fundamental principles of computing are understood. Thus this book is language independent. It has been designed for use in a lecture-laboratory course. In such a course the lecture portion should concentrate upon the fundamentals of the computing process while the laboratory portion should show how a particular programming language can be used to develop programs to carry out the computational concepts discussed in the lecture.

The first eight chapters of this book concentrate upon the computing process and the development of an algorithm to describe the solution of a given problem. The last seven chapters then illustrate how these ideas can be applied to a number of important problem areas.

At the University of Connecticut this book is used in an introductory computing course. It is assumed that the students have a mathematical maturity equivalent to that required by the first calculus course. The course consists of two one-hour lectures and one two-hour laboratory period, and meets for fourteen weeks. During this time we cover all thirteen chapters and the students master a major programming language (PL/C). The laboratory and lecture work are fully integrated so that many of the lectures have assignments corresponding to problems that must be solved as laboratory exercises. Alternative course outlines and laboratory suggestions are contained in the Instructor's Manual, which is available from the publisher.

Any of the standard teaching languages, such as BASIC, PL/C or WATFIV, can be used for the laboratory portion of the course.

The sequence in which the material is presented provides an orderly and logical transition from the fundamental ideas involved in carrying out a computation in a mechanical manner through the basic methods that may be used to carry out a number of the common information-processing tasks.

Chapter 1 provides an overview of the computing process and establishes the idea of an algorithm. Chapters 2 and 3 then consider the general organization of a computer and how the basic computational operations are performed on information. The use of flowcharts to represent algorithms is treated in Chapter 4, and Chapter 5 considers the techniques that can be used to reduce a general problem statement to flowchart form. Chapter 6 presents the concept of functions and subroutines, and discusses how they can be used to simplify the programming process. The different factors that influence the cost of developing and executing a computer program are considered in Chapter 7. Chapter 8 discusses the different types of errors introduced by the computing process and some of the things that can be done to minimize these errors.

The last five chapters consider ways of applying computers to the solution of many common information-processing problems. An introduction to searching and sorting techniques is presented in Chapter 9. Chapters 10 and 11 discuss how list and tree structures can be used to represent different types of data in a way that makes it easier to process. The final two chapters discuss many of the basic computational techniques that can be used to process numerical information.

We are indebted to many people who have helped in the development of this book. The following persons read the manuscript at various stages of its development and offered a number of very helpful suggestions: A. R. Beckett; Professor C. Davidson, University of Wisconsin; Professor R. E. Fairley and Professor R. C. Gammill, University of Colorado; Professor J. J. Forsyth, Michigan State University; Professor R. F. Mathis, Ohio State University; Professor T. A. Morrell, University of Illinois; Professor L. P. McNamee and Dr. J. A. Rader, U.C.L.A.; Professor A. Pearson, University of Texas, Professor E. Rategan, College of San Mateo; and Professor S. F. Weiss, University of North Carolina.

We were also very fortunate in having the opportunity to have this material class-tested at the University of California at Los Angeles by Dr. J. A. Rader.

Our colleague Harold M. Lucal also made extensive comments and suggestions during the final stages of developing this book. The detailed review of the final manuscript by James Perry was also very helpful.

The task of writing this book has been considerably aided by the helpful guidance and encouragement we have received from Donald C. Ford, of Hamilton Publishing Company. The ability of Mrs. Jean Hayden to transform our handwritten notes into typed copy is also deeply appreciated. Finally we thank our wives, Aline Booth and Janet Chien, for their patience and encouragement throughout the development of this book.

Storrs, Connecticut   *Taylor L. Booth*
                                                          Yi-tzuu Chien

about the authors

Taylor L. Booth is Professor of Electrical Engineering and Computer Science at the University of Connecticut, where he has been on the faculty of the Electrical Engineering Department since 1959. He has actively participated in the development of the department's graduate and undergraduate computer science program. This activity led to two previous books, *Sequential Machines and Automata Theory* (1967) and *Digital Networks and Computer Systems* (1971).

As a member of the COSINE Committee of the National Academy of Engineering Dr. Booth chaired two task-force studies dealing with undergraduate digital laboratory programs and the use of minicomputers in undergraduate laboratories. In 1972 Dr. Booth received the Frederick Emmons Terman Award for his contributions as an electrical engineering educator. Dr. Booth's research interests lie in the area of computer system design and analysis. He is the Associate Editor for Switching and Automata Theory of the Institute of Electrical and Electronics Engineers Transactions on Computers. He is also a member of the Association for Computing Machinery.

Dr. Booth received his Ph.D., M.S., and B.S.E. degrees from the University of Connecticut in 1962, 1956, and 1955 respectively. From 1956 to 1959 he was an analytical engineer for the Air Arm Division of Westinghouse Electric Company in Baltimore, Maryland. He is currently a consultant to several companies on problems involving computer system design and application.

Yi-tzuu Chien is Professor of Electrical Engineering and Computer Science at the University of Connecticut, where he has been on the faculty of the Electrical Engineering Department since 1967.

He was born in China, where he received his B.S. degree from the National Taiwan University in 1960. He received his M.S. and Ph.D. degrees from Purdue University in 1964 and 1967, respectively. From 1966 to 1967 he was a member of the technical staff at Bell Telephone Laboratories, Inc. in Holmdel, N.J.

Dr. Chien's research interests lie in the areas of interactive computer graphics, automatic pattern recognition, and artificial intelligence. He has published a number of journal articles in these areas. He is a member of the Machine Pattern Analysis Committee of the Institute of Electrical and Electronics Engineers, Computer Society. He is also a member of the Association for Computing Machinery.

contents

Computing:
fundamentals
and applications

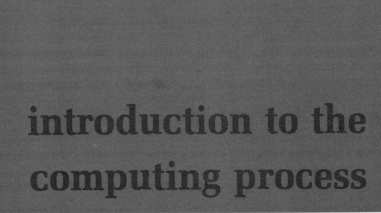

1

**introduction to the
computing process**

1 ■ Introduction

Information is one of the mainstays of modern society. There is hardly a task that we perform that does not involve the generation, transmission, or reaction to information in some form. When we are hungry, nerve impulses are sent to our brain telling us it is time to eat. Books convey information in the form of ideas and facts. A modern business samples public opinion and reaction whenever it introduces a new product. An engineer determines the distance to the moon by measuring the time it takes a radar signal to travel from the earth to the moon and back. All these tasks involve information.

For centuries man has tried to develop tools to ease his physical and mental work loads. The electronic computer is the latest in a long line of devices that have been developed to help process information. Scientists, engineers, and businessmen can now carry out in a few hours information-processing tasks that would be impossible without the computer. Social scientists have found computers to be invaluable in studying the complex interrelationships that exist in society and our institutions. Even artists and musicians have found the computer an interesting new medium for creative expression.

When digital computers were first introduced, many of the basic principles behind using a computer to perform a given task were not well understood. Initially computer programming was an esoteric art form into which only a few individuals were initiated. However, since the mid 1960's the art of using a computer to solve problems has evolved into a science of computing.

This book has been developed to introduce the basic concepts that lie behind the computing process. Therefore it does not deal with the specific techniques of writing a program in one of the standard programming languages such as PL/I, FORTRAN, or BASIC. The emphasis is, instead, upon the basic structure of the computing process and how it is influenced by both the way in which a computer is organized to operate upon information and the properties of the different types of information processing tasks that can be executed on a computer. Once these ideas are understood it is a relatively easy task to develop a computer program in an appropriate programming language.

2 ■ The Computing Process

A computer is an automatic device that is constructed in such a way that it can carry out any one of a number of well-defined basic information-processing operations. Before considering how a computer is organized let us consider the types of tasks that must be performed in carrying out a calculation.

Recently a large number of electronic hand-held calculators have appeared on the market. These calculators, which have many of the basic properties of a digital computer, usually are similar to that shown in Fig. 1-1. The accumulator holds the result produced by the latest calculation. There are five

Accumulator —

FIGURE 1-1 ■ Illustration of typical hand-held electronic calculator.

basic operations; addition (+), subtraction (−), multiplication (×), division (÷), and clear (c). The clear operation serves the function of setting the accumulator to all zeros.

The calculator operates in the standard manner. For example, the calculation

$$176.23 + 642.24 = 818.47$$

would be carried out by the following sequence of steps

Step 1 Push clear key.

Step 2 Enter 176.23 by touching the keys 1,7,6, ., 2, and 3 and then the addition key. This places 176.23 in the accumulator.

Step 3 Enter 642.24 by touching the keys 6, 4, 2, ., 2, and 4. 642.24 is then added to the number 176.23 in the accumulator by pushing the addition key. The result, 818.47, appears in the accumulator.

Any computational task performed on this calculator must be described by a similar sequence of well-defined steps. This sequence of steps is called an algorithm. Taken individually each step of the algorithm is of limited value. However, when they are carried out in the particular sequence described by the algorithm, the net result is to carry out a very complex information-processing task.

Algorithms

From an abstract viewpoint, any computation can be formally represented by the mathematical relationship

$$y = F(x)$$

where x represents the input information needed to make the computation, $F(x)$ represents the computation performed on x, and y represents the results of the computation.

If the computation represented by $F(x)$ is to be performed by an automatic device, such as a calculator or a computer, then there must be an explicit and unambigious set of steps or rules that tell us how to perform the desired computation. These requirements are summarized in the following formal definition of an algorithm:

An algorithm for the computation

$$y = F(x)$$

exists if there is an ordered sequence of discrete steps that can be automatically performed by a device, each step requiring only a finite amount of time, such that given x the device either:

1. forms $y = F(x)$ by executing these steps in the prescribed order.

or

2. indicates that no y exists that satisfies the conditions of the computation.

The device must require only a finite number of steps to reach one or the other of these decisions.

To illustrate what we mean by an algorithm consider the following two sets of instructions that you might be given to carry out a simple algebraic calculation

First Set of Instructions

Step 1 $x = 1.5$

Step 2 $y = 5x^2 + 3x + 2$

Second Set of Instructions

Assumption: Calculation $y = (5x + 3)x + 2 = 5x^2 + 3x + 2$ done on a hand calculator.

Step 1 Clear the accumulator by pressing the key c.

Step 2 Enter 5 into the accumulator by pressing the keys 5, and $+$.

Step 3 Multiply the number in the accumulator by 1.5 by pressing the keys 1, ., 5, and $\times$.

Step 4 Add 3 to the number in the accumulator by pressing the keys 3, and $+$.

Step 5 Multiply the number in the accumulator by 1.5 by pressing the keys 1, ., 5, and ×.

Step 6 Add 2 to the number in the accumulator by pressing the keys, 2, and +.

Step 7 Read the number in the accumulator as the desired value for y.

The first set of instructions does not form an algorithm for a computation to be carried out on a hand calculator, since we have not indicated how the computations are to be performed. These instructions do, however, represent a mathematical description of the calculation and could be carried out by anyone with a knowledge of algebra. The second set of instructions is much more explicit and represents the general form of an algorithm. Each step in the task is given explicitly and can be carried out in an automatic manner.

As long as we are dealing with a hand calculator we have little difficulty in describing the steps of an algorithm in a natural language. In this case the algorithm is interpreted by a person and we can rely upon his ability to understand the "meaning" of the different statements that make up the algorithm and carry out the indicated task even if it requires the filling in of particular details from "past experience." The flexibility of expression provided by natural languages is not acceptable if we must communicate the exact structure of an algorithm to a computer. To overcome this problem, special user-oriented programming languages have been developed to perform this task.

Programming Languages

Programming languages are designed to perform a very narrow and well-defined function: that of allowing a computer user to communicate with computers. Every computation performed by a computer must be described by an algorithm. Each step of the algorithm must be defined in an exact and unambigious manner so that there will be no "misunderstanding" between what the programmer wishes the computer to do and what the computer actually does. Consequently most programming languages have a very artificial structure that sometimes resembles, but never has, the richness of a natural language.

Over a hundred programming languages have been developed and new languages are continually being introduced. The main goal of each new language is to reduce the work needed by a programmer to describe a given computational algorithm. Of all the languages that have been developed, only a few have gained any widespread use.

The three earliest languages to become widely used were FORTRAN, ALGOL, and COBOL. FORTRAN was first introduced by IBM in the late 1950's as a programming language for engineering and scientific calculations. At about the same time an international committee developed the language ALGOL which was intended as an international standard for user-oriented programming languages. ALGOL has found limited acceptance in the United States but it has enjoyed greater popularity in Europe.

TABLE 1-1 ■ Typical programs written in major programming languages

```
                     FORTRAN
C        PROGRAM TO SUM 10 NUMBERS
C        INPUT VALUES FOR THE A'S
         READ (5,10)    (A(I),I = 1, 10)
    10   FORMAT (F10.2)
C        START CALCULATIONS
         B = 0.
         DO 20 I = 1,10
    20   B = B + A(I)
C        PRINT RESULTS OF CALCULATIONS
         WRITE (6,10) B
         STOP
         END
```

```
                     ALGOL
            COMMENT PROGRAM TO SUM 10 NUMBERS
BEGIN: ARRAY A[1,10]; REAL B; INTEGER I;
       FORMAT F1 (E10.5);
       COMMENT INPUT VALUES FOR A'S;
       READ (F1, FOR I:=1 UNTIL 10 DO A(I));
       COMMENT START CALCULATIONS;
       B:= 0.;
       FOR I:=1 STEP 1 UNTIL 10 DO B:=B+A(I);
       COMMENT PRINT RESULTS OF CALCULATIONS;
       PRINT (F1,B);
       END;
```

```
                     PL/I
/*  PROGRAM TO SUM 10 NUMBERS */
SUM: PROCEDURE OPTIONS (MAIN);
       DECLARE (A(10), B) FLOAT;
/* INPUT VALUES FOR THE A's */
       GET LIST (A);
/*  START CALCULATIONS */
       B = 0;
       DO I = 1 to 10;
       B = B+A(I);
       END;
/*  PRINT RESULTS OF CALCULATIONS */
       PUT LIST (B);
       END SUM;
```

```
                     APL
ρ    PROGRAM TO SUM 10 NUMBERS
     A ← 10.1  4.3  6.5  4.2  2.2  .1  .65  8.2  1.0  11.0
     B ← +/A
ρ    PRINT RESULTS OF CALCULATIONS
     B
```

BASIC

```
 10  REM THIS PROGRAM FINDS SUM OF TEN NUMBERS
 20  DIM A(10)
 30  REM TEN NUMBERS ARE READ INTO THE ARRAY A(10)
 40  FOR J = 1 TO 10
 50  READ A(J)
 60  NEXT J
 70  DATA  10.1, 4.3, 6.5, 4.2, 2.2
 80  DATA  .1, .65, 8.2, 1.0, 11.0
 90  REM STARTS CALCULATION OF SUM B
100  LET B = 0
110  FOR I = 1 TO 10
120  LET B = B + A(I)
130  NEXT I
140  REM OUTPUT B
150  PRINT B
160  END
```

COBOL

(Procedure Division only)

```
PROCEDURE DIVISION.
BEGIN.
        NOTE THIS SECTION OPENS THE INPUT AND OUTPUT FILES,
        READS THE DATA FROM THE INPUT FILE INTO A TABLE,
        COMPUTES THE SUM OF ALL VALUES IN THE TABLE AND
        PRINTS THE RESULT.
INITIALIZE.
        OPEN INPUT FILE
            OUTPUT OUTFILE.
READ-DATA.
        NOTE THE FOLLOWING READS ONE INPUT VALUE, PUTS IT INTO
            A TABLE AND COMPUTES THE SUM.
        READ INFILE.
        ADD ONE TO I.
        MOVE ELEMENT-VALUE TO A(I).
        ADD A(I) TO B.
        IF I IS EQUAL TO 10 GO TO WRITE-COMPUTED-SUM,
            ELSE GO TO READ-DATA.
WRITE-COMPUTED-SUM.
        NOTE PRINTS OUT COMPUTED RESULT.
        MOVE B TO DATA-SPACE
        MOVE LINE 1 TO DATA-LINE.
        WRITE OUTFILE AFTER ADVANCING SOME LINES.
END-OF-JOB.
        CLOSE INFILE OUTFILE.
        STOP RUN.
```

Both FORTRAN and ALGOL were designed primarily for scientific work. The need for a language for business applications led to the development of COBOL under the sponsorship of the United States Government. This language was designed to handle data of the type found in business data processing.

FORTRAN and COBOL proved to have many shortcomings and IBM has since introduced a new language, PL/I, which provides capabilities to do both scientific and business-oriented information-processing tasks. PL/I is slowly gaining in popularity as more people become familiar with this language. Industrial, scientific, and business users have a very large economic and educational commitment to FORTRAN and COBOL. These computer languages will thus continue to be important for many years to come.

The general nature of these programming languages is illustrated in Table 1-1. This table shows how an algorithm to compute

$$B = \sum_{I=1}^{10} A_I$$

would be described by the different languages. For this example the values of A_I are assumed to be

$$A_1 = 10.1 \quad A_2 = 4.3 \quad A_3 = 6.5 \quad A_4 = 4.2 \quad A_5 = 2.2$$

$$A_6 = 0.1 \quad A_7 = 0.65 \quad A_8 = 8.2 \quad A_9 = 1.0 \quad A_{10} = 11.0$$

Each line of a program is called a *statement.* To execute a program the statements must be entered into the computer. One of the commonest methods is to punch the statements on a punched card of the type shown in Fig. 1-2 and then use a card reader such as the one shown in Fig. 1-3 to read

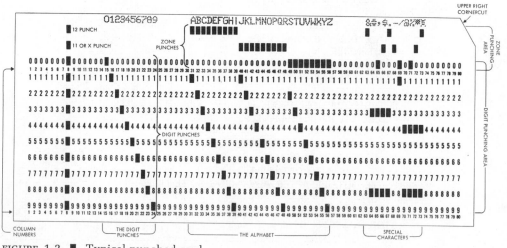

FIGURE 1-2 ■ Typical punched card.

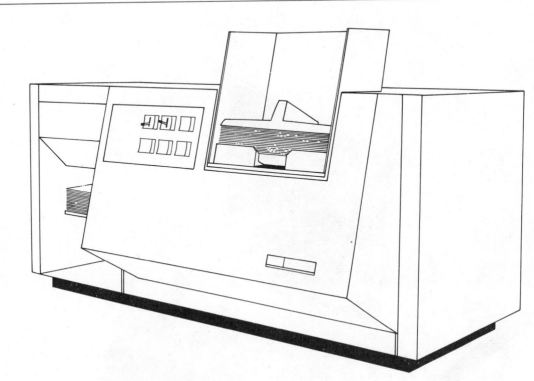

FIGURE 1-3 ■ Card reader.

the complete program into the computer. This approach is useful when very large programs are being used, or when a large number of users must be serviced with a minimal equipment investment. One disadvantage in this approach is the amount of time it takes to obtain results after the initial program has been developed.

This difficulty can be reduced by using a typewriter-like terminal of the form shown in Fig. 1-4. Each program statement is typed in and an immediate response to the statement or a group of statements is possible. A terminal of this type allows the user to interact or carry on a dialog with the computer. This means that the user can develop a comprehensive program by first developing the important parts of the program, checking that they perform properly, and then organize the parts into a complete program. One disadvantage is that only one person can use a terminal at a given time.

The use of interactive terminals has expanded very rapidly and several interactive languages have been designed for this type of computer/user interaction. BASIC and CPS, a language very similar to PL/I, are two languages that have been developed to facilitate numerical calculations on a time-sharing computer system. Both of these languages were designed so that they are easy to learn and use. A powerful new interactive language, APL, has

FIGURE 1-4 ■ Interactive computer terminal.

received increasing attention. This language differs in structure from all the other languages in that it makes no attempt to keep any semblance to a natural language. APL is a concise and consistent system of mathematical notation that allows a programmer to easily carry out complex information-processing tasks.

From the above discussion one might reach the conclusion that the study of computing would involve learning the details and methods of application of one or more of the languages mentioned above. Although this was the approach that was taken when computers first came into general use, it is now recognized that it is not the language used to represent a computation but the algorithm that describes the calculation that is of fundamental importance.

Consequently in this book we concentrate upon the basic principles of the computing process itself rather than upon how the process is represented by a particular programming language. Once these principles are mastered it is an easy task to translate any algorithm into a computer program using an appropriate programming language.

There are several excellent reference manuals available that may be used to learn the details of the major programming languages. Once the skill of programming in one programming language is mastered it is quite easy to extend this skill to one or more of the other standard languages.

3 ■ Areas of Computer Application

Historically the first electronic computers were developed to carry out long and repetitive numerical calculations. These calculations were needed in order that the behavior of different physical processes being studied by engineers and scientists might be understood. However, it was soon realized that computers were not simply "number crunchers," but could also be used for tasks requiring the symbolic manipulation of information. Current computer applications have penetrated into nearly every industrial, governmental, and academic field. The following discussion indicates some of the more important areas of application.

Scientific and Engineering Calculations

Computers have been used extensively in nearly all scientific and engineering fields. They have relieved scientists and engineers from having to carry out tedious numerical calculations by hand and they have also extended the range of problems that can be investigated. More importantly, many scientific and engineering problems often defy closed-form solutions. Often the only alternative is to attempt an approximate solution with the assistance of a computer. The computer, in this application, becomes a design tool that allows a number of possible approximate solutions to a problem to be tried before a final solution is selected.

Business Data Processing

Another major application of computers is found in the business world. A computer may be used to carry out such routine tasks as computing the weekly payroll of a company, or keeping track of the inventory of a business. The inventory can be constantly monitored and when the quantity of any stocked item falls below a critical level the computer can automatically initiate the steps necessary to reorder that item. In large businesses, computers are used to analyze the vast amount of data generated by that business's day-to-day operation. The results of this analysis are used to provide the necessary information to assist the management in their decision-making processes.

Most of the operations just mentioned are commonly referred to as *data processing.* Typically, data-processing operations are characterized by the fact that they involve the transferring of large amounts of data in and out of a computer, with only a limited amount of numeric calculation carried out on the data. Thus, computers and programming languages that are designed for data-processing applications must have extensive input and output capabilities. In contrast, scientific and engineering applications that require large amounts of numeric calculations may be more efficiently handled by computers and programming languages with extensive facilities for calculations. For problems with varied needs, we need a computer and a programming language that possess the best of both capabilities.

Natural Language Processing

Computers are symbol manipulators. They deal with characters or other symbolic data in essentially the same way that they deal with numeric quantities. Because of this, computers have been used as a language processor to carry out tasks set by linguists, educators, and even social and political scientists. For example, computers have been programmed to help the preparation of the detailed word-index in a given text that linguists call a concordance. They have also been used to collect statistical information from particular texts which may be of interest in the determination of their authorship. Computer-assisted instruction systems, which have the capability of providing individualized education in a natural language environment, are now in existence. Legal and medical services, and other knowledge-based fields have been computerized to achieve greater efficiency and availability. Finally, serious efforts have been made, with varing degrees of success, to use computers to assist in automatic language translation.

All these examples suggest that the time soon may come when the humanist will take the computer as much for granted as they do the typewriter and the tape recorder, and when educators will consider the computer as an important teaching tool. Social and political scientists may soon find they too can rely upon computers to provide them with instant, timely information about the behavior of social and political systems.

Control and Automation

Perhaps the most hidden application of computers is that of the control and automation of industrial processes. Because of their speed, precision, and reliability, computers have been used to monitor and control many of the production processes required in our modern technology. In many factories, the manufacturing process frequently requires a sequence of decisions for which alternatives exist. The goal here is to arrive at the sequence of decisions which result in the greatest efficiency, productivity, and versatility of the manufacturing plant. By means of a computer, instantaneous analysis can be made on the processes involved, and the result of this analysis can be used immediately to find the "optimal" sequence of decisions. This decision-making process can be carried out with a minimum of human supervision. Control and automation of this kind also increases our capability to design and experiment with more complicated processes which would not be feasible using conventional techniques and human monitoring.

The reader at this point may well wonder how a computer, historically developed to carry out numeric calculations, can also perform complicated tasks that require the processing of nonnumeric data. It turns out that this is easily achieved if we think of a computer as a symbol manipulator rather than as a desk calculator. As we shall discuss in our subsequent chapters, all nonnumeric data, as well as numeric, must be encoded into the same computer-acceptable form before they are stored and operated upon by the computer. Once we understand how the different tasks are performed on a computer it is a relatively easy matter to develop a computer program to carry out any task of interest.

4 ■ The Cost of Computing

Whenever we introduce a labor-saving device, we must be prepared to pay for the use of that device. Using a computer can be a very costly experience. It is not unusual to be charged from $150 to $600 an hour for computer time. Happily, many of the programs that are run on a computer require only a few seconds or minutes. Thus, the cost of solving a problem can be kept within bounds if one is careful in the way one uses a computer. These costs are not, however, the only costs involved in using a computer to solve a given information-processing problem.

Besides the cost of computer time, there is the *programming cost* associated with developing the program necessary to carry out a given computation, and the cost of *computer misapplication*. Many computer users are completely unaware of these cost factors until they are dramatically brought to their attention in some shocking way. In this section we briefly review some of the major factors which influence these costs. Details concerning specific ways to minimize computer costs are given throughout the book.

Programming Costs

In many instances people develop an algorithm to solve a problem and then rush to a computer to carry out the required calculations. A considerable amount of thought should be given to the algorithm before preparing a computer program to implement the algorithm. Close examination may even show that the calculations can be simplified and satisfactory results can be obtained by a few simple hand calculations. If that is not possible, the examination might show how to simplify the calculation or how to better organize the algorithm so that a smaller amount of computer time is needed to carry out the calculation.

Programming itself can be very expensive. The cost of programming represents the time spent by the programmer to develop a program and the cost of the computer time necessary to remove all the programming and other errors during the development phase. A complete mastery of the local programming language and careful attention to detail will go a long way in minimizing programming costs.

The programming process has a number of steps that must be understood if the overall programming costs are to be minimized. The first step is to define the problem in enough detail to identify what must be done by the program. At this point the programmer should think of other possible ways to carry out the calculation instead of starting the development of a new program. One of the alternatives that is often overlooked is the fact that a program to carry out the desired task might already exist, in the computer center or in a standard reference. A brief search for such a program will often save a considerable amount of the time and effort which would be expended in "reinventing the wheel." If a complete program to do the job cannot be found, it may still be possible to find other programs that will be useful in the programming effort or that will suggest a method of approach.

The next step in the programming process is to plan the complete program. This step starts by first developing the algorithm that describes the desired computational task. Several algorithms may have to be considered before the best method of solution is discovered. The function of each part of the algorithm should be clearly understood and checked to make sure it carries out the desired task.

Once the algorithm is defined the task of converting it into an operational program is undertaken. At this point it is important to organize the program in such a way as to make most effective use of the computer and to make it easy to test the program to detect any programming or logical errors. The process of removing errors from a program, called *debugging,* can represent a major cost. No matter how experienced a programmer may be, there will usually be a number of errors that must be removed before any given program operates correctly. Anything that is done to minimize the debugging task will not only reduce the overall programming cost but will also reduce the amount of frustration that a programmer must endure to obtain a working program.

As soon as a program is operating correctly there is a very strong temptation to leave it and go on to some other task. This decision can be very costly if, at a later date, one wishes to use the program for another application. The final task in programming is that of documentation. The final program should be described in a report that provides not only a listing of the programming-language statements that make up the program but also a discussion of the algorithm used to develop the program and a description of how the program is to be used. It is surprising how fast the details of a particular program are forgotten by a programmer after that program is finished. Poor documentation often means that a considerable amount of time and effort will be required for someone to use a program at a later date. This unnecessary cost can be avoided by spending the time to provide the necessary documentation while all of the important details are still fresh in one's mind.

Computer Misapplication

The cost of computer misapplication represents a hidden cost. Unexpected errors made during a computation often give output results that appear correct. Decisions based upon these results may lead to very costly mistakes. For example, a computer used to prepare bills for a large department store might mix up the accounts of a large number of customers because of a program bug. The store would then be required to spend a considerable amount of money in salaries for the personnel needed to deal with the customers and to correct the billing errors. It is all too easy to blame the computer for the error. Unfortunately, in too many cases the error is introduced by the human who developed the program rather than the computer.

The best way to minimize the overall cost of a program to solve a given problem is to have a thorough understanding of both the problem and the computing techniques that can be used to solve problems on a computer.

5 ■ Summary

The effective use of a computer to solve complex problems requires more than that one become proficient in the use of a particular programming language. It requires a thorough understanding of how a computer processes information and how the calculations necessary to solve a problem can be organized so that they can be efficiently carried out by a computer. In this book we take a comprehensive look at the computing process in a manner that is independent of any particular programming language.

The next chapters deal with the general organization of a computer and the structure of algorithms and their representation. That discussion shows that all algorithms can be represented by a set of basic building blocks and introduces the idea that they can be represented graphically by a flowchart. These ideas are then used to discuss the process of reducing a general problem statement to an algorithm that describes the computations necessary to solve the problem. After we have developed an understanding of the general problem-solving process we turn our attention to the limitations imposed upon the computing process by the way a computer is constructed and how it operates. The succeeding chapters consider some of the basic techniques that can be used to solve numerical and nonnumerical problems. These discussions introduce many of the standard computing methods that are useful in different information-processing and computational tasks.

Since each chapter contains several new and important concepts, the following chapter organization is used to help the reader identify and understand these concepts. At the end of each major section a set of short exercises is inserted to illustrate the important ideas of that section. The answers to many of these exercises are included at the back of the book. In addition, a set of more comprehensive problems is included at the end of each chapter. Most of these problems require the development and execution of a complete computer program for their solution. These problems are quite extensive and are designed to further illustrate the material contained in the chapter and to introduce the actual programming techniques that are necessary to make effective use of the ideas presented. References are included at the end of each chapter to indicate where more advanced discussion of the material can be found.

References

The following references have been selected to provide a sampling of the many applications of computers. [8] and [9] present a general overview of the different programming languages and programming systems that have been developed to handle a wide range of problems. [2], [3], and [10] provide a general discussion of digital computers and their applications. The remainder describe ways in which computers have been applied to a large number of different disciplines.

1. Alt, F., and Rubinoff, M. (1971) *Advances in Computers, Vol. 11,* Academic Press, New York.
2. Baer, R. M. (1972) *The Digital Villain,* Addison-Wesley, Reading, Mass.
3. Desmonde, W. H. (1964) *Computers and Their Uses,* Prentice-Hall, Englewood Cliffs, N.J.
4. Feigenbaum, E. A., and Feldman, J. eds., (1963) *Computers and Thought,* McGraw-Hill, New York.
5. Ledley, R. (1960) *Digital Computers and Control Engineering,* McGraw-Hill, New York.
6. Locke, W. and Booth, A. eds., (1955) *Machine Translation of Language,* The MIT Press, Cambridge, Mass.
7. Myers, C. A. (1970) *Computers in Knowledge-Based Fields,* The MIT Press, Cambridge, Mass.
8. Rosen, S. (1972) "Programming Systems and Languages," *Communications of the ACM,* Vol. 15, No. 7, pp. 591–600.
9. Sammet, J. (1972) "Programming Languages: History and Future," *Communications of the ACM,* Vol. 15, No. 7, pp. 601–610.
10. Taviss, I., ed. (1970) *The Computer Impact,* Prentice-Hall, Englewood Cliffs, N.J.

basic computer organization

1 ▍ Introduction

One of the major tasks in computing is that of defining an algorithm to describe the computation we wish to perform. This task is influenced to a considerable extent by the structure of the computer on which the computation is to be executed. Thus, before we study the structure of algorithms we must first consider the organization of a digital computer to obtain an understanding of how a computer uses a program to perform a calculation and how it stores the data needed in that calculation.

2 ▍ Computer Organization

If an algorithm is to represent a particular computational task, it must be represented in such a manner that it can be executed by an automatic device. To see what this requirement means consider how an algorithm to compute,

$$Y = U^2 + V^2 + W^2$$

might be expressed if it were to be executed on a hand calculator by someone who knows no mathematics. This algorithm must be expressed in such a way that the computist can carry out all of the steps in a mechanical manner. To do this assume that the work area is organized as shown in Fig. 2-1. In addition to the hand calculator we have a list of instructions that the computist is to follow, a sheet of paper with numbered lines on which numerical values can be recorded, three slips of paper with the values of U, V, and W written on them and a fourth slip of paper with the symbol Y written on it. The computist will take the three slips with the values of U, V, and W on them and carry out the instructions given by the instruction list. At the completion of the calculation the computed value of Y will be written on the slip marked Y.

The list of instructions to be used by the computist are expressed in an abbreviated form to save space. For our example the instructions, and their meaning are as follows:

1. COPY {symbol indicating data item} TO {number of line in record list}
   Meaning: Copy the number on the slip marked with the symbol or the number in the accumulator onto the indicated line of the record list.
   Examples: COPY U TO 1
   COPY ACCUMULATOR TO 5

2. CLEAR
   Meaning: Push clear key (key marked C) on hand calculator

3. ADD {number of line in record list}
   Meaning: Push the keys on the calculator corresponding to the digits

of the number found on the indicated line of the record list. Then push the + key of the calculator.

Example: ADD 4

4. MULTIPLY {number of line in record list}

Meaning: Push the keys on the calculator corresponding to the digits of the number found on the indicated line of the record list. Then push the × key of the calculator.

Example: MULTIPLY 3

5. OUTPUT {number of line in record list} TO

{symbol indicating data item}

Meaning: Copy the number on the indicated line of the record list onto the slip marked with the indicated symbol.

Example: OUTPUT 5 TO Y

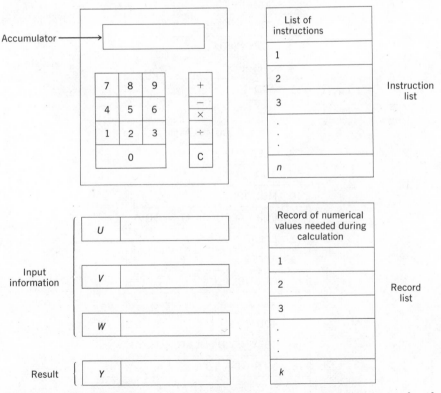

FIGURE 2-1 ■ Organization of the work area for a computation on a hand calculator.

Additional abbreviations can be introduced for the other operations that might be performed by the computist. This list is sufficient for the current example.

The instruction list describing the algorithm to compute

$$Y = U^2 + V^2 + W^2$$

is given in Fig. 2-2.

To see how this list is used, assume that the slips U, V, and W have the values shown in Fig. 2-3 written on them when the computation is started. The contents of the record list, the accumulator, and the slip Y are also shown during the different stages of the calculation.

At this point you should check the values shown in Fig. 2-3 to make sure that you understand how each entry in the history of the calculation was obtained.

1.	COPY U TO 1
2.	COPY V TO 2
3.	COPY W TO 3
4.	CLEAR
5.	ADD 1
6.	MULTIPLY 1
7.	COPY ACCUMULATOR TO 4
8.	CLEAR
9.	ADD 2
10.	MULTIPLY 2
11.	COPY ACCUMULATOR TO 5
12.	CLEAR
13.	ADD 3
14.	MULTIPLY 3
15.	ADD 5
16.	ADD 4
17.	COPY ACCUMULATOR TO 6
18.	OUTPUT 6 TO Y
19.	END OF COMPUTATION

FIGURE 2-2 ■ Instruction list to compute $Y = U^2 + V^2 + W^2$.

Input information

U	2.1

V	1.2

W	3

Last instruction executed		4	6	10	14	16	18
Accumulator		0	4.41	1.44	9	14.85	14.85
Record list	1	2.1	2.1	2.1	2.1	2.1	2.1
	2	1.2	1.2	1.2	1.2	1.2	1.2
	3	3	3	3	3	3	3
	4			4.41	4.41	4.41	4.41
	5				1.44	1.44	1.44
	6						14.85
Slip Y							14.85

FIGURE 2-3 ■ History of calculation performed according to the instruction list of Fig. 2-2.

If we examine this example we can identify the following basic tasks that must be performed during the calculation:

1. Read in information (steps 1 through 3 in Fig. 2-2).
2. Temporarily store information for later use (steps 7, 11, and 17).
3. Operate upon stored information (steps 5, 6, 9, 10, 13, 14, 15, and 16).
4. Control the sequence in which the different tasks are performed (the way the instruction list is organized).
5. Output the results of the calculation (step 18).

All of these operations can be carried out by the computist without any knowledge of why they are being performed or of the results expected. In fact the computist can easily be replaced by an electronic device if the instruction list and record list are represented using electronic techniques.

Organization of a Typical Computer

Modern computers are engineering masterpieces. Consequently the first encounter one has with a computer can be an overwhelming experience. This apparent complexity is very deceiving. While it is true that a modern computer is a very complex electronic device, the basic tasks that it performs are essentially identical to the tasks needed to carry out the computation on a hand calculator discussed in the previous example. To see this, consider the basic organization of a computer shown in Fig. 2-4.

There is a direct correspondence between the major units shown in Fig. 2-4 and the tasks carried out in the previous example. The control unit takes

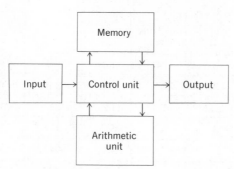

FIGURE 2-4 ■ A simple diagram illustrating the organization of a computer.

the place of the computist, the arithmetic unit takes the place of the hand calculator, and the input and output units take the place of the data slips that were labeled U, V, W, and Y. The list of instructions and the list of data used by the control unit to perform the calculation are stored in memory in an electronic form that can be read and interpreted by the control unit. The following discussion presents a general overview of the properties of the major components of a typical digital computer and the way in which this organization influences the way that computers operate on information.

The input to a computer can take many forms depending on the type of information which must be delivered to the computer. The most common input device is a punched-card reader which can transfer a large amount of information into the computer in a relatively short period of time. For those situations where direct man–machine communication is desired, a typewriter is often used. With this latter type of input device, an operator can guide the operation of a computer by instructing it to perform various operations as intermediate results are made known. There are many other input devices but the two that we have just discussed are the ones most commonly used for general programming tasks.

The arithmetic unit of a computer is the center in the computer where the basic information-processing tasks, such as addition, multiplication, comparisons, and decisions take place. This unit must be able to hold and manipulate data under the direction of the control unit. One or more storage areas that can temporarily hold a small amount of data during a given processing operation are included in the arithmetic unit. These special storage areas are also called accumulators.

The memory of the computer serves two very important purposes. It stores both the data needed in a calculation and a coded version of the algorithm that the computer is to use to process the data. The memory is often divided into primary memory and secondary memory.

Primary memory stores information so that it is directly accessible to the computer. This memory is usually made up of an ordered array of little rings of magnetic material called *cores.* Because of this the primary memory is called *core memory.* Many of the larger computers have an additional form of bulk *secondary information storage,* such as magnetic tapes, drums or disks. These devices can store vast amounts of data and information in a relatively small space. This data is not directly available. If during a calculation some of the information stored in secondary storage is needed, it must be transferred into the core memory unit.

The final major unit is the output device. Data can be transferred from the computer in many forms. For a computer mainly devoted to computations, the output is usually printed on a printer or, less often, punched on cards. Many computers can also display output information on some form of graphic display so that the user can obtain a dynamic interpretation of the interaction between the various variables of his problem. Outputs of this type are very useful in design problems where the operator can vary the value of one variable in a problem and see how this variation influences the rest of the problem.

Digital Information Representation

Digital computers do not operate upon numbers or symbols of the type we commonly use when carrying out a computation or information-processing task. In a digital computer all information is represented by a finite-length sequence of binary digits each of which can take on the value of either 0 or 1. For example, if we wish to represent the symbol A in a digital computer we might encode it as 11000001.

In general we can represent such an ordered sequence as

$$x_1 x_2 \ldots x_i \ldots x_r$$

where each x_i can take on a value of 0 or 1. We say that each x_i represents one *bit* of information. A sequence of r binary digits represents r bits of information.

Inside a computer we must have the ability to store, transmit, and modify information. The way chosen to store information has an important influence upon the design of a computer. Once we select a convention concerning the way information is stored, the design of the necessary devices to transmit and modify information is easily accomplished.

There are a wide variety of information storage devices. For our discussion it is not necessary to know how these devices operate. Instead we take the basic information storage element to be a *cell* and assume that it can store a single binary digit. The content of the cell is assumed to remain constant until some particular action is taken to change the information stored in the cell.

Single information storage cells are of limited value since they can only store a single bit of information. If more information must be stored, a collection of cells can be joined together, as shown in Fig. 2-5, to form a *register.* A register with r cells is called an *r-bit register.*

The information contained in the register is indicated by giving the sequence of 0's and 1's stored in the register. For example, the 8-bit register

Cell 1	Cell 2	. . .	Cell r

FIGURE 2-5 ∎ A representation of an r-bit register.

shown in Fig. 2-6 contains the sequence 11000001 that we indicated might represent an encoded form of the letter A.

In a computer information is represented and stored in bit sequences of standard length. Such a standard bit sequence is called a *computer word.* Every computer manufacturer selects a word size for their computers on the basis of a number of different technical considerations. For the current generation of computers word sizes range from 12 to 64 bits.

The primary memory of a computer is made up of a large collection of identical registers. Each register stores one computer word. The registers are arranged in an orderly manner as illustrated in Fig. 2-7. Each register is assigned a unique identifying number, called the *address of the register,* from 0 to $N_{max} - 1$, where N_{max} is the number of registers that make up the memory unit. Usually N_{max} is a power of 2. For example, we might have $N_{max} = 2^{14} = 16{,}384$. A memory unit with this number of registers is referred to as a *16K word memory* where in computer terminology K is an abbreviation to indicate $2^{10} = 1024$.

The arithmetic unit also contains a few registers for temporary information storage during a computation. The amount of storage space is limited so that as soon as one step of a computation is completed all of the information in these temporary storage registers that will be needed later must be transferred to core memory. The information needed in the next step of the computation is then taken from core memory and placed in the temporary storage registers.

To carry out an automatic calculation on a hand calculator we needed an instruction list and a record list. In a computer an encoded representation of the instruction list that describes the calculations to be performed and an encoded representation of the data and information needed in the calculation are stored in the main memory. Each of the basic operations that the computer can perform is represented by a unique binary code. The sequence of coded instructions that make up the algorithm to be executed by the computer is called a *machine-language program.*

1	1	0	0	0	0	0	1

FIGURE 2-6 ∎ Illustration of how information may be stored in an eight-bit register.

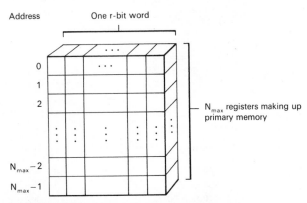

Address   One r-bit word

N_{max} registers making up
primary memory

FIGURE 2-7 ■ Basic organization of a core memory unit.

The control unit must interpret the machine-language program. It takes the first instruction from memory, determines the operation to be performed, executes the operation and then proceeds on to the next instruction to be executed. Normally this instruction is the one found in the next consecutive memory location. However, in some cases, the control unit will determine that the next instruction is to be found in a different location. The control unit continues operation until it reaches an instruction that indicates the computation is complete. It then halts the operation of the computer and waits for the computer operator to load a new machine-language program.

Machine-Language Programs

Anyone interested in entering the field of computer science must be intimately familiar with the operation of computers at the basic machine language level and be able to write machine-language programs. It is unreasonable and unnecessary to expect that every computer user must have this ability. If one is to fully appreciate many of the features of the standard programming languages, it is necessary, however, to have an understanding of the structure of machine-language programs and how they are represented in a computer.

Let us assume that we wish to carry out the calculation

$$Y = U^2 + V^2 + W^2$$

using a hypothetical computer with a 12-bit word size. The first thing we must do is decide where to locate the machine-language program (corresponding to the instruction list) and the data (corresponding to the record list) in the computer's memory. One such organization is illustrated in Fig. 2-8.

The machine-language program must then be generated. The program for our hypothetical computer is also shown in Fig. 2-8 along with the interpretation given to each instruction. An examination of this simple machine-language

Memory register number	Coded contents of memory register	Meaning
Instruction list		
1	110001011110	Copy value of *U* from input device and place in memory register 30
2	110001011111	Copy value of *V* from input device and place in memory register 31
3	110001100000	Copy value of *W* from input device and place in memory register 32
4	111100000010	Clear the computer's accumulator
5	001000011110	Add number in memory register 30 to accumulator
6	101000011110	Multiply number in memory register 30 by number in accumulator, leave result in accumulator
7	011000100001	Deposit number in accumulator into memory register 33
8	111100000010	Clear the computer's accumulator
9	001000011111	Add number in memory register 31 to accumulator
10	101000011111	Multiply number in memory register 31 by number in accumulator; leave result in accumulator
11	011000100010	Deposit number in accumulator into memory register 34
12	111100000010	Clear the computer's accumulator
13	001001100000	Add number in memory register 32 to accumulator
14	101000100000	Multiply number in memory register 32 by number in accumulator; leave result in accumulator
15	001000100001	Add number in memory register 33 to accumulator
16	001000100010	Add number in memory register 34 to accumulator
17	011000100011	Deposit number in accumulator into memory register 35
18	110010100011	Print number in memory register 35 on computer's printer
19	111010000000	Halt computer
⋮		
Record list		
30		Register to store value of *U*
31		Register to store value of *V*
32		Register to store value of *W*
33		Temporary location to store value of U^2
34		Temporary location to store value of V^2
35		Temporary location to store computed value of *Y*

FIGURE 2-8 ■ A typical machine-language program.

program shows that it would be of very little value to the computer user since it is impossible to understand without a considerable amount of detailed study.

The standard user-oriented programming languages discussed in Chapter I have been developed to allow computer users to develop a computer program in an easily understandable language. A special translator program, called a *compiler,* then converts the program written in the user-oriented programming language into a machine-language program. Some of the important properties of compilers and user-oriented languages will be discussed later. But before we can do this we must first briefly investigate how different types of information are represented inside a computer.

Exercises

1. The following list gives the sequence of instructions to be carried out to compute a formula. Trace through this list and determine what formula is being computed.

Instruction List

Input information

U	

V	

Output information

Y	

1. COPY U TO 1
2. COPY V TO 2
3. CLEAR
4. ADD 1
5. ADD 2
6. COPY ACCUMULATOR TO 3
7. MULTIPLY 3
8. COPY ACCUMULATOR TO 4
9. OUTPUT 4 TO Y
10. END OF COMPUTATION

2. An algorithm is to be developed to compute the formula

$$Y = 1 + X + X^2 + X^3$$

using the instruction set given on p. 18 above:
   (a) Give the instruction list describing the algorithm.
   (b) Show the history of calculation performed according to the instruction list of (a) for $X = 1.2$, in a way similar to that shown in Fig. 2-3.

3. For the computation

$$Y = \sum_{I=1}^{100} A_I^2$$

determine the sequence of instructions that must be written into the instruction list 100 times in order to carry out the sum operation.

3 ▮ Information Representation

The information used in a computer must be stored in the space provided by one or more computer words. This property has a very important, but often overlooked, influence upon the methods used to carry out a computation. This section discusses the ways that nonnumeric character information and numeric information is stored in a computer.

If a computer word has r bits, then there are 2^r distinct sequences of r binary digits that can appear in a computer word. For example, if $r = 2$, then the $2^2 = 4$ different sequences would be

$$[0,0] \quad [0,1] \quad [1,0] \quad [1,1]$$

The meaning that we assign to any particular sequence of r bits depends upon the type of information that we wish to store in a computer word.

The requirement that all data or information stored in memory must fit into one or more computer words imposes limitations on the type of information that can be stored. In some situations these limitations are of minor importance, while in other cases they strongly influence the quality of the calculations that we can perform. The following important properties of both numeric and character information should be familiar to anyone using computers.

Decimal Number

Whenever we carry out a calculation we automatically use decimal numbers such as 256, 36.765, or 100,126.72 without paying much attention to the actual form that the number takes. In a computer program both the form the number can take and the number's size are strongly influenced by the computer's construction and the programming language being used.

Any number used in a computer program must be representable by a finite number of digits. Numbers such as $\sqrt{2}$ or π, which require an infinite number of digits to represent exactly, must be approximated. For example, suppose that a number can have no more than five decimal digits. Then

$$\sqrt{2} \cong 1.4142 \qquad \pi \cong 3.1416$$

are two such approximations.

Integers, Fractions, and Fixed-Point Numbers

When a number is written as a finite-length sequence of decimal digits and an included decimal point, we say that the number is expressed in *fixed-point* form. For example

$$17.6345 \quad -2567.46 \quad 002.320$$

are six-digit fixed-point numbers. Where appropriate, leading and trailing zeros may be omitted. Thus,

$$002.320$$

may be written as

$$2.32$$

without any loss of meaning.

Any fixed-point decimal number is divided into two parts by the decimal point. The part of the number to the left of the decimal point is called the *integer part* of the number and the part of the number to the right of the decimal point is called the *fractional part* of the number.

In the very important but special situation where the decimal point appears at the right end of the number, then the number is called an *integer*. Similarly, any number in which the decimal point appears at the left end of the number is called a *fraction*.

When dealing with fixed-point numbers we must define the maximum number of digits that may be used to represent the number and the location of the decimal point. This establishes the size of the largest and the smallest nonzero number that we can use in our calculation. For example, assume that we have a six-digit fixed-point number with the decimal point two places from the right end of the number. Such a number has the following general form

$$\pm XXXX.XX$$

Thus the largest number that can be represented is

$$9999.99$$

and the smallest nonzero positive number that can be represented is

$$0000.01$$

Numbers such as 86543.24 (too large) or 0000.001 (too small) cannot be represented within the specified form assumed for the number. Numbers such as 7654.326 cannot be represented (too many digits) even though it falls between 7654.33 and 7654.32. The total number of digits allowed in a number together with the defined location of the decimal point determines the *precision* of a number.

There are many applications where the fixed-point representation of numbers are used. For example, an accounting program written to keep track of the financial transactions in a business would normally use fixed-point numbers to record the dollar amounts of all business transactions. For many situations a fixed-point representation is too restrictive. Since the largest and smallest numbers that can be represented are determined by the number of digits allowed to the left and right of the decimal point. This restriction can be overcome by introducing the idea of floating-point numbers.

Floating-Point Numbers

When numbers are too large or too small it becomes unwieldy to write down all of the digits. For example it would be bothersome if the number

$$-30000000000000000000$$

or

$$.0000000000000000168$$

has to be written a large number of times. Since most of the digits in these two numbers are zeros, they can be expressed as a fixed-point number multiplied by 10 raised to an appropriate power. For example,

$$-30000000000000000000 = -3.0 \times 10^{19}$$

and

$$.0000000000000000168 = 1.68 \times 10^{-17}$$

Numbers written in this manner are called *floating-point* numbers. For convenience floating-point numbers can be written as

$$-3.0 \times 10^{19} = -3.0E19$$

or

$$1.68 \times 10^{-17} = 1.68E - 17$$

where E is read as "times ten-to-the."

Every floating-point number has the following two-part structure:

$$\underbrace{\langle \text{Fixed-point number} \rangle}_{\text{First part}} \; E \; \underbrace{\langle \text{Integer} \rangle}_{\text{Second part}}$$

The first part is called the *mantissa* of the number and the second part is called the *exponent* of the number. The precision of a floating-point number is defined by the precision of the mantissa. The sign of the number (+ or −) is the sign associated with the mantissa. The sign associated with the exponent indicates the number of positions that the decimal point is shifted to the right (+) or left (−).

A floating-point representation is used to represent numerical information that may take on very large or very small values or numerical information that might vary over a considerable range of values. As illustrated by the following examples, all fixed-point numbers can be represented in floating-point form and all floating-point numbers can be represented in fixed-point form. The representation in floating-point form, however, is not unique.

The mantissa of a floating-point number may be any fixed-point number. For uniformity of internal storage and printed results, most programming lan-

Fixed point	Floating point
219.25	.21925E3
3.141593	3.141593E0
0.0005	5.0E−4
455	4.55E2
−7452	−.7452E4

guages and computer systems establish a standard form of representation for the mantissa. The two most common standards assume the mantissa is represented as either a fixed-point number between 1 and 10 or a fraction between .1 and 1. The precision of the mantissa, and consequently the precision of the floating-point number, will usually fall in the range of 6 to 12 decimal digits, although other precisions are possible.

The range of numbers that can be represented in floating-point form is essentially determined by the maximum value that can be assigned to the exponent. If the largest integer value that can be assigned to the exponent is N then the largest floating-point number that can be represented is approximately 10^N and the smallest number is approximately 10^{-N}. The value of N depends upon the particular computer and programming language being used but will usually fall in a range of 40 to 100. Other values of N are, of course, possible.

Binary Numbers

All the information stored in a computer word is encoded as a sequence of zeros and ones. To encode numerical information in this form we must agree upon how numerical values are to be assigned to each such sequence. One way to do this is to represent numerical information in the binary number system rather than the more familiar decimal number system.

Decimal numbers are so common to our culture that when we see a symbol such as 286.54 we immediately feel that we understand its numerical meaning. This reaction is so natural that we forget that each digit of a decimal number has a place value. Thus, 286.54 is really a shorthand way of expressing the number

$$N_{10} = 2(10)^2 + 8(10)^1 + 6(10)^0 + 5(10)^{-1} + 4(10)^{-2} = 286.54_{10}$$

This decimal number is said to be expressed in terms of the *base 10* since each digit is multiplied by an appropriate power of 10. The number forming the base of a number system is called the *radix* of the system.

The use of 10 as a radix for our number system probably occurred as a natural consequence of the fact that man has ten fingers. All information in a computer is represented in terms of the two distinct binary digits, 0 and 1.

This suggests that we should use 2 rather than 10 as a radix. If we select this convention the resulting number is called a *binary number*.

We can represent a binary number as

$$N_2 = a_{n-1}(2)^{n-1} + a_{n-2}(2)^{n-2} + \cdots + a_1(2)^1 + a_0(2)^0 + a_{-1}(2)^{-1} + \cdots + a_{-m}(2)^{-m}$$

The coefficients a_{n-1} through a_{-m} are either 0 or 1. This number can be represented in positional notation as

$$N_2 = a_{n-1}a_{n-2} \cdots a_1a_0.a_{-1} \cdots a_{-m}$$

The point between a_0 and a_{-1} is a *binary point* and serves to separate the *integer portion* of the number $a_{n-1}a_{n-2} \cdots a_1a_0$ from the *fractional part* of the number $.a_{-1} \cdots a_{-m}$. Some typical binary numbers are

$$101101.110$$
$$-101.01101$$
$$1.1110101$$

The decimal equivalent of any binary number can be found using the above relationship. For example, the decimal number corresponding to the binary number

$$11011011.01$$

is found as follows: for this number $n = 8$ and $m = 2$, thus,

$$
\begin{aligned}
a_{n-1}(2^{n-1}) &= 1\,(2^7) = 1\,(128) = 128 \\
a_{n-2}(2^{n-2}) &= 1\,(2^6) = 1\,(64) = 64 \\
a_{n-3}(2^{n-3}) &= 0\,(2^5) = 0\,(32) = 0 \\
a_{n-4}(2^{n-4}) &= 1\,(2^4) = 1\,(16) = 16 \\
a_{n-5}(2^{n-5}) &= 1\,(2^3) = 1\,(8) = 8 \\
a_{n-6}(2^{n-6}) &= 0\,(2^2) = 0\,(4) = 0 \\
a_{n-7}(2^{n-7}) &= 1\,(2^1) = 1\,(2) = 2 \\
a_{n-8}(2^{n-8}) &= 1\,(2^0) = 1\,(1) = 1 \\
a_{-1}(2^{-1}) &= 0\,(2^{-1}) = 0\,(\tfrac{1}{2}) = 0 \\
a_{-2}(2^{-2}) &= 1\,(2^{-2}) = 1\,(\tfrac{1}{4}) = \tfrac{1}{4} \\
\end{aligned}
$$
$$\text{Total} = 219\tfrac{1}{4} = 219.25$$

We can talk about binary integers (binary point at the right of all digits), binary fractions (binary point at the left of all digits) and binary fixed-point numbers in the same way that we discuss the equivalent decimal numbers. It is also possible to talk about binary floating-point numbers. Normally the mantissa of a binary floating-point number is a binary fixed-point number and the exponent is given as a decimal integer. The exponent in this case represents the number of places the binary point must be moved.

Some typical binary floating-point numbers are

$$1.101 \times 2^3 = 1.101E3 = 1101$$

and

$$101.1101 \times 2^{-3} = 101.1101E - 3 = .1011101$$

The binary point is moved three positions to the right in the first number and three positions to the left in the second number.

Binary numbers can be used to carry out any numerical calculation that can be done using decimal numbers. As we have seen above, it is always possible to determine the decimal number equivalent to a given binary number. Similarly, as is shown in Appendix I, it is possible to translate any decimal number into a binary number. As discussed in the Appendix, this conversion is exact for some numbers and only a good approximation for others if the precision of the resulting binary number is limited to a fixed number of binary digits.

Most computer users will not encounter binary numbers in their work. However, a general understanding of binary numbers, their relationship to decimal numbers, and the way numerical information is represented in a computer is necessary if one is to understand some of the factors that limit computational accuracy and computation speed. These problems are taken up in later chapters.

Computer Representation of Binary Numbers

There are a number of ways that numerical information can be stored in a computer word. The easiest way is to assume that the number being stored corresponds to the bits in the word. For example, a 12-bit computer word can store the binary integer

$$b = a_{11}a_{10}a_9a_8a_7a_6a_5a_4a_3a_2a_1a_0$$

as shown in Fig. 2-9.

If a computer word has r bits, it is possible to represent any positive binary integers between 0 and $(2^r - 1)_{10}$. Similarly, the r binary digits can be used to represent the r-bit binary fractions between 0 and $(1 - 2^{-r})_{10}$. If the number has n integer digits and m fractional digits, any r-bit positive binary number between 0 and $[(2^n - 1) + (1 - 2^{-m})]_{10}$ can be represented. For example, let $r = 3$. Then Table 2-1 indicates the different three-bit positive binary numbers that can be stored in a three-bit register. The location of the binary point for a fixed-point number is usually not encoded. The machine-level program which operates on information stored in this form must be written so that

a_{11}	a_{10}	a_9	a_8	a_7	a_6	a_5	a_4	a_3	a_2	a_1	a_0

12-bit word

FIGURE 2-9 ∎ Binary integer storage in a 12-bit word.

TABLE 2-1 ■ Possible three-bit binary numbers that can be stored in a three-bit register

$n = 3, m = 0$	$n = 2, m = 1$	$n = 1, m = 2$	$n = 0, m = 3$
000	00.0	0.00	.000
001	00.1	0.01	.001
010	01.0	0.10	.010
011	01.1	0.11	.011
100	10.0	1.00	.100
101	10.1	1.01	.101
110	11.0	1.10	.110
111	11.1	1.11	.111

the location of the binary point is properly accounted for in any computations. This task is usually carried out by the compiler.

Negative fixed-point numbers can be encoded in the same way except that one bit of the word, usually the leftmost bit, is used to indicate the sign of the number. If the bit is 0 the number is positive, and if the bit is 1 the number is negative. This means that an r-bit word can store $(r - 1)$-bit binary integers between $\pm(2^{r-1} - 1)_{10}$ and $(r - 1)$-bit binary fractions between $\pm(1 - 2^{1-r})_{10}$. Similar results hold for fixed-point numbers.

The specification of any floating-point binary number requires two quantities; the mantissa and the exponent. If a computer word is large enough to accommodate the desired precision and range of the floating-point numbers, then the two parts can be stored in an r-bit word using a method such as is shown in Fig. 2-10(a). Sometimes greater precision is required in the representation of the number. In that case, two or even more computer words can be used to store a floating-point number, as is illustrated in Fig. 2-10(b). Of course, the computer is required to do more work when it processes numbers stored in this manner.

Computer Representation of Decimal Numbers

Most numerical calculations included in a program written in a higher-level programming language involve decimal numbers. But the information stored inside a computer is expressed as sequences of zeros and ones. Thus, if decimal calculations are to be performed, some type of convention must be used to represent this decimal information. There are two approaches that can be used:

1. Convert all decimal numbers to a binary-number representation.
2. Use an internal coding which retains the decimal form of the information.

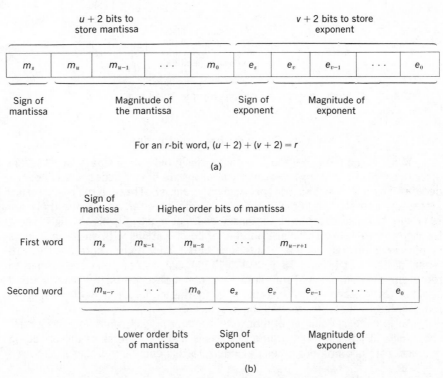

FIGURE 2-10 ■ Storage of floating-point numbers. (a) Storage of a floating-point number in one computer word. (b) Storage of a floating-point number in two computer words.

The final choice depends upon the type of computer being used and the compiler program used to produce the machine-level program. In some cases the programmer can select the method best suited to the calculations being carried out.

Binary Representation of Decimal Information

An algorithm is given in Appendix I that may be used to convert a decimal number to a corresponding binary number. One way to store decimal information is illustrated in Fig. 2-11, where all decimal numbers are first converted to an equivalent binary form. After the calculations are completed the results are then converted from binary back into decimal form.

The chief cost in this method is that involved in carrying out the two different types of conversions. This is not particularly bothersome if there is only a small amount of input and output information that must be processed relative to the number of calculations to be performed.

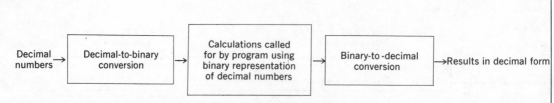

FIGURE 2-11 ■ Steps in storing decimal numbers in binary form.

Binary-Coded Decimal Information

Many computers, particularly those designed for business application, store decimal information by assigning appropriate binary codes to each of the decimal digits that make up the decimal number. These binary codes are stored and operated on in place of their decimal counterparts. Since there are ten digits to be represented by a binary code, at least four binary digits must be used to generate a sufficient number of combinations with one's and zero's to represent the ten decimal digits. For four binary digits there are $2^4 = 16$ binary patterns of 1's and 0's (0000 to 1111). Only ten of them are needed to represent the ten decimal numbers. One common code is the *binary-coded decimal* (BCD) code given in Table 2-2. In this code, each decimal digit is represented by its corresponding binary number.

To encode a decimal number we transform each digit into its corresponding BCD code. The decoding process is just the reverse of the encoding process. The following examples demonstrate this encoding process:

Integer BCD encoding:
$$\underbrace{0111}_{7} \quad \underbrace{0110}_{6} \quad \underbrace{0011}_{3} \quad \underbrace{0100}_{4} \quad \underbrace{1001}_{9}$$

Fixed-point BCD encoding:
$$\underbrace{0110}_{6} \quad \underbrace{1001}_{9} \quad \underbrace{0011}_{3} . \underbrace{0100}_{4} \quad \underbrace{0010}_{2}$$

Floating-point BCD encoding:
$$\underbrace{0111}_{7} \quad \underbrace{0001}_{1} \quad \underbrace{0010}_{2} \quad E \quad \underbrace{0010}_{2} \quad \underbrace{0101}_{5}$$

The storage of BCD encoded numbers in a computer's memory is accomplished in essentially the same way that binary numbers are stored. The only difference is that each decimal digit is stored in four bits of the computer word. For example a 24-bit computer word can store a 24-bit binary integer or a six-digit decimal number. Figure 2-12 shows how a decimal integer might be stored in a 24-bit computer word. In this case, the largest decimal integer that can be stored is $999999 = 10^7 - 1$. The largest binary number that can be stored in the same 24-bit word is equivalent to the decimal number $2^{24} - 1 = 16,777,215$.

TABLE 2-2 ∎ The binary-coded decimal (BCD) code

Decimal number	BCD code	Decimal number	BCD code
0	0000	5	0101
1	0001	6	0110
2	0010	7	0111
3	0011	8	1000
4	0100	9	1001

The storage of fixed-point and floating-point decimal numbers in BCD form is also equivalent to the storage of the corresponding binary number except that four bits are needed to store each decimal digit. Decimal numbers can thus be stored in memory in encoded decimal form. The price we pay is a reduction in the magnitude of the numbers that can be stored. This is compensated for by the fact that we do not have to go through the conversion process of transforming decimal numbers to binary numbers and vice versa. This can be an important consideration in business applications where we must work with a large amount of numerical data in a way which requires only a relatively minor amount of numerical calculation.

Storing of Characters

Since a computer is an information-processing device, it can work on nonnumeric as well as on numeric information. Nonnumeric information corresponds to such things as names, words, or any sequence of symbols that we wish to associate with a meaning such as an algebraic equation. All nonnumeric information is represented by a string of characters from some basic character set. This character set usually includes the 26 letters of the alphabet, A through Z, the ten digits 0 through 9, the different punctuation symbols, the standard mathematical symbols, and some special symbols designed for particular needs.

The typical character set used on the punched cards for a computer contains 64 different symbols. In a computer it is quite common to use an eight-bit code to represent the characters. Some of the typical encodings are dis-

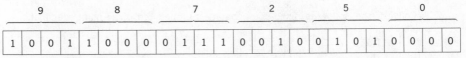

FIGURE 2-12 ∎ BCD encoding of a six-digit decimal number in a 24-bit computer word.

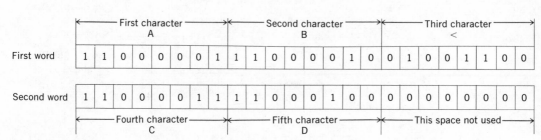

FIGURE 2-13 ■ Storage of a sequence of characters.

cussed in Appendix II. Referring to this Appendix, we see that the following EBCDIC code can be used to represent the following characters:

A	11000001	·	01001011
B	11000010	<	01001100
C	11000011		
D	11000100		

If we must store character information in an r-bit word, we must arrange one or more eight-bit codes in each word. For example, assume that each word is 24 bits long. Then we can store three eight-bit characters in a word. For example, let us assume that we wish to store the following character sequence in memory where each memory word has 24 bits.

$$AB < CD$$

This sequence has five characters. Thus, we need two memory words to store the sequence. If we use the eight-bit code given above, then the given sequence is packed into memory in the manner shown in Fig. 2-13. The number of bits needed to store one character is called a *byte*.

If we know how the character information is packed into a word it is possible to locate and make computations on one or more characters at a time, as well as upon whole character strings. This means that we are able to carry out information-processing tasks involving characters and sequences of characters with the same ease that we can carry out numerical calculations. Throughout the rest of this book we are therefore justified in assuming that any algorithm can use numerical or nonnumerical information with equal ease.

Exercises

1. Convert the following fixed-point binary numbers to fixed-point decimal numbers:
   (a) −111.011
   (b) 11101
   (c) 11010011.01
   (d) −100.11

2. Write each of the following decimal numbers in its standard floating-point form (mantissa normalized between .1 and 1) with a precision of five decimal digits:
   (a) 3.141593
   (b) 4752.6
   (c) −778.52
   (d) −0.0000164759

3. What is the range of values for the numbers whose magnitudes are specified by the following precisions:
   (a) Fixed-point decimal integer with a precision of four digits.
   (b) Fixed-point decimal number with a precision of five digits including two digits to the right of the decimal point.
   (c) Fixed-point binary integer with a precision of 15 digits.

4. Determine the largest decimal number that can be stored in a 32-bit computer word, if the encoding is:
   (a) in BCD form
   (b) in binary number form

4 ■ Compilers

The writing of a machine-language program, even for simple calculations, takes a large amount of time, even for professional programmers. A considerable amount of effort must be expended in simple tasks such as deciding how to arrange the information and instructions in memory, or generating standard sequences of machine-language code to carry out standard tasks. To relieve the ordinary computer user of these problems, many user-oriented programming languages, of the type discussed in Chapter I, have been developed. The computer user can then describe the algorithm he wishes to execute on the computer in one of these languages, and a special computer program, called a *compiler,* converts the program into an appropriate machine-language representation.

The initial program written by the programmer in the user-oriented language is called the *source program,* while the resulting machine-language program is called the *object program.* The relationship between these programs and the compiler is illustrated in Fig. 2-14.

Once we decide to use a user-oriented programming language to describe our computations, we become isolated from the minute programming details that would have to be considered if we were working at the machine-language level. The basic operations that we may use in our program are determined by the source language, while the compiler takes care of assigning storage space in memory and generating the machine-language instructions necessary to carry out our program. Although the compiler removes the necessity for us to know machine-language programming, we must keep in mind the general organization of a computer, how it processes information, and how it

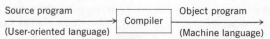

FIGURE 2-14 ■ Illustration of the relationship between a source and object program.

stores information, since these features often influence the behavior of our calculations.

When we use a user-oriented programming language we can think of the computer's memory as a sequence of boxes each one of which can store either a finite-length number, a finite-length character string or an instruction that can be executed by the computer. Figure 2-15 illustrates this type of organization. Each box may correspond to one or more memory words. It is impractical to think of referencing each item of information by giving the actual memory location where that information is stored. We therefore assign a special symbol sequence, called an *identifier,* as a name for each box. Whenever we wish to indicate a particular item, all we must do is give the identifier associated with the item.

Each storage location used to store data can contain any type of information allowed by the particular programming language with which we are dealing. The only constraint is that we must use a finite number of digits to indicate any numerical information and a finite number of characters to indicate any nonnumeric information.

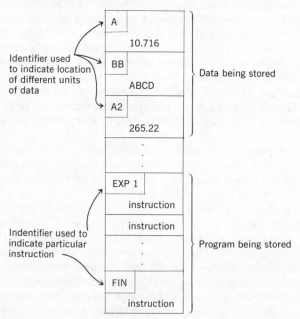

FIGURE 2-15 ■ Hypothetical structure of memory from users viewpoint.

The need to attach identifiers to instructions may not appear as necessary as the need to identify information. However, it is often necessary to indicate a particular section of a machine-language program or a particular point in the program. Thus, the ability to attach identifiers to instructions gives us an easy way to reference any instruction or set of instructions in which we are interested.

The Compiling Process

The object program generated by a compiler represents the machine-language-level program that will be executed by the computer. To form this program the compiler must decide how and where all the data is to be stored in memory, and must generate the appropriate machine-language instructions necessary to carry out the computations represented by the source-language statements. A compiler can do this only if the source-programming language is defined in an exact and unambiguous manner.

A source program is made up of a series of statements. Each statement, written according to the rules of the source language, either provides information to the compiler concerning how the program or data are to be organized, or it describes a computation that must be translated into machine language. For example, the following FORTRAN statements

$$REAL\ X, Y, Z$$
$$X = 26.5$$
$$Y = 36.82$$
$$Z = X + Y$$

would tell the compiler that it must reserve three information-storage boxes, labeled with the identifiers X, Y, and Z, respectively, to hold the floating-point numbers† associated with these identifiers. Next, the compiler would generate the necessary instructions to load the number 26.5 into the location indicated by the identifier X and 36.82 into the location indicated by the identifier Y. The final statement would generate the machine language program necessary to take the number stored in Y, add the number stored in X, and then place the resulting value in the location indicated by the identifier Z. The corresponding PL/I statement sequence would be

$$DECLARE\ (X, Y, Z)\ FLOAT;$$
$$X = 26.5;$$
$$Y = 36.82;$$
$$Z = X + Y;$$

Even though a compiler can carry out most of the routine tasks of translating a source program to an object program, the computer user must supply a considerable amount of guidance concerning how the program is to

---

† In FORTRAN a floating-point number is called a real number.

be organized and the type of data to be expected. Each programming language has a particular way of supplying this information to the compiler. A computer user who does not fully understand how these tasks are accomplished usually does not make effective use of the computer when attempting to carry out a particular computational task.

Computing Cost

Computer time is expensive and can easily be wasted by improper program design or inappropriate use of the computer facilities. Each computer installation has a set of special systems programs that are designed to help the user run his program. These systems programs, which include the compilers associated with the programming languages that may be used on the computer, require a certain amount of computer time to perform their functions. The cost of this time is, of course, charged to the user. Once an object program has been generated, the computer uses this program to carry out the desired information processing task. The cost of the time needed to execute the object program is the cost of the actual calculation. All of the other costs are overhead charges incurred in the preparation of the final object program. The interrelationship of these costs are illustrated in Fig. 2-16.

As illustrated in Fig. 2-16, it is possible to avoid compiling costs once a program has been fully developed and tested by obtaining a copy of the object program and then using that object program every time additional calculations are needed. This approach, which is often overlooked, should be used whenever it is planned to use the resulting program for a large number of calculations over an extended period of time.

Most computer centers have a number of different compilers that can be used to translate a given programming language. Some of the compilers are designed to generate an optimized object program that makes most efficient use of the available computing facilities. Although this type of compiler should be used whenever it is desired to generate an object program for use over an extended period of time, it is not necessary to carry out this type of optimization until all other programming errors have been removed. Thus, one or more "fast" compilers are usually available that carry out a rapid, but not necessarily optimum, translation. These compilers are designed to aid the programmer detect programming errors while minimizing the processing cost. If the pro-

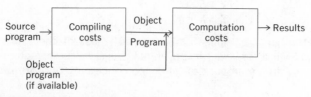

FIGURE 2-16 ■ Breakdown of computing costs.

gram being developed is a relatively short program that is only to be used a few times, it is usually not economically necessary to generate a permanent object program. For these cases all of the programming effort, including the final calculations, can be carried out using the "fast" compiler.

Exercises

1. A computer installation charges the user $180 an hour for computer time. A computer program has been developed to carry out a certain job which must be repeated for a large number of times. Suppose it takes the program a total of 5 minutes to run—2 minutes to compile and 3 minutes to execute for each job:
 (a) Calculate the computing cost (computer time only) if the same program is to be run (compiled and executed) 100 times.
 (b) Calculate the computing cost if an object program is obtained first and the object program is then executed 100 times.
 (c) Compute the difference in cost between (a) and (b) above.
 (d) Compute the difference in cost between (a) and (b) above if the same program must be run 10,000 times.

2. In exercise 1, suppose that a professional programmer claims that he could improve the program to cut the computer time in half (i.e., 1 minute to compile and $1\frac{1}{2}$ minutes to execute) for each job. However, it will take the programmer an estimated 50 hours to develop the improved program at the rate of $10 an hour. (You may assume that the option of obtaining and running object programs is available.) Determine whether or not the improvement is economically worthwhile:
 (a) if the improved program is to be run 100 times;
 (b) if the improved program is to be run 10,000 times.

5 ■ Summary

Computers come in all sizes, from mini-computers with 12-bit words and 4096 words of memory to super-computers with 64-bit words and memories with over a million words. All of these computers carry out calculations in essentially the same way. A machine-language program is stored in memory along with the information needed by the program. The computer's control unit supervises the execution of the machine-language program taking information out of memory or from an appropriate input device as needed and sends the final results to an appropriate output device.

As we will see in later discussions, the way that information must be stored internally is often of importance in a given computer application. In particular, any item of information must be of finite length. When working with numeric information this will mean that some numbers cannot be represented exactly and must be approximated by a number with a fixed, finite number of digits.

Programming languages insulate the computer user from the details of developing the final machine-language program executed by the computer. The programming language must be designed, however, so that the user can supply the compiler enough information so it "knows" how the program and data should be organized in the computer's memory.

The following chapters discuss various aspects of the computing process and ways to use the computer to carry out different classes of computations. Much of this material will be easier to understand if it is interpreted in terms of the concepts presented in this chapter.

References

The following references provide an extensive description of the structure of computers and the way in which information is actually represented inside of a computer. [5] discusses the different types of number systems and how they evolved. [3], [6], and [7] deal with the different ways information can be represented inside of a computer. [3] also discusses how electronic circuits can be designed to carry out many of the standard information processing tasks found in a computer. [1], [2], and [4] discuss many of the current computer systems and the different pieces of equipment that might be included in a computer system.

1. Bohl, M. (1970) *Computer Concepts,* Science Research Associates, Chicago, Ill.
2. Bohl, M. (1971) *Information Processing,* Science Research Associates, Chicago, Ill.
3. Booth, T. L. (1971) *Digital Networks and Computer Systems,* John Wiley & Sons, New York.
4. Chapin, N. (1971) *Computers: A Systems Approach,* Van Nostrand Reinhold Co., New York.
5. Gardner, M. (September, 1968) "Counting Systems and The Relationships Between Numbers and the Real World," *Scientific American,* Vol. No. 3, pp. 218–230.
6. Knuth, D. E. (1968) *The Art of Computer Programming, Vol 1, Fundamental Algorithms,* Addison-Wesley, Reading, Mass.
7. Ralston, A. (1971) *Introduction To Programming and Computer Science,* McGraw-Hill, New York.

Home Problems

1. Expand the number of instructions that can be used by a computist on a hand calculator to include division. Give an algorithm describing how the following calculation may be performed:

$$Y = (U^2 + V^2)/W^2$$

2. Assume that we have a computer with a memory made up of 32-bit words. Estimate the following quantities:
   (a) The number of characters which can be stored in 1000 words of memory.
   (b) The number of seven-digit, BCD-encoded, signed-decimal, fixed-point numbers which can be stored in 1000 words of memory.

(c) The number of 12-digit, BCD-encoded, signed-decimal, fixed-point numbers which can be stored in 1000 words of memory.

(d) The number of binary-encoded, seven-digit, decimal integers that can be stored in 1000 words of memory.

(e) The number of binary-encoded, seven-digit, floating-point, decimal numbers which can be stored in 1000 words of memory.

3. Assume that we have a computer program that carries out all floating-point calculations with a mantissa precision of four decimal digits. Let

$$A = 8.456E8 \qquad B = 8.454E8 \qquad C = 7.231E5$$

(a) What will be the value of W, X, Y, where

X = A−B (the mantissa of X only has four decimal digits)

Y = A+C (the mantissa of Y only has four decimal digits)

W = X+C

Z = Y−B

(b) How large is the difference between W and Z?

(c) Explain why W and Z have two different values even though mathematically they should be the same (W = A − B + C, Z = A + C − B).

4. Let A, B, and C be three binary fixed-point numbers:

$$A = 1010.1101 \qquad B = 101.11 \qquad C = 110.11$$

Carry out the following calculations

(a) B + C

(b) C − B

(c) A × B

(d) A/B

5. Assume that a computer has a memory word size of r-bits.

(a) Prove that there are 2^r distinct patterns of r binary digits that can appear in each word.

(b) Prove that the decimal value of the largest unsigned binary integer which can be stored in a word is $(2^r - 1)_{10}$.

6. Make a table for the computer language you are using which shows:

(a) the different data types which can be represented by identifiers

(b) the convention used to determine the data type associated with each identifier

(c) the precision limits associated with each data type

7. Assume that π and $\sqrt{2}$ are to be represented as two 12-bit, binary, fixed-point numbers. Let PI and SQ2 be the identifiers which represent these two numbers.

(a) Give the binary representation for both PI and SQ2.

(b) What is the equivalent fixed-point decimal value of PI and SQ2?

(c) What is the approximate error introduced by the requirement that π and $\sqrt{2}$ must be represented as 12-bit, binary, fixed-point numbers?

8. Assume that the following bit pattern is stored in a 16-bit word.

0	1	0	1	0	0	0	0	0	1	1	.0	0	0	0	1

What information is represented by this bit pattern if:
   (a) the information is coded as EBCDIC characters?
   (b) the information is encoded as a positive binary integer?
   (c) the information is encoded as a BCD decimal integer?
      Is there any way to determine what type of information is represented by
the given bit pattern?

3

**information representation,
expressions and assignment
statements**

1 ▌ Introduction

Mathematical notation was developed so that symbols could be used to represent information and the operations performed on this information in a compact and concise manner. As long as we work problems using pencil and paper, we automatically associate meaning to the symbols that we see and we interpret this meaning according to our previous experience. Computers, unfortunately, do not have the flexibility of humans. Therefore, we must be very precise in the way we describe information and how it is to be used in a computer. In Chapter II we investigated the methods that could be used to represent and store information inside of a computer. In this chapter we discuss information representation and the operations that can be performed upon information from a computer user's viewpoint.

2 ▌ Basic Data Types

When dealing with information, the following three distinct data types can be identified:

1. Numeric
2. Character
3. Logical

Numeric Information

Numeric information corresponds to information that is represented by a number or numerical value. For example we can talk about 100 dollars or 12 eggs. The numbers 100 and 12 represent numerical information. Any number that is given in explicit form is a *constant,* while any quantity that is given a name and is allowed to take on a range of values is called a *variable.* The name associated with the variable is called an *identifier.* For example, the following mathematical formula

$$A = (3.16 + X + Y)/23$$

contains two constants, 3.16 and 23, and three variables represented by the identifiers A, X, and Y.

The information represented by the variables and constants must be stored in individual and unique storage locations. As discussed previously, we can represent these locations as a stack of boxes as shown in Fig. 3-1. Each box holds the computer encoded value of each constant or variable. It is up to the compiler program to allocate the storage space and decide how the particular information is to be represented.

When the compiler encounters a symbol that represents a constant, such as 3.16, it immediately knows that it must store the value of that constant in a

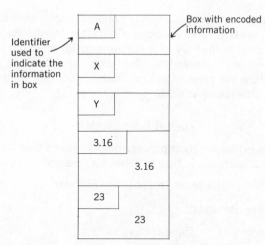

FIGURE 3-1 ■ Method of visualizing information storage.

box it labels 3.16. However, when the computer encounters an identifier that represents a variable, such as X, then it knows that it must provide a box labeled X. However, the computer has no way of telling what value the variable X will have during a computation, so it leaves the contents of the box undefined. During some part of the program there will be a calculation that assigns a value to the variable X. When this calculation is completed the value generated is placed in the box named X which has been reserved as the storage location for this information.

A computer is a symbol manipulator. Therefore, there is no reason to restrict ourselves to numeric information.

Character Information

Character information corresponds to any sequence of characters to which we might wish to assign a meaning. For example, in a payroll calculation the names of the different people who receive paychecks represent character information. Character information is difficult to distinguish from other symbolic quantities. Thus the convention is adopted that the value of all character information is delimited as

'Character Information'

The following examples illustrate this idea.

'TOM'   'NEXT⌴VALUE'   '1,012'

In this example, ⌴ denotes a blank space and the set of symbols 1,012 is a five-symbol character sequence rather than a number.

Just as we can talk about numerical constants and variables, we can talk about character constants and variables. Character constants, such as 'TOM' or '1,012', are stored in memory in a manner similar to numerical constants. Character variables are indicated by identifiers that have the same form as numerical identifiers. We must therefore "remember" that a particular identifier represents a character variable.

Logical Information

There are many information processing operations that involve making a decision whether a sentence is true or false. For example, the statement

The Moon is a satellite of Earth

is true. However the statement

The girl has red hair

may be either true or false depending upon which girl is being discussed. Logical information deals with truth and falsity. If a data element represents a logical value, then that element must have a value either TRUE or FALSE. In some programming languages logical values are represented by spelling out the worlds TRUE or FALSE. For our discussion we accept the more common convention of allowing 1 to represent TRUE and 0 to represent FALSE. The problem of distinguishing between the numbers 0 and 1 and the logical values 0 and 1 is usually settled by the particular context in which the value is used.

Logical constants are either 0 or 1. Logical variables are indicated by identifiers that have the same form as other identifiers except that they indicate a logical value that may be either 0 or 1. In the following discussion the values 1 and 0 will be used interchangeably with TRUE and FALSE, respectively, to indicate logical values.

Representation of Identifiers

In developing an algorithm we must define identifiers to represent variables corresponding to different types of information. Identifiers are represented by character sequences such as A, NEXT, VALUE or A10 and are distinguished from character information by the absence of the delimiting single quote marks. In many programming languages the convention is also used that the first character in an identifier must be a letter and no blank spaces can be included in the sequence. We use this convention in this book.

Exercise

1. Determine for each of the following data items whether it is a constant, a variable, or neither, and whether the information it represents is numeric, character, or either:

(a) 3.14159
(b) '3.14159'
(c) 'AVERAGE'
(d) A1001
(e) PAYAMOUNT
(f) PAY AMOUNT

---

3 ∎ Operators

Mathematical operators tell us how we are to process the mathematical information represented by constants and variables to obtain an explicit value. There are four major classes of operators that are found in programming languages:

1. Arithmetic operators
2. Character operators
3. Relational operators
4. Logical operators

Although these operations are familiar to anyone who has worked with mathematical concepts, we must be very careful when using these operators to understand the exact form of the operation they represent within a computer.

Arithmetic Operations

The basic mathematical operations are:

1. (+) addition
2. (−) subtraction
3. (*) multiplication†
4. (/) division

These operators are called *binary operators* since normally they describe a *binary operation,* which consists of combining two numbers, called *operands,* to form a new number.

Unfortunately, there is a small problem with the use of the + and − signs that occurs in some situations. When an operator acts on only one operand the operation is called a *unary operation.* Two unary operations are

$$+V \text{ (unary addition)}$$

and

$$-V \text{ (unary negative or unary minus)}$$

---

† The * symbol is used to indicate the multiplication operation in an algorithm in order to avoid the confusion inherent in some of the other notations used to represent multiplication such as A · B, A × B, or AB.

since

$$+V = V$$

we do not encounter any trouble in evaluating any arithmetic expressions if we disregard the unary $+$. However, we cannot disregard the unary minus since this operation tells us to form the negative value of a number.

In addition to the four arithmetic operations above, most programming languages include exponentiation as a standard binary operation. The operation of *exponentiation* has the general form V^U. This notation is difficult to use in preparing programs since all the symbols do not fall on the same line. A number of conventions have been adopted to represent this binary operation. The two most popular are

$$V**U \quad \text{and} \quad V \uparrow U$$

We use the first convention in this book.

Binary and unary arithmetic operators operate on numerical information and the resulting value is a number.

Character Operations†

The basic binary operation associated with character information is the operation of concatenation. Let 'ABC' and 'UVW' be two character sequences. Then the binary operation of *concatenation,* denoted by $\|$, is defined as

$$\text{'ABC'} \parallel \text{'UVW'} = \text{'ABCUVW'}$$

The concatenation operation thus forms a new character sequence 'ABCUVW' by adjoining the character sequences 'ABC' and 'UVW' into a single sequence. The operands of the concatenation operation are character sequences and the resulting value is a character sequence.

When we work with numbers we find the numbers 0 and 1 of particular importance since they act as identities (i.e., $0 + x = x$, $1 * x = x$). There is a special character value that serves as an identity value for concatenation. The *null sequence* or *null character* is the character sequence without any characters. The null sequence is indicated by

''

and should not be confused by the blank character

'␣'

that we use to represent a space in a character sequence. To see the dif-

---

† Not all programming languages allow the use of the concatenation operation. However, it is often possible to formulate equivalent results through programming tricks.

ference, we have

$$\text{'AB'}\|\text{''} = \text{'AB'}$$

while

$$\text{'AB'}\|\text{'}\sqcup\text{'} = \text{'AB}\sqcup\text{'}$$

In the first example the result of the concatenation is a character sequence made up of two characters, while in the second example the result is a character sequence made up of three characters.

Relational Operations

There are many situations where it is necessary for us to compare two quantities of information and make the logical decision that either

(a) "it is TRUE that the two quantities compare in the required manner"

or

(b) "it is FALSE that the two quantities compare in the required manner"

Mathematically the task of making a comparison is accomplished by introducing the idea of relational operators.

Relational operators are binary operators. The operands of a relational operator will be either numerical values or character sequences and the result of applying the operators to the operands is a logical value. A relational operation has the following general form

$$\langle\text{operand}\rangle\langle\text{relation}\rangle\langle\text{operand}\rangle$$

When the two operands being compared according to the indicated relation satisfy the condition indicated by the relation, then the resulting logical value is 1 (TRUE). If the relation is not satisfied, then the resulting logical value is 0 (FALSE).

Table 3-1 lists the standard relational operators used in this book. These,

TABLE 3-1 ■ Relational operators

Symbol	Meaning
1. $<$	less than
2. $\leq$	less than or equal
3. $=$	equal
4. $\neq$	not equal
5. $>$	greater than
6. $\geq$	greater than or equal

or an equivalent set of operators, are found in most programming languages.

The relational operators are most familiar as they apply to numerical values. For example

$$25 < 36$$

has a logical value of 1, while

$$A \geqslant B$$

has a logical value that depends upon the numerical values associated with the identifiers A and B. If A has a value of 5 and B a value of 6, then $A \geqslant B$ has a logical value of 0. It is not, however, necessary to limit the operands to numerical values.

Relational Operations Involving Character Sequences

If the two operands of a relational operation are character sequences, then the relation is evaluated according to a "natural ordering" that is induced by the code used to store character information in a computer. This code establishes a numerical order on the individual characters of the character set which is generally referred to as the *collating sequence* of the character set. The particular collating sequence used in a particular programming language depends upon the conventions associated with that language. For our discussion, the collating sequence for the letters A through Z, the decimal digits 0 through 9, and the space character (⊔) or blank is assumed to have the following form

$$⊔ < A < B \cdots < Z < 0 < \cdots < 9$$

We use the less than relation $<$ to denote that the character on the left "comes before" or is "less than" the character on the right.

Once the collating sequence has been decided, the ordering of any two character sequences can be decided very easily. Starting on the left of both sequences, a character-by-character comparison is carried out until two dissimilar characters are found. The two character sequences are then ordered according to the ordering of these two characters. For example,

$$'ABC' \neq 'DBC'$$
$$'A10' < 'A11'$$
$$'X5' > 'X2'$$

all have a logical value of 1. While

$$'AC' = 'BC'$$
$$'A1' < 'AA'$$

both have a logical value of 0.

As long as both operands are character sequences of the same length there is no problem. When the two sequences are of different lengths we assume that blanks (⊔) are added to the right of the shorter sequence until it has the same length as the longer sequence. The comparison is then carried out on this modified sequence. For example,

$$'A' < 'AA'$$
$$'ALEX' < 'ALEXANDER'$$

both have a logical value of 1 while

$$'A5' < 'AA6B'$$
$$'JOHNSON' < 'JOHN'$$

both have the logical value of 0.

At first the idea of applying relational operators to character strings may appear a little unfamiliar. However, as this type of operation becomes more familiar we will see that it provides us with a very powerful computational tool. The rules regarding the ordering of character sequences must be well understood or serious errors may result.

Logical Operations

Any variable that represents a logical quantity takes on a value of 1 (TRUE) or 0 (FALSE). There are three basic logical operations that are used in this book to combine logical variables. These operations are sufficient to carry out any logical computation.

The three logical operations that we will use are the *NEGATION* or *NOT* operation, the *AND* operation, and the *OR* operation. The first operation is a unary operation and the last two are binary operations. The operands of the operations are assumed to be logical variables (or logical constants) and the resulting value of the operation is a logical value. The three operations are defined as follows:

Let A and B be identifiers that represent logical variables

NOT $\neg A$
   $\neg A$ has the value TRUE if A has the value FALSE and has the value FALSE if A has the value TRUE
AND $A \wedge B$
   $A \wedge B$ has the value TRUE if and only if both A and B have the value TRUE. Otherwise the value is FALSE.
OR $A \vee B$
   $A \vee B$ has the value TRUE if and only if either A or B or both have the value TRUE. Otherwise the value is FALSE.

These three operations are summarized by Table 3-2.

Logical operations provide a compact way to represent logical rela-

TABLE 3-2 ■ Basic logical operations and their symbols[a]

NEGATION (¬)			AND (∧)				OR (∨)		
A	¬ A		A	B	A ∧ B		A	B	A ∨ B
1	0		0	0	0		0	0	0
0	1		0	1	0		0	1	1
			1	0	0		1	0	1
			1	1	1		1	1	1

[a] Note: 1 indicates TRUE and 0 indicates FALSE.

tionships. For example, the general statement

"Fred and Mary will go to the movies if each one has the price of admission."

can be represented by the following logical expression

$$A \wedge B$$

where A, B are identifiers which represent logical values as follows:

A—Fred has the price of admission
B—Mary has the price of admission

and the operation A ∧ B represents the logical condition

Fred and Mary are going to the movies

The result of this operation is 1 (TRUE) if A is 1 (TRUE) and B is 1 (TRUE) Otherwise the expression is 0 (FALSE).

The usefulness of these operations will become more apparent when we investigate how they are used in different classes of expressions. Table 3-3 provides a summary of the basic properties of all the different types of operations we have just discussed. These operators form the building blocks that we may use to carry out complex computations.

Exercises

1. Determine the result of the operations $A + B$, $A - B$, $A * B$, A/B, and $A * * B$ for:

    (a) A = 12.5   B = 2.0
    (b) A = .55E2   B = .2E1
    (c) A = .12E3   B = −.2E1

2. Determine the result of the operations A∥B and B∥A for

(a) A = 'MY␣NAME␣'   B = 'IS␣JOHN␣'
(b) A = 'A␣COMPUTER␣'   B = 'PROGRAM␣'
(c) A = ''   B = 'PEOPLE'
(d) A = '␣'   B = ''

3. Let A and B be the following statements:

$$A - X \text{ is less than or equal to } Y$$
$$B - X \text{ is greater than } Z$$

Determine the logical value of the operations $\neg A$, $\neg B$, $A \wedge B$, and $A \vee B$ if:

(a) X = 3   Y = 5   Z = 4
(b) X = 7   Y = 7   Z = 2
(c) X = 5   Y = 3   Z = 8

TABLE 3-3 ■ The basic operations and their properties

Operation	Symbol	Data type of Operand(s)	Result	Type
Addition	+	number	number	binary
Subtraction	−	number	number	binary
Multiplication	*	number	number	binary
Division	/	number	number	binary
Exponentiation	**	number	number	binary
Unary minus	−	number	number	unary
Concatenation	∥	character string	character string	binary
Less than	<	number or character string	logical value	binary
Less than or equal	≤	number or character string	logical value	binary
Equal	=	number or character string	logical value	binary
Not equal	≠	number or character string	logical value	binary
Greater than	>	number or character string	logical value	binary
Greater than or equal	≥	number or character string	logical value	binary
NOT	¬	logical value	logical value	unary
AND	∧	logical value	logical value	binary
OR	∨	logical value	logical value	binary

4 ■ Expressions, Precedence Rules, and Assignment Statements

An *expression* is a formula constructed from the basic operations that tells us how to combine a collection of variables and constants to obtain a value. The most common type of expressions are arithmetic expressions, which only involve arithmetic operations, and logical expressions, which only involve logical operations. However, as we will shortly see, it is possible to combine all the different basic operations in a mixed expression.

Some typical expressions of the different types are:

1. Arithmetic expressions

$$((X+Y)-(4*Z))$$
$$(((X**Y)**Z)+(2-(3*X)))$$

2. Character expressions

$$(('COMPUTER'\|'\sqcup SCIENCE')\|'\sqcup STUDENTS')$$

3. Logical expressions

$$(A \lor (((\neg B)\land C)\land(\neg D)))$$

4. Mixed expressions (B and X are identifiers representing character sequences)

$$((('AB'<'CD') \lor ('A'>B)) \lor (('AB'\|'C') < X)$$

In all these expressions we have included all the parentheses to show which terms are acted on by which operators. The value of any term inside parentheses is determined before it is used as an operand. The use of parentheses to indicate the order in which the different operators are to be applied insures that the expression is evaluated in the correct order. Parentheses, however, introduce an unnecessary cumbersomeness in the representation of the expression. We may omit most if not all the parentheses from an expression if we set up an explicit set of rules to tell us how to evaluate the parenthesis-free expression.

Rules of Precedence in Expressions

A binary operation is said to be written in *infix notation* when the operator is written between the operands that it operates on. There is thus no difficulty in evaluating simple expressions such as

$$A + 1.6 \qquad B \land C$$

However, when we are dealing with complex expressions without parentheses, we must be careful to define a fixed convention that defines the order in which the operations are to be carried out. For example, the expression

$$X - Y/C * * A$$

could be interpreted as

$$((X - Y)/C) * * A \quad \text{or} \quad X - ((Y/C) * * A) \quad \text{or}$$
$$(X - Y)/(C * * A) \quad \text{or} \quad X - (Y/(C * * A)) \quad \text{or} \quad (X - (Y/C)) * * A$$

where each expression inside parentheses is evaluated before the external operator is applied. To overcome this interpretation problem, we define a set of rules to indicate the order of precedence in which the operators are applied.

All programming languages have a set of precedence rules that are defined for the language. It is an unfortunate fact of life that these rules differ from language to language. In most cases this does not lead to any problems, particularly if the programmer is aware of this fact and fully understands the precedence rules of the different languages being used and how they differ. It does mean particular care must be taken if a program written in one programming language is to be rewritten in another programming language. The only sure way to avoid any difficulties of this type is to use parentheses, when necessary, to indicate the correct meaning for any operation that might be misunderstood.

There is no accepted standard for precedence rules. The rules given below are the ones in common use for FORTRAN and, except in the instances noted, can be used for PL/I. For this discussion it is assumed that no expression contains two operators in succession. Thus, if we wish to have an expression for the operation

$$U^{-V}$$

we must write it as

$$U * * (-V)$$

rather than

$$U * * -V$$

The rules of precedence to be used in this text are given in Table 3-4.

The examples on top of p. 60 illustrate the use of these precedence rules. In each example the implied parentheses are shown to indicate the way each expression is evaluated.

When a complex expression is used to represent a calculation it is very important that the appropriate precedence conventions be followed exactly. Failure to do this can lead to very serious errors which are often difficult to locate. For example, one very common error that many programmers make is to write the expression A/B− C, which equals (A/B) − C, when they really wish to

Expression	Implied parentheses
X+Y**2*Z	(X+((Y**2)*Z))
A*B*C/E*F−G+2*A	((((((A*B)*C)/E)*F)−G)+(2*A))
−A**B*C	((−(A**B))*C)
A+(B‖C>D‖E ∨ C‖D<E)	(A+(((B‖C)>(D‖E)) ∨ ((C‖D)<E)))
A ∨ (¬B)∧C∧(¬D)	(A ∨ (((¬B)∧C)∧(¬D)))
10*A−B**C≠C**2−B*A	(((10*A)−(B**C))≠((C**2)−(B*A)))

compute A/(B − C). It is easily seen that these two expressions produce different results.

When a program written in one language is translated into another language, problems often occur because of different precedence rules. For example, in FORTRAN the expression

$$A**B**C \text{ means } ((A**B)**C)$$

TABLE 3-4 ▌ Typical rules of precedence for the basic operators

1. All expressions contained in parentheses are treated as a single term whose value is obtained by evaluating the expression inside the parentheses as an independent expression.
2.† All exponentiations (**) are performed first.
3.† All unary minuses are performed second.
4. All multiplications (*) and divisions (/) are performed third.
5. All additions (+) and subtractions (−) are performed fourth.
6. All concatenation operations (‖) are performed fifth.
7. All relational operations (<, ≤, =, ≠, >, ≥) are performed sixth.
8.†† All logical NOT (¬) operations are performed seventh.
9. All AND (∧) operations are performed eighth.
10. All OR (∨) operations are performed ninth.
11.† When an expression contains a sequence of consecutive operations of the same level in which the order of applying these operations is not completely specified by parentheses, then the evaluation is from left to right.

The following important differences exist in the precedence rules for PL/I. Details of these differences can be found in a PL/I programming manual.
† Exponentiations (**) and unary minus are assumed to be of the same level. When an expression contains a sequence of consecutive exponentiations and unary minuses in which the order of applying these operations is not completely specified by parentheses, then the evaluation is from *right* to *left*.
†† The NOT operation in PL/I shares the priority with exponentiation and unary minus. The reason behind this is covered in some PL/I manuals.

while in PL/I

$$A**B**C \text{ means } (A**(B**C))$$

These two interpretations give different results. If $A = 2$, $B = 2$, and $C = 3$, then the FORTRAN expression has the value $(2^2)^3 = 64$ while the PL/I expression has the value $(2)^{2^3} = 256$.

From the above example we see it is possible to make very serious mistakes through misapplying the precedence rules associated with a given language. If in doubt, the best rule is to use parentheses to indicate the exact sequence in which the expression or part of the expression is to be evaluated.

Functions

It is possible to carry out all the mathematical computations called for in an algorithm using the simple operations just discussed. However, we often find it convenient to use functions such as $\sin(x)$, $\log_{10}(x)$, or e^{-x} in a calculation. To define the value of functions such as these in terms of the basic operations is an unnecessary waste of time. Thus, all major computer programming languages provide means to use standard mathematical functions as part of a computation.

A function has the general form

$$\langle value \rangle = f(x_1, x_2, \ldots, x_n)$$

where the x_i, $i = 1, \ldots, n$, are the *arguments* of the function and $\langle value \rangle$ represents the quantity obtained after the function is evaluated. We can have *arithmetic functions* where <value> will be a number, *logical functions* where <value> will be either 1 (TRUE) or 0 (FALSE), or a *character function* where <value> is a character sequence. The arguments may represent numeric, logical, or character information.

Functions are used in expressions just like variables or constants. A typical expression containing a function has the form

$$A**B-SIN(X)*B$$

In evaluating this expression the function SIN(X) is evaluated first, before any of the other computations are carried out.

It is also possible for the programmer to define special functions that are of use in carrying out special computations. The definition and use of these types of functions is discussed in Chapter VI.

Assignment Statements

An algorithm is made up of a sequence of *statements* that uniquely indicate how the different steps of an algorithm are carried out. One important class of statements are assignment statements.

Each identifier indicates a storage space in the computer's memory. The information stored in this space is undefined until a value is assigned to the variable represented by the identifier by some action of the program. This value is then retained in the location indicated by the identifier until a new value is assigned to the variable. An *assignment statement* is used to assign a value to a variable.

Assignment statements have the following general form

$$V \leftarrow \langle \text{value} \rangle$$

where V is an identifier and $\langle \text{value} \rangle$ indicates the value to be assigned to the variable represented by the identifier. The operation of assignment† is indicated by the left arrow operator $\leftarrow$ and indicates that the quantity represented by $\langle \text{value} \rangle$ has been stored in the location indicated by the identifier.

The simplest situation occurs when the value that we wish to assign to an identifier is a constant. Typical statements of this type are

$$\text{TEN} \leftarrow 10.6$$
$$\text{A100} \leftarrow 1.67E17$$
$$\text{LEFT} \leftarrow \text{'PROGRAM'}$$

In the first statement TEN is assigned a fixed-point value of 10.6, A100 is assigned a floating-point value of 1.67×10^{17}, while the third variable is assigned the character sequence 'PROGRAM'.

Under more general conditions, the value term in the assignment statement is the result of a calculation performed by the computer before the result is assigned to the variable V. The form of the calculation is determined by an expression.

When evaluated during a computation, an expression produces a value that must be used immediately or it will be lost. The most common use of this value is in an assignment statement to set a value for a variable. A typical assignment statement of this type would be

$$X \leftarrow A/(B - C)$$

This means that we take the values assigned to A, B, and C, compute $A/(B - C)$, and *then* place the result in the storage location identified by X.

It is important to note that an assignment statement does not represent equality, such as we are accustomed to in mathematics. For example, the following is a perfectly legitimate assignment statement involving an expression.

$$N \leftarrow N + 1$$

This statement, which is quite common in computing, means that we take the value saved in storage location N, add 1 to it and store the new value in

† The left arrow $\leftarrow$ is used to emphasize that the assignment is an operation which is not the same as the equal ($=$) relational operator. FORTRAN and PL/I use $=$ to represent the assignment operation. APL uses $\leftarrow$. Some implementations of ALGOL use $:=$ as the assignment operator.

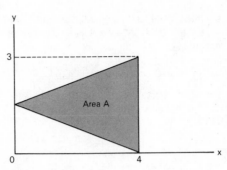

FIGURE 3-2 ■ An area $A = \frac{1}{2} xy$.

storage location N in place of the value that was stored there originally. To illustrate this idea consider the following sequence of assignment statements and the value stored in location N after each is executed

$$N \leftarrow 1 \qquad \text{1 is stored in location N}$$
$$N \leftarrow N + 1 \qquad \text{2 is stored in location N}$$
$$N \leftarrow N + 1 \qquad \text{3 is stored in location N}$$

This example illustrates that N represents a location in memory which contains a value and that the assignment statement is used to modify this value.

As we will see in the next chapter, assignment statements and expressions play a key roll in representating the steps in an algorithm to perform a given computation. To obtain an idea of how they are used, assume that we wish to compute the area of the figure shown in Fig. 3-2. One sequence of statements that would accomplish this task is

$$X \leftarrow 4$$
$$Y \leftarrow 3$$
$$A \leftarrow X * Y/2$$

Exercises

1. Use parentheses to indicate how the following expressions are evaluated:
   (a) $A * * B/C - D * E * * F$
   (b) $A * B > C * D < E \wedge F \| G = H$
   (c) $\neg B \wedge A > C \wedge E \leqslant F * * G$

2. Assume that the initial value of the indicated variables are $N = 2$, $V = 5$, $C = 0$, $A = 1$, $X = 5$, $Y = 6$, $Z = 2$. What will be the value of N and V after the following statements are executed?
   (a) $N \leftarrow N * 2$
   (b) $V \leftarrow X - 3 * Z \leqslant Z + Y - 2 \wedge C \vee (\neg A)$
   (c) $V \leftarrow 2 * X/Z * Y$

3. Assume that the initial value of the indicated variables are A = 'BIG', B = 'DEAL',
C = 'JOHN', D = 'JO', E = 'HN'. What will be the value of V after the following
statements are executed?

   (a) V ← A‖B

   (b) V ← D‖E ≤ A‖B ∨ D‖E=C

4. The following assignment statements are to be executed in the order in which
they are written

$$
\begin{aligned}
\text{TEN} &\leftarrow 10 \\
\text{FIVE} &\leftarrow 5 \\
\text{TEMP} &\leftarrow \text{TEN} \\
\text{TEN} &\leftarrow \text{FIVE} \\
\text{FIVE} &\leftarrow \text{TEMP}
\end{aligned}
$$

What will be the information stored in TEN and FIVE after all the assignment
statements are executed?

5 ■ Summary

In this chapter we have investigated the different types of information
that can be used in a computation and the basic operations that can be used
to combine and transform information. These concepts form the backbone of
all computer programs. A clear understanding of operators, expressions, precedence rules, and assignment statements is particularly important in the follow-
in chapters, where we use these basic concepts to develop the rest of the
tools we need to describe algorithmic processes.

References

Each programming language has a well-defined set of conventions concerning how
the basic operations are carried out. Except for reference [3], all the references
describe the features of a particular programming language. A very large number
of programming manuals are available which cover a given language. The following
were selected as representative of the manuals for each language. [3] presents a
very comprehensive treatment of the problem of defining mathematical operations
in a consistent manner. It is also the basic work behind the development of the
APL programming language.

1. IBM (1972) *IBM System 360 FORTRAN IV Language,* International Business
Machines Corp., New York.
2. IBM (1972) *IBM System/360 PL/I (F) Language Reference Manual,* International Business Machines Corp., New York.
3. Iverson, K. E. (1962) *A Programming Language,* John Wiley & Sons, New York.
4. McCracken, D. D., and Umberto, G. (1970) *A Guide to COBOL Programming,*
2nd ed., John Wiley & Sons, New York.

5. Peluso, A., and Bauser, C., and Debruzzi, D. (1972) *Basic BASIC Programming,* Addison-Wesley, Reading, Mass.

6. Sprowls, R. C. (1972) *PL/C: A processor for PL/I,* Canfield Press, San Francisco, Ca.

Home Problems

1. List the precedence rules for each of the major programming languages that are available in your computer center. This list should include one or more of the following languages:

FORTRAN, ALGOL, PL/I, BASIC, APL.

Determine, using the precedence rules for each language, how the following expressions are interpreted:

   (a) $A**B**C**D$ (b) $(-A)**B**(-C)**D$

2. Discuss the problems introduced by the internal representation of information if we allow a completely mixed mode of operations in expressions. For example, what problems arise if A is a floating-point identifier and B is an integer identifier and we are given the expression $A < B$.

3. Make a table of all the built-in functions available for use in the local programming language. Summarize the characteristics of these functions in terms of:

   (a) type of arguments
   (b) maximum number of arguments
   (c) type of values returned
   (d) special restrictions placed on the arguments

4. Discuss the problems involved in assigning different types of data to an identifier in the programming language or languages available in your computer center. For example, assume that I and J are identifiers which represent integers and X is an identifier that represents a floating-point number. How does the programming language handle the following assignment statements:

   (a) $X \leftarrow I*J$ (b) $I \leftarrow J*X$ (c) $I \leftarrow X**J$

5. Deterimine the collating sequence of all the characters in the character set allowed in the programming language that is available to you for your programming work. Using the established collating sequence, determine the ordering relationship for the character sequences in each of the following data sets:

   (a) A5, B4, C3, D2, E1, F0
   (b) 1X, 2Y, 3Z
   (c) .A1, ⊔*A, A__B, A+B, A/B

6. Using the precedence rules established in this chapter determine the assignment statement needed to accomplish each of the following computations:

   (a) $X = A + \cfrac{B}{C + \cfrac{D}{E + \cfrac{F}{G}}}$

(b) $Y = -\dfrac{A^B \, C^D}{A^C + B^D}$

(c) $Z = \sqrt{\sin^2(x) + \cos^2(y)}$

Assume that sin(x) and cos(y) are built in functions. Express each statement so that the use of parentheses to indicate the order of computations is minimal.

**structure of algorithms
and their flowchart
representations**

1 ■ Introduction

To understand the computing process we must have a way to talk about the process and communicate our ideas and problem solutions to other people. Algorithms allow us to do this. However, we need an effective method to express algorithms in a concise and unambiguous manner.

Experience has shown that graphical techniques are very effective in communicating the operations that are performed by an algorithm and the interrelationships that exist between the different sections of an algorithm. This has led to the development of a formal graphical technique, called a *flowchart,* to represent the behavior of algorithms.

Many beginning programmers think that flowcharts are unnecessary since it appears that they are able to write their computer programs directly in a given programming language without bothering to first express their algorithm in flowchart form. This is, in reality, a very false security. There is no question that simple programs can be written and run on a computer without first developing a flowchart representation of the underlying algorithms. However, as the algorithms being developed become more complex, it becomes impossible to keep track of all of the details and interrelationships that exist in an algorithm without writing them down in some manner. A person who has mastered the art of flowcharting through practice on simple problems finds this a straightforward process.

Flowcharts are of more importance than simply being a programming aid, since the information represented by a flowchart is independent of the programming language being used to code the algorithm for use on a particular computer. Consequently flowcharts are a very powerful problem-solving tool in their own right.

In the next chapter we examine the problem-solving process. Flowcharts provide an important conceptual tool which can be used to study the properties of the different methods that are available to solve a problem. They also provide a means to communicate the exact form of our ideas to others who are working with us on the problem or to explain our solution to those who are interested in its ultimate application.

Once an algorithm is transformed into a computer program, the flowchart is useful for developing the tests that can be run on the program to see if it is performing properly. Finally, a flowchart is an important part of the final documentation of the finished computer program. Often this part of a programming effort is disregarded by the person developing the program. Without this documentation a program is of little value to other users since they will not be sure of the exact algorithm represented by the program. In fact, it is not uncommon to find, at a later date, that the original programmer is unable to recall important programming details about the structure of the program if proper documentation is omitted when the original work on the program is finished.

This chapter is concerned with the basic techniques used to represent an algorithm by a flowchart. For this discussion it is assumed that the structure of the algorithm is already known. The more important problem of developing the original algorithm to be represented is discussed in the following chapters.

2 ■ Computations and Decisions

The size of an algorithm needed to solve a given problem is related to the problem's complexity. If we examine the algorithm or flowchart representing the solution to any problem, even one of very high complexity, we find that the flowchart is built up of a few basic concepts used over and over again. The following five tasks serve as the basic building blocks from which any flowchart is formed:

1. Input information
2. Perform computations
3. Make decisions
4. Repetition of a step a number of times
5. Output information

If the ways these tasks are performed are understood, it is a relatively easy matter to form a flowchart representation of any algorithm.

Computations

The simplest type of algorithm is one that only requires the evaluation of a few expressions. For example, assume we wish to find the values for the variables x_1 and x_2 when the values of the variables y_1 and y_2 are given according to the following set of equations

$$3x_1 + 2x_2 = y_1$$
$$x_1 + 4x_2 = y_2$$

These two equations can easily be solved for x_1 and x_2. Doing this gives the following

$$x_1 = \frac{2y_1 - y_2}{5} \qquad x_2 = \frac{3y_2 - y_1}{10}$$

Assume $y_1 = 5$ and $y_2 = 6$. The flowchart describing the evaluation of x_1 and x_2 is shown in Fig. 4-1.

Every flowchart has one starting point and one or more possible ending points. These points are indicated by ovals with an appropriate term inside indicating how the point is used in the flowchart. The computations involved in the different steps of the algorithm are indicated in one or more rectangles. The grouping of computations is arbitrary. However, the usual practice is to

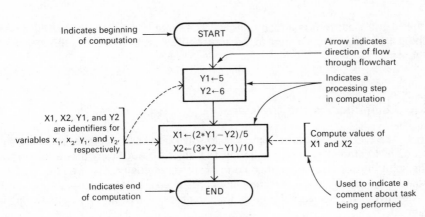

FIGURE 4-1 ■ Flowchart of a simple calculation.

include, if possible, all the computations involved in a given step in a single rectangle. The relationships between the steps of a computation are indicated by the arrows that connect the different parts of the flowchart. The computation is carried out in the sequence indicated by the arrows. The symbol

$$\leftarrow\text{----}[\langle\text{comment}\rangle$$

is used to provide explanatory comments particular to the particular task being performed by the section of the flowchart being pointed at.

Decisions and Branching

In many algorithms we may reach a point where the next step depends upon the current status of the calculation at that point. For example, assume that we wish to make a calculation that involves the function g(x) defined by

$$g(x) = \begin{cases} \sin(x) & \text{for } \sin(x) \leq 0.7 \\ 0.7 & \text{for } \sin(x) > 0.7 \end{cases}$$

This function is shown in Fig. 4-2.

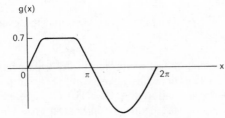

FIGURE 4-2 ■ Graph of g(x).

To evaluate g(x) we first compute f(x) = sin(x) and then test f(x) to see if it is less than or equal to 0.7. If it is, g(x) = f(x). Otherwise g(x) = 0.7. Situations of this type represent a branch point in our calculations.

A *branch point* is a point in an algorithm where it is necessary to make a decision, based upon conditions at the time the branch point is encountered, concerning the next statement to be executed. The simplest type of branching decision is made by evaluating a logical expression. Figure 4-3(a) illustrates this situation. If the logical expression is TRUE, then the outgoing path labeled TRUE (often indicated as T) is taken. Otherwise the path labeled FALSE (often indicated by F) is taken. An example of the use of this type of branch point is given in Fig. 4-3(b), where the function g(x) of Fig. 4-2 is evaluated.

There are many conditions where the decision required at a branch point may have more than two alternatives. For example, we might have to evaluate a function h(x) defined by the conditions

$$h(x) = \begin{cases} x^2 & \text{for } x > 0 \\ -5 & \text{for } x = 0 \\ -x^2 & \text{for } x < 0 \end{cases}$$

In this situation we must compare x to 0 and then compute a value for h(x) depending upon the result of this comparison. The general flowchart form of this type of comparison is illustrated in Fig. 4-4(a). The decision is made in two

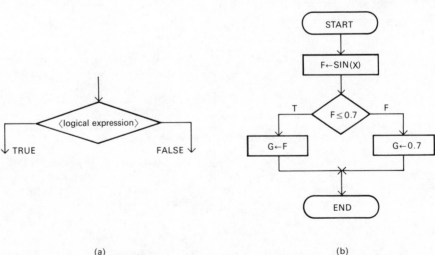

(a)   (b)

FIGURE 4-3 ■ Branch points based upon a logical expression. (a) Flowchart representation of a general logical expression branch point. (b) Use of logical expression branch point.

steps. First x is tested to see if it is greater than zero. If not, it is tested to see if it is equal to 0. If both tests fail, the result is that x is less than 0.

There are many situations where a multiple stage decision process is required. To simplify the flowchart representation, a multiple decision can be represented as shown in Figs. 4-4(b) and (c). The decision is made by comparing the term represented by ⟨expression 1⟩ and ⟨expression 2⟩ according to the mutually exclusive relations indicated by the labels on the paths leaving the branch point. The colon (:) indicates that the relation associated with each branch is to be used to compare the two expressions. One and only one of the relations can be true. The branch corresponding to the true relation is the one that is followed to the next step of the calculation.

As an example of how a logical expression can be used in a branch point consider the problem shown in Fig. 4-5. In this problem we must determine if

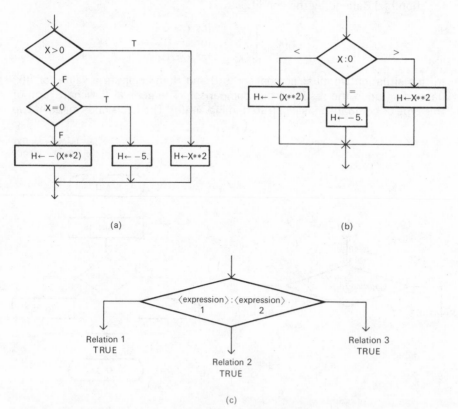

(a)

(b)

(c)

FIGURE 4-4 ■ Branch point based upon multiple conditions. (a) A flowchart representation of a multiple decision. (b) Simplified flowchart representation of a multiple decision. (c) General flowchart representation of a three-way decision (three mutually exclusive relations).

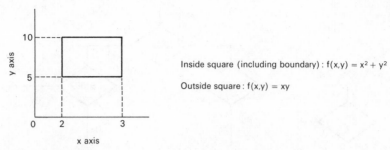

FIGURE 4-5 ■ Problem involving a logical branch point.

the point (x,y) falls within or on the boundary of the square or outside the square before we compute the function f(x,y). Figure 4-6 illustrates how we determine which expression is to be used to compute the function f(x,y). Although the logical expression used at the branch point involves the relations $\leq$ and $\geq$, the overall expression is a logical expression since each relational subexpression, such as $(X \geq 2)$, has a logical value depending upon the value of X or Y.

There are many situations where it is necessary to make a number of comparisons. For example, assume that a student receives a score S on a test and we desire to assign a grade according to the following system

Grade	Condition
A	$S \geq 90$
B	$80 \leq S < 90$
C	$70 \leq S < 80$
D	$60 \leq S < 70$
F	$S < 60$

This task can be represented by the partial flowchart shown in Fig. 4-7.

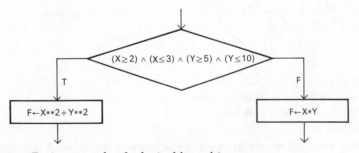

FIGURE 4-6 ■ An example of a logical branching process.

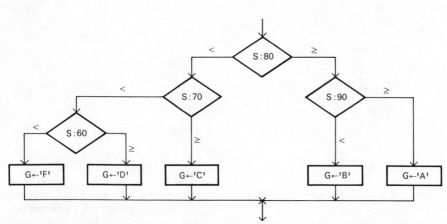

FIGURE 4-7 ■ A multiple decision task.

Decision processes are important in their own right. However, a simple extension of the idea will allow us to carry out repetitive calculations that a computer is often asked to do.

Exercises

1. Draw a partial flowchart to represent the following calculation. If John is older than Henry but younger than Sally, then he will be given 5 dollars. Otherwise he gets 10 dollars.

2. Assume that the radius of a circle is 10.

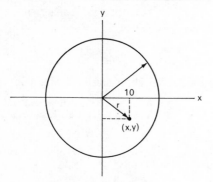

f(x,y) = x − y for all points inside circle

f(x,y) = 0 for all points on circumference of circle

f(x,y) = x + y for all points outside circle

FIGURE E4-1

Show how f(x,y) is computed by a partial flowchart. (Reminder: $r^2 = x^2 + y^2$.)

3 ∎ Looping and Repetitive Calculations

One of the important advantages of a computer is that it can repeat the steps in a repetitive task as many times as are necessary to complete the task. To introduce the idea of a loop consider the following simple problem.

Suppose we wish to compute

$$T = \sum_{N=1}^{N=NMAX} \frac{1}{N} = 1 + \frac{1}{2} + \frac{1}{3} + \cdots + \underbrace{\frac{1}{NMAX}}$$

$$\text{NMAX terms}$$

If we tried to represent this calculation using the techniques of the last section, we would obtain a flowchart of the form shown in Fig. 4-8. In this flowchart T is initially set to zero. The summation is carried out by successively adding 1/N to T and then incrementing N by 1 in preparation for the next step.

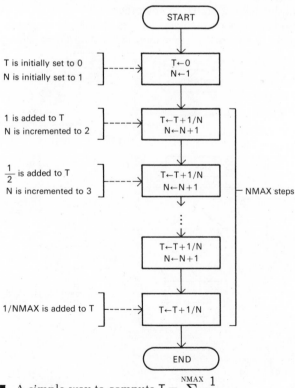

FIGURE 4-8 ∎ A simple way to compute $T = \sum_{N=1}^{NMAX} \frac{1}{N}$.

Obviously this is a very inefficient method for carrying out this summation process, particularly if NMAX is very large. The problem with this approach is that it does not make use of the inherent repetition in the summation process.

A much more realistic way to compute T is shown in Fig. 4-9. In this case the summation is carried out by going around the indicated loop NMAX times. The variable N is used as a *counter* to keep track of the number of terms in the series that have been summed. As soon as N > NMAX the summation process is stopped.

As a second example, consider the function

$$F(n) = (5)^n \sin(3.1n)$$

The problem is to find the first positive integer n such that F(n) > 25. One way of solving this problem is to carry out a systematic search process of the type described by the flowchart of Fig. 4-10(a). In this approach, successive values of N are used to compute F(n) until a value is found such that F(n) > 25. The problem that may occur is that there may not be any value of N that satisfies the requirement F(n) > 25. If this condition exists, the search is known as an *infinite loop* and is unacceptable in any program.

For those calculations that may lead to an infinite loop it is necessary to take precautions to insure that the loop is terminated in a finite number of

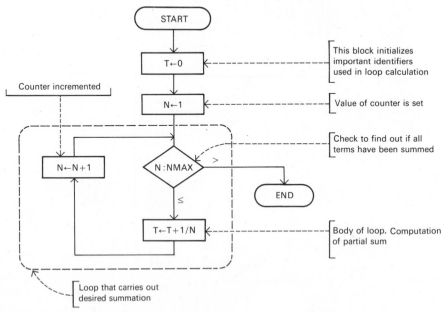

FIGURE 4-9 ■ Flowchart of algorithm to compute $T = \sum_{N=1}^{NMAX} \frac{1}{N}$.

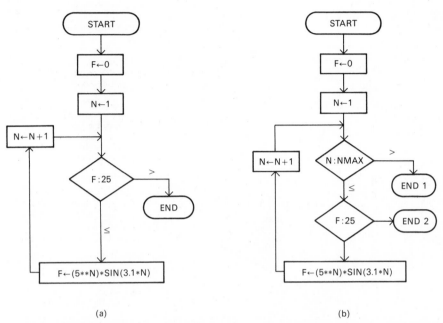

(a)   (b)

FIGURE 4-10 ■ Two ways to find a value of n such that F(n) > 25. (a) Unlimited search. (b) Limited search.

steps. One way to do this is to include a counter in the loop and stop the loop when the counter reaches a value greater than some maximum value. This modification is indicated in Fig. 4-10(b) where only NMAX tries are made to find the desired value of n.

These two examples demonstrate the general structure of a simple loop. The first example demonstrates the simplest situation, where the loop is terminated after a prespecified number of repetitive calculations. A counter is needed to keep track of this number. In the second example, the termination of the loop is carried out by checking the status of the calculation inside the loop. It is not necessary to have a counter although a counter is often included to avoid the possibility of an infinite loop. Let us now generalize these ideas.

Simple Loops

Figure 4-11 indicates the general components that may be included in any simple loop. Almost every loop has a counter of some type to ensure that the conditions of an infinite loop never occur. In some loops this is the only mechanism used to determine when to terminate the loop.

The body of the loop represents the main computational task performed by the loop. Usually there will be one or more identifiers involved in these calculations that must be set to an initial value before the loop is entered. This

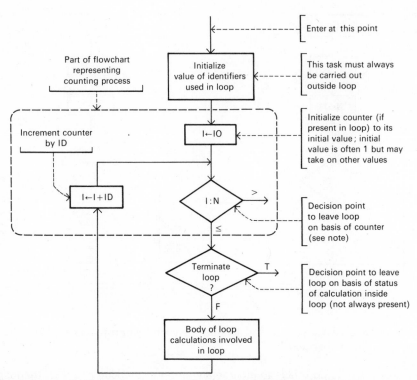

FIGURE 4-11 ■ General structure of a simple loop. (Note: In some repetitive calculations, it is not necessary to check the counter to decide when to leave the loop. It is recommended to include this point to prevent the possibility of an unintentional infinite loop.)

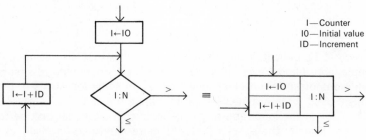

FIGURE 4-12 ■ Counter service flowchart symbol.

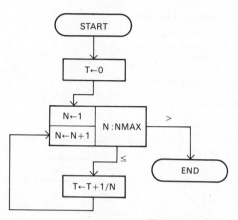

FIGURE 4-13 ■ Flowchart to compute $T = \sum\limits_{N=1}^{NMAX} \dfrac{1}{N}$ using the counter service symbol.

is accomplished by the initialization box before the loop is entered. Failure to properly initialize the identifiers in the body of the loop often leads to disastrous results.

The need for an internal decision point to terminate the loop will depend upon the computation being performed. Quite often this part of the loop is omitted.

The initialization, incrementing, and testing of the counter variable is standard for all loops involving a counter. To emphasize this interdependence we combine all three of these steps in the single flowchart symbol illustrated in Fig. 4-12. In the most general situation, the counter is initialized to a value of IO and incremented by ID after each execution of the body of the loop.

Figure 4-13 shows how the counter service symbol of a loop is now used in the flowchart of the algorithm to compute

$$T = \sum_{N=1}^{NMAX} \frac{1}{N}$$

described in Fig. 4-9.

Exercises

1. Develop a flowchart that uses a simple loop to perform each of the following calculations:
    (a) the sum of all the odd integers from 1 to 100
    (b) the sum of all the even integers from 1 to 100
    (c) the sum of all the multiples of 3 from 1 to 100
Use the counter service flowchart symbol to represent the loop.

2. For the flowchart shown below:

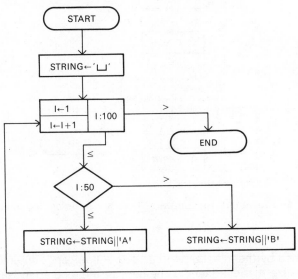

FIGURE E4-2

(a) How many times is each of the assignment statements in the body of the loop executed?

(b) Determine the value stored in the identifier STRING when the task described in the flowchart is completed.

3. Give a flowchart to compute the sum

$$T = \sum_{N=NMAX}^{1} \frac{1}{N}$$

so that N starts with the largest value NMAX, and progresses toward 1.

4. A sequence of numbers is generated according to the following rule: Starting with the first two numbers 0 and 1, each number is the sum of the two preceding ones. Thus, for instance, the first ten numbers in the sequence are

0, 1, 1, 2, 3, 5, 8, 13, 21, 34

The sequence so generated is called the Fibonacci sequence.

Develop a flowchart that uses a loop to keep generating the numbers in the Fibonacci sequence until either a number generated has exceeded 1000 or 100 numbers have been generated.

4 ■ Arrays and Loops

The idea of loops allows us to repeat the steps in a repetitive task in an efficient manner. Frequently, the use of loops can be further enhanced if the data needed in the steps of a calculation is stored in an organized way. We now discuss some of the basic properties and uses of loops when arrays are used to store data.

Subscripted Variables

Quite often in mathematics we encounter a formula of the form

$$T = \sum_{i=1}^{10} a_i$$

where the terms a_i correspond to a list of ten numbers. We could represent each number by a separate identifier. However, it is more convenient to talk about each number in terms of its place in the list and to give the list itself a name. The list in this example is made up of ten numbers. We can indicate each number by the identifiers A_1 through A_{10}, where A_1 represents the first

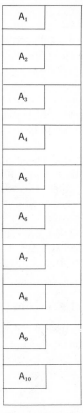

FIGURE 4-14 ■ Storage of a one-dimensional array.

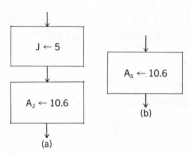

FIGURE 4-15 ■ Selection of an item from an array. (a) Selection of a particular element of an array. (b) Equivalent flowchart representation indicating a particular element of an array.

number of the list and A_{10} represents the tenth number. The Jth number in the list would then be A_J. In this example J is called a *subscript* and A_1 through A_{10} are called *subscripted variables.*

Subscripted variables are used to represent information stored in consecutive storage locations. Figure 4-14 illustrates how the ten numbers would be stored. Such a collection of data elements is called a *one-dimensional array.* A collective identifier, A, will be used when we refer to all the elements in the array.

The subscript, J, of the array can take on integer values from 1 to 10. To assign a value to a particular element of the array we first assign a specific integer value to J and then use this value to indicate which storage position is to receive the value. This can be done by using the process illustrated by the flowchart in Fig. 4-15(a). The representation of Fig. 4-15(a) is equivalent to the representation of Fig. 4-15(b). This example illustrates how the value of 10.6 is assigned to the fifth element of the array. The important concept being introduced in Fig. 4-15(a) is that we can select a different variable in the array by simply changing the value assigned to J.

Arrays with a single subscript are called *one-dimensional arrays* or *vectors.* There is no reason to limit ourselves to one-dimensional arrays. But before we consider more complex arrays let us briefly investigate how we can use these one-dimensional arrays.

Use of Arrays in Loops

To illustrate how an array is useful consider the simple task of summing a collection of numbers. Mathematically this is represented as

$$T = \sum_{i=1}^{N} a_i$$

Let us assume that the values of the a_i's are stored in the one-dimensional

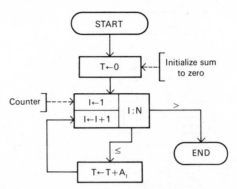

FIGURE 4-16 ∎ Flowchart of a simple summation.

array A with elements A_I, $I = 1, 2, \ldots, N$. The flowchart of Figure 4-16 illustrates how the desired summation is carried out using a simple loop. In this loop the integer I serves two purposes. Its first task is to act as a counter to count the number of times that we execute the statement

$$T \leftarrow T + A_I$$

Its second function is to act as a *pointer* to point to the element in the array that is currently being used in the summation process.

After each summation the value of I is incremented by 1 using

$$I \leftarrow I + 1$$

Since I is initially set to 1 when entering the loop, I takes on the successive values 1, 2, 3, 4, and 5. For each of these values, except the last, I points to a different element of the array. The idea of I pointing to an element of an array is illustrated in Fig. 4-17. When I reaches the value of 5 the summation processes is completed and we leave the loop. Later on we will encounter situations where separate variables are used for pointers and counters.

The last thing we notice about this example is the fact that we must initialize the value of T to 0 before we enter the loop. The initial value of 0 is

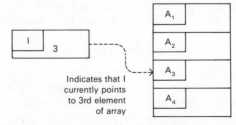

FIGURE 4-17 ∎ Visualization of the idea of using I as a pointer.

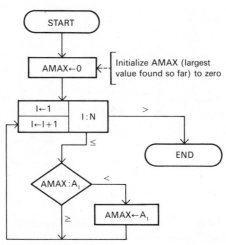

FIGURE 4-18 ■ Flowchart to find the largest number of an array.

selected since this is the value of the sum before any terms are added. If we overlook this step, then our calculations may be in error depending upon the value in T when we reached the part of the calculations represented by the flowchart.

As another example of a simple loop involving a one-dimensional array consider the following problem. Assume that we have an array A of N nonnegative numbers and we wish to find the largest number in the array. The Ith element of the array is A_I. To solve this problem we can use the algorithm represented by the flowchart of Fig. 4-18.

The value of the largest number in the array is to be placed in AMAX when the calculation is finished. Thus, before we enter the loop we set the initial value of this variable to 0 since we do not know *a priori* if there are any nonzero elements in the array. Then we initialize I, which is used as both a counter and a pointer, and start through the loop. Each time we go through the loop we compare A_I with the current value of AMAX. If A_I is larger, the value of A_I becomes the new value of AMAX. Otherwise the value of AMAX doesn't change. The value of I is then incremented again and the loop is repeated until the count exceeds N. When this occurs we exit from the loop.

Multidimensional Arrays

It is often desirable to arrange information in an array with two or more subscripts. For example, assume that we have a class of five students and wish to record the mark they received on each of four exams. A convenient way to arrange this information would be in a two-dimensional array that has the following form:

$$
\begin{array}{c}
\text{Column} \downarrow \\
\text{Row} \longrightarrow \quad S = \begin{bmatrix}
76 & 85 & 90 & 72 \\
80 & 78 & 96 & 80 \\
65 & 71 & 84 & 70 \\
90 & 89 & 99 & 89 \\
45 & 50 & 75 & 60
\end{bmatrix}
\end{array}
$$

The array S has five rows and four columns. The Ith row corresponds to the Ith student and the Jth column corresponds to the Jth exam. The element $S_{I,J}$ corresponds to the mark the Ith student received on the Jth exam.

A two-dimensional array, A, which is usually called a *matrix* if the elements of the array are numbers, has the following general form:

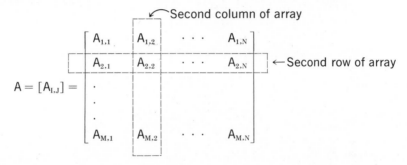

This array, which has M rows and N columns, is called an M by N array or matrix. The information represented by the array A may be organized in memory as shown in Fig. 4-19.

There is no reason to limit ourselves to two subscripts. An array could have r subscripts. In this case it is an *r-dimensional array.* Multiple-dimensional arrays can be used in algorithms just as easily as single dimension arrays.

Assume we are given an M by N matrix and that we wish to find the largest number in each row. To do this we can use the algorithm illustrated in Fig. 4-20. In this algorithm B_I is used to store the value of the largest number in the Ith row. The two variables I and J do double duty as pointers and counters. The variable I points to the row of the matrix that contains the term currently being processed and also the position in the one-dimensional vector B_I where the largest number is to be stored. When we start checking the Ith row we initially set B_I to $A_{I,1}$ and then check if the other $N-1$ terms are larger than this initial value. This saves one pass through the inner loop. In addition I also counts the number of rows we have investigated. Similarly, the variable J points to the column that contains the term currently being processed and counts the number of columns that we have investigated. Figure 4-21 shows a graphical interpretation of the use of I and J as pointers.

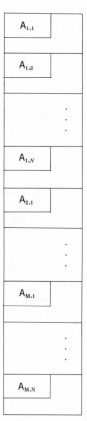

FIGURE 4-19 ■ Illustrating a possible memory organization for the M × N array A = [A$_{I,J}$].

Nested Loops

The flowchart of Fig. 4-20 is an example of a loop within a loop. Such a situation is called a *nested loop*. Flowcharts involving nested loops are quite common when working with multi-dimensional arrays. There are properties of nested loops that should be understood in order to appreciate how their operation might influence the overall performance of an algorithm.

The general structure of a typical nested loop is illustrated in Fig. 4-22. The outer loop has the standard form of any loop. The body of the outer loop contains one or possibly more inner loops. The inner loop must be initialized before the calculations are carried out. The complete calculation represented by the inner loop is then performed before the calculation of the outer loop is continued. From this we see that for every pass through the outer loop we carry out N passes through the inner loop.

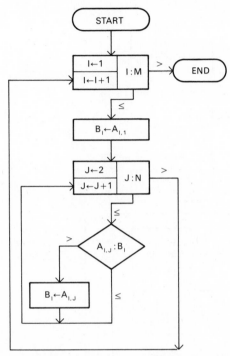

FIGURE 4-20 ■ An example involving a two-dimensional array.

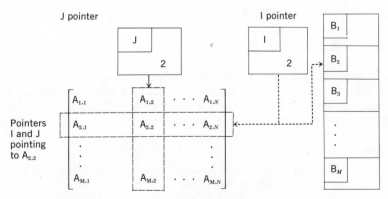

FIGURE 4-21 ■ Illustration of the idea of using I and J as pointers.

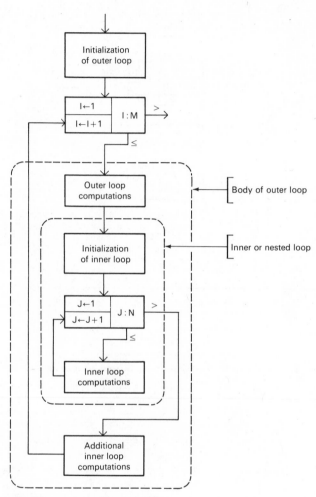

FIGURE 4-22 ∎ Illustration of a nested loop.

Throughout this book we will find that simple loops and nested loops have a large number of different applications. As long as the basic organization of a loop is understood there should be no difficulty in their use no matter how complex the calculations within the loop may be.

Exercises

1. Let $[A_{I,J}]$ and $[B_{I,J}]$ be two M by N matrices. Give a flowchart that shows how the M by N matrix $[C_{I,J}]$ can be formed where

$$C_{I,J} = A_{I,J} + B_{I,J}$$

2. For the flowchart of Fig. E4-3, determine the number of times each of the three statements is executed when the computation represented by the flowchart is completed.

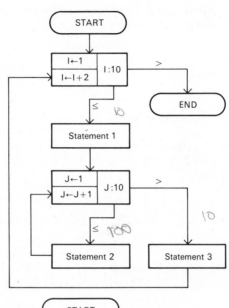

FIGURE E4-3

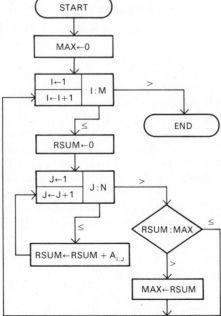

FIGURE E4-4

3. In the flowchart of Fig. E4-4, $A = [A_{I,J}]$ is an M by N matrix of nonnegative numbers.

(a) Trace through the flowchart and determine the task to be carried out.
(b) What would happen if the initialization statement

$$RSUM \leftarrow 0$$

was left out before entering the inner loop of the flowchart?

5 ■ Completing the Flowchart: Input and Output

Up to this point only assignment statements have been used to associate values with the identifiers in an algorithm. In this case a value could either be assigned directly, such as

$$A \leftarrow 4.256$$

or a value could be assigned as a result of a computation such as

$$A \leftarrow A * B + 3.2$$

This method is satisfactory as long as we are dealing with information that is easily included in the algorithm. However, this is not always the case.

Input Boxes

Almost all computations performed by a computer require that a certain amount of information be supplied at the time the program is run on the computer. This information can be supplied in a number of ways. For our discussion we assume that all external information is punched on a stack of punched cards and that the computer can read this information off the cards and assign the indicated values to the proper identifiers.

The reading in of input information is indicated by the flowchart symbol shown in Fig. 4-23. It is shaped like a computer card to remind us that we are dealing with input data. The identifiers listed in the box are assumed to be assigned values read from the input in the order indicated. Thus in Fig. 4-23 the first input value is assigned to A, the next value is assigned to B, the third value is assigned to N, and the fourth value is assigned to K. The read-in process is destructive in that the value of an identifier before the input value is read is lost as soon as the new value is received from the input device.

FIGURE 4-23 ■ Flowchart representation of input data.

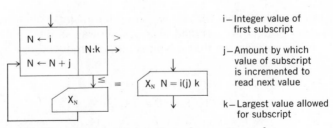

i — Integer value of
first subscript

j — Amount by which
value of subscript
is incremented to
read next value

k — Largest value allowed
for subscript

FIGURE 4-24 ■ Flowchart representation of array input data.

When we are dealing with arrays we often wish to read in a value for all elements of the array at a given time. To indicate this we can modify the flowchart input representation to the form shown in Fig. 4-24. As shown in this figure, a simple loop is used to read in the data in the proper sequence. This complete operation is compressed into the notation $N = i(j)k$ inside of the reading box symbol.

Output Boxes

The results of a computation are of little value unless they are available for external use. There are many different ways of obtaining information from a computer. For our purposes, we assume that all output information is printed on a printer. The flowchart symbol used to indicate output information is shown in Fig. 4-25.

Two different cases are indicated. Figure 4-25(a) shows the symbol that will produce a printout of the four variables on a single line. Typical output for this case might be

$$A = 10.6 \qquad B = 5.43 \qquad N = 10 \qquad K = 15$$

There are many cases where we wish to have headings or other explanatory information printed out along with the data. In addition, we may not wish to have all of the data on the same line. Figure 4-25(b) shows how we can indicate this. Each time we wish to print a new line we put the identifiers that make up that line on a new line. If we wish to print out an alphanumeric head-

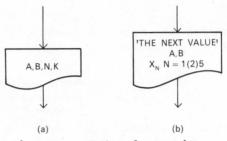

(a)   (b)

FIGURE 4-25 ■ Flowchart representation of output data.

ing, we enclose the characters that we wish to print in single quotation marks as shown. Arrays of data are handled in the same way as input information. Using these rules, we then see that a typical output produced by Fig. 4-25(b) might be

THE NEXT VALUE

$A = 10.1$ $B = 11.62$

$X_1 = 4.5$ $X_3 = 6.2$ $X_5 = 14.7$

The act of printing does not change the values associated with the identifiers that were printed out. Thus, if A had a value of 10.1 before it was printed, it will have the same value afterwards.

Interconnections

When the size of a flowchart gets large we often find that it is difficult to fit it all on a single page, or that the number of interconnecting lines on the chart becomes confusing. To overcome these problems we can use connector symbols of the form illustrated in Fig. 4-26 to indicate interconnections without needing to draw the connecting lines. The following simple example of a complete flowchart illustrates how these symbols are used.

An Example

To illustrate how we input and output information, consider the flowchart shown in Fig. 4-27. This flowchart is used to determine if a point whose x and y coordinates have been read into the program is inside or outside a circle of radius R. There are assumed to be M values for the coordinate pair (x,y). As each pair is read, $d^2 = x^2 + y^2$ is calculated and the result is compared to R^2. The output then prints the value of x and y and the result of the test. A typical output for $R = 4$ and $M = 4$ might be

5.2	6.1	OUTSIDE
2.1	2.5	INSIDE
1.5	3.6	INSIDE
10.7	11.5	OUTSIDE

From the above discussion we see that indicating input and output information in a flowchart is very easy. However, the way these tasks are carried out

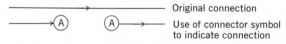

FIGURE 4-26 ■ Methods of replacing a connecting line with a connector symbol.

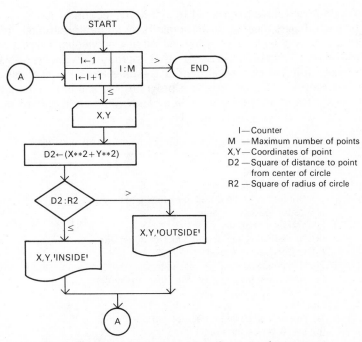

FIGURE 4-27 ■ A simple program to read and print information.

in a program depends upon the programming language being used. The need for well-designed output organization should not be overlooked when a program is being developed, since the usefulness of any computation can often be limited by the way information is made available to the user.

Exercise

1. Develop a flowchart for an algorithm that will:
   (a) Read in five positive numbers and store them in a one-dimensional array $A = [A_I]$.
   (b) Find the largest of these numbers.
   (c) Print the output

   THE LARGEST NUMBER IS ⟨value of number⟩

---

6 ■ Information Structures

Up to this point we have considered two methods of information storage. Single identifiers have been used to indicate the storage of a single item of information and arrays have been used to store a collection of items all of the same type (i.e. integers, floating-point numbers, or character strings). Information represented by a single data type is called *homogeneous.* There are many situations where we must deal with data that is grouped in such a way that it does not easily fit into a single identifier or a simple array. For example, let us assume that we are trying to develop a program that will automatically keep track of the grades of all the students in a course. For each student we must store the information given by Table 4-1.

TABLE 4-1 ■ Information to be recorded about a student

1. Name of student
2. First examination
   (a) Numerical grade on each of four questions
   (b) Letter grade for exam
3. Second examination
   (a) Numerical grade on each of five questions
   (b) Letter grade for exam
4. Third examination
   (a) Numerical grade on each of four questions
   (b) Letter grade for exam
5. Final exam
   (a) Numerical grade on each of ten questions
   (b) Letter grade for exam
6. Numerical grade on 14 homework assignments
7. Numerical grade given for classroom participation

If we examine this list, we see that we must store 43 different items of information. Some of the items, such as the student's name and the letter grade of each exam, are character sequences, while the other information is numeric. Information of this type is called *nonhomogeneous.*

We could store this information in an array if all of the character sequences were first transformed into numerical values by some type of simple coding. Assuming that we do this, we still have the problem of deciding what type of array to use.

For example, this information could be stored in a three-dimensional array

$$A = [A_{I,J,K}]$$

The index I would indicate the record of the Ith student, the index J would indicate which one of the seven categories of information was of interest, and the K index would be used to indicate which item of the Jth category was being consulted. If we assume that the class contains 25 students, then the indices I, J, and K take on integer values in the range

$$1 \leq I \leq 25 \quad 1 \leq J \leq 7 \quad 1 \leq K \leq 14$$

This means that we need an array of

$$25 \times 7 \times 14 = 2450$$

elements. Since we only need 43 elements per student, this means that $2450 - 25 \times 43 = 1375$ of the array positions would be empty. This method of storing information is wasteful of memory space although it is easy to locate any desired item of information.

Another approach is to use a two-dimensional array $[B_{I,J}]$. In this case the index I is still used to indicate the record of the Ith student. The index J is used to locate all of the other information in the following way.

$B_{I,1}$	encoded name of Ith student
$B_{I,2}-B_{I,6}$	information about first examination
$B_{I,7}-B_{I,12}$	information about second examination
$B_{I,13}-B_{I,17}$	information about third examination
$B_{I,18}-B_{I,28}$	information about final examination
$B_{I,29}-B_{I,42}$	information about homework grades
$B_{I,43}$	grade for classroom participation

This method requires $(25)(43) = 1075$ storage locations, the minimum number needed to store the desired information. Although this approach does not waste any storage space it has the disadvantage that it is much more difficult to locate the desired information. To read a specific set of data from the array it is necessary to first identify the values of J that correspond to that data and then read the data out of the array. The problem which occurs is that the desired data items are not in consecutive memory locations. Thus, a considerable amount of extra processing is needed to compute the correct values of J.

Both of the above arrays also suffer from the limitation that we had to use a numerical encoding for character data. This, along with the other difficulties in trying to fit the information into a convenient arrangement to store it in a single array, indicates that we need a more general concept than an array if we are going to be able to store and discuss nonhomogenous information.

Two essentially similar concepts have been developed to represent the storage of nonhomogenous information. Both concepts provide a systematic representation of information so that it is possible to reference and use this information without becoming involved in unnecessary and often cumbersome bookkeeping problems.

Records and Files

The earliest work which dealt with the processing of nonhomogenous information involved business data-processing applications. This approach removes the limitation, present in arrays, that all the information has to be of the same type. The basic collection of information was called a *record* and a collection of records was called a *file*. A record is a logical collection of information consisting of one or more items. Each item is represented by a location in the record called a *field*. When a collection of records is formed into a file each record is assigned an ordered place in the file. The logical location of a record in a file is called the *position* of the record.

To illustrate these ideas let us consider how we could represent the information in Table 4-2. This requires a file with ten records. Each record consists of four fields: student name, student number, semester standing, and examination score. There are ten record positions, each position corresponding to one of the ten records. For example position 4 contains the record.

FINCH, B	047 465 261	6	88
First field	Second field	Third field	Fourth field

Some programming languages provide special facilities for defining and handling files. However, it is possible to create files using languages without this capability by using a collection of one-dimensional arrays.

Assume we wish to represent a file with r records and that each record has k fields. This file can be represented by using k one-dimensional arrays where each has r elements. Each field corresponds to one of the arrays and the Jth record corresponds to the information contained in the Jth element of each array.

The information contained in Table 4-2 can be stored in a file formed from four ten-element arrays. Let these arrays be

$[SNA_l]$ student name character array
$[SNU_l]$ student number character array
$[SS_l]$ semester standing integer array
$[ES_l]$ examination score integer array

TABLE 4-2 ■ A file of student records

Position	Student name	Student number	Semester standing	Examination score
1	ALAN, A.	028 362 808	4	78
2	BAYLOR, M.	041 425 766	4	92
3	COOPER, G.	078 280 108	5	65
4	FINCH, B.	047 465 261	6	88
5	IVES, K.	012 484 783	5	45
6	MORRIS, R.	213 448 950	4	96
7	NELSON, H.	043 422 544	4	80
8	SMITH, F.	015 560 480	5	75
9	TEED, S.	143 321 766	4	58
10	WALTER, D.	071 406 659	4	85

SNA_1	SNU_1	SS_1	ES_1
SNA_2	SNU_2	SS_2	ES_2
SNA_3	SNU_3	SS_3	ES_3
SNA_4	SNU_4	SS_4	ES_4
.	.	.	.
.	.	.	.
.	.	.	.
SNA_9	SNU_9	SS_9	ES_9
SNA_{10}	SNU_{10}	SS_{10}	ES_{10}

FIGURE 4-28 ■ Illustration of the organization of a file using one-dimensional arrays.

Then the file would have the form shown in Fig. 4-28. The fourth record of this file is

$$SNA_4 = FINCH, B \quad SNU_4 = 047\ 465\ 261 \quad SS_4 = 6 \quad ES_4 = 88$$

To illustrate how we would use information stored in this manner, assume that we wish to process the file of Table 4-2 to obtain a list of all students who received a grade of 80 or better on the examination. It is assumed that this file is stored as shown in Fig. 4-28. The desired algorithm is represented by the flowchart of Fig. 4-29.

In this flowchart, I is used as both a counter and a pointer. For each value of I, ES_I is compared to 80. If the examination score is less than 80, no action is taken and we go to the next file position. Otherwise we use I, which points to the Ith file position, to printout the name of the student and the student's score. After that is completed, the next record in the file is tested.

One problem in representing a file as a collection of one-dimensional arrays is that we lose all the fine structure corresponding to different interrela-

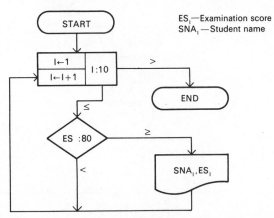

FIGURE 4-29 ■ Flowchart to determine all students with an examination score of 80 or over.

tionships that exist between the items that make up the file. These interrelationships can be preserved if we introduce the idea of a structure.

Structures

When we discussed arrays all elements of the array were implicitly of equal rank. In dealing with structured data we introduce the idea of the level of a data item. Each item in a structure has a *level number* which relates it to other items in the structure. This interrelationship can be likened to the way headings, subheadings, and subsubheadings are used in an outline to organize ideas in a book. The level numbers indicate the hierarchy of the items. The first level, level 1, is the name of the structure. The elements of the levels are then subdivided into other elements until we reach a point where no additional subdivisions are introduced. These final elements are called the *elementary elements* of the structure. Figure 4-30 illustrates a graphical way that we can use to represent the information contained in a structure. This graph is called a *tree*.

The structure in Figure 4-30 has four levels. The name of the structure is STUDENT GRADES. The items of information stored in the structure are indicated by the elementary elements of the graph. On level 2 we have two elementary elements, STUDENT NAME and SEMESTER STANDING. No information is stored at level 3. All the elements at level 4 are elementary elements representing information. If we examine the elementary elements at level 4, we see that four are identified by the name EXAM GRADE and four by the name FINAL GRADE. To distinguish which item of information we are dealing with, we must identify the element on level 3 that is associated with the desired elementary element at level 4. Thus, COURSE 1 FINAL GRADE serves to identify uniquely a specific element at level 4.

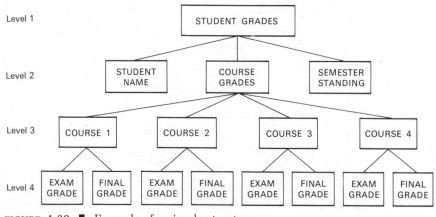

FIGURE 4-30 ■ Example of a simple structure.

Just as a record consists of a collection of information items grouped together for some purpose, so does a structure. Thus, it is possible to talk of a collection of identical structures forming a file just as a collection of records form a file. Some programming languages include structures as one of the basic methods of storing information and provide techniques both for defining structures and for carrying out operations on the elements of the structure.

In those languages that do not provide this facility we can still simulate a structure by using a collection of arrays. In this case some of the arrays may have more than one dimension. To illustrate how this can be done, assume that the records of ten students are to be recorded in a file using the structure shown in Fig. 4-30. To create this file we need the following arrays:

$[SN_I]$— one-dimensional array for student names
$[SS_I]$— one-dimensional array for semester standing
$[CG_{I,J,K}]$— three-dimensional array for grade information

The index I is used to indicate which student record is being considered. The index J is used to indicate which course is being considered while the index K is used to indicate which grade is being considered. Thus, I, J, and K are integers, where

$$1 \leq I \leq 10 \qquad 1 \leq J \leq 4 \qquad 1 \leq K \leq 2$$

The exam grade obtained by the fifth student in the second course is obtained by setting $I = 5$, $J = 2$, $K = 1$, and looking at the value of $CG_{5,2,1}$.

To show how a structure is used, let us consider a situation where we

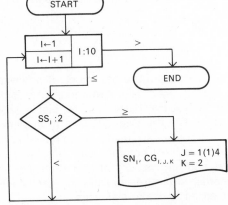

FIGURE 4-31 ■ Flowchart of an algorithm to print final exam grades of all second-semester students.

wish to make a list of the final exam grades for all students in their second semester. The flowchart of Fig. 4-31 gives an algorithm to carry out this task. Here again we see that I is used as both a counter and a pointer to the structure associated with the Ith student.

Exercises

1. Assume that the ten student records shown in Table 4-2 are stored in four one-dimensional arrays represented in Fig. 4-28. Give portions of a flowchart that will perform *each* of the following tasks:

(a) Determine and print the name of the student who has the highest examination score.

(b) Determine and print the names of the students who are in their fifth semester.

(c) Compute the average score and output the names of the students whose scores are above the average.

(d) Determine and print the names of any students who are juniors or seniors (fifth semester or beyond) and have an exam score below 80.

2. Consider a collection of 100 employee records to be used by a company to figure a weekly payroll. A typical record is shown below, along with the names associated with each field.

ADAM	JOHN	C	17952	35	5	4	6
Last name	First name	Middle initial	Pay number	Regular hours	Overtime hours	Regular rate	Overtime rate

Each record is to be organized into a single structure of several levels with the information contained in the record being the elementary elements.

(a) Display a graphical form (tree form) of the structure for a record.

(b) Show how a file of the 100 structured records can be stored in arrays.

---

7 ■ Summary

This chapter has introduced the basic idea of a flowchart and the techniques that can be used to organize information for a computation. All flowcharts are constructed using five basic building blocks. Table 4-3 illustrates the basic flowchart tasks and the symbols used to implement any flowchart.

Four basic techniques that are useful in representing stored information have been introduced. The most common ones for simple computations are individual identifiers and arrays. However, when we encounter nonhomogeneous data records, structures provide greater flexibility in organizing data so that they are easier to use in algorithms.

Throughout the rest of the book these information storage and flowchart techniques will be used to describe ideas, new concepts, and specific calcula-

TABLE 4-3 ■ Summary of basic flowchart elements

1. Input

2. Computation

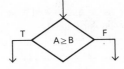

$A \leftarrow B + B*C$

3. Decision

T $A \geq B$ F

< $A : B$ >
         =

4. Looping

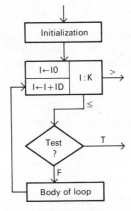

Initialization

$I \leftarrow I0$ $I : K$ >
$I \leftarrow I + ID$
                    ≤

Test ?   T

F

Body of loop

5. Output

A,B,C

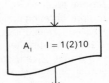

A_i $I = 1(2)10$

TABLE 4-3 ■ Continued

6. Special symbols

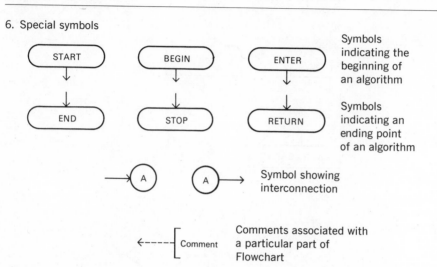

Symbols indicating the beginning of an algorithm

Symbols indicating an ending point of an algorithm

Symbol showing interconnection

Comments associated with a particular part of Flowchart

tions. In this way we are able to present a large amount of information in a very compact manner.

As you become more familiar with these ideas you will also find that they are an aid to your own thinking as you try to solve a particular problem. In doing this you must remember that flowcharts are only a tool and never an end in themselves. They allow you to express yours ideas in a clear and compact manner and to understand the structure of the algorithm with which you are working. The actual decisions concerning how a problem is to be solved and how information is to be organizaed are your responsibility and must be completed before the flowchart can be developed. These more challenging and difficult problems are considered in the next chapter.

References

An attempt has been made to standarize flowchart symbology. The standards are discussed in [2] and used in [1] and [6]. Several other flowchart conventions are also used in [4]. Anyone entering the computer field soon learns the local conventions for flowchart representation and should adhere to those conventions. [1], [4], and [6] illustrates how a formal approach to flowchart representation is helpful in carrying out standard computing tasks. [3], [5], and [7] discuss problem solving using a computer. [5] and [7] are somewhat oriented to business applications, while [3] is a general discussion of problem solving aimed at high-school students.

1. Bohl, M. (1971) *Flowcharting Techniques*, Science Research Associates, Chicago, Ill.

2. Chapin, N. (June 1970) "Flowcharting With The ANSI Standard: A Tutorial," *Computing Surveys,* Vol. 2, No. 2, pp. 119–146.

3. Forsythe, A. I., Keenan, T. A., Organick, E. I., and Stenberg, W. (1969) *Computer Science—A First Course,* John Wiley & Sons, New York.

4. Schriber, T. J. (1969) *Fundamentals of Flowcharting,* John Wiley & Sons, New York.

5. Vazsonyi, A. (1970) *Problem Solving By Digital Computers With PL/I Programming,* Prentice-Hall, Englewood Cliffs, N.J.

6. Wayne, M. N. (1973) *Flowcharting Concepts and Data Processing Techniques: A Self-Instructional Guide,* Canfield Press, San Francisco, Calif.

7. Wilde, D. U. (1973) *An Introduction To Computing; Problem-Solving, Algorithms, and Data Structures,* Prentice-Hall, Englewood Cliffs, N.J.

Home Problems

If possible, the algorithms developed to solve the following problems should be programmed and tested on a computer.

1. Let A be an array that stores the student names of Table 4-2. Give the flow-chart of an algorithm which will print out the names in reverse alphabetical order.

2. Give the flowchart of an algorithm which will find the largest and smallest number in an array. The numbers in the array may be positive, negative, or zero.

3. Many programming languages must use special techniques to work with character information. To avoid this problem it is often desirable to develop a code which assigns a unique number to each distinct character sequence. Assume that all character sequences of interest are made up of from one to five letters. Develop a code which gives a unique numerical value to each distinct character sequence. The code should be designed so that the ordering relationship of the encoded character sequences is the same as the ordering relationship of the original character sequences.

4. Assume that the information listed in Table 4-1 is to be stored in a three-dimensional array A. The name of the student does not have to be stored but all of the other information does.
   (a) Indicate how each item of information is to be stored as a numerical value.
   (b) Give a flowchart of a program which computes the number of students who have passed all four examinations.

5. Repeat home problem 4, but this time try to store the information in a two-dimensional array B.

6. Repeat home problem 4 but this time store all the information, including student names, as a structure. Realize this structure by using arrays.

7. In a rectangular coordinate system, every point in the x, y plane is identified by an ordered pair of numbers (x,y) where x is the x-coordinate and y is the y-coordinate. Each point in the plane can be classified into one of the following regions:

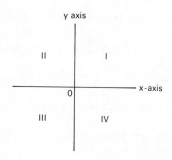

1. Quadrant I ($x > 0$, $y > 0$)
2. Quadrant II ($x < 0$, $y > 0$)
3. Quadrant III ($x < 0$, $y < 0$)
4. Quadrant IV ($x > 0$, $y < 0$)
5. The positive x-axis ($x > 0$, $y = 0$)
6. The positive y-axis ($x = 0$, $y > 0$)
7. The negative x-axis ($x < 0$, $y = 0$)
8. The negative y-axis ($x = 0$, $y < 0$)
9. The origin ($x = 0$, $y = 0$)

Give a detailed flowchart of an algorithm which will input N pairs of numbers corresponding to the x-coordinate and the y-coordinate of N points and, on the basis of the two numbers in each pair, assign each point to one of the nine regions listed above. Assume that the N input points are stored in two one-dimensional arrays $[X_I]$ and $[Y_I]$.

8. Repeat home problem 7, but this time do not store the input points in an array. Instead, each point (x- and y-coordinate) is inputted and on the basis of the x- and y-value an identification will be made and results printed. Show how the algorithm in problem 7 should be modified to solve this problem.

9. A sequence of u data elements can be stored in one of two ways in a two-dimensional array $[A_{I,J}]$, $I = 1(1)M$ and $J = 1(1)N$, where $M \cdot N = u$. They are said to be stored in row-major order if the data is assigned to the subscripted variables such that the subscript J is varied first through its full range of N values before the subscript I is varied. They are stored in column-major order if the way that the subscripts are varied is reversed. For example, the two ways that a sequence of 12 data elements can be stored in a 3 by 4 array are shown below:

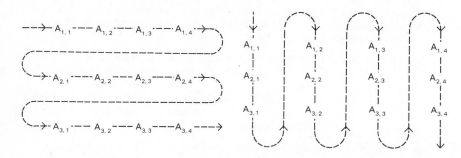

Row-major order   Column-major order

$----\rightarrow$ Order of storage

Assume that a sequence of u data elements are punched on cards that are sequentially read into the computer memory.

(a) Develop a flowchart of an algorithm that will read in and store the data in an M by N array in row-major order.

(b) Do (a) again, but in column-major order.

[Note that in some programming languages, it is possible for the programmer to read in and store all the input data in an array in a single step by simply referencing the array indicated by the identifier A. In using this language feature, the programmer must fully understand how the array elements are stored (i.e., in which order) before carrying out any computation on the data array.]

10. Extend the flowcharts developed in home problem 9 so that they will handle a three-dimensional array $[A_{I,J,K}]$, $I = 1(1)M$, $J = 1(1)N$, and $K = 1(1)P$ when $M \cdot N \cdot P = u$. In this case, the row-major order refers to the fact that the rightmost subscript, K, is varied most rapidly, and the leftmost subscript, I, is varied least rapidly. If the way the subscripts are varied is reversed, it is called the column-major order.

11. Let, A, B, C, and D be the logical variables (i.e., have a value of either TRUE or FALSE). In mathematical logic we say that two logical expressions, F(A, B, C, D) and G(A, B, C, D) are equivalent or equal if the logical relation

$$F(A,B,C,D) = G(A,B,C,D)$$

is true for all of the possible values that can be assigned to the logical variables A, B, C, and D. Since there are only 16 different combinations of variables that must be checked it is possible to prove the equivalence of the logical expressions by showing that the above equivalence relation is true for each of the 16 different combinations of variables.

Let

$$F(A,B,C,D) = (A \lor B) \land (C \lor D)$$
$$G(A,B,C,D) = (A \land C) \lor (A \land D) \lor (B \land C) \lor (B \land D)$$

Develop the flowchart of an algorithm which will check these two logical expressions to see if they are equivalent.

12. A teacher's rating sheet is prepared to determine the student's evaluation of a particular instructor. The rating consists of ten questions. To each question, the student is to answer with one of the four responses.

1. Excellent   3. Fair
2. Good   4. Poor

Assume that, for each student, the responses (1, 2, 3, or 4) to the ten questions are recorded on an input card. Give a flowchart of an algorithm that will tabulate and print out the evaluation results from a class of N students. A suggested printout is shown below.

Tabulation of Evaluation Results		$N = 100$	
	Excellent	Good	Fair	Poor
Question 1	52	30	17	1
Question 2	60	28	12	0
.	.	.	.	.
.	.	.	.	.
.	.	.	.	.
Question 10	35	40	22	3

problem analysis and
flowchart synthesis

1 ■ Introduction

Once a flowchart representation of a given computation has been developed, it is a relatively easy matter to transform the information contained in that flowchart into a computer program. The task of developing the flowchart is often the most difficult and time consuming step in carrying out a computer solution of a problem. There are a number of reasons why this is so.

When a problem is initially presented it often appears to be very clearly defined. However, as we evaluate the problem we often find that conditions occur which were not even considered when the problem was initially formulated. Sometimes this occurs because the person who originated the problem is not aware of how computers are used in the problem-solving process. In other cases, the preliminary analysis of the problem is sufficient to uncover the difficulties that turn up when an attempt is made to develop the complete problem solution.

After the general method for solving a problem has been established, the next task consists of developing a flowchart to represent the steps that a computer must carry out to compute the desired solution. For most problems there are a number of different approaches that can be used to carry out the necessary tasks. The one that is finally selected must not only provide the desired solution to the problem but should also carry out the solution using the minimal amount of computer resources.

The cost of any computation usually depends upon the amount of time needed to carry out the task and the amount of storage space needed to store the program and data associated with the computations. Thus, the organization of the sequence of instructions that make up a program and the way that the data associated with the program is organized have a strong influence upon the program's overall efficiency.

Each algorithm involves a number of self-contained subtasks. If we are able to identify these tasks as we develop our algorithm, the resulting flowchart will take on a modular nature. This means that we can develop a complete problem solution by first developing algorithms to carry out solutions for each of the subtasks and then interconnect these results to obtain the overall solution. This approach makes it easier to debug the computer program resulting from the flowchart. We first make sure that the subprograms associated with each subtask are operating correctly. After all these subprograms have been checked, we then verify that the main program is correct.

Unfortunately, the task of synthesizing an efficient flowchart to carry out a given task is not an algorithmic process. Currently, a considerable amount of research is directed at this problem. However, many of its aspects are still not well understood. Consequently, we find that the ability to develop an efficient flowchart to represent a given computation depends upon both previous experience and a complete knowledge of the different factors that influence the efficiency of a computation. Past experience has shown that most people are able to develop their flowcharting ability as they develop solutions to a sequence of problems that increase in difficulty and breadth.

In this chapter, we first explore the general methods that can be used to generate an efficient flowchart representation of the computations called for by a given algorithm. This discussion implicitly assumes that we have a well-defined description of the desired problem solution. Our goal is to develop an understanding of the various factors that influence the efficiency of a program and the different decisions that must be made in designing it.

Most problems one attempts to solve using a computer are not well defined. They are often initially formulated in a somewhat general manner, which indicates the desired objectives of the computation but has a minimal amount of detail about how the computation is to be carried out. This is true not only for large scale information-processing tasks but also for rather small tasks that at first may appear to be well-defined problems. Thus, the major task faced by the person carrying out the analysis is to reduce the initial problem statement to an algorithm that describes the actual calculations to be carried out to solve the problem. The second part of this chapter considers the general methods which can be used to reduce complex problems to well-defined problems that can be solved.

Throughout this chapter examples are used to illustrate the advantages and limitations of the different concepts being discussed. These examples are presented in enough detail to make evident the way in which they can be implemented by any one of the standard programming languages. In later chapters these techniques are used without repeating the complete details of their implementation.

2 ∎ Well-Defined Problems

The easiest types of flowcharts to develop are those associated with problems having a predefined exact solution. Problems of this type are called *well defined.* Although most problems cannot initially be classified as well defined, the problem-solving process that we present in the next sections shows that the solution to a complex problem involves the reduction of the complete problem to a sequence of well-defined problems that can be solved to give the solution to the main problem. Thus, before we consider this more complex analysis problem, we will consider the basic structure of well-defined problems and how a flowchart representation of their solution can be developed.

A well-defined problem may take a number of different forms. In some cases the problem will be of a mathematical nature and its solution is described by a set of equations. At other times the problem will be an information-processing task involving making decisions and/or manipulating information that is in known form. Before looking at specific problems, let's stand back and examine the types of tasks that must be carried out to develop a flowchart representation of the solution to a particular problem.

Initial Analysis

The initial description of a well-defined problem is the result of an analytical study which is usually not concerned with the fact that a computer is to be used in the solution process. The development of an algorithm to carry out the solution means that the information contained in the problem statement must be reduced to a sequence of steps that will be carried out to arrive at the solution. The selection of this sequence of steps requires careful planning and organization if the resulting flowchart is to describe an algorithm that makes efficient use of the available computing facilities.

To develop a flowchart for a given problem, it is necessary to obtain answers to the following questions:

1. What output information is to be produced by the calculation?
2. What information is known and available as input information during the calculation?
3. What information is known and available to establish values for the initial conditions of the identifiers used in the calculation?
4. What internal information must be generated and stored for later use in the calculations?
5. What is the best way to organize the stored information so that it is easy to work with and uses a minimal amount of memory space?
6. What calculations must be performed to generate the internal information and the output information?
7. What is the best way to organize the calculations to minimize the number of steps needed to perform a given task?
8. How will each of the variables associated with any type of information be represented?

After we answer these questions we are in a position to develop the flowchart to describe the exact method that will be used to carry out the desired calculations.

The following examples illustrate how each of these questions is answered for a sequence of well-defined problems of increasing difficulty. It should become evident as these problems are being considered that a considerable amount of planning and evaluation is needed to develop an efficient flowchart for the solution of well-defined problems.

Evaluation of Linear Equations

In many numerical applications it is often necessary to calculate the values of one set of variables from the known values of another set of variables. One typical type of calculation is that expressed by the set of linear equations of the form

$$y_1 = a_{11}x_1 + a_{12}x_2 + a_{13}x_3$$
$$y_2 = a_{21}x_1 + a_{22}x_2 + a_{23}x_3$$
$$y_3 = a_{31}x_1 + a_{32}x_2 + a_{33}x_3$$

In this problem the output information is to be the values associated with y_1, y_2, and y_3 and the input information corresponds to the values assigned to x_1, x_2, and x_3. The coefficients a_{ij} represent internal information that must be initialized before the calculation begins.

Next we must decide how to organize the calculation. We see that, for $i = 1, 2, 3$,

$$y_i = \sum_{j=1}^{3} a_{ij}x_j$$

This means that we must provide storage space for the coefficients a_{ij} and the values of x_1, x_2, and x_3. From the statement of the problem we do not know how the results are to be used, so we will store the results and also print them out. This means that we need a place to store the computed values of y_1, y_2, and y_3.

From these considerations we decide to use three arrays to represent this information. They are

$$\text{Input array } X = [X_I] = \begin{bmatrix} x_1 \\ x_2 \\ x_3 \end{bmatrix}$$

$$\text{Output array } Y = [Y_I] = \begin{bmatrix} y_1 \\ y_2 \\ y_3 \end{bmatrix}$$

$$\text{Coefficients array } A = [A_{I,J}] = \begin{bmatrix} a_{11} & a_{12} & a_{13} \\ a_{21} & a_{22} & a_{23} \\ a_{31} & a_{32} & a_{33} \end{bmatrix}$$

The arrays X and Y have three elements and the array A is a three by three matrix.

The calculation can now be carried out using the algorithm represented by the flowchart of Fig. 5-1. Examining this figure we can observe a number of common features of a flowchart. First we observe that the algorithm involves nested loops. The inner loop computes the value for each y variable while the outer loop controls which y variable is being evaluated. The first task performed on entering the flowchart is to initialize the array A. Next the input values for X are read in and stored. The outer loop is very simple. We note that each time we pass through the outer loop we must initialize the value of Y_I to zero before we start the computations indicated by the inner loop. If we did not do this, we might find that an error could occur because Y_I might have a nonzero value.

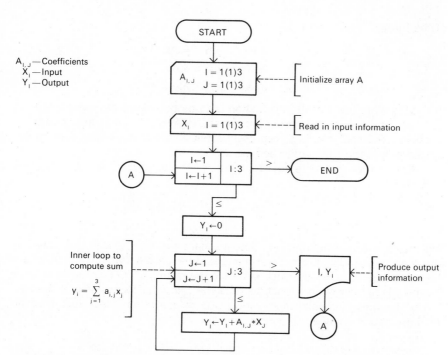

FIGURE 5-1 ■ Flowchart of an algorithm to compute the values of a set of linear equations.

This is due to the fact that the storage location associated with Y_I might contain a nonzero value generated during another phase of the calculation, or when the computer was solving another problem.

A Table Lookup Algorithm

One common task in computing is to locate a name corresponding to some quantity in a table and then use this name to find a value for the associated quantity. For example, let us assume we wish to encode a message by translating each letter into a number that was previously fixed by some random selection process. The letters and the corresponding numbers are shown in Table 5-1.

Using this table we see that the input sequence

'A'   'C'   'B'   'F'   'G'   'Z'   'X'

would be transformed into the sequence

25   36   15   10   9   20   19

TABLE 5-1 ▪ Coding table for the alphabet

Letter	Code number	Letter	Code number	Letter	Code number
A	25	J	17	S	31
B	15	K	6	T	38
C	36	L	35	U	24
D	41	M	4	V	12
E	26	N	11	W	3
F	10	O	27	X	19
G	9	P	1	Y	2
H	42	Q	18	Z	20
I	23	R	40		

The development of a flowchart representing this encoding process is a little more complex than the previous example, since we must decide how to carry out the transformation. Examining the problem statement we see that the output will be a sequence of numbers between 1 and 42 and that the input will be a sequence of letters. A method for carrying out the conversion process must now be developed.

If we do the conversion process by hand, we take the input letter, scan Table 5-1 until we find the letter, then read out the number that is associated with that letter. From this we see that we must provide a means for storing the equivalent of Table 5-1 in memory.

One approach is to use two one-dimensional arrays of 26 elements, $L = [L_i]$ which will store the letters and $N = [N_i]$ which will store the number corresponding to the letter. For example, the fifth letter in the table is E which is encoded as 26. Thus, location L_5 of L contains 'E', while location N_5 of N contains 26. To carry out the encoding process we take the input letter and compare it sequentially with each term of the array L until a match is found. The corresponding element of the N array is then read as the encoded value of the input letter. Finally, we must introduce some convention to indicate the end of the input sequence. One way to do this is to use a special character, say a period ('.'), as an end delimiter.

The above information can be used to develop the flowchart shown in Fig. 5-2. The input character is assigned to the identifier Y. The two arrays L and N are initialized before entering the main part of the algorithm. The exact details of this initialization process are not presented since they can be carried out in a number of different ways depending upon the particular programming language used to realize this flowchart.

The identifier Y and array L represent character information and the array N represents numerical information. Both decision points test non-numeric quantities. The first decision point is used to determine if the end of

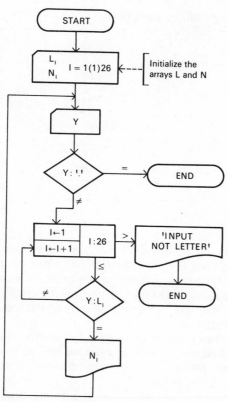

FIGURE 5-2 ■ Flowchart of a character encoder using table lookup techniques.

the input sequence has been reached. If the character is a period, then the processing is complete. Otherwise the input is a character that must be located in the array L. This is done by sequentially comparing the input with each element of the array until a match is found. The output corresponding to the matched character is then read from the array N and printed out. In this way I acts as a counter and as a pointer to the current entry in the table. If the character is not found in the table, an error message is printed out and processing halts.

Calculation of sin(x)

The two previous examples consider well-defined problems in which the final flowchart very closely corresponded to the way the problem was initially represented. There are many situations where it is desirable to reorganize the problem description so that a more efficient flowchart can be developed. The following example illustrates this approach.

Assume that we wish to develop a program to compute sin(x) for a given input value of x. The output is the value sin(x) and the input is the value of x in radians. From mathematics we know that we can represent the value of sin(x) as

$$sin(x) = x - \frac{x^3}{3!} + \frac{x^5}{5!} - \cdots + (-1)^{m+1} \frac{x^{2m-1}}{(2m-1)!} + \cdots$$

$$= \sum_{m=1}^{\infty} (-1)^{m+1} \frac{x^{2m-1}}{(2m-1)!}$$

where $n! = n(n-1)(n-2)(n-3) \cdots 2 \cdot 1$. This series representing sin(x) is an alternating series. As m increases the mth term

$$U(m,x) = (-1)^{m+1} \frac{x^{2m-1}}{(2m-1)!}$$

decreases towards zero. Thus, the infinite summation for sin(x) converges for all values of x. In particular, if, as we must in developing a computer program, we approximate sin(x) by only using the first N terms, then

$$sin(x) \cong \sum_{m=1}^{N} (-1)^{m+1} \frac{x^{2m-1}}{(2m-1)!}$$

will have an error E that is bounded by the relationship

$$E < \left| \frac{x^{2N+1}}{(2N+1)!} \right|$$

That is, the error is bounded by a value equal to the magnitude of the $(N+1)$st term of the sequence. To compute sin(x) we can thus carry out the indicated summation until we reach a value of N such that the magnitude of the $(N+1)$st term is less than our desired error.

An inexperienced programmer would probably decide to compute sin(x) by simply evaluating the series

$$sin(x) = \sum_{m=1}^{N} (-1)^{m+1} \frac{x^{2m-1}}{(2m-1)!}$$

where N is selected such that

$$\left| \frac{x^{2N+1}}{(2N+1)} \right| < ERROL$$

where ERROL is the allowable error. The resulting flowchart would have the form shown in Fig. 5-3. For a number of reasons this is a very poor method for carrying out this calculation. First of all the calculation of $(2M-1)!$ for each term of the summation is wasteful because, as we will soon see, it involves a large number of unnecessary steps. Similarly, the calculation of U is also done in an inefficient manner.

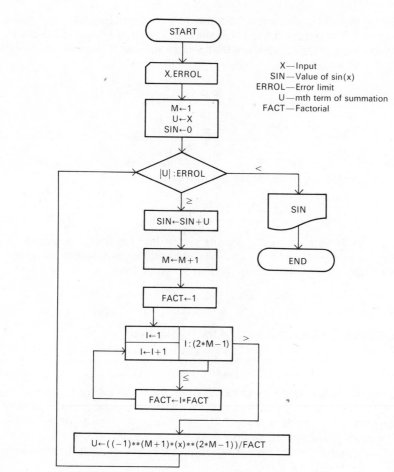

FIGURE 5-3 ▮ First attempt to compute sin(x).

We can make our summation process more efficient and cut down the number of calculations required if we do a little preplanning concerning how we might carry out the summation process. As a first step let us represent the sum as

$$sin(x) = \sum_{m=1}^{N} U(m,x)$$

where

$$U(1,x) = x$$

and the mth term is

$$U(m,x) = \frac{(-1)^{m+1}x^{2m-1}}{(2m-1)!}$$

The next term in the summation, $U(m+1,x)$, is related to $U(m,x)$ by

$$U(m+1,x) = \frac{(-1)^{m+2}x^{2m+1}}{(2m+1)!} = \frac{(-1)x^2}{(2m+1)(2m)} U(m,x)$$

The value of x is fixed during the summation. Thus, if we define

$$f(x) = \frac{-x^2}{(2m+1)(2m)} = \frac{C(x)}{(2m+1)(2m)}$$

we obtain the relationship

$$U(m+1,x) = f(x)U(m,x)$$

This method for computing $U(m+1,x)$ from $U(m,x)$ is much simpler than using

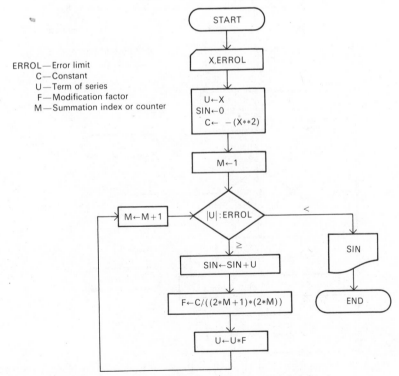

ERROL—Error limit
   C—Constant
   U—Term of series
   F—Modification factor
   M—Summation index or counter

FIGURE 5-4 ■ Flowchart of an algorithm to compute sin(x).

the original formula, since we do not have to evaluate $(2m + 1)!$ and x^{2m+1} at each step. A flowchart using this new method of computing sin(x) to within an error limit ERROL is given in Fig. 5-4. Comparing this flowchart with the one in Fig. 5-3, we see that we have significantly reduced the number of calculations performed in the body of the loop.

There is one addition that we should make to the flowchart. As it now stands, there is no limit to the number of times we execute the loop. If x is too large, possibly because of some error in specifying x, we might end up going around the loop an undesirable number of times. It is always good practice to include a counter to limit the number of times any loop is executed. This is easily accomplished as shown in Fig. 5-5.

This example has illustrated the need for a careful analysis of any well-defined problem before selecting the algorithm that is to be used to solve the problem.

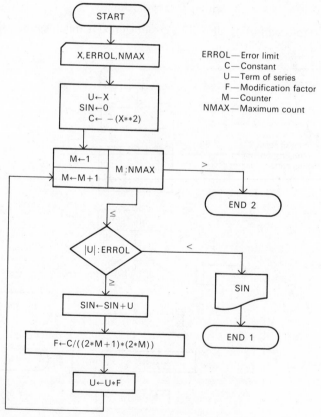

FIGURE 5-5 ∎ Flowchart of an algorithm to compute sin(x) in NMAX or fewer steps.

Exercises

1. The cosine function is defined as

$$\cos(x) = 1 + \sum_{m=1}^{\infty} (-1)^m \frac{x^{2m}}{(2m)!} = 1 - \frac{x^2}{2!} + \frac{x^4}{4!} - \frac{x^6}{6!} + \cdots$$

Develop a flowchart that will compute cos(x) without directly calculating the factorial. Assume that the error in calculating the function on the computer must be within the limit ERROL. The error in taking the sum of the first N terms in the infinite series is bounded by the magnitude of the (N + 1)st term.

2. For the exponential function defined below

$$e^x = 1 + \sum_{m=1}^{\infty} \frac{x^m}{m!} = 1 + x + \frac{x^2}{2!} + \cdots$$

(a) Let the general term in the infinite series be

$$U(m,x) = \frac{x^m}{m!}$$

Derive a formula for U(m + 1,x) in terms of U(m,x).
(b) We let

$$e^x \cong 1 + \sum_{m=1}^{N} \frac{x^m}{m!}$$

Develop a flowchart to compute this approximation using the result from (a). Assume that the error in taking the sum of the first N terms in the infinite series is bounded by the magnitude of the (N + 1)st term which must be within the limit ERROL.

3 ■ Multiple-Step Algorithms

The examples just discussed involved simple calculations which could be carried out as a single task. Most problems to be solved on a computer are much more complex. The easiest way to solve a complex problem is to break it into a number of interrelated subproblems. An algorithm is then developed to solve the original problem under the assumption that we already have an algorithm that solves each of the subproblems. The solution is completed by developing the necessary solution algorithm for each subproblem.

The calculations necessary to carry out the solution to a particular subproblem must, of course, eventually be represented by a complete flowchart. While developing the overall flowchart for the complete problem it is unnecessary to include a complete flowchart of the solution of each subproblem. Instead we can use the symbols shown in Fig. 5-6 to represent the calculations.

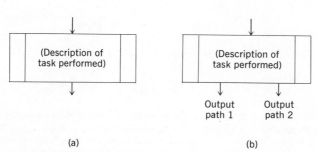

FIGURE 5-6 ■ Flowchart symbols to indicate complex subtasks. (a) Single output path. (b) Multiple output path.

The details of these calculations are indicated by a separate flowchart.

The simplest type of calculation is indicated by the symbol given by Fig. 5-6(a). The box indicates that as soon as the particular task is performed we proceed to the next task. There are situations where the task being performed may include a branch point. The next task thus depends upon the result of the calculation represented by the box. Situations of this type are represented as shown in Fig. 5-6(b).

As an example of how a multiple-step algorithm is developed consider the following problem.

Normalization of Grades

When a large number of students take an examination the distribution of grades may have a form similar to that shown in Fig. 5-7(a). The average value

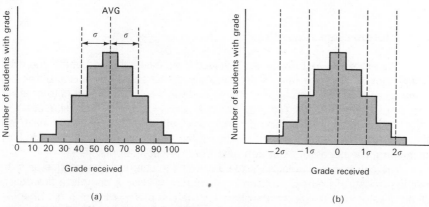

FIGURE 5-7 ■ Illustration of the effect of normalizing a set of grades. (a) Unprocessed examination grades. (b) Normalized grades.

of the grades is

$$AVG = \frac{1}{NS} \sum_{I=1}^{NS} G_I$$

where G_I is the numerical grade of the Ith student and there are assumed to be NS students.

The dispersion of the grades around this average value is measured by the standard deviation $\sigma = SIGM$ defined as

$$SIGM = \left[\sum_{I=1}^{NS} \frac{(G_I - AVG)^2}{NS - 1} \right]^{1/2}$$

The normalized grade is then obtained by the following relationship

$$GN_I = \frac{G_I - AVG}{SIGM}$$

where GN_I is the normalized grade of the Ith student. Figure 5-7(b) shows the effect that normalizing the grades has upon the way that the distribution of grades is represented.

To develop an algorithm to carry out this normalization process, we proceed in stages. First we note that we must have an array G to represent the initial student grades and we must produce an array GN of normalized student grades. An initial flowchart of this problem would have the form shown in Fig. 5-8(a). Examining the flowchart, we see that we have three subtasks to perform. Each of these subtasks is described by the flowcharts of Figs. 5-8(b) to (d).

The use of subtasks to simplify flowcharts allows us to discuss general information-processing concepts without having to be distracted by all of the details necessary to carry out the subtasks that are used to represent these concepts.

Internal Information Storage

The sequence in which we carry out the subtasks of an algorithm depends upon how these subtasks are interrelated. For example, assume that an algorithm requires us to carry out three subtasks, say Task A, Task B, and Task C. If the information generated by Task A is needed to perform Task B, and if the information generated by Task B is needed to perform Task C, then we must carry out our computations in the following sequence

Task A → Task B → Task C

This means that the information needed by Task B from Task A must be temporarily stored until Task B is performed. A similar situation exists for Task C. The way we choose to store this intermediate information for later use must be carefully considered as we develop our algorithm.

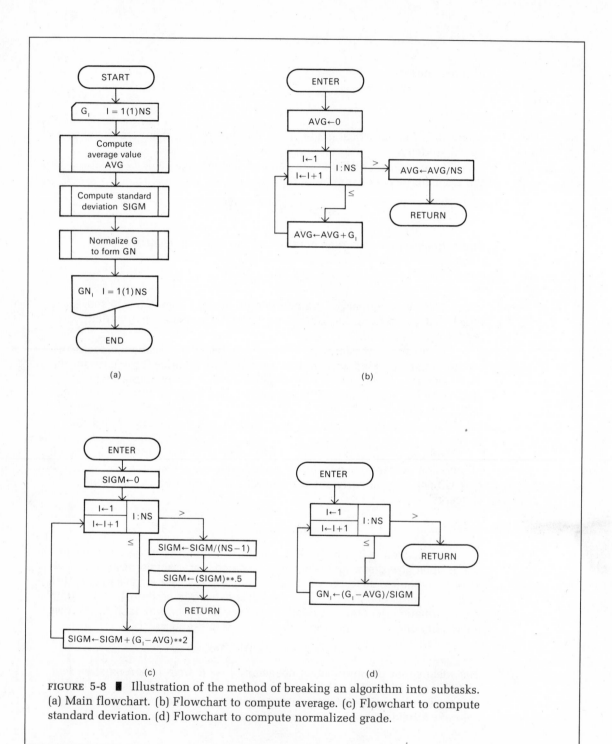

FIGURE 5-8 ■ Illustration of the method of breaking an algorithm into subtasks. (a) Main flowchart. (b) Flowchart to compute average. (c) Flowchart to compute standard deviation. (d) Flowchart to compute normalized grade.

Temporary Variables and Arrays

One of the commonest forms of temporary storage techniques is to use a single identifier or an array to hold intermediate information. The only restriction on the number of times such a storage area can be used in a program is that new information cannot be stored in the area until the old information is no longer needed. The multiple use of a given array for temporary storage is very useful in large programs since it can considerably reduce the amount of memory space required in the computer for the execution of a program. This is often a very important consideration when a large and complex program is being developed.

To illustrate how temporary storage may be used, consider the following problem. Assume that a program is to be developed to help in the grading of an examination. The input information is to consist of

1. The number of students taking the examination
2. For each student:
   (a) The student's name
   (b) The grade received on each of five examination questions

The output information is to be

1. The student's name
2. The examination score
3. The grade received by the student on the basis

A	90–100
B	80–89
C	70–79
D	60–69
F	less than 60

4. The class average

Examining this problem statement, we see that the input information consists of the number of students, N, taking the examination and N data groups consisting of a student's name and five numbers representing the student's grade on each problem. Assume that this information is arranged on cards in the sequence shown in Fig. 5-9.

At this point we must make a decision concerning how this information is to be stored. One approach would be to read all of the information in at once. If we take this approach, we would have to have an N-element array to store the student names and an N × 5-element array to store all of the examination scores. This approach is unnecessarily wasteful of storage space, since there is no need to read in all the student information at one time. Instead, after reading N, we can process the input information concerning each student on a card one at a time.

Taking this approach means that we must provide temporary storage for the name of the student whose record is currently being processed and a tem-

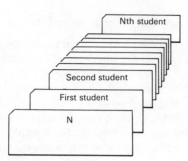

FIGURE 5-9 ■ Student data arranged on input punched cards.

porary five-element array to hold the student's five examination grades. When the processing of the current student's record is complete the desired output information about the student is printed and the processing continues by reading in the information on the next student.

There is one other task that must be performed. At the end of the computation we must calculate the average examination grade. This means that we must keep a running total of the examination scores. At the end of the computation we divide this running total by N to obtain the class average.

Figure 5-10 gives a general flowchart of the tasks that must be performed. Examining this flowchart, we see that we use the array ES for the temporary storage of the student's examination scores, SN for the temporary storage of the student's name, TS for the temporary storage of the student's total examination grade, and SG for the temporary storage of the letter grade earned on the examination. The running sum of the examination scores is indicated by RS.

To see how this program operates assume that the following information is on the input cards:

```
Card 1    3
Card 2    JONES 20 16 17 15 18
Card 3    SMITH 10 19 20 20 16
Card 4    BROWN 20 20 16 15 20
```

Then the output of the calculation would be

```
JONES      86      B
SMITH      85      B
BROWN      91      A
AVERAGE    87.3
```

This discussion has served to emphasize the relationship between the computations carried out as part of an information-processing task and the intermediate information that must be stored as the task progresses. The way in which the calculations and storage are organized plays an important roll in

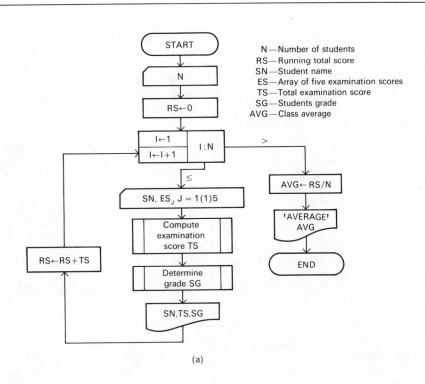

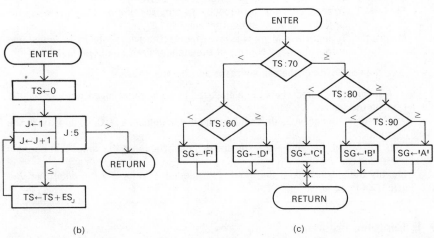

FIGURE 5-10 ■ Flowchart of an algorithm for processing examination scores. (a) General flowchart of program. (b) Computation of examination score. (c) Determination of grade.

determining the overall efficiency of the resulting computer program and the ease with which the actual computer program can be developed. In the following section we investigate how we can reduce a general problem to a set of well-defined problems. These problems can then be solved using the approaches which have just been discussed in this and the preceding sections.

Exercises

1. Assume that we are given an N-element array A of nonnegative numbers that may take on values between 0 and 100. We wish to standardize this array so that all the numbers fall between 0 and 1. If we assume that at least one of the elements of A is nonzero, then we can carry out this standardization process by first finding the largest number in the array and then dividing each term of the array with this number. Develop an algorithm to carry out the standardization process which consists of two subtasks and a main task:

Subtask 1   Finding the largest number in A
Subtask 2   Standardizing the array by dividing the numbers in A by the number found in subtask 1
Main task   To input the array, execute the two subtasks and output the standardized array

Give the flowcharts of the two subtasks and the main task.

2. This exercise is an extension of exercise 1. Assume that we are given a two-dimensional array $A = [A_{I,J}]$ of nonnegative numbers where $I = 1(1)M$ and $J = 1(1)N$. We wish to standardize this array by standardizing each and every row of the array. Develop an algorithm which consists of two subtasks and a main task:

Subtask 1   To determine the largest number of a given row of N numbers
Subtask 2   To standardize a given row by dividing the numbers in the row by the largest number found in that row
Main task   To input the M by N array, execute the two subtasks M times, and output the M by N array of the standardized numbers

Give the flowcharts of the two subtasks and the main task.

3. A string of N characters is to be analyzed by a computer algorithm that will determine the following:
 (a) the number of times that each of the five vowels (A, E, I, O, U) appears in the string,
 (b) the vowel that appears in the string most often, and the vowel that appears least often.
Identify the subtasks and the main task needed to carry out the algorithm and give their flowcharts.

4 ■ Complex Problems

The ability to solve complex problems is a combination of art, experience, and a broad background of knowledge concerning the problem area under investigation. We too often overlook the amount of work necessary to solve a problem when the solution is explained to us. Once a problem has been solved and the method of solution is stated in a clear and logical manner, most traces of the thought process used to develop the solution are effectively lost. A person inexperienced in the art of problem solving often interprets his inability to develop a lucid and elegant solution to a complex problem in a short period of time as an indication that he does not have the capability of solving such problems. This, however, is not the case. Although each new problem we encounter appears to have a unique form, we usually find that its solution requires one or more fairly standard subcalculations. If we can identify these subcalculations, we may reduce our work by organizing our algorithm in such a way that it is only necessary to develop the steps that link these calculations together.

Problem Solving

Problem solving is hard work. It requires considerable patience coupled with the perseverance to stay with the problem through a number of false starts until the solution is discovered. The amount of work required to solve a problem can be reduced if one develops a systematic method of approach that searches for a solution in small steps rather than trying to define the complete solution in a single large step.

We now investigate the problem-solving process from a general viewpoint. Each problem has its own peculiarities, and at some point in the problem-solving process it is necessary to use special techniques to overcome these peculiarities.

The problem-solving process begins with the initial statement of the problem to be solved. This statement can originate from a number of different sources. If the problem originates with the person that is going to solve it, the whole process is self-contained since there is no need to deal with other parties. But there are many cases where the problem is originated by an outside party and the analyst developing the solution must work closely with this person to see that the proposed solution is an acceptable solution.

When the problem is first presented, it must be thoroughly examined to obtain as much factual information as possible about its parameters, the *a priori* information available for use during the problem-solving process, the information that must be generated while the problem-solving process is underway, and the results desired when the problem is finally solved. At this point, several unknown quantities are often identified and they must be defined before work on the solution can be started. The needed information about these unknowns can be obtained in a number of ways. Ideally, the source of the original problem can supply the needed information. If all the questions cannot be answered, it then becomes necessary to make reasonable assumptions about this information and proceed with the problem-solving process. These assumptions should be noted and checked for suitability as the problem-solving process proceeds.

Once the preliminary familiarization phase has been completed and the general objectives are well understood, we begin the analysis phase. The objective of this phase is to reduce the problem to the point where the tasks required to carry out the necessary computations can be identified.

The Preliminary Analysis

Many people make the mistake of trying to carry out the problem-solving process in one massive step. They often become bogged down in extensive detail long before they have fully digested the various aspects of the problem or understand the best way to carry out the solution.

The best method of solving a problem is to divide it into subproblems, such that each subproblem is less complex than the original problem. Each new subproblem is then attacked as a problem itself. If the solution to the subproblem can be obtained in a straightforward manner, we develop the solution and go on to solve the other subproblems that are in need of solution. Otherwise, we redivide the subproblem into more refined subproblems and search for solutions to these new subproblems.

This method of problem solving is effective because we do not try to do everything at once. Conceptually, we can think of this problem-solving process being carried out in a sequence of steps of the form shown in Fig. 5-11. This figure indicates that we first divide the main problem into a set of subproblems

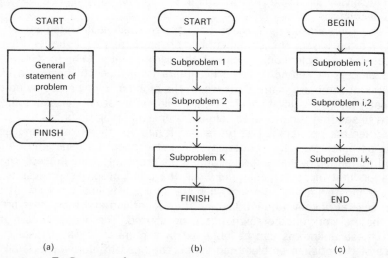

FIGURE 5-11 ■ Conceptual representation of the process of subdividing a complex problem into subproblems. (a) Initial problem statement. (b) Division of main problem into major subproblems. (c) Division of a major subproblem into finer subproblems.

related to the main problem. Hopefully, each of these subproblems will be easier to solve. Examining the subproblem, we may again discover that each subproblem could be solved if we had the answer to a subproblem of the subproblem. The division of problems into subproblems continues until we reach a point where each subproblem is a well-defined problem that we can solve. We then work our way back through the division process, using the newly developed information to solve the more complex problems. Graphically, the task of dividing a complex problem into major subproblems appears very easy. In a normal problem-solving situation we sometimes make mistakes and overlook important subproblems or we assume that a subproblem exists which has no bearing on the calculation being performed. This is normal in any complex situation and it need not worry us. All we have to do is add or delete a box in the general flowchart representation of our solution. Although this may influence other parts of our proposed solution, we find that it is usually not necessary to restart the whole problem-solving process from the beginning. Proceeding in this manner, we finally produce a general outline of how the problem is to be solved. Each box in the general flowchart represents a well-defined calculation. The methods in the previous sections are then used to develop the complete flowchart of the computations necessary to carry out the desired calculations.

This method of problem solving is applicable to all problems. However, the number of subproblems that must be considered and their complexity depends upon both the problem under investigation and the experience of the person carrying out the problem-solving process. The following example will illustrate the steps in the problem-solving process from the viewpoint of the inexperienced problem solver. Thus, we will consider each step in considerable detail. By the time we complete the discussion we will assume that the reader has become familiar with the basic ideas behind the problem-solving process and is ready to apply these ideas to other problems. To become an accomplished problem solver requires practice. Some of this practice can be obtained by solving the problems presented throughout the rest of this book.

The following realistic, but somewhat simplified, problem has been developed to illustrate the problem-solving process. Several of the parameters of the problem have been simplified so that the main ideas are not lost in unnecessary detail. The problem is based upon a very real system that has been suggested as an aid in the grading of large classes.

An Automated Grade-Evaluation Program

In large classes a considerable amount of information is collected about each student during a semester. The calculations necessary to reach a final grade for each student can be quite extensive and subject to computational error if they are entirely left up to a teacher or teaching assistant. To assist teachers with this task, it has been decided to develop a standard program to aid in the bookkeeping and numerical calculations necessary in grading a class. For each student the program is to accept the raw information, such as examination question grades, laboratory grades, class participation grades, and final examination question grades and compute a performance profile of the student's overall performance. The program is to compute a suggested appropriate course grade but the final decision concerning the student's grade is to be made by the professor. This decision will be based upon the student's performance profile generated by the program and the professor's own observation of the student's performance during the semester.

Initial Problem Evaluation

The problem statement indicates the tasks that the program must perform, but gives very little information about how the program should be organized. The first step is to identify the major subtasks that must be performed. An initial evaluation of the stated objectives shows that the problem can be divided into the following major subtasks:

1. Process hour examination results.
2. Process laboratory performance results.
   (a) This is an option that must be provided for those courses with an associated laboratory.
3. Process classroom participation results.
4. Process final examination results.
5. Combine all of the generated data for each student and estimate a reasonable grade to match the performance of the student.
6. Print out results in the form of a student profile.

These tasks form the major blocks of the preliminary flowchart description of the problem given in Fig. 5-12.

The next step is to obtain a better understanding of the requirements that must be satisfied by each of the subtasks. To do this, we seek out advice from a professor who is an expert on educational testing to help identify the different types of information-processing tasks that must be performed and the mathematical representation of these tasks.

The professor explains that since this program is intended for use with large classes we may assume that the performance of the class can be represented by a normal curve.† As a result of this assumption the professor has developed the following set of equations that describe how the information associated with the class is to be processed.

---

† For the reader who is not familiar with statistics, it is not necessary to understand all the details of how the following equations are derived. We assume that the professor has done all of the necessary analytical work and our job is simply one of using the results. A brief discussion of the normalization process used is given in section III, page 120 of this chapter.

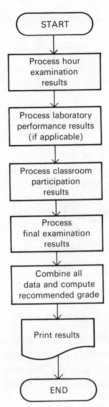

FIGURE 5-12 ■ Preliminary flowchart illustrating division of the main problem into major subtasks.

Processing of Examination Scores

For each course there are KS students and NE examinations. The jth examination has u_j questions. On each examination the raw score obtained by each student is

$$S_{k,j} = \sum_{m=1}^{u_j} Q_{j,m}$$

where $S_{k,j}$ is the raw score of the kth student on the jth examination and $Q_{j,m}$ is the score on the mth question on the jth exam. Since the difficulty of an examination can vary, the raw scores on each examination are normalized by using the following equations:

$$A_j = \frac{1}{KS} \left(\sum_{k=1}^{KS} S_{k,j} \right) .$$

which is the average score on the jth examination,

$$SIGMA_j = \left[\frac{1}{KS - 1} \sum_{k=1}^{KS} (S_{k,j} - A_j)^2 \right]^{1/2}$$

which is the standard deviation of examination raw scores on the jth examination, and

$$SN_{k,j} = \frac{S_{k,j} - A_j}{SIGMA_j}$$

which is the normalized score of kth student on the jth examination. The normalized test scores for each examination are then combined to compute a normalized total test score for all NE examinations:

$$STE_k = \frac{1}{NE} \left(\sum_{j=1}^{NE} SN_{k,j} \right)$$

which is the average normalized hour examination score for the kth student.

Processing of Laboratory Performance

Not all courses have laboratory sections associated with them. But for those that do there are L laboratory periods, and for each period the student receives a numerical laboratory grade. The normalized laboratory grade for each student is derived from the following equations:

$$G_k = \sum_{l=1}^{L} GL_{k,l}$$

which is the kth student's raw laboratory score for all L laboratory periods, and $GL_{k,l}$ is the grade for the lth laboratory period,

$$AL = \frac{1}{KS} \left(\sum_{k=1}^{KS} G_k \right)$$

which is the average laboratory score,

$$SIGML = \left[\frac{1}{KS - 1} \sum_{k=1}^{KS} (G_k - AL)^2 \right]^{1/2}$$

which is the standard deviation of laboratory scores, and

$$GLN_k = \frac{G_k - AL}{SIGML}$$

which is the normalized total laboratory score for the kth student.

Processing of Classroom Participation Results

At the end of the course the instructor for the course may wish to evaluate the student's classroom participation during the semester. This is done by assigning a participation score to each student indicating the quality of the student's performance. This score, if it is to be included in making up the student's grade, is processed in the following manner:

$$CS_k$$

which is the raw assigned classroom participation score for the kth student,

$$AC = \frac{1}{KS} \left[\sum_{k=1}^{KS} CS_k \right]$$

which is the average classroom participation score,

$$SIGMC = \left[\frac{1}{KS-1} \sum_{k=1}^{KS} (CS_k - AC)^2 \right]^{1/2}$$

which is the standard deviation of the classroom participation scores, and

$$CSN_k = \frac{CS_k - AC}{SIGMC}$$

which is the normalized classroom participation score of the kth student.

Processing of Final Examination Results

The final examination consists of R questions. The results are processed separately from those of the hour examinations because they are included in the final grade separately from the other grades. The raw score of the kth student on the final examination is

$$SF_k = \sum_{j=1}^{R} F_{k,j}$$

where $F_{k,j}$ is the score on the jth question. These raw scores are then processed by the following equations:

$$AF = \frac{1}{KS} \left[\sum_{k=1}^{KS} SF_k \right]$$

which is the average score on the final examination,

$$SIGMF = \left[\frac{1}{KS-1} \sum_{k=1}^{KS} (SF_k - AF)^2 \right]^{1/2}$$

which is the standard deviation of the final examination scores, and

$$SFN_k = \frac{SF_k - AF}{SIGMF}$$

which is the normalized final examination score for the kth student.

This completes all of the steps necessary to process the raw data collected about each student. The final task is to combine this data and come up with a recommended grade for each student.

Course Score

In each course each professor will wish to apply a different measure of importance to each of the preceding evaluations. The following numbers represent the importance the professor assigns to each area.

WE—importance of hour examinations
WL—importance of laboratory work
WC—importance of classroom participation
WF—importance of final examination

If the professor does not wish to include laboratory work or classroom participation in the evaluation, then WL and/or WC, respectively, are set to zero.

The normalized final score for the semester is given by

$$FS_k = \frac{WE * STE_k + WL * GLN_k + WC * CSN_k + WF * SFN_k}{(WE^2 + WL^2 + WC^2 + WF^2)^{1/2}}$$

Using the normalized final score, the estimated final grade for each student is defined by the following relationships:

A   if $FS_k \geq 1.18$
B   if $0.53 \leq FS_k < 1.18$
C   if $-0.53 \leq FS_k < 0.53$
D   if $-1.18 \leq FS_k < -0.53$
F   all other values of FS_k

Organization of System Information

Now that the various computational tasks have been established, our next problem is to decide upon the data structures we will need to represent all the information that must be stored during the computation. To do this we first investigate the computations and identify the different classes of information that are present.

Tables 5.2, 5.3, and 5.4 summarize the parameters and information that we are working with and their symbols. The range of values associated with each parameter is obtained by investigating the types of examination and grading policy present in the large courses.

Now that the input information is identified, it is necessary to consider the information that is created as part of the program and how it is stored.

TABLE 5-2 ■ Parameters of class

Parameter	Symbol	Range of values
Number of students	KS	50–500
Number of hour examinations	NE	1–5
Number of laboratory sessions	L	0–15
Weighting factors	WE	0.1–10
	WL	0.1–10
	WC	0.1–10
	WF	0.1–10

TABLE 5-3 ■ Input information about students

Parameter	Symbol	Range of values
Number of questions on jth examination	U_j	1–10
Score on a question	$Q_{j,m}$	0–50
Laboratory grades	$GL_{k,l}$	0–100
Classroom participation score	CS_k	0–100
Number of questions on final examination	R	1–30
Score on final examination question	$F_{k,j}$	0–50
Student name	$NAME_k$	5–20 characters

TABLE 5-4 ■ Arrays used to realize structure of Fig. 5-13

$NAME_I$	Array of student names	I—student
$SCORE_{I,J,K}$	Array of examination scores	I—student J—examination K—raw or normalized score
$SCORT_I$	Array of total normalized examination scores	I—student
$SCORL_{I,K}$	Array of laboratory scores	I—student K—raw or normalized score
$SCORC_{I,K}$	Array of classroom scores	I—student K—raw or normalized score
$SCORF_{I,K}$	Array of final examination scores	I—student K—raw or normalized score
$COMSC_I$	Composite score of all scores	I—student
$GRAD_I$	Final letter grade	I—student

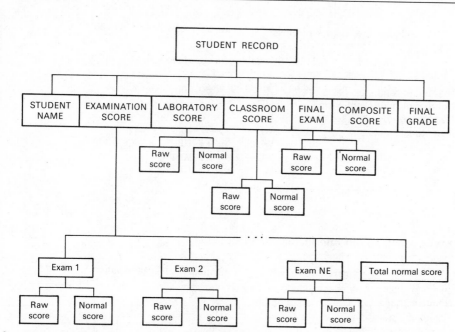

FIGURE 5-13 ■ Structure showing information stored about each student.

This problem generates a considerable amount of information about each student. Thus, we must create a file where each entry in the file is a structure that contains all the information that must be stored about each student. After examining all of the tasks a structure organized as shown in Fig. 5-13 is selected to store the information. This structure can be represented by related arrays given in Table 5-4. In these arrays

$1 \leq I \leq KS$ indicates the ith student
$1 \leq J \leq NE$ indicates the jth hour examination
$K = 1$ indicates raw score
$K = 2$ indicates normalized score

Now that we have a general idea of the information processing tasks that must be carried out, we can go back to our preliminary flowchart of Fig. 5-12 and expand upon the steps that must be performed to complete the major subtasks that were initially identified. The expanded flowchart that results from this step is given in Fig. 5-14.

If we examine Fig. 5-14, we see that we have reduced our subproblems to a number of tasks which are well defined. Our final step is to develop a complete flowchart showing all of the details of the calculation. Before doing this, let us take a look at the flowchart of Fig. 5-14 and note one interesting feature that we will discuss later in Chapter VI.

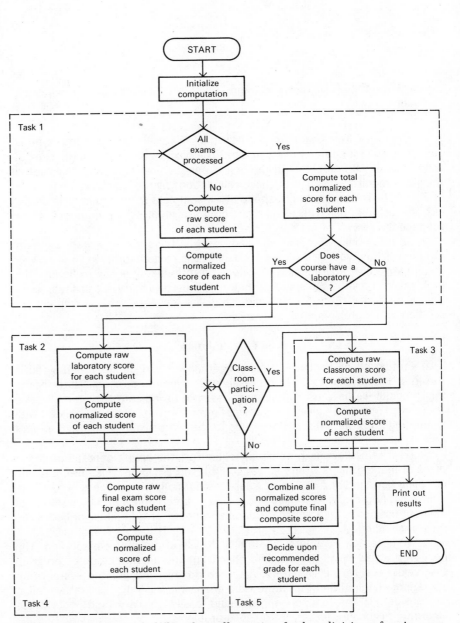

FIGURE 5-14 ■ Expanded flowchart illustrating further division of main computational tasks.

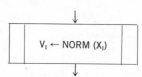

FIGURE 5-15 ■ Special flowchart representation to indicate the normalization operation.

There are four boxes in the flowchart that call for the same type of calculation on four different sets of data. The box is labeled "Compute Normalized Score of All Students." In the first expanded flowchart we indicate all of the steps required to carry out these calculations by the special symbol shown in Fig. 5-15. This symbol corresponds to a complete subprogram that carries out the computations necessary to normalize an array of numbers X and produce the array V of normalized values.

So far in our discussion we must describe the steps of a standard computation of this type each time it is used. In the next chapter we show how we can improve our programming efficiency by introducing a way to handle this problem whereby the same subcomputation is used to carry out this task every time it is needed. Before we consider this new concept, let us complete the solution to the problem being discussed.

The Final Solution

Putting all of this information together we can obtain the flowcharts shown in Fig. 5-16(a) to (e) to represent the complete program. Note that in this program we have used the special symbol to indicate the normalization operation. Figure 5-17 gives the general flowchart of the steps associated with generating an array V that corresponds to the normalized values of the input array X.

To use this flowchart, we simply substitute the appropriate identifiers in place of the identifiers X_I and V_I. We could insert a copy of this flowchart into our main flowchart at every point where the normalization process is required. This is not necessary, as we see in the next chapter, and would be wasteful of memory besides requiring a considerable amount of additional unnecessary programming effort.

We have now completed the major details of our problem solution. The next step would be to develop and check out the actual computer program that would realize the algorithm. After we do this and get the system into operation, we might find that there were one or more conditions that we failed to consider. If this happened, we could easily go back and modify our algorithm to account for any unforeseen problems.

This problem and the assumptions that we made to solve the problem somewhat limit the number of different types of course structures to which the system could be applied. There would be no trouble extending the capability of

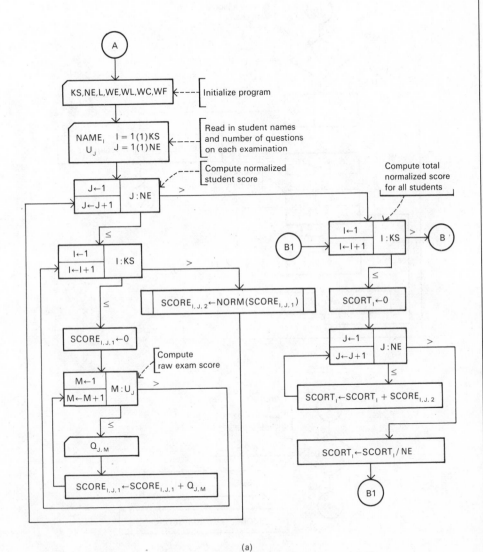

(a)

FIGURE 5-16 ■ Expanded flowchart for all major tasks of Fig. 5-14. (a) Flow-chart for Task 1: processing of examination scores.

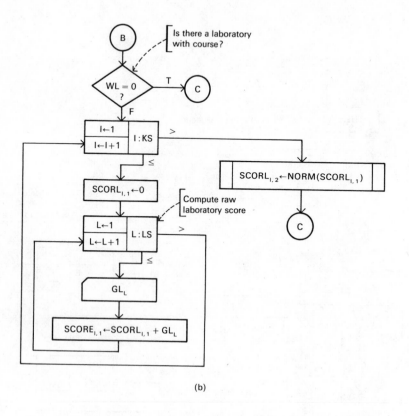

(b)

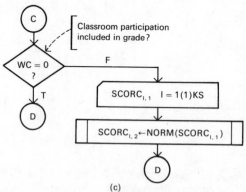

(c)

FIGURE 5-16 ■ (b) Flowchart for Task 2: processing of laboratory scores. (c) Flowchart for Task 3: processing of classroom scores.

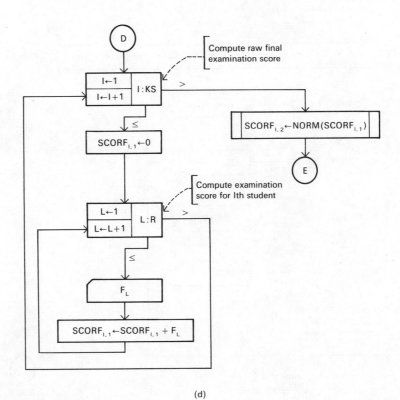

(d)

FIGURE 5-16 ■ (d) Flowchart for Task 4: processing of final examination scores.

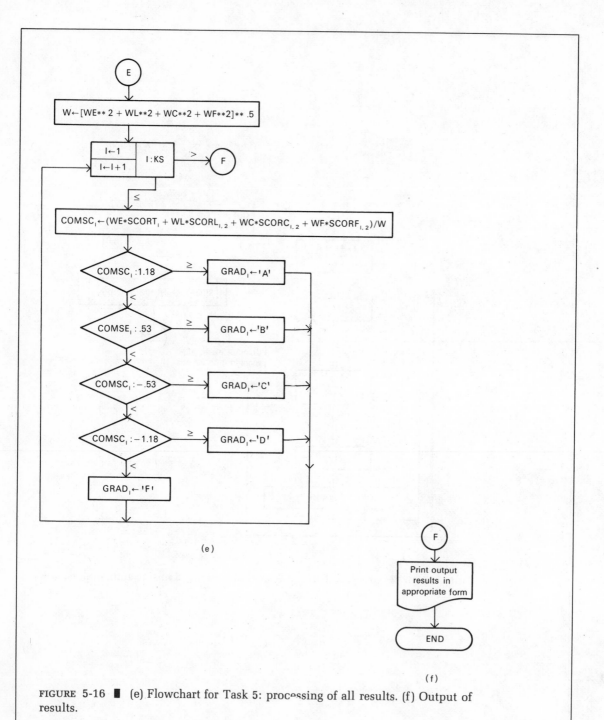

(e)

(f)

FIGURE 5-16 ■ (e) Flowchart for Task 5: processing of all results. (f) Output of results.

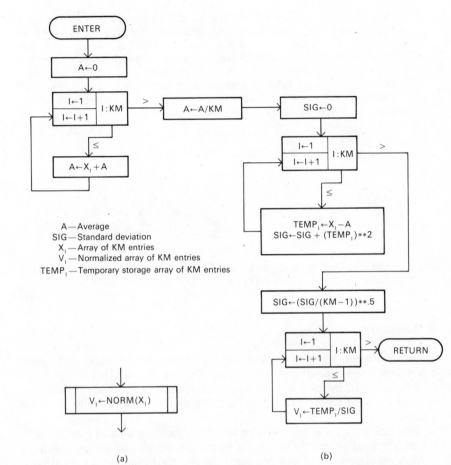

FIGURE 5-17 ■ Flowchart representing the general task of normalizing an array. (a) Flowchart representation. (b) Computation represented in flowchart form.

the program to consider more variations in the way courses might be organized since the general approach would still be the same. The only difference would be in the complexity of the calculations and decisions that would have to be included in the problem solution.

Exercise

1. Modify the automated grade-evaluation program discussed in this section to include the following additional capabilities:

(a) For *each* subtask, before normalization, the median grade† of the class is determined and the student's score is compared to the median. The result of this comparison (below or above the median) is stored ('BELOW' score < median, 'ABOVE' score ≥ median) as part of the student's record. This information is to be printed out in the final printout.

(b) For *each* subtask, before normalization, a letter grade is assigned to the student's score as part of the student's record. The assignment is as follows: (Assume all scores fall in range of 0–100.)

Letter grade	Total score
A	90–100
B	80–90
C	70–80
D	60–70
F	below 60

Show how these capabilities are incorporated into the program. Give both the general and expanded flowchart for the modified program.

5 ▌ Summary

In this chapter we have investigated the general problem-solving process and considered a systematic way in which this process can be handled. One does not, however, become a proficient problem solver by reading examples that other people have developed; proficiency requires considerable practice and experience.

The problem-solving process can be aided if we are able to use the work of others who have solved similar problems or have developed general methods to solve a class of well-defined problems. In the next chapter we consider a technique that makes it easy for us to incorporate the work of others in our solution as well as to develop algorithms of our own.

References

The most extensive discussion of the general approach to problem solving is found in [7]. [5] and [8] discuss the art of problem solving as it applies to engineering and mathematics. Automating the problem-solving process has been studied extensively in artificial intelligence research. [2] and [6] presents some of the results in this area. [3] is on infinite series and their properties. [1] discusses the relationship between the structure of a programming language (PL/I) and the

† The median is defined as the number such that half of the student grades are greater than or equal to this number and half are less than this number.

problem-solving process. [4] has many useful algorithms which can be used in developing solutions to problems.

1. Conway, R., and Gries, D. (1973) *An Introduction To Programming: A Structured Approach Using PL/I and PL/C*, Winthrop, Cambridge, Mass.
2. Feigenbaum, E. A., and Feldman, J. (1963) *Computers and Thought*, McGraw-Hill, New York.
3. Knopp, K. (1956) *Infinite Sequences and Series*, Dover, New York.
4. Knuth, D. E. (1969) *The Art of Computer Programming, Vol. 2, Seminumerical Algorithms*, Addison-Wesley, Reading, Mass.
5. Kovach, L. D. M. (1964) *Computer-Oriented Mathematics*, Holden-Day, San Francisco, Ca.
6. Nilsson, N. J. (1971) *Problem-Solving Methods in Artificial Intelligence*, McGraw-Hill, New York.
7. Polya, G. (1957) *How To Solve It*, Doubleday–Anchor, Garden City, N.Y.
8. Weinstein, A. S., and Angrist, S. W. (1970), *An Introduction To The Art of Engineering*, Allyn and Bacon, Boston, Mass.

Home Problems

If possible, the algorithms developed to solve the following problems should be programmed and tested on a computer.

1. Let x be any real number. Develop a flowchart for an algorithm which will compute the following functions:

   (a) Floor of x, $\lfloor x \rfloor$ = the greatest integer less than or equal to x. (Example, $\lfloor \frac{1}{2} \rfloor = 0$ $\lfloor -\frac{1}{2} \rfloor = -1$ $\lfloor \sqrt{2} \rfloor = 1$.)

   (b) Ceiling of x, $\lceil x \rceil$ = the least integer greater than or equal to x. (Example $\lceil \frac{1}{2} \rceil = 1$ $\lceil -\frac{1}{2} \rceil = 0$ $\lceil \sqrt{2} \rceil = 2$.)

   (c) x mod y = the remainder when x is divided by y, y > 0. (Note: x mod y = $x - y \lfloor x/y \rfloor$, if y > 0. For example, 3 mod 2 = 1, 5 mod 3 = 2, 16.2 mod 3 = 1.2.)

2. *Pseudo-random number generator.* Pseudo-random numbers are numbers generated by a deterministic method which produces numbers which appear to be random. Knuth (reference [4]) suggests that the following method can be used to generate pseudo-random numbers. Whenever a new random number is required, set

$$X \leftarrow (a * X + C) \bmod m$$

[see problem 1(c) for a definition of mod]

$$U \leftarrow X/m$$

and use the new value of U as the desired random value. The following conditions determine the behavior of this generation technique:

1. X, a, C and m are integers. U is a fraction.
2. The first value of X may be chosen arbitrarily.
3. If a different sequence of random numbers is desired, a new first value of X should be used.
4. The value of m is the word size of the computer.

5. a = 3141592621.
6. Select C with the following conditions
   (i) C is an odd number
   (ii) C should be approximately (.2113248654)m
7. The pseudo-random number U is uniformly distributed in the interval [0,1].

Develop a flowchart of a program that will generate a sequence of 100 pseudo–random numbers.

3. *Shuffling algorithm* (see Knuth reference [4]). Assume that $X_1, X_2, \ldots, X_T$ are the T elements of an array and that it is desired to rearrange the array in a random order (i.e., such as in shuffling a deck of cards). This can be done by the following algorithm:

1. Set J←T.
2. Generate a random number U, uniformly distributed between zero and one (see problem 2).
3. Set
   $K \leftarrow \lfloor J*U \rfloor + 1$
   K is a random integer between 1 and J
   $\lfloor x \rfloor$ is defined in problem 1.
4. Exchange X_K and X_J.
5. Decrease J by 1. If J > 1, return to step 1. If J = 1, the shuffling is complete.

Develop a flowchart of an algorithm that will shuffle a 52-element array. The elements of the array represent the different cards in a deck of cards.

4. Use the shuffling algorithm of problem 3 to develop the flowchart of a program that will deal four different bridge hands. Print out each hand showing the cards dealt to each player.

5. Develop a flowchart of an algorithm that will automatically balance the checking account of a customer for a bank. The algorithm should include the following capabilities:

1. Read in a sequence of input data corresponding to the transactions of a particular month. Each input data consists of the following information: Date of Month, Deposit or Withdrawal, Amount.
2. Determine the balance of the account after each transaction. Assume a beginning balance for the month.
3. Calculate the total service charge to be subtracted from the account if the balance at any time of the month runs below a predetermined amount. The total service charge is computed on the basis of a fixed rate for each check processed by the bank during the month.
4. Print out a monthly statement that includes the beginning balance, the ending balance, and the balance after each transaction, as well as the record of all transactions.

6. Develop a flowchart of an algorithm that will set up a schedule for a league of N teams to play each other twice during a playing season. Assume that each week of the season will have contests held on Sunday with all N (N even) teams playing, and that two teams will not play each other for the second time until each team has played the other teams once. Print out the weekly schedule for the entire season.

7. Assume that a file of records stored in a computer memory contains information that is of a proprietary nature and is to be accessed only by authorized persons. In order to prevent unauthorized use of the file, a security check system is established. First, an access list consisting of all the authorized users is created and maintained in the computer. Each user on the list is identified by his name (or account number) and a "secret" password assigned to him. A typical organization of the access list is shown below:

User's name	Password
User's name	Password
. . .	. . .
User's name	Password

A user trying to access the file is checked against the access list by requiring him to supply his password as well as his name. The user is allowed to have access to the file only if he has correctly supplied both his name and the secret password issued to him. The password in the access list is therefore used as a double check on the user's true identity.

Assume that an access list for a file has been created and stored in the computer. Develop an algorithm that will carry out the security-check system described above.

8. Develop a flowchart of an algorithm that will implement an inventory system for a company to control its stocked items. The inventory system is to carry out the following tasks:

1. Maintain an up-to-date inventory list. This list includes the description of items and the number of each item currently in stock.
2. Initiate a reorder as soon as an item has reached a predetermined minimum number.
3. Update the inventory list when new orders are received.
4. Add a new item to the list and remove an item from the list as determined by the management of the company.

9. Assume that an initial list of student names who signed up for a particular course during the preregistration period is stored in a computer. At the beginning of the new semester, students are allowed to add or drop the course within an ADD/DROP period. Develop a flowchart of an algorithm that will prepare a final list of student names enrolled in the course after the ADD/DROP period. The major tasks of this algorithm should include:

1. Add names to the initial list.
2. Delete names from the initial list.
3. Print out the final list of student names in alphabetical order.

10. A local hospital wishes to develop a computer program which will keep track

of the status of all doctors on the staff of the hospital. Whenever an inquiry is made concerning a given doctor the computer prints out one of the following messages.

1. The doctor is not in the hospital.
2. The doctor is in his office.
3. The doctor is visiting patients.
4. The doctor is in the operating room.

It has been decided to use the following data structure to represent the information used in this program. Whenever an inquiry is made, the name of the doctor is located in the name array. The corresponding pointer value is then used to locate which message is to be printed. Whenever the program is notified that the status of the doctor has changed all the program has to do is to change the value of the pointer associated with that doctor's name to point to the message indicating the doctor's new status. Develop the flowchart of an algorithm which will carry out this task.

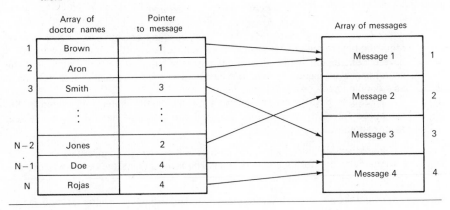

procedures, functions, and subroutines

1 ▌ Introduction

In the previous chapter we have concentrated upon the techniques that can be used to develop and describe algorithms. This discussion was essentially independent of the fact that the computations were eventually to be executed on a computer. At some point in the problem-solving process we must develop a computer program to carry out the computations called for by a given algorithm. When this stage is reached we must consider how the structure of the resulting computer program is influenced by the structure of the algorithm being implemented.

The programming task is very strongly influenced by the particular programming language being used. Most of the standard computational tasks discussed in the previous chapters are easily represented in any of the standard programming languages. However, there is one important programming technique that we have not explicitly discussed because it deals with programming and the efficient utilization of a computer rather than with the development of the algorithm representing the solution of a given problem.

The computer program developed to realize a given algorithm is called a *procedure* or a *routine.* When an algorithm is divided into a series of subtasks, then the computer program segments necessary to carry out these tasks are called *subprocedures* or *subroutines.*

There are two classes of subprocedures that can be identified in a problem. Figure 6-1 is a simplified flowchart of an algorithm, developed in Chapter V, which can be used to carry out the grading process in a course. Examining this figure we see that the algorithm is made up of a number of different subtasks. Each subtask will give rise to a subprocedure. Some of these subprocedures are unique, since the subtask that they perform occurs only once in the algorithm. Other subprocedures are repeated a number of times. For example, there is one subtask, labeled "normalize score," that appears at four different locations in the flowchart of Fig. 6-1. The way in which this task is realized as a subprocedure has a very important influence on the structure of the computer program used to implement the algorithm represented by the flowchart.

Every programming language has special provisions for realizing subprocedures that occur at a number of different places in a program. Unfortunately, the method used varies from language to language. In fact, different compilers for the same language often translate subprocedures in a slightly different way. The following discussion therefore emphasizes the general principles that are involved in using subprocedures. An appropriate language manual should be consulted for the exact details of how subprocedures are realized in any particular programming language.

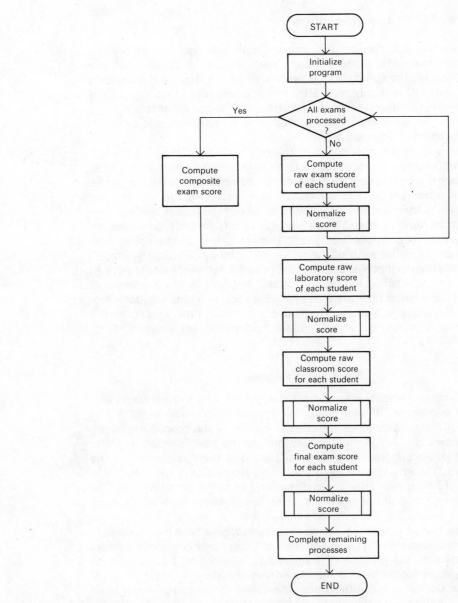

FIGURE 6-1 ■ A simplified flowchart of an algorithm to compute course grades.

2 ■ Open and Closed Subprocedures

When we translate an algorithm into a complete program, there are two ways to treat the subprocedures associated with each subtask of the algorithm. The simplest approach is to write a distinct subprocedure to carry out each of the indicated subtasks. The complete procedure then consists of all of these subprocedures collected together in the proper order. When a subprocedure is included as part of a procedure in this manner, it is called an *inline subprocedure* or *open subprocedure.*

An open subprocedure is designed to carry out a specific calculation. If these calculations appear only once in a procedure, then this is often the most reasonable approach to use. When essentially the same calculation must be performed at a number of different places in a procedure the use of open subprocedures to carry out this calculation is usually inefficient, since a specific subprogram must be coded and stored in memory for each open subprocedure. For example, consider the flowchart of Fig. 6-1. If an open subprocedure were used to realize each of the tasks indicated by "Normalize Score," four essentially identical copies of the same program sequence would have to be created and included in the main program. Not only is there a waste of memory space in storing what are essentially identical machine-language program segments, there is also a considerable amount of time wasted by the programmer in reproducing copies of essentially equivalent program statements.

Closed Subprocedures

A much more efficient way to handle the problem of a subprocedure that appears in a number of different places in a procedure is shown in Fig. 6-2. A single copy of the subprocedure is available for use by the procedure. Whenever the needed calculation must be performed, the main procedure shifts control over to the subprocedure. The calculation is then performed by the subprocedure. When the calculation is completed the results of the calculation and control are returned to the main procedure, at the appropriate point, to carry out the next task in the main procedure. Subprocedures of this type are called *closed subprocedures* or *closed subroutines.*

By using closed subprocedures where applicable, we save a considerable amount of programming effort and conserve computer memory space. We do, however, introduce the problem of transmitting information back and forth between the main procedure and the closed subprocedure. In fact, the technique we may use to carry out this information transfer forms the major topic of discussion in the rest of this chapter.

This need to transfer information requires that special linking program sequences must be included in the internal machine-language program to interconnect the main procedure to the subprocedure. Thus, the use of closed subprocedures requires more effort on the part of the computer. The pro-

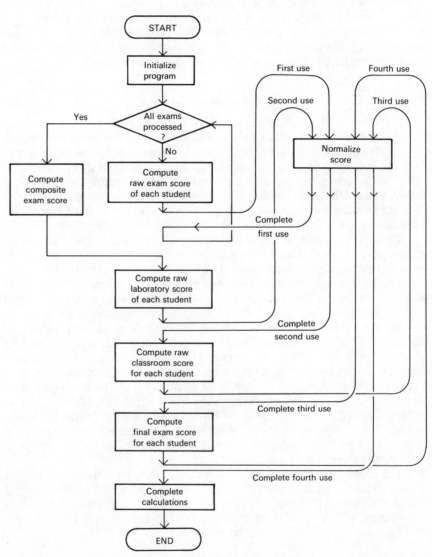

FIGURE 6-2 ■ Illustrating use of a closed subprocedure in a program.

grammer using closed procedures must also be very careful to use the proper techniques to establish the desired linkage.

In some cases the subtask performed by the subprocedure may be less complex than the linkage problem involved in the transfer of control and information between the main procedure and the closed subprocedure. For this case an open subprocedure would be more appropriate than a closed one. The programmer must be responsible for making such a decision.

Use of Subprocedures

The division of a computer program into various subprocedures provides a special convenience to the programmers working on the program. By segmenting a large and complex program into separate, small, well-defined subprograms, it is possible to carry out the programming tasks in steps. First, each of the subprograms can be written, compiled, and executed as a separate subprocedure. After each subprocedure has been programmed and tested, the complete program can be developed by interconnecting these subprocedures in the proper order.

Besides convenience, there are other reasons for dividing a computer program into smaller units. In many instances, a large complex program is developed by a group of programmers working together. Each programmer is responsible for the development of one or more of the subprocedures that appear as part of the main procedure. These subprocedures are then tied together by the person in overall charge of developing the main program.

Once a subprocedure is designed to carry out a given task, it may be used in many main procedures. This allows us to use a subprogram written by someone else as part of our own programming efforts. Not only does this save us time, it also means that we do not have to duplicate the programming effort already carried out by someone else. Most computer manufacturers provide a substantial number of general-purpose subprograms as part of the software package supplied to a computer installation. Some computer installations and their users also develop their own specialized subprograms, which are made available to other users who may wish to carry out the same computations represented by these subprograms.

The following very simple example will illustrate the difference between an open and a closed subprocedure. This example is intended to illustrate the important problems that must be considered in developing a subroutine. *It is not intended to illustrate the practical use of subroutines.* Examples of this latter type are presented in later discussions.

A Simple Example

Assume that we wish to compute

$$D = F(A) + F(B)$$

where A and B are constants and the function F(x) is defined as

$$F(x) = \begin{cases} x^4 + x^2 - 1 & x < 0 \\ 2x^2 - 1 & 0 \le x \le 1 \\ x^3 & x > 1 \end{cases}$$

We now illustrate how this calculation can be carried out using an open and a closed subprocedure.

The flowchart shown in Fig. 6-3(a) shows how this calculation can be carried out as a sequence of subtasks. Figure 6-3(b) gives the general flowchart of a subprocedure for the evaluation of F(x).

To show the difference between open and closed subprocedures, we expand the general flowchart of Fig. 6-3(a) in two different ways. In Fig. 6-4 we have the flowchart that would be programmed if the computation were carried out using open subprocedures. Examining this flowchart we see that, except for a change of identifiers, the computation for R and S are of identical form. This suggests that we might wish to use a closed subprocedure to compute both F(A) and F(B).

Since we have not introduced any special techniques to handle closed subprocedures, let us try to apply the techniques that we are already familiar with to turn the computation represented by the flowchart of Fig. 6-3(b) into a closed subprocedure. (This, of course, is not the way we will actually handle closed subprocedures, but the following discussion indicates the problems as-

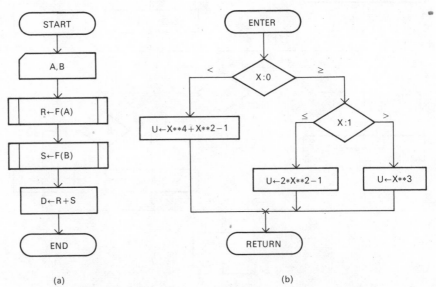

(a)   (b)

FIGURE 6-3 ■ Major tasks involved in computation for D. (a) Major subtasks of computation. (b) Flowchart to compute U←F(x).

sociated with closed subprocedures.) Figure 6-5 is one possible way to introduce the idea of a closed subprocedure into the calculation.

Examining the flowchart of Fig. 6-5, we see that we must use a special technique to transfer information between the main procedure and the subprocedure. For this example we introduce a special identifier T to act as an indicator. When T has a value of 0 we know that A is the input to the subprocedure and we must return from the subprocedure with a value for R. We next set T to 1 to indicate that the next time we use the subprocedure we must use B as the input and return from the subprocedure with a value for S.

The reason we have to employ this rather cumbersome coupling process

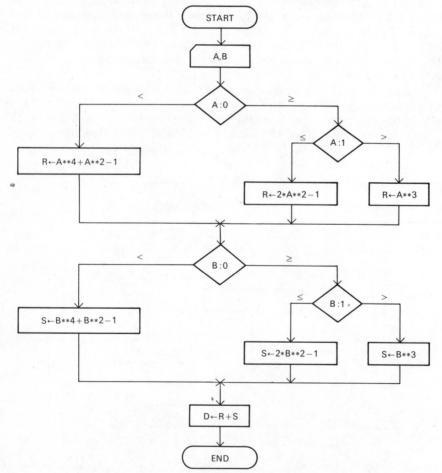

FIGURE 6-4 ∎ Using open subprocedures to compute D.

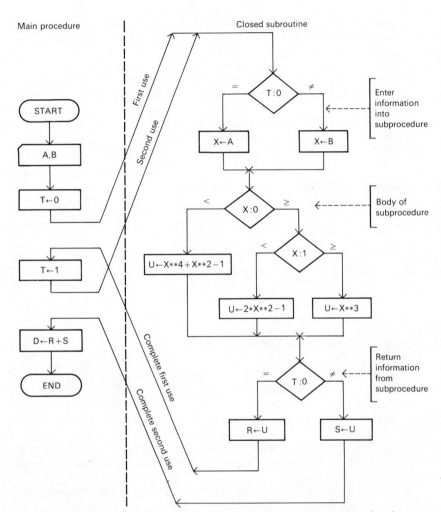

FIGURE 6-5 ■ One way to realize a computation using a closed subroutine.

to use a closed subprocedure is that the idea of a closed subprocedure is mainly a computer programming technique. As far as a flowchart is concerned, all we need is a symbol such as

$$R \leftarrow F(A)$$

to indicate that some type of subprocedure calculation is carried out. To understand how closed subprocedures are used in a computer program, we must investigate the special features of a programming language that are available to represent subprocedures. In particular, we must understand how the programmer can:

1. Define the computations to be performed by a subprocedure
2. Identify which subprocedure is to be used at a given point in the main procedure
3. Transfer information from the main procedure so that the subprocedure can carry out the desired computation
4. Transfer the results of a subprocedure computation to the main procedure so that they may be used in the main procedure.

We consider these problems in the next section.

Exercise

1. Expand Figs. 6-3, 6-4, and 6-5 to the case where

$$D = F(A) + F(B) + F(C)$$

---

3 ■ Structure and Control of Procedures

A complete computer program may consist of a single procedure or an interconnection of subprocedures. If the computer program consists of only a single procedure, the internal control of the program execution does not present any additional problem. In virtually all computers in use today, control is passed sequentially from one statement to another in the normal execution of the procedure. The only possible deviation from the normal sequence of execution is at the point where a branching statement is encountered in the procedure.

When an algorithm for a given problem involves several subtasks, a subprocedure can be developed to carry out the specific computation associated with each subtask. The complete program representing this algorithm then consists of a main procedure and the set of subprocedures associated with the subtasks. The main program acts as a "supervisor" or a "dispatcher." It calls upon the subprocedures to carry out their specific calculations at the appropriate time and it carries out the necessary computations to provide the proper interconnection of the results produced by the subprocedures.

One of the greatest differences between the major programming languages is the way in which the languages handle open and closed subprocedures. All languages provide a formal mechanism to incorporate closed subprocedures in a program. Open subprocedures usually receive no special attention or only limited attention in most of the major programming languages. Because of this the following discussion concentrates on closed subprocedures, although many of the ideas also relate to open subprocedures.

Representation of Subprocedures

In a programming language, a subprocedure represents a collection of statements that are executed as a unit to carry out a given computational task. Each such subprogram is given a *name* by which the particular subprocedure can be referenced or called upon. The end of the subprogram corresponding to a particular subprocedure is signified by a statement of the form

END <name>

Figure 6-6 shows a graphical representation of the general form that a subprogram corresponding to a subprocedure named FIRST would take. The line segments represent the program statements of the subprocedure, while the rectangle enclosing the subprocedure indicates the physical boundary of that subprocedure as it appears in a program.

We must now consider how we can join the various subprocedures so that they can carry out a complete computation. To do this, we first consider the problem of how the actual appearance of subprocedures in a program affect the control of the program execution.

The Main Procedure

In most computer languages, the physical position of the subprogram that represents a subprocedure does not determine how it is to be executed in relation to other subprocedures. Control of program execution does not pass automatically from one subprocedure to the next in the sequential order that they appear in the program. Each subprocedure must be *invoked*, or *called*, from either the main procedure or some other subprocedure. This invocation

FIGURE 6-6 ■ A graphical representation of the procedure named FIRST.

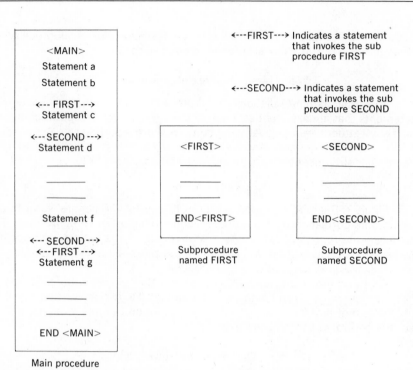

Main procedure

FIGURE 6-7 ■ A main procedure with two subprocedures.

of a subprocedure is done with a statement that in some way calls, or references, the name of the subprocedure to be invoked.

To illustrate the general ideas presented above, assume that we have a program made up of a main procedure, named MAIN, and two subprocedures named FIRST and SECOND. These procedures are arranged as shown in Fig. 6-7. When the program is to be executed, we start by executing statement a of the main procedure and then execute the statements in order until we come to a statement which invokes a subprocedure. When we invoke a subprocedure, control is transferred from the main procedure to the subprocedure, and the computations represented by the subprocedure are performed. When the subprocedure is completed, control is returned to the main procedure. For the arrangement shown in Fig. 6-7 the execution sequence of the main procedure can be summarized as follows:

Start here
↓
Statement a → Statement b → invoke FIRST → Statement c ⌐
└→invoke SECOND → Statement d · · · → Statement f → invoke SECOND ⌐
└→invoke FIRST → Statement g · · · → END

If we look at this example, we can identify the following tasks that must be performed when a subprocedure is invoked:

1. Identify which subprocedure is invoked and transfer control to that subprocedure.
2. Transfer needed information to the subprocedure so that it can carry out the desired computation.
3. Transfer the results of the subprocedure computations back to the main program so that they may be used in the computations represented by the remainder of the main procedure.
4. Return control to the point where the subprocedure was invoked.

The first task, that of identifying which subprocedure is invoked and the transfer of control, is carried out by the computer by using the name associated with the subprocedure. The fourth task, that of returning control to the invoking procedure, is also carried out by the computer. The problem of transferring information between the main procedure and a subprocedure is more involved and is now discussed in detail.

Communication between Procedures and Subprocedures

When a subprocedure is used to perform a particular task, it must be able to receive a particular set of data values from the invoking procedure each time the subprocedure is invoked. It must also be able to return the result of the computation to the invoking procedure. The usefulness of subprocedures depends very much upon how well this communication process can be performed.

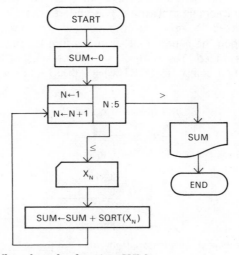

FIGURE 6-8 ∎ A flowchart for forming SUM.

Consider the problem of summing five data values in the following formula:

$$SUM = \sum_{N=1}^{5} SQRT(X_N)$$

where $SQRT(X_N)$ corresponds to the task of finding the square root of X_N. Each data value to be summed is the result of first computing the square root of some number X_N, $N = 1, 2, \ldots, 5$. Let us develop an algorithm to form this sum. The primary task of this problem consists of performing the five successive additions to form the value associated with the identifier SUM. This can be easily accomplished using the flowchart shown in Fig. 6-8. In this flowchart we assume that there is a subprocedure to evaluate the value of the square root of X_N. This subprocedure represents a separate program which must receive the value of X_N from the main procedure and return a value to the main procedure corresponding to the positive root of X_N.

Assume that we have a subprocedure which carries out the computations necessary to calculate the square root of X_N. This subprocedure is represented by the flowchart shown in Fig. 6-9. In this figure we use the special notation

to indicate the passing of information between the main flowchart and the flowchart representing the subprocedure. Consider the case where

$$X_1 = 12 \quad X_2 = 4 \quad X_3 = 7 \quad X_4 = 2 \quad X_5 = 6$$

When $N = 1$, for the first iteration, the square-root subprocedure receives the value $X_1 = 12$ from the main procedure, computes $SQRT(X_1) = 3.4641$ and returns this value to the main procedure. This square root is then added to SUM which was initialized to zero. For the second iteration, $N = 2$, the main procedure calls upon the square-root subprocedure for the second time when $SQRT(X_2)$ is to be added. The value $X_2 = 4$ is transmitted to the square-root subprocedure, which computes $SQRT(X_2) = 2.0000$ and returns this value to

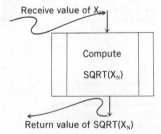

Receive value of X_N

Compute

$SQRT(X_N)$

Return value of $SQRT(X_N)$

FIGURE 6-9 ∎ Flowchart representation of subprocedure for computing $SQRT(X_N)$.

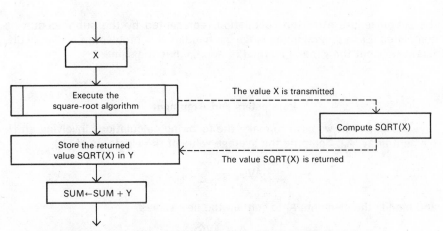

FIGURE 6-10 ∎ Expanded addition operation in the main flowchart.

the main procedure where it is added to SUM. This process goes on until all five square roots have been successfully computed and added to SUM. Notice that the square-root subprocedure is called upon to perform its task only when the square root of a certain number is needed in the main procedure; its primary function is simply to assist the main procedure in carrying out the successive additions required in solving the problem. Conceptually, the addition operation

$$SUM \leftarrow SUM + SQRT(X_N)$$

in the loop of the main flowchart can be considered as consisting of a sequence of operations as illustrated in Fig. 6-10.

What we have demonstrated above are two important concepts of information transfer between procedures. First, the problem of successively adding the five square roots can be carried out by developing two separate procedures: a main procedure that is to carry out the main task of five successive additions, and a subprocedure which is called upon by the main procedure whenever there is a need to perform the task of extracting the square root of a number. Secondly, there is a certain amount of information that must be transferred back and forth between the main procedure and the subprocedure whenever the latter is called upon to perform the assigned task. In the above example, the value of X_N must first be sent to the square-root subprocedure from the main procedure, and subsequently, the computed square root must be returned to the main procedure before the addition can take place.

The establishment of the communication link that transfers information between the invoking procedure and the invoked procedure is the responsibility of the compiler. If the compiler is to accomplish this task, it is necessary to establish a standard way to indicate what information must be transferred to the subprocedure when it is invoked and what information is returned from the subprocedure after the calculation represented by the subprocedure is completed. Each programming language handles this problem in a slightly different way, but the general method of approach is the same.

Parameters and Arguments

Assume that we wish to make the following calculations involving an N-element array $[A_I]$. Compute the average value of the elements of $[A_I]$

$$AVG = \frac{1}{N} \sum_{I=1}^{N} A_I$$

and modify the elements A_I to contain the new values

$$A_I - AVG$$

in the modified array. If we realize this computation as a single main procedure, we have a flowchart of the form shown in Fig. 6-11(a). In this case, the value for N and the array $[A_I]$ are read into the computer, processed, and the results printed out. Now let us consider what changes occur if we have the subprocedure described by the flowchart of Fig. 6-11(b) already programmed.

Examining the flowchart of Fig. 6-11(b), we see that the identifiers used correspond to an array X with elements X_I, a single identifier Y that is associated with the average value of the array elements, and the identifier M corresponding to the dimension of the array. In addition, we note that there is no input block or output block associated with the flowchart. We must now consider how this subprocedure can be used.

The subprocedure, to be useful, must be able to receive information from the main procedure and return the results of the computation it performs to the main procedure. Input information is passed to the subprocedure by way of a parameter list. Information is returned either by way of a parameter list or by associating a value with the subprocedure itself.

Every subprocedure is identified by giving its name and an associated *parameter list.* For example, in Fig. 6-11(b) the name of the subprocedure and the parameter list is indicated by

Name of subprocedure ⟍   ⟋ Parameter list

ARAVG(X,M)

The identifiers in the parameter list are called *parameters* and serve as place-markers. When the subprocedure is invoked each of these parameters is associated with an identifier known to the invoking procedure. For example, in Fig. 6-11(c) the subprocedure ARAVG(X,M) is invoked by use of the statement

$$AVG \leftarrow ARAVG(A,N)$$

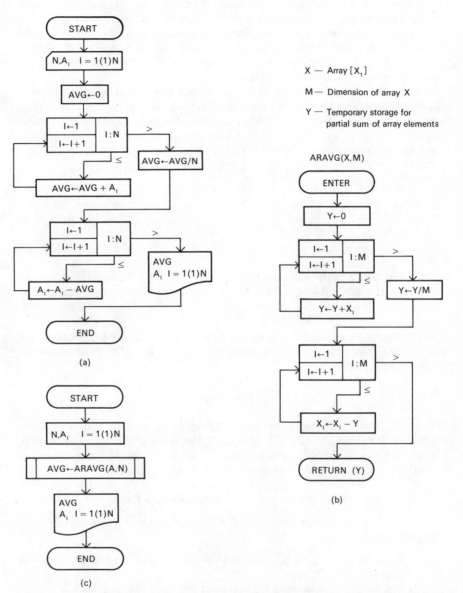

FIGURE 6-11 ■ Illustrating how a subprocedure is used in a main procedure. (a) Flowchart of a main procedure. (b) Flowchart of a subprocedure to carry out task. (c) Flowchart of a main procedure using a subprocedure.

In this case, the parameter X is now associated with the array indicated by A and the parameter M is associated with the identifier N. The identifiers A and N are called *arguments*. These arguments effectively take the place of their respective parameters when the calculation represented by the subprocedure is carried out. They represent the information that must be transmitted to the subprocedure from the main procedure.

When the subprocedure ARAVG is invoked the computer establishes a coupling mechanism so that the subprocedure has access to the information represented by the arguments A and N. Entering the subprocedure we first initialize an identifier Y to zero. The first loop calculates a value for Y by effectively replacing X_I by A_I and M by N. This means that Y has the value

$$\sum_{I=1}^{N} A_I$$

Next we compute

$$Y \leftarrow Y/N$$

which corresponds to the value we wish to assign to AVG. Before doing this, we go through the second loop which modifies A_I according to the relationship

$$A_I \leftarrow A_I - Y$$

When this task is executed, the values associated with the elements of the array A are actually changed. Finally, we arrive at the end of the subprocedure which is indicated as

$$\downarrow$$
$$\boxed{RETURN(Y)}$$

This causes two things to occur. First, the value associated with Y is made available to the main procedure. In this case, the value of Y is assigned to AVG. Second, the calculation of the subprocedure is completed and the control of execution is returned to the invoking procedure at this point.

Principle Properties of Subprocedure Use

This example has illustrated the following important properties of a subprocedure.

1. Every subprocedure is identified by a name and a parameter list. For example, ARAVG(X,M).
2. The parameters in the parameter list serve as placemarkers.
3. When a subprocedure is invoked, arguments are substituted for the parameters. The arguments must have the same attributes as the parameters. *An argument must be specified for each parameter in the parameter list of the invoked subprocedure.*

4. The arguments represent the identifiers that the subprocedure will use in the calculation to replace the parameters that appear in the uninvoked description of the subprocedure.
5. Information is passed to the subprocedure by the arguments. The value associated with any argument is the value used by the subprocedure in carrying out the calculation.
6. Information may be returned from a subprocedure in two ways.
   (a) Whenever a parameter appears on the left-hand side of an assignment statement, the argument associated with that parameter will be modified when that statement is executed.

   For example, if A is the argument associated with the array parameter X then

   $$X_I \leftarrow X_I - Y$$

corresponds to

   $$A_I \leftarrow A_I - Y$$

and the value of A_I is modified. A numeric example is shown below:

	Identifier	Value
	Y	5
Initial	A_I	7
Final	A_I	2

   (b) A value can be returned to the invoking procedure by using a return statement of the form (or its equivalent depending upon the language)

   $$\text{RETURN } (<\text{value}>)$$

This value must be used immediately by the invoking procedure. Note that it is not necessary to return any information from a subprocedure (for example, the subprocedure might simply print out some information). Similarly, either or both of the above methods may be used to return information.

There are two types of subprocedures that are usually distinguished by a programming language. These are *function subprocedures*, usually called *functions,* and *subroutine subprocedures,* usually called *subroutines.* The difference between these two classes of subprocedures is in the way they are invoked and returned to the invoking procedure.

Functions

A function is a subprocedure that associates a value with the name of the subprocedure. This value is used at the point of invocation immediately upon return from the subprocedure. The subprocedure used in the previous example was a function subprocedure. Since a function returns a value, it can be invoked by simply writing the name of the function with the appropriate arguments at the point where we wish to use the value associated with the function. In the last example, the statement

$$AVG \leftarrow ARAVG(A,N)$$

invoked the subprocedure ARAVG, which returned a value corresponding to the average value of the elements of array A. The array was also modified.

Functions do not have to be restricted to assignment statements. For example, consider the main procedure and function subprocedure, named MARK, described in Fig. 6-12. The input to the main procedure is the student name, indicated by the identifier NAME, and a numerical test score between 0 and 100, indicated by the identifier GRADE. The function subprocedure computes a letter grade corresponding to the value of the argument associated with the parameter X and transfers the letter grade to the argument associated with Y. The function also returns a value of 0, if the student fails, or a value of 1, if the student passes, directly to the point where the function was invoked. In this case, the function appears at a decision point. Thus, the returned value associated with the function is used in deciding which branch to follow.

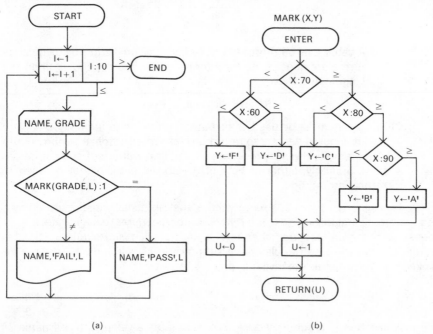

(a)   (b)

FIGURE 6-12 ■ Illustrating use of a function subprocedure in a decision. (a) Main procedure. (b) Function subprocedure.

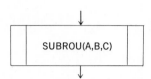

FIGURE 6-13 ■ Flowchart representation of a subroutine call.

Subroutines

Subroutines are subprocedures that do not associate values directly with the name of the subprocedure. This means that any information transferred from the subprocedure to the main procedure is accomplished by assigning values to one or more of the arguments associated with the subprocedure. Since a value is not associated with the name of the subroutine, we need a special program-language statement that can be used to invoke a subroutine. Suppose we have the subroutine

$$SUBROU(X,Y,Z)$$

that we wish to use. To invoke this subroutine, we would use a statement of the form

$$CALL\ SUBROU(A,B,C)$$

where the parameters X, Y, and Z have been replaced by the arguments A, B, and C, respectively. To indicate the use of subroutines in a flowchart, we can use the representation shown in Fig. 6-13.

To illustrate the use of a subroutine, consider the subroutine

$$NORM(X,Y,N)$$

where the parameters X and Y represent two one-dimensional arrays of N elements. The computations performed by NORM(X,Y,N) are

$$AVG = \frac{1}{N} \sum_{I=1}^{N} X_I$$

$$SIGM = \left[\frac{1}{N-1} \sum_{I=1}^{N} (X_I - AVG)^2 \right]^{1/2}$$

$$Y_I = \frac{X_I - AVG}{SIGM}$$

The flowchart for this subroutine is given in Fig. 6-14(a). In Fig. 6-14(b), this subroutine is used to compute the normalized value of an array that is read in. The input array is A and the resulting normalized array is B. Both arrays have K elements, thus the arguments are A, B, and K, and these are used in place of the parameters X, Y, and N.

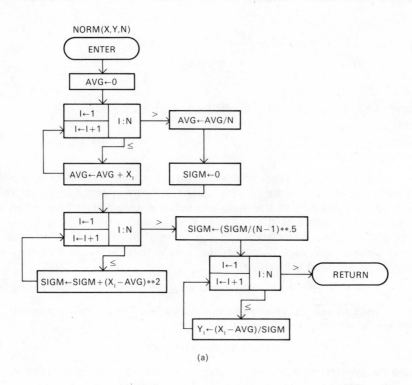

(a)

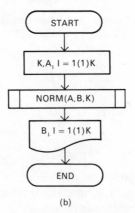

(b)

FIGURE 6-14 ■ Illustration of the use of a subroutine. (a) Flowchart of NORM(X,Y,N) subroutine. (b) Using NORM(X,Y,N) subroutine.

We can tell that NORM(X,Y,N) is a subroutine rather than a function by examining the point where we return to the invoking procedure. At this point we simply have RETURN, which indicates the return of control to the main procedure, without any value associated with the return operation. Consequently, the subprocedure must be a subroutine instead of a function.

Built-in Functions and Subroutines

In many computer languages, a set of commonly used functions or subroutines is provided as part of the compiler. These built-in subprocedures need not be written by the programmer as separate programs: they are a part of the language and any of them may be invoked merely by a function reference or a subroutine call. Some of the typical built-in functions are

SIN(X)
COS(X)
LOG(X)
LENGTH(X)   (X is a character sequence
            and the result is the length
            of the sequence.)

Many computer manufacturers also supply standard subroutines as part of the compiler, to allow programmers to use certain subprocedures without having to develop them separately. The availability of these subprocedures, if used properly, can be a great time saver to the programmer. Very general programs can be written by developing a main procedure that uses these subprocedures to carry out a major part of the required computational tasks. Since the subprocedures have already been checked out, all the programmer must do is make sure that the main program is correct.

Exercises

1. (a) Describe the tasks that the flowchart in Fig. E6-1 performs:
   (b) Develop the two function subprocedures MAX and MIN. Show their flowcharts.
   (c) Can you suggest a method that will accomplish the same tasks in (a) by developing only one function subprocedure (MAX or MIN)?

2. The ELSUM, ELPRO, and TRACE of an $n \times n$ matrix

$$A = [A_{I,J}] = \begin{bmatrix} A_{1,1} & A_{1,2} & \cdots & A_{1,n} \\ A_{2,1} & A_{2,2} & \cdots & A_{2,n} \\ \cdot & \cdot & & \cdot \\ \cdot & \cdot & & \cdot \\ \cdot & \cdot & & \cdot \\ A_{n,1} & A_{n,2} & \cdots & A_{n,n} \end{bmatrix}$$

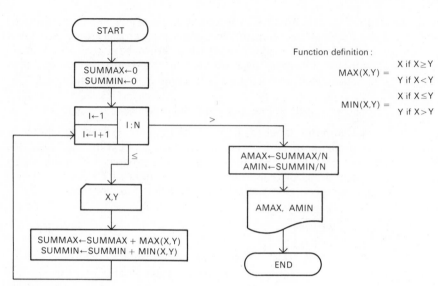

Function definition :

$$MAX(X,Y) = \begin{cases} X \text{ if } X \geq Y \\ Y \text{ if } X < Y \end{cases}$$

$$MIN(X,Y) = \begin{cases} X \text{ if } X \leq Y \\ Y \text{ if } X > Y \end{cases}$$

FIGURE E6-1

are defined as follows:

ELSUM = the sum of all the elements of the matrix = $\sum\limits_{I=1}^{n} \sum\limits_{J=1}^{n} A_{I,J}$

ELPRO = the product of all the elements of the matrix = $\prod\limits_{I=1}^{n} \prod\limits_{J=1}^{n} A_{I,J}$

TRACE = the sum of the diagonal elements of the matrix = $\sum\limits_{I=1}^{n} A_{I,I}$

(a) Develop three function subprocedures that will compute ELSUM, ELPRO, and TRACE for any given n × n matrix. You may assume that a two-dimensional array A storing the elements of a matrix can be used as a single parameter.
(b) Develop a subroutine named SUMPROTRA that will compute *all* three functions, ELSUM, ELPRO, and TRACE.

3. A subroutine procedure QUAD(A,B,C,R1,R2) for solving the quadratic equation

$$ax^2 + bx + c = 0 \quad a \neq 0 \quad \text{and} \quad b^2 - 4ac \geqslant 0$$

is to be developed. The parameters A, B, and C are the three coefficients of the equation, and R1 and R2 are two identifiers that are used to return the two computed roots to the main procedure. The two computed roots are

$$x_1 = \frac{-b + \sqrt{b^2 - 4ac}}{2a} \qquad x_2 = \frac{-b - \sqrt{b^2 - 4ac}}{2a}$$

(a) How many arguments are needed in the invoking procedure? What are these arguments?

(b) Give a detailed flowchart for the subroutine QUAD. Assume that $b^2 - 4ac \geq 0$ so that we will not have problems with the square root.

(c) Show how QUAD is used in the main flowchart that performs the task of solving N quadratic equations with N sets of coefficients using a simple loop.

4. This exercise deals with a modified version of the QUAD subroutine developed in Exercise 3. Assume that the N sets of coefficients are read into three one-dimensional arrays, $[A_I]$, $[B_I]$, and $[C_I]$, $I = 1(1)N$. The N pairs of roots will also be returned and stored in two one-dimensional arrays, $[ROOT1_I]$, $[ROOT2_I]$, $I = 1, 2, \ldots, N$.

(a) Develop a new flowchart for the subroutine QUAD so that it will use arrays as parameters and arguments and so that all the N equations are solved before the N pairs of roots are returned to the main procedure.

(b) Show, by way of a flowchart, how this new subroutine is used in the main procedure, which simply reads in the N sets of coefficients, *calls QUAD once,* and prints out the N pairs of roots.

4 ▊ Summary

The efficient solution of complex problems requires us to break the overall problem down into a set of simpler subproblems. This approach not only allows us to gain a better understanding of the steps needed to solve a problem, it also allows us to use much more efficient programming techniques. These subproblems can often be grouped into classes of problems that are carried out in essentially the same manner. These calculations can then be performed by using either functions or subroutines.

Functions and subroutines have the same generality as any other program unit. Thus, any subtask can be carried out using these subprocedures. In later chapters we investigate many different types of problem-solving techniques in both numerical and nonnumerical applications. These techniques can easily be transformed into a function or subroutine using the ideas discussed in this chapter.

The way in which subprocedures are realized differs for each programming language. A complete understanding of how the programming language that you plan to use handles subprocedures is very important if you wish to make maximum use of this very important programming technique.

References

The way functions and subroutines are realized in each of the different programming languages is covered in the reference manuals which describe each language. The discussion in [2], [3], and [5] give a general insight into how closed subprocedures are implemented. [1], [3], [5], and [7] are of a more advanced nature and consider some of the problems that must be handled by the compiler when closed subprocedures are translated into machine-language programs.

1. Flores, I. (1966) *Computer Programming,* Prentice-Hall, Englewood Cliffs, N.J.

2. Forsythe, A., Keenan, T., Organick, E., and Stenberg, W. (1969) *Computer Science—A First Course,* John Wiley & Sons, New York.

3. Higman, B. (1967) *A Comparative Study of Programming Languages,* American Elsevier, New York.

4. Knuth, D. E. (1969) *The Art of Computer Programming, Vol. 1, Fundamental Algorithms,* Addison-Wesley, Reading, Mass.

5. Ralston, A. (1971) *Introduction To Programming and Computer Science,* McGraw-Hill, New York.

6. Sherman, P. M. (1970) *Techniques in Computer Programming,* Prentice-Hall, Englewood Cliffs, N.J.

7. Stone, H. S. (1972) *Introduction To Computer Organization and Data Structures,* McGraw-Hill, New York.

Home Problems

If possible, the algorithms developed to solve the following problems should be programmed and tested on a computer.

1. Use the algorithm of home problem 2 Chapter V to develop a function subprocedure which produces pseudo-random numbers uniformly distributed in the interval [0,1].

2. Modify the function subprocedure developed in problem 1 so that the pseudo-random numbers are distributed in the interval [a,b], where a and b are two real numbers and $a < b$.

3. Use the algorithm of home problem 3, Chapter V to develop a subroutine subprocedure that will shuffle the information stored in an array.

4. Form a group of three or more students and implement the automatic grading system discussed in Section IV of Chapter V. Each of the subtasks should be carried out by an appropriate closed subprocedure. These subprocedures should be developed independently. One student should then be responsible for forming the complete program by writing a main procedure which invokes each subprocedure at the proper time.

5. Make a summary of the subprocedures available in the local computer center library which can be used to develop programs in the programming language you are using.

6. Develop a flowchart of a function subprocedure that will compute the factorial of n, FACT(n) = n!, for any given nonnegative integer n. FACT(n) is defined as follows:

$$FACT(n) = \begin{cases} 1 & \text{if } n=0 \\ n(n-1)(n-2) \cdots 3 \cdot 2 \cdot 1 & \text{if } n > 0 \end{cases}$$

Note that the factorials increase very rapidly. For example, FACT(5) = 120, FACT(10) = 3,628,800, and FACT(1000) is an integer with over 2500 decimal digits. Explore the characteristics of the local computer to see what limitations must be placed in your function subprocedure in order to calculate and store the exact value returned by FACT(n).

7. The function FACT(n) defined in problem 6 can be approximated by what is known as *Stirling's formula.*

$$FACT(n) \approx \sqrt{2\pi n} \left(\frac{n}{e}\right)^n$$

Stirling's formula allows us to compute the factorial function without having to carry out the laborious multiplications. Develop a function subprocedure that will compute the factorial function using the Stirling approximation. Determine the errors in the approximations for various integers n.

8. A set of objects without reference to the order in which they are arranged is called a *combination.* The number of combinations of n different objects taken r at a time has been found to be

$$\binom{n}{r} = \frac{n!}{r!(n-r)!}$$

where n! is the factorial of n. The number $\binom{n}{r}$ is called a binomial coefficient.

These numbers have a large number of applications in mathematics and engineering. Develop a function subprocedure that will compute the binomial coefficient $\binom{n}{r}$ for any given nonnegative integers n and r (r $\leqslant$ n).

9. Develop a subroutine that will plot a mathematical function

$$y = f(x)$$

Assume that the x- and y-values of the function have already been stored in two arrays $[X_i]$ and $[Y_i]$. The subroutine must use the x- and y-values to calculate an appropriate scaling for the size of the output page in your local computer, and plot the points (each x-value and its corresponding y-value is a point) in the x–y plane.

10. Develop a subroutine that will locate all the occurrences of a given word in a text and replace it with a new word.

7

computational costs
and program optimization

1 ■ Introduction

There are a large number of factors that influence the amount of money it costs to develop and use a computer program to solve a given problem. Some of these costs, such as the salary of the programmer and the computer time needed to develop and test a program, are developmental costs. These costs can be minimized if an experienced and well-organized programmer is responsible for program development.

Each computation performed by computer takes a finite amount of time. In addition, each program utilizes a portion of the computer's resources. The cost of a calculation is a direct function of the time required to perform the calculation and the resources that must be allocated to process the program. Anything that can be done to minimize computer time or the amount of resources required will minimize computation cost.

Every computer manufacturer designs a computer according to a set of principles that the manufacturer believes will produce the best profit. Thus, the time required to carry out a given computation varies from computer to computer depending upon the computer's design. It is therefore impossible to give exact timing information about all the basic operations that are performed in the execution of a program. What is possible, however, is to provide a general ordering of the basic operations in terms of their relative speed and the reason for this ordering. This information can then be used to minimize the time needed to conduct a computation.

Of all the computer resources, a programmer can usually only influence such things as the amount of memory required for the program, the way that information is read into and out of the computer, and the way that large data sets are stored and referenced by the system. As a program increases in size, it is quite common to encounter the situation where the amount of memory space required to accommodate the program and its associated data exceeds the space available. At this point the program must be reorganized to make more efficient use of available memory space. If this is not possible, the program will have to be reorganized so that it can be carried out in parts.

In this chapter we examine some of the factors which influence computational speed and the efficient use of computer resources. These results are used to show how several common mistakes which waste computing time can be avoided. Finally, we consider some of the techniques that can be used to minimize the amount of memory space needed to handle a program. Our discussion is of a general nature and the techniques are useful no matter which programming language is used for writing the program. In fact, many of these techniques were developed and formalized as part of an attempt to develop compilers which perform program optimization as part of the translation process. Each programming language also has special features which influence the efficiency of a program written in that language. These features are covered in the program-language manuals.

2 ▮ Program Operations and Machine Operations

As was discussed in Chapter II, all computers have a set of basic machine-language operations that can be used to process the information stored in the computer's memory. These operations are usually not identical to the operations that are provided as part of the higher-level programming language used to program the computer. The computer's compiler must therefore translate each program operation into one or more machine-language operations. The more complex the higher-level operation, the more machine-language instructions needed to perform the computation called for by the operation.

In most modern computers it takes between 0.1×10^{-6} to 10×10^{-6} seconds (0.1 to 10 microseconds) to execute a machine-language instruction. If a program-language operation is quite simple, it might only require one or two machine instructions to realize the operation. Operations of this type can be executed at the same speed as the machine level instructions. There are other program-language operations that may take between 10 to 100 or even more machine-language instructions to realize. In this case, it might take as long as 100 to 1000 microseconds to carry out a single program-language operation.

Before we consider the relative ordering of operation speeds, let us estimate how many operations can be performed per minute on a modern computer. Since there are 60 seconds in a minute there are 60×10^6 microseconds in a minute. If the average higher level program instruction takes 10 microseconds to execute, we see that approximately 6,000,000 program operations can be carried out in a minute. This number illustrates why modern computers are such powerful information-processing tools.

Representation of Numeric Information

As we saw in Chapter II, there are two ways that can be used to store numerical information in binary form. The easiest is to represent all numerical information as a binary number and store this number directly in the computer's memory. A somewhat more complex approach is to use a binary coded decimal (BCD) representation where each decimal digit of a number is encoded as a four-bit binary sequence before the number is stored in the computer's memory.

Most small computers have been designed so that they assume that all numerical information is represented by a binary number. A relatively few computers, especially those designed for business use, are designed to work only with numbers represented in BCD form. The larger and more complex computers are often designed so that the computer user may use either number representation. When there is a choice, it is important to understand the advantages and limitations of each system so that the best one may be selected to do the desired job.

Inside a computer the logic circuits necessary to do binary arithmetic are simpler and faster than the logic circuits necessary to carry out the same arithmetic operations on BCD numbers. Thus, arithmetic operations are faster if binary numbers rather than BCD numbers are used.

When information is transferred into or out of a computer, we might use one of the standard codes given in Appendix II. Each decimal digit has a separate code sequence which can easily be transformed into the BCD representation of the digit. Similarly, any BCD encoded digit can be very easily transformed into the proper output-code sequence. Thus, it is very easy to transfer numerical information into and out of a computer if it is stored in the computer in BCD form.

If the numerical information is to be stored in binary form, we must introduce an intermediate processing step. When numerical information is read into the computer, we must convert the decimal number into the corresponding binary number. After a computation involving binary numbers is completed and we wish to output information, we must convert the result from binary form to the proper decimal form. Each of these conversion processes takes time. Thus, the time required to input and output numerical information might be more critical in determining the speed of a computation than the time actually needed to carry out the desired arithmetic operations.

When there is a choice in the type of number system to use, the following guideline is helpful: If a computation involves a high ratio of arithmetic operations to input/output operations, numbers should be represented in binary form. If a computation involves a low ratio of arithmetic operations to input/output operations, then a decimal (BCD) number representation should be used. Each particular computer will have a different set of characteristics that determine what should be considered as a high or low ratio. The following example illustrates how the time required to carry out calculations is influenced by the different factors.

Assume that a computer system has the relative timing requirements listed in Table 7-1. Consider the two calculations represented in Fig. 7-1. The first calculation involves a large number of input and output operations, while the second involves a small number of input and output operations.

TABLE 7-1 ■ Relative timing requirements

Operation	Time required (general units)
Binary addition	1
Decimal (BCD) addition	3
Input decimal numbers	4
Output decimal numbers	4
Input binary numbers	8
Output binary numbers	8

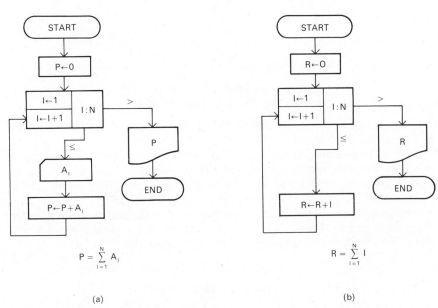

$$P = \sum_{I=1}^{N} A_I$$

(a)

$$R = \sum_{I=1}^{N} I$$

(b)

FIGURE 7-1 ■ Two different types of calculations. (a) Calculation involving a large number of input/output operations. (b) Calculation involving a small number of input/output operations.

In the calculation of Fig. 7-1(a) we must, in addition to the processing of the loop counters, read in N data terms, perform N additions on the terms, and output one result. Since the time it takes to process the counter and initialize the loop is the same, we can concentrate upon how the number representation influences the time required to perform the operations in the body of the loop. For this assumption we see that it takes

T = N(time to read a number + time to do an addition)

+ (time to output a number)

units to carry out the calculation in the body of the loop and output the results. Thus, we have the following:

Time required if decimal numbers are used $7N + 4$
Time required if binary numbers are used $9N + 8$

The time saved by using decimal numbers is $(2N + 4)$ units. For large N this can be a meaningful saving.

Now consider the calculation of Fig. 7-1(b). In this calculation we initialize R to 0, perform N additions, and then output a single number. If we disregard the time required to initialize and process the counter, then the time required for this calculation is

$$T = N \text{ (time to do an addition)} + \text{(time to output a number)}$$

units. Thus, we have the following:

Time required if decimal numbers are used $3N + 4$
Time required if binary numbers are used $N + 8$

If we use binary numbers, we save $(2N - 4)$ units of time. For large N, this can be a very important saving.

The above examples are only illustrative. The relative times required to carry out the different operations vary from computer system to computer system. Thus, the trade off between using a decimal or a binary representation must be considered in terms of the particular computer being used. In the rest of this section, we will use decimal numbers in the discussion, since the ideas being presented are the same no matter which number system is actually used inside the computer to represent numerical information.

Integer Arithmetic

Any fixed-point number that does not have a fractional part is an integer. Examples of integers are 265, 56, 3. Numbers in floating-point form, such as 2E6 or 2.56E2, are not considered to be integers although there are integers that have the same numerical values. Integer numbers are the easiest type of numbers to work with since we do not have to worry about the location of a decimal or binary point. Thus, integer arithmetic is the fastest type of arithmetic that can be performed on a computer.

There are five basic arithmetic operations; addition, subtraction, multiplication, division, and exponentiation. Addition and subtraction are the fastest operations and they both take approximately the same amount of time to perform. Multiplication and division are the next fastest, but they require a longer time to carry out since they involve a number of intermediate addition or subtraction operations. Exponentiation is the slowest operation since the steps necessary to carry it out are much more complex than those needed for the other four operations.

In all computers, addition and subtraction are basic hardware operations. In some computers, multiplication and division are carried out by machine-language subroutines while in others these operations are included in the set of basic hardware operations. Exponentiation is quite often carried out by machine-language subroutines. The algorithm used for exponentiation is often done in different ways depending on the values and forms of the two operands. The following examples illustrate the reason for the above orderings of computational speed.

The operations of addition, subtraction, multiplication, and exponentiation to positive powers always generate integers if the two operands are in-

Operations involving one step

Addition	Subtraction
176	265
232	−124
408	141

Operations involving multiple steps

Multiplication	Division	Exponentiation[a]
256	25	$(2)^3 = (2)(2)(2) = 8$
125	25⟌625	
1280	50	
512	125	
256	125	
32000		

[a] One possible way when an integer is raised to a positive integer power.

tegers. This is not true for division. For example.

$$
\begin{array}{r}
51.44 \\
25 \overline{)\,1286} \\
125 \\
\hline
36 \\
25 \\
\hline
110 \\
100 \\
\hline
100
\end{array}
$$

The result is a number with an integer part and a fractional part. The way that the result will be handled depends to a considerable extent upon the language being used. In some situations, only the integer part of the number is retained, while in other situations, that may be present in the same language, the result is treated as a fixed-point or floating-point number. When developing a program in any programming language, it is important to understand the conventions used by that language to handle the division of two integer numbers.

Fixed-Point and Floating-Point Numbers

Whenever numerical information is not representable as an integer, we must use either a fixed-point or a floating-point number representation. Arithmetic operations involving numbers in either of these forms is complicated by the need to keep track of the location of the binary or decimal point.

To carry out addition or subtraction, we must first align the decimal point before we carry out the operation. This adds additional steps to the computational process since the alignment process must be carried out first, followed by the execution of the operation. The following examples illustrate this problem.

Fixed-point addition	Floating-point addition
76.324 + .2564	7.423E4 + 2.165E2
76.3240	7.42300E4
.2564	.02165E4
76.5804	7.44465E4

Note that when floating-point addition or subtraction is carried out, one of the numbers must be modified so that the exponent associated with both numbers are the same.

Multiplication and division of fixed-point numbers is carried out in the standard way except that the position of the decimal point must be accounted for by the computer. This requires additional computer instructions. Floating-point multiplication and division is carried out very easily, as indicated by the following examples

Floating-point multiplication	Floating-point division
1.63E4	3.6E4/1.5E3
2.10E2	
000	2.4 E1=E(4−3)
163	1.5⟌3.6
326	3.0
3.4230E6=E(4+2)	60
	60

In both cases, we operate on the mantissas and exponents separately. The mantissas are either multiplied or divided, while the exponents are added or subtracted depending upon the operation being performed.

The exponentiation operation on fixed-point or floating-point numbers usually involves a machine-language subroutine and is much more time consuming than the other operations.

From the above, we see that arithmetic operations performed on fixed- or floating-point numbers are slower than the corresponding operations performed on integers. The speed of addition and subtraction is still faster than the speed of multiplication and division for fixed- and floating-point numbers. Exponentiation is the slowest operation.

Character Operations

Any operation on character sequences involves a sequence of machine-language instructions that perform the operation on a character by character basis. Thus, the basic operations involving character sequences are often the slowest operations. The actual time required will be proportional to the length of the sequences involved.

Relational Operations

Relations such as equal, less than, or greater than can be applied to either numerical or character information. Two integers can be compared in about the same time that it takes to perform addition or subtraction of integers. If two fixed-point or floating-point numbers are compared, additional time is required to account for the proper positioning of the decimal or binary point. Thus, relational operations applied to numbers of this type take about the same amount of time as fixed-point or floating-point addition.

When two character sequences are compared, it is done on a character by character basis. Thus, the amount of time required by any relational operation involving two character sequences is a function of the length of the sequences. In general, the time required to process character sequence comparisons will be longer than that needed to compare numerical information.

Logical Operations

The basic logical operations of NEGATION, AND, and OR are quite easy to do on a computer. From a time viewpoint, these operations are usually performed as fast as the addition and subtraction of integers.

Assignment Operations

The assignment operation indicates that a value is to be stored in a particular memory location. The amount of time required to carry out this operation depends upon the type of information being operated upon. If the value is an integer, a fixed-point number, or a floating-point number, the operation is performed essentially as fast as integer addition, fixed-point addition, or floating-point addition, respectively. Logical values are stored as fast as the logical operations are performed. Character sequences take the most time to store and the storage speed depends upon the number of characters in the sequence.

Functions

Each programming language provides a number of standard functions, such as $\sin(x)$ or e^x, that can be used by the programmer. Whenever a function of this type is used, it is usually evaluated by a machine-language subroutine.

The evaluation of a function takes a much longer time than the multiplication and addition arithmetic operations.

Every computer program is constructed from the basic operations just discussed. If we are not careful in designing a flowchart, we can waste a great deal of time carrying out unnecessary calculations, or we can spend more time on a calculation than is actually required. Although each programming language has particular features that can be used to reduce computation time, there are many things we can do that will minimize the computation time of any program. Some of these techniques are presented in the next section.

Exercises

1. Using the time requirements given in Table 7-1, determine the units of time required to perform the task represented in the flowchart shown below:

   (a) if decimal numbers are used

   (b) if binary numbers are used

Disregard the time needed to initialize and increment the counter variable, but include the time it takes to test the counter variable in the iteration boxes. Assume that the time required to perform the test is the same as that required to perform an addition operation.

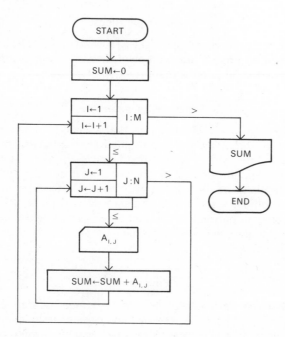

FIGURE E7-1

2. The flowchart shown below describes an algorithm that counts the number of alphabetic characters in a character string ended with an asterisk '*'. The characters are read in, one at a time, from punched cards.

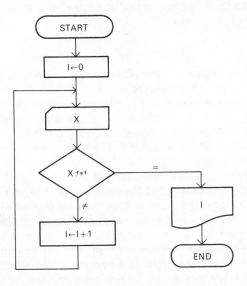

FIGURE E7-2

(a) Trace through the flowchart to see if it performs the task as described.
(b) Determine the units of time required to execute the algorithm. Assume that the time required to process a character (input, output, comparison) is 10 units. Use Table 7-1 for other time requirements.

3 ▊ Program Optimization

The best way to obtain a program that does not waste computation time is to be aware of the factors that influence computational speed and then use this information, along with past experience, to pick the most efficient way to perform each task called for in the program. The discussion in this section illustrates many of the factors that should automatically be considered during the development of a program. As you gain experience and understanding of the computing process, you will be able to identify other things that can be done to make your programs operate faster.

Some of the techniques discussed in this section achieve improvements in operating time simply by changing the order in which a computation is carried out. Other techniques require us to increase the number of instructions in the program and use additional storage space. There are no hard and fast rules to tell us when it is worthwhile to apply a particular time-saving technique.

If a program is to be run a large number of times, then it is justifiable to spend a reasonable amount of time trying to eliminate features that increase running time. On the other hand, the extra programming cost associated with trying to eliminate small inefficiencies in programs that are to be used only once or twice is not justified.

Expression Evaluation

A fundamental cause of computational inefficiency is the evaluation of unnecessary expressions or subexpressions. It is not uncommon to find programs where the same expression is recalculated a number of different times. Each time a recalculation takes place, computer time is wasted. The solution to this problem is to make the calculation once and store the resulting value for use in later parts of the program. For example, consider the calculation indicated in Fig. 7-2.

If we examine Fig. 7-2(a), we see that the expression $(B**2-4*A*C)$ must be evaluated three times, that the square root of this expression must be evaluated twice, and that the product $2*A$ must be evaluated twice. Since the operations of multiplication and exponentiation take a considerable amount of time, we should minimize the number of times we perform these operations. Figure 7-2(b) shows how the program segment can be reorganized to eliminate unnecessary steps. First, we introduce a new variable E which is assigned the value $B**2-4*A*C$. Although we do not save any time when we make the comparison of E to 0, we have eliminated the need to compute this value

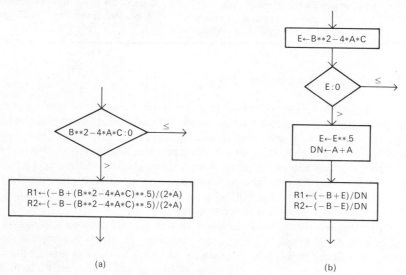

(a)   (b)

FIGURE 7-2 ■ Flowchart modification to reduce calculation time. (a) Original calculation. (b) Reduced time calculation.

TABLE 7-2 ■ Comparison of the two program segments of Fig. 7-2

Operations	Relative time needed for operation	Original program segment	Revised program segment
Unary minus	1	2	2
Additions	1	1	2
Subtractions	1	4	2
Multiplications	10	8	2
Divisions	10	2	2
Exponentiations	50	5	2
Comparisons	1	1	1
Assignments	1	2	5
Total number of operations		25	18
Relative total computation time		360	152

again. We then redefine E as

$$E \leftarrow E**.5$$

This means that we do not have to repeat the operation $(B**2-4*A*C)**.5$ twice. Next, we note that the denominator in the calculation of both R1 and R2 contains $2*A$. But addition is faster than multiplication. Thus, we compute

$$DN \leftarrow A+A$$

which is equivalent to $2*A$ but much faster to compute, and use this value in the evaluation of R1 and R2.

Table 7-2 compares the number of operations needed for both program segments and the relative computation time. Examining this table, we see that we have reduced the number of time-consuming operations (multiplication and exponentiations) as well as the total number of operations needed to carry out the calculations. More important, we see that the total computation time has been more than halved. The price we had to pay was the introduction of two additional terms, E and DN, to store the intermediate information.

The elimination of redundant subexpressions can be summarized by the following rule: If there is a subexpression that appears in a sequence of expressions and if the value of the subexpression does not change between occurrences, then the subexpression should be evaluated only once and its value assigned to a new variable which replaces all subsequent occurrences of the original subexpression.

Looping

The ability of a computer to repeat a sequence of calculations a large number of times while the value of one or more variables are changed is one of

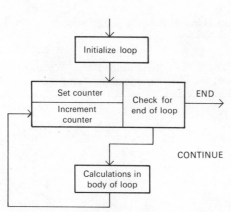

FIGURE 7-3 ▮ General form of a program loop.

the features that make computers so useful. It is also one of the potential
sources of inefficient computer usage. Repetitive calculations are performed
using a program segment with the general structure shown in Fig. 7-3. Any
inefficiencies in the body of the loop are magnified by the number of times the
loop is executed. There are two major things that can be done to improve loop
performance. First, we should make sure that the expressions that make up
the calculations in the body of the loop are as efficient as possible. Second, we
should not include any expressions in the loop that could be evaluated before
the loop is entered. Such expressions are called *loop-independent* expressions.

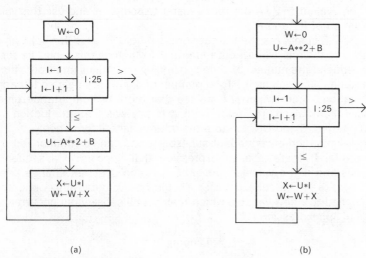

FIGURE 7-4 ▮ Illustration of flowchart simplification. (a) Original flowchart. (b)
Revised flowchart.

To show how the removal of loop-independent expressions can be accomplished, consider the simple program segment shown in Fig. 7-4. In Fig. 7-4(a), the computation $U \leftarrow A**2+B$ is carried out 25 times. But we only need to make this calculation once, since the value of U is not changed during any portion of the calculation described by the loop. Thus, if we move the calculation outside the loop, as shown in Fig. 7-4(b), we save 24 unnecessary calculations. This would mean that we perform 24 less additions, exponentiations, and assignments.

The servicing and testing of the counter in a loop requires a number of calculations. Sometimes two or more individual loop calculations can be combined into a single loop. This reduces the number of loop counters that must be serviced. For example, the computation represented by the flowchart of Figs. 7-5(a) and (b) are identical as long as there is no interaction between the results of loop 1 and the computations in loop 2. However, using the second arrangement reduces the number of calculations required for servicing the counters.

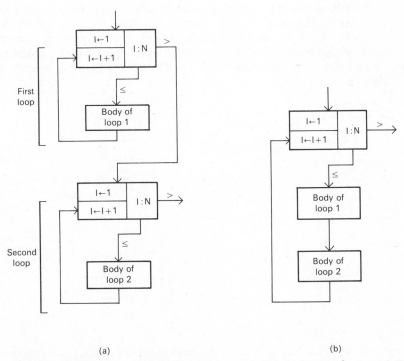

(a)   (b)

FIGURE 7-5 ■ Computing time reduction by combining disjoint loops. (a) Two separate loops. (b) Combined loops.

Input/Output

Inexperienced programmers often make very inefficient use of a computer when it comes to utilizing input information or printing output information. When developing a program, care should be taken to identify the actual input information that is required by the calculation and how it is to be used. Sometimes a considerable amount of extraneous information is available, and it is read by the program and stored in the computer although it is never used. In other cases, information may be read in and stored before it is processed when a different sequence of calculations would not require that this information be stored. For example, consider the flowchart of Fig. 7-6.

In the first flowchart a loop is used to load 20 consecutive numbers into an array A of 20 elements. A second loop is then used to compute the sum of these 20 elements. A much more efficient method, assuming that the array A is not needed in a later calculation, is shown in the second flowchart. In this case, the summation process occurs as soon as a number is read and no attempt is made to store the array. This approach not only reduces the amount of storage needed in the computer, it also reduces the number of loops in the program by one.

Since it is very easy to print output information, many programmers generate more output data than is really needed. Not only is this a waste of paper and computer time, it can add to the difficulty of finding the output information that is of real importance. During the initial development of a program, a considerable amount of output is of value to check the program and verify that

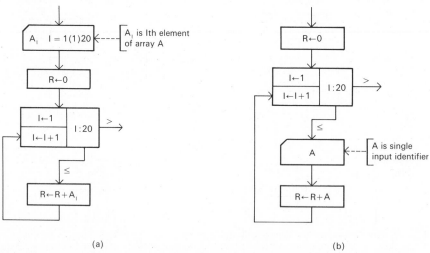

(a)   (b)

FIGURE 7-6 ■ A possible method to improve input efficiency. (a) A program in which an array is initially stored and then processed. (b) Revision of a program so that the input is not stored in an array.

it is operating correctly. However, once all of the errors have been removed from the program, all of the unnecessary output instructions should be deleted from the program.

Every computer and programming language has special features that can be used to improve computational efficiency. As you become more familiar with a given computer installation and the facilities provided, you will learn other methods to improve program performance. The ideas presented in this section are easily applied and should be automatically employed while a program is being developed.

Exercises

1. Show how the following calculations can be reorganized to minimize computing time.

(a) XP ← X∗SIN(TH) + Y∗COS(TH)
   YP ← X∗COS(TH)−Y∗SIN(TH)

(b)

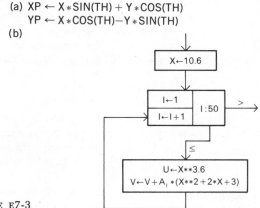

FIGURE E7-3

2. The following flowchart is used to obtain the two sums, called ODD and EVEN, respectively, of alternate terms in $[A_I]$, I=1(1)100. Show how the two loops can be combined to improve the efficiency of the calculation.

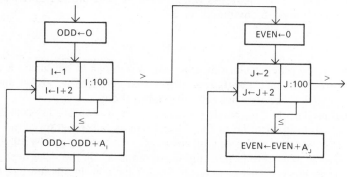

FIGURE E7-4

4 ■ Minimization of Memory Requirements

Every program we develop must eventually be transformed into a machine-language program that is executed by a computer. This program, together with sufficient space to store the data used by the program, must be stored in the computer's memory. In large computer systems, there will be two types of memory: main memory and auxiliary memory. Some small computers may not have any type of auxiliary memory.

The part of the machine-language program being executed and the data associated with this program must reside in main memory. If part of the program or part of the data needed is stored in auxiliary memory, the computing task must be temporarily suspended whenever this information is needed and must be transferred to main memory.

In large computer systems, the computer may take on the responsibility of automatically partitioning a given program into sections. Some of these sections are stored in main memory and some are stored on an auxiliary memory device such as a magnetic tape or a magnetic disk. The program sections in auxiliary storage are transferred to main memory as needed. The smaller the memory size needed to run the program, the fewer the number of transfers which will be required.

In small computer systems, and even some of the larger ones, each user is assigned a maximum amount of memory space that can be used for a program. If that space allocation is exceeded, then the program is rejected. When this happens, there is no alternative but to reduce the amount of memory space needed to store the machine-language program and the information needed by the program.

The methods discussed in the last section are sometimes useful in reducing memory requirements, although in some cases an increase in execution speed is obtained by using additional memory space. In this section, some of the techniques that can be used to conserve memory are discussed. This saving in memory may result in an increased execution time. Most programming languages include features which make it possible to implement these memory management techniques.

Reuse of Memory

Most large programs are divided into a number of subtasks. Each subtask is carried out by a program segment that requires a certain amount of data. Figure 7-7 illustrates this type of organization.

Assume that the program is divided into three separate tasks as shown in Fig. 7-7(a). The organization of the machine-language program corresponding to each task and the area reserved for data is shown in Fig. 7-7(b). The data storage area in this case is not minimized since all of the data used in each program is assigned a special memory area. This is an inefficient use of memory. To see this, consider the data areas indicated by "Data area needed for

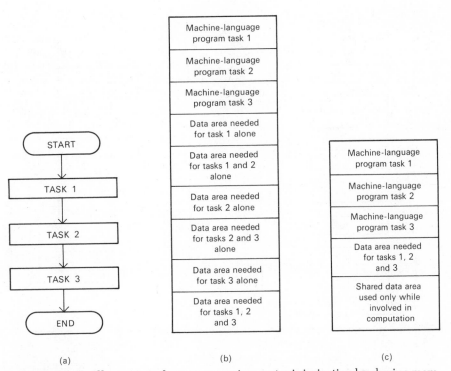

FIGURE 7-7 ■ Illustration of memory requirement minimization by sharing memory locations. (a) Division of a program into individual tasks. (b) Memory allocation without sharing. (c) Memory allocation with sharing.

task 1" and "Data area needed for task 2." As soon as we finish task 1, we no longer need any of the information stored in the data area needed for task 1. We could thus use this same area to store some or all of the information needed only for task 2. Thus, the two areas could, in reality, occupy the same memory locations without interfering with the computations. In a similar way, the other areas that are not needed for all tasks could be shared. This idea of using a shared area is illustrated in Fig. 7-7(c).

To show how this sharing takes place, consider the flowchart segment shown in Fig. 7-8(a). The two tasks are independent, except that they both compute a value for the identifier D. Without memory sharing, the data associated with the two tasks might be arranged as shown in Fig. 7-8(b). Eleven locations must be used to store this information.

An examination of the flowchart shows the data indicated by AVG and A_1 through A_4 are independent of the data indicated by W_1 through W_5. One or the other of these data sets will be used to compute D, but not both. Thus, the shared memory arrangement shown in Fig. 7-8(c) can be used.

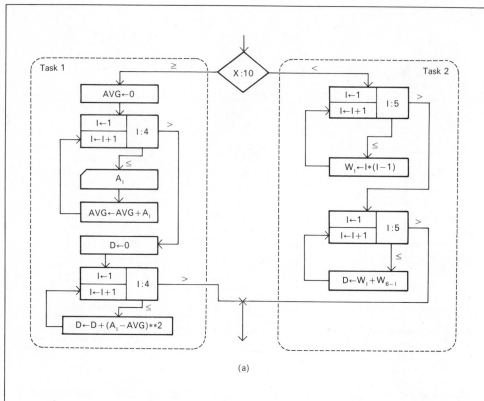

(a)

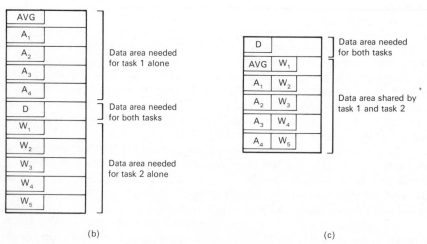

(b)   (c)

FIGURE 7-8 ■ An example of memory sharing. (a) Flowchart segment with two tasks. (b) Data storage without sharing. (c) Memory allocation with sharing.

The location reserved for D is needed for both tasks, but the rest of the locations can do double duty. If task 1 is performed, the information will be stored in the locations indicated by the identifier in the first identifier box, and if task 2 is performed, the information will be stored in the location indicated by the identifier in the second identifier box. This data organization requires only six locations.

Definition of Constants

Each constant used in a program must be stored in memory. Care must be taken in defining the constants, in order to minimize memory utilization. For example, consider the statement

$$A \leftarrow (3/2) * (X+Y) ** 1.5$$

that might appear in a typical program. This statement is inefficient for two reasons.

Note that $3/2 = 1.5$. If we use this statement as shown, we must provide a location in memory to store the three numbers 3, 2, and 1.5. In addition, we must generate a machine-language program segment to compute 3/2. Both of these problems could be avoided if the statement was written as

$$A \leftarrow (1.5) * (X+Y) ** 1.5$$

Such simple reductions of this type are often left in a program because the programmer is lazy. For example, we might wish to carry out an evaluation of the expression

$$Y + \sqrt{2}$$

and store the result in X. Since the $\sqrt{2}$ has to be looked up if it is to be used directly, there is a tendency to write the program statement corresponding to this evaluation as

$$X \leftarrow Y + (2) ** (1/2)$$

when it should be written as

$$X \leftarrow Y + 1.41421$$

By doing it this way, we only need to store a single constant and we do not have to include the machine-language program to do the division and compute $(2) ** .5$. This simplification also speeds up the execution of this statement.

Character constants can also cause unintentional wastage of storage space. For example, consider the flowchart of Fig. 7-9. In this example, the sentences to be printed are very long and require a considerable amount of memory to store. Shorter sentences such as

$$\text{'X LESS THAN 10'}$$

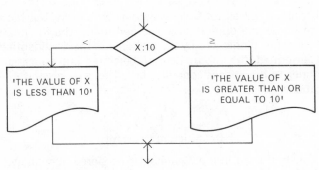

FIGURE 7-9 ■ Illustration of how character constants waste storage space.

and

'X GRTER OR EQUAL 10'

would convey the same information but require less storage. Anything that can be done to shorten or eliminate character-string constants will reduce memory space storage requirements.

Overlays

Even with very careful planning and attention to detail, we may find that our resulting program cannot fit into the available space in the main memory. When this happens, we must segment our program in such a way that part of the machine-language program can be temporarily stored outside the main memory. As we complete the execution of one segment, the next segment of the program to be executed is transferred to main memory replacing the just completed segment of the program. This process is known as *overlaying,* since one segment of a program overlays, or replaces, another segment.

Overlaying can be accomplished in a number of ways depending upon the computer system being used and the particular features of the programming language used to describe the computation. For large systems, much of the overlaying task is carried out automatically by the computer. The programmer can, however, influence the efficiency of the process by planning his program so that it is easy to determine how it should be segmented.

Many computer systems do not have the automatic overlay capability and require that the programmer develop a *planned overlay policy.* This policy may be implemented under the control of the computer's operating system or, for some small computer, manually by the user.

To illustrate how an overlay policy is used, consider a program with the general structure shown in Fig. 7-10. Each task in this program is defined by a subprogram. In addition, there is a main program that ties all these subprograms together.

The memory organization needed to run this program using overlays is

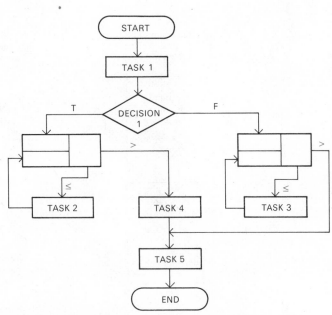

FIGURE 7-10 ■ General outline of a complex program.

illustrated in Fig. 7-11. A small percentage of main memory is devoted to a permanent control program that consists of the encoded main program and the instructions necessary to bring in the different subprograms as needed. In addition, a special area is set aside for data that must be available to all parts of the program.

When the computation is started, the control program brings in the program necessary to perform task 1. The memory organization has the form shown in Fig. 7-11(b) at this point. When task 1 is completed, decision 1 is made. If the decision is True, the programs for task 2 and task 4 replace the program for task 1 [Fig. 7-11(c)]. Otherwise, the program for task 3 is entered into memory [Fig. 7-11(d)]. Finally, the program for task 5 is loaded [Fig. 7-11(e)] and executed to complete the total computation.

The use of overlays increases computation time and should only be used when the complete program cannot be executed as a unit. When a program exceeds the available main-memory capacity, overlays must be used. The increased cost is the price that must be paid in order to be able to carry out the desired computation.

This section has indicated some of the techniques that can be used to overcome the problems associated with the common situation of having programs expanded to the point where they exceed the computer's available memory capacity. There are other techniques that can be used to reduce memory requirements. Some of these will be discussed in later chapters.

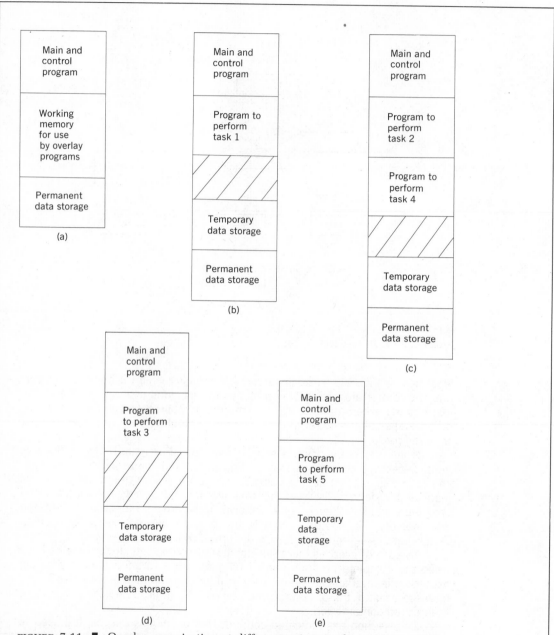

FIGURE 7-11 ■ Overlay organization at different points in the execution of the program of Fig. 7-10. (a) Memory organization at start of program. (b) First overlay. (c) Overlay if decision 1 is TRUE. (d) Overlay if decision 1 is FALSE. (e) Final overlay.

Exercises

1. The general outline of a complex program is given in the following flowchart:

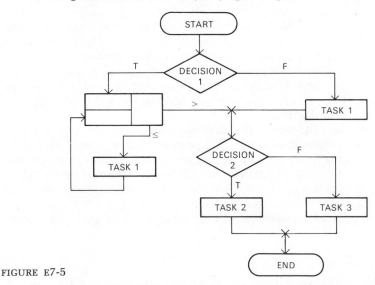

FIGURE E7-5

Develop a planned overlay policy for this program and show your overlay organization at different points in the execution of the program.

2. Modify the statements in the following flowchart so that the desired calculations can be performed and results printed out using only one of the two temporary arrays $[C_i]$ and $[D_i]$. Assume the elements of the arrays $[A_i]$ and $[B_i]$ are read into the computer memory before they are operated upon. Can you carry out the same task without using any temporary arrays? Explain your answer.

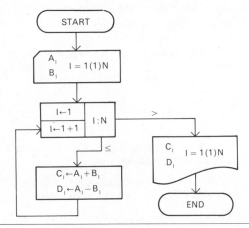

FIGURE E7-6

5 ■ Summary

In this chapter, we have presented some of the factors which must be considered when a program is developed to realize a given algorithm. From this discussion, we see that information is a dynamic quantity. It must be stored, modified, and transmitted in the proper sequence if correct results are to be obtained at minimal overall cost in computer time and memory space. If one develops the ability of thinking about a calculation in these dynamic terms, rather than as a sequence of instructions in some programming language, one quickly finds that it is easy to avoid undesirable situations in the computations needed to solve a given problem.

The importance of many of the ideas presented in this chapter depends upon the particular computer system and programming language being used. As the size and importance of the problems being solved increase, it becomes necessary to have a complete understanding of how the internal structure and organization of the local computer system influences the characteristics and efficiency of a program. Programs which are developed without considering this information often are wasteful of both computer resources and money.

References

Methods of improving the efficiency of a program are discussed in [1] and [2]. Most of the standard programming languages provide methods to manage the storage of data. Reference should be made to an appropriate manual for the techniques used by a particular language. [3] and [4] discuss some of the problems involved in data management and the use of overlays.

1. Allen, F. E. (1969) "Program Optimization," in *Annual Review in Automatic Programming,* Pergamon Press, Elmsford, N.Y., pp. 239–307.
2. Kreitzberg, C. B., and Scheiderman, B. (1972) *The Elements of FORTRAN Style: Techniques for Effective Programming,* Harcourt Brace Jovanovich, New York.
3. Rosin, R. F. (March 1969) "Supervisory and Monitor Systems," *Computing Surveys,* Vol. 1, No. 1, pp. 27–54.
4. Sherman, P. M. (1970) *Techniques in Computer Programming,* Prentice-Hall, Englewood Cliffs, N.J.

Home Problems

If possible, the algorithms developed to solve the following problems should be programmed and tested on a computer.

1. Summarize the different techniques available in the local programming language to control memory allocation for information storage.

2. Assume that A is an identifier representing an integer while B and X are iden-

tifiers representing floating-point numbers. If we try to carry out the computation

$$X \leftarrow A+B$$

we find that the internal representation of A is different than the internal representation for B and X. In some languages, the compiler will use a special internal machine-language subroutine to convert A into floating-point form before the value of A is used to evaluate the given expression. This extra conversion step takes additional time.

Assume that A is a given integer and that $[B_I]$ is a floating-point array. Develop a program which computes

$$Y = \sum_{I=1}^{N} (B_I - A)^2$$

in minimum time (Y represents a floating-point number).

3. Summarize the different techniques available in the programming languages available for your use to perform overlaying.

4. Discuss the characteristics (computing costs, speed, limitations, etc.) of the "Fast Compilers" that are available for certain programming languages available for your use (for example, PL/C compiler for PL/1 and WATFOR for FORTRAN).

5. A polynomial of degree n,

$$P(x) = a_n x^n + a_{n-1} x^{n-1} + \cdots + a_1 x + a_0$$

may be evaluated on a computer in two different ways for a given value of x. It can be evaluated by calculating the terms of the polynomial using a single assignment statement involving addition, multiplications, and exponentiation. This is the direct method.

The second and more efficient method, which involves a succession of multiplication and addition, is obtained by rewriting the polynomial in the following form

$$P(x) = ((...(a_n x + a_{n-1})x + a_{n-2})x + a_{n-3})x + \cdots)x + a_0$$

For example, if $n = 4$

$$P(x) = a_4 x^4 + a_3 x^3 + a_2 x^2 + a_1 x + a_0$$

$$= (((a_4 x + a_3)x + a_2)x + a_1)x + a_0$$

Develop a flowchart of an algorithm that will evaluate a polynomial of degree n using the method of successive multiplication and addition. Compare this method with the direct method in terms of the time and memory space requirements.

6. There are many situations in which the elements of a two-dimensional array $[A_{I,J}]$ are symmetric, i.e.,

$$A_{I,J} = A_{J,I} \qquad \text{for all values of I, J} = 1, 2, \ldots, N.$$

An array with this property is called a *triangular matrix*. For a triangular matrix, we need only to store the upper or lower half of the elements in the original array, i.e.,

$$
\begin{bmatrix}
A_{1,1} & & & \\
A_{2,1} & A_{2,2} & & \\
\cdot & \cdot & \cdot & \\
A_{N,1} & A_{N,2} & \cdots & A_{N,N}
\end{bmatrix}
\quad \text{or} \quad
\begin{bmatrix}
A_{1,1} & A_{1,2} & \cdots & A_{1,N} \\
 & A_{2,2} & \cdots & A_{2,N} \\
 & & \cdot & \\
 & & & A_{N,N}
\end{bmatrix}
$$

Develop an efficient scheme for storing two triangular matrices $[A_{I,J}]$ and $[B_{I,J}]$ and give a flowchart of an algorithm to carry out the addition of corresponding array elements, i.e.,

$$[C_{I,J}] \leftarrow [A_{I,J}] + [B_{I,J}]$$

errors in numerical computation

1 ■ Introduction

Up to this point we have concentrated upon the techniques that can be used to reduce a complex problem to a form that can be solved using a computer. Our discussion has been concerned mainly with the problem of developing an algorithm that describes the desired solution. However, the successful translation of the algorithm into a computer program does not always produce the desired result when the program is finally executed. Because of its physical limitations, the computer has certain characteristics that place various restrictions on the numerical results we can obtain from a computer program. These characteristics and limitations must be understood if we expect the computer program to give us accurate results. This chapter considers the types of numerical errors introduced by the structural limitations of a digital computer when it is used to perform numerical calculations.

Three general questions are considered in this chapter:

1. What is a numerical computation? How does it differ from an ordinary analytical computation such as is carried out in arithmetic or algebra?
2. What are the special characteristics and limitations of a computer that must be considered when it is used to carry out a numerical computation?
3. How do these limitations affect the results obtained from numerical computations and how should these affects be handled from the standpoint of a computer user?

The errors introduced in a calculation due to the structural characteristics of a digital computer are called *computational errors.* By understanding the reasons for these errors it is often possible to plan a computation so that their influence can be minimized.

In addition to the computational errors, systematic errors may also occur which are no less important. For example, errors which are inherent in the data-acquisition process often present serious problems for numerical computation. These inherent errors may be introduced by the conditions under which numerical data are collected: noise in experimental measurements, human blunder, statistical fluctuation, and imperfect data transmission from one medium to another, etc. Exact sources of these errors are often difficult to determine and even if they have been determined, they are not easily correctable in the computational procedure. They must therefore be treated as a separate problem and hence are not discussed in this book.

2 ■ Representation of Errors

In mathematics numerical information is usually represented by a number referred to as a *real number.* We can represent the set of all real numbers by a line that extends from $-\infty$ to $+\infty$. Any point on the line corresponds to a real number. Figure 8-1 illustrates the real number system with two numbers, n_1 and n_2, indicated:

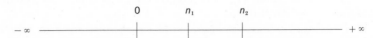

FIGURE 8-1 ■ Graphical representation of the real numbers.

Real numbers have a number of properties that make them very useful in making calculations. The real numbers are dense. By this we mean that no matter how close we may pick n_1 and n_2 to each other there is always a real number that lies between n_1 and n_2. If we perform any of the standard mathematical operations, such as addition, subtraction, multiplication, or division, on real numbers the result is a real number. The real numbers include the transcendental numbers such as π and e, and the irrational numbers such as $\sqrt{2}$ and $\sqrt{3}$. Numbers of this type require an infinite number of digits in their representation.

Computers cannot, unfortunately, represent all of the real numbers. In a computer all numerical information must be represented by a number with a finite number of digits. The maximum number of digits that can be used is fixed by the particular computer being used. This means that the set of numbers that we can use in a calculation is a subset of the real numbers. This subset does not possess many of the important properties of the real numbers.

This set of numbers is not dense. There is always a finite distance between any two consecutive numbers without any intervening number. For example, assume that every number has six or fewer digits. Then the two floating-point numbers 1.99999E10 and 1.99998E10 are two adjacent numbers. The distance between these numbers is 10^5 and *there is no floating-point number with a precision of six in this interval.* We cannot represent transcendental numbers with a finite number of digits. Thus, if we must perform a calculation involving transcendental numbers, a very common requirement, we must approximate the number using a finite number of digits. Finally, we note that when we apply any of the standard numerical operations to the finite-length numbers, the result may be a number that requires more digits for representation than are available. Thus, we must approximate the result. For example, 1.99999E10 + 9.99998E10 = 11.99997E10, but if we are limited to six digits, we must use 1.19999E11 as the resulting sum. Note that this approximation has forced us to introduce an error of 7E5 in our result.

In this section we consider how finite-length representation of numerical information may introduce numerical errors. The following sections consider how these errors influence the results of numerical calculations.

Precision

Different computers and programming languages have different conventions for representing numerical information. The number used to specify the total number of significant digits (binary or decimal) that may be associated with a given numerical variable is called the *precision* of the variable. An identifier is said to have a precision N if the number associated with the identifier can have no more than N digits.

The maximum number of digits that can be assigned to represent a number is a function of the computer's word length. Precision specifications need not coincide with a computer's word length.

For our discussion the precision of an integer or fixed-point variable will correspond to the maximum number of digits that can be used to represent the value of the variable. The precision of a floating-point variable is taken as the number of digits that are used to represent the mantissa of the variable. The following numbers all have a precision of six although they represent vastly different numerical values.

$$163221 \qquad 1.26348 \qquad 1.63221E20$$

Resolution

The *resolution* of a variable is the magnitude of the difference that exists between two adjacent numbers. For integers and fixed-point variables the resolution is constant over the entire range of the variables. The resolution of a floating-point variable is not fixed. Instead, it increases as the size of the exponent associated with the number increases.

Assume that we specify that the precision of a decimal integer variable I is 3. Then this means that I can be assigned any value between $+999$ and -999. The resolution of this and any other integer variable is 1, since the difference between any two adjacent integer values is 1.

The resolution of a fixed-point variable depends upon both the precision associated with the variable and the location of the decimal (or binary) point. Assume that the fixed-point variable has the following form:

$$\pm d_m d_{m-1} \cdots d_1 . d_{-1} d_{-2} \cdots d_{-n}$$

Then the precision is $m + n$ and the corresponding resolution is 10^{-n} in the decimal system. If $m = 2$ and $n = 4$, then the precision of a fixed-point variable is 6, and its resolution is .0001.

The resolution of a floating-point number is not constant. It depends upon the value of the exponent. Assume that floating-point numbers are represented in the standardized form

$$\pm d_1 . d_{-1} d_{-2} \cdots d_{-n} Eu$$

where d_1 is not zero and u is an integer with a value between $\pm K_m$. If $u = K_m$ then the resolution is $10^{-n} (10^{K_m})$, while if $u = -K_m$, the resolution would be $10^{-n} (10^{-K_m})$.

Since the resolution varies depending upon the value of u we can speak of the *local resolution* as 10^{-n} (10^u). For example, let $n = 5$ and $K_m = 20$. Then the precision of the floating-point variable is 6 and the resolution will vary from a minimum value of

$$.00001E{-}20$$

which is a very small number, to

$$.00001E{+}20$$

which is a large number. This variation in the resolution of a floating-point variable can lead to large errors when floating-point calculations are performed.

Range

In computing, we use identifiers to indicate numerical variables. The *range* of an identifier is the set of all numbers that can be assigned to that identifier. The precision attribute associated with an integer identifier immediately fixes its range. The precision and precision specification indicating the location of the decimal point (or binary point) determines the range of a fixed-point identifier. The range of a floating-point identifier is determined by both the precision of the mantissa and the largest magnitude that the exponent can be assigned.

For example, let I be an integer identifier with a precision of 6. Then the range of I is from -999999 to $+999999$. Assume that F is a fixed-point identifier with a precision and resolution of the following form:

$$\pm d_m d_{m-1} \cdots d_1. d_{-1} d_{-2} \cdots d_{-n}$$

The range of this number is from $-(10^m - 10^{-n})$ to $+(10^m - 10^{-n})$. For example, if $m = 3$, $n = 2$, then the range is from

$$-(10^3 - 10^{-2}) = -999.99$$

to

$$+(10^3 - 10^{-2}) = +999.99$$

Floating-point identifiers have the largest range. If the identifier has a precision of n and the exponent has a value between $\pm K_m$, then the range of the identifier is

$$\pm(10 - 10^{-(n-1)})10^{K_m}$$

Whenever we work with numerical quantities in a computer, there is always the possibility that a situation will occur that generates a number having more digits than can be accommodated by the precision and range of the identifier associated with that number. It is extremely important that we understand how the computer handles problems of this type.

Overflow

An *overflow* condition exists whenever a mathematical computation generates a number which falls outside the allowable range of the identifiers associated with that number. For example, assume that the integer identifiers A, B, and C have a precision of 2 and we wish to calculate C

$$C \leftarrow A * B$$

Now if A has a value of 2 and B has a value of 5, then the resulting value of C is 10 which is well within the range of C. However, if A = 25 and B = 15, then C would have a value of 375 which is outside the range of C. This is an overflow condition.

Different computer systems and programming languages handle the occurrence of an overflow in different ways. Some computers will generate an error message telling the programmer that an overflow condition has occurred. This is particularly true when the numbers involved in the calculation are floating-point numbers. In some systems, particularly when the numbers are integers, the computer will simply drop the leftmost digits until the resulting number is in the allowable range. For our example, the number 375 would become 75 and this would be the value assigned to C. An error message may or may not be printed.

Truncation

Another problem occurs when a number is generated which has a smaller resolution than the resolution of the identifier to be associated with the number. For example, assume that A is a fixed-point identifier with a resolution of .001 and a precision of 6. Then all numbers associated with A have the form

$$d_3 d_2 d_1 \cdot d_{-1} d_{-2} d_{-3}$$

Now A can take on such values as +126.240, −26.32, or 999.128. However, suppose that A is generated by

$$A \leftarrow 12.235 * .33$$

The resulting value would be 4.03755, which is outside the resolution specification associated with A. There are two approaches that may be used to resolve this problem.

A number may be *truncated* by simply dropping all the digits on the right that do not fit into the precision specification. If this approach were used, then A would be assigned the value 4.037 and the last two digits on the right would be lost. Similarly, if the value resulting from another calculation were 27.6309999, the truncated value assigned to A would be 27.630.

Whenever truncation is used we introduce an error corresponding to the information represented by the last digits. Thus, when 4.03755 was truncated to 4.037 the error was 0.00055 and when 27.6309999 was truncated to 27.630 the error was 0.0009999. The error is never larger than the resolution of the

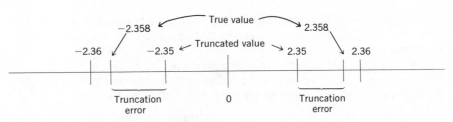

FIGURE 8-2 ■ Illustration of truncation error for fixed-point numbers with resolution of .01.

identifier used to represent the number. Figure 8-2 illustrates the form that truncation error takes when we are dealing with both positive and negative numbers.

If we indicate the true value of the number as x, its truncated value as x_T and the truncation error as ϵ_T, then we have the following relationships:

$$x - x_T = \epsilon_T \qquad |x - x_T| < (\text{resolution interval})$$

The magnitude of the truncated number is always less than the magnitude of the true number.

Rounding

Another approach to the problem instead of truncation is to select a value of the variable which is closest to the true value of the variable. This process is referred to as *rounding*. The value assigned to the variable is found by first computing the magnitude of the truncation error, $|\epsilon_T|$. If

$$|\epsilon_T| \leq \frac{(\text{resolution interval})}{2}$$

then the rounded value becomes simply the truncated value of the variable. If

$$|\epsilon_T| > \frac{(\text{resolution interval})}{2}$$

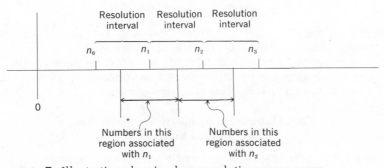

FIGURE 8-3 ■ Illustration showing how resolution errors occur.

then the magnitude of the rounded value is obtained by taking the next allowed value of the variable that has a magnitude larger than the magnitude of the truncated variable.

Figure 8-3 illustrates how rounding errors occur.

If we indicate the true value of the number as x, its rounded value as x_R, and the rounding error as ϵ_R, then we have the following relationships:

$$x - x_R = \epsilon_R \qquad |x - x_R| \leq |\epsilon_T| \leq \frac{\text{(resolution interval)}}{2}$$

Table 8-1 illustrates these two types of errors.

TABLE 8-1 ■ Truncation and rounding errors

Form of variable	Original value	Truncated value	Magnitude of truncated error	Rounded value	Magnitude of rounding error
dd.ddd	17.6324	17.632	.0004	17.632	.0004
dd.ddd	−25.6328	−25.632	.0008	−25.633	.0002
d.dddEu	2.76445E6	2.764E6	.00045E6	2.764E6	.00045E6
d.dddEu	3.76655E−2	3.766E−2	.00055E−2	3.767E−2	.00045E−2

Underflow

The final type of problem that may occur is a result of calculations that produce a nonzero value smaller than the smallest allowed number used by an identifier. This problem is of particular importance for floating-point numbers. For example, assume that the smallest floating-point number that can be assigned to an identifier A is

$$1.0E-20$$

Then a calculation such as

$$A \leftarrow (2.01E-10) * (1.05E-15)$$

would give a value of 2.110E−25, which represents a number much smaller than that allowed for A. This is an example of *underflow*.

In most computer systems a value of zero will be assigned to the identifier. Depending upon the particular system, an error message may also be printed indicating that an underflow condition existed.

**Errors Introduced by Binary Representation
of Decimal Numbers**

As discussed in Chapter II, decimal numbers may be stored in a computer by converting the decimal number to its equivalent binary value. For many decimal numbers, their conversion to binary notation is straightforward because they can be readily expressed in terms of powers of two. In particular, all decimal integers can be converted to binary form by finding the right combinations of the unit, two, four, and so on. The following are examples of decimal integers and their binary equivalent:

$$25_{10} = 11001_2 = (1)2^4 + (1)2^3 + (0)2^2 + (0)2^1 + (1)2^0$$
$$12_{10} = 1100_2 = (1)2^3 + (1)2^2 + (0)2^1 + (0)2^0$$
$$5_{10} = 101_2 = (1)(2)^2 + (0)2^1 + (1)2^0$$
$$2_{10} = 10_2 = (1)2^1 + (0)2^0$$

Decimal fractions, however, may or may not be representable by powers of two. For example, the decimal fraction 0.5 can be converted to binary notation as

$$0.5_{10} = .1_2 = (1)(2^{-1})$$

and the decimal fraction 0.625 can be converted to binary notation as

$$0.625_{10} = .101_2 = (1)2^{-1} + (0)2^{-2} + (1)2^{-3}$$

In the event that a decimal fraction cannot be exactly converted to an equivalent binary number, some approximation must be made in order to store that number in the computer. Let us look at this situation with an example.

Using the decimal fraction to binary fraction conversion technique presented in Appendix I, we can show that

$$0.4_{10} = (.0110011001100110011 \ldots)_2$$

Notice that the exact binary equivalent of 0.4 requires an infinite repetition of the binary digit pattern 1100. Thus, a decimal fraction with a finite number of decimal digits is represented by a binary fraction with an infinite number of binary digits. To store this binary number in a computer it must be truncated. Assume that a 12-bit word is available to hold this information. Then, internally the decimal number 0.4 would be approximated by

$$.011001100110$$

Converting this stored number back to a decimal value gives

$$\frac{1}{4} + \frac{1}{8} + \frac{1}{64} + \frac{1}{128} + \frac{1}{1024} + \frac{1}{2048} = \frac{819}{2048} = 0.39990234375$$

rather than 0.4. The error in converting to a binary representation is thus 0.00009765625.

This truncation has an interesting side effect. Consider the flowchart sequence shown in Fig. 8-4. If this task is carried out using one of the standard programming languages, the printed result might be

$$Y = .399902$$

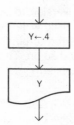

FIGURE 8-4 ■ A simple program to print a value of .4.

if Y was an identifier known to have a precision of 6. The error comes from the internal representation of .4 as a binary fraction.

In some situations it is important not to allow conversion errors. One way to do this is to store all decimal numbers in binary coded decimal (BCD) form. Unfortunately, not all computer systems and programming languages provide this option.

The errors discussed in this section arise because of the internal structure of the computer. Errors can also occur external to the computer and can be present when numerical information is read into a given program. In the next section we investigate how numerical errors influence the overall results of a computation.

Exercises

1. Assume that the fixed-point variable has the following form

$$\pm d_m d_{m-1} \cdots d_1 . d_{-1} d_{-2} \cdots d_{-n}$$

For each of the precisions given below, determine its range and resolution:
   (a) $m = 3, n = 2$ (b) $m = 0, n = 5$ (c) $m = 5, n = 0$

2. Find the magnitude of both the truncation error and the rounding error for the following numbers.

Form of Variable	Original Number
(a) dd.ddd	45.0472
(b) ddd.ddd	392.1078
(c) d.dddEu	3.63999E−2
(d) d.dddEu	1.36524E6

3. Assume the assignment statement

$$X \leftarrow A * B/C$$

is to be executed on a computer which can handle numbers between $-1.0E-35$ (the smallest) and $+1.0E35$ (the largest). Determine, for each of the following set of data, whether the execution would result in an overflow condition, an underflow condition, or neither:

(a) A = 1.0E10   B = 1.0E20   C = 1.0E−10
(b) A = 1.0E−10   B = 1.0E−30   C = 1.0E10
(c) A = 1.0E−10   B = 1.0E−20   C = 1.0E10

4. Determine the error in converting

$$0.4_{10} = (.0110011001100...)_2$$

to a binary representation if a six-bit word is available to hold this information.

3 ■ Computational Error

One of the consequences of using a computer for numerical computation is the introduction of computational errors. Computational errors occur whenever some form of approximation must be made in the process of computation which produces a difference between the *computed result* arising from the approximation and the *exact result* that would be obtained if no approximation was made. There are two related problems we must deal with as a result of these computational errors. One problem is that of trying to determine the accuracy of the computed results; that is, how close they are to the exact result. The other problem is how to analyze the effect of error accumulation due to the immense number of calculations often needed in solving numerical problems on a computer. This section provides an introductory discussion of these problems from the view-point of a computer user. A much more extensive discussion of computational errors and how they can be minimized in large computational problems can be found in the references listed at the end of this chapter.

Classification of Errors

To talk about errors, we must develop a mechanism for describing errors resulting from various sources. It is important to emphasize that the term computational error does not mean a blunder or mistake made by the computer. Modern computers can carry out computations involving millions of operations without making a single operational mistake. The concept of error refers to the errors that are introduced in the computational procedures as a result of computer limitations.

There are two ways to characterize the kinds of errors that are encountered in a computation:

Actual Error = Exact Value − Computed Value

$$\text{Relative Error} = \frac{\text{Actual Error}}{\text{Exact Value}} = \frac{\text{Exact Value} - \text{Computed Value}}{\text{Exact Value}}$$

The exact value refers to the ideal analytical result that would be achieved without any approximation; the computed value is the numerical result achieved when some form of approximation is made in the computation.

As an example of these errors, the fraction $\frac{2}{3}$ can be approximated by 0.666, accurate to three decimal places. The exact value is $\frac{2}{3}$ and the computed value is 0.666. Thus we have

$$\text{Actual Error} = \frac{2}{3} - \frac{666}{1000} = \frac{2000 - 1998}{3000} = \frac{2}{3}(10^{-3})$$

$$\text{Relative Error} = \frac{\frac{2}{3}(10^{-3})}{\frac{2}{3}} = 0.001$$

Notice that the actual error is determined by the difference between the exact value and the computed value of the same number; the size of the actual error is a direct measurement of how the computed value deviates from the exact value. The relative error, however, is a relative measure of the difference; it is in a sense normalized by the exact value and consequently does not depend upon the units of the number under computation.

On many occasions, when the sign of the error is not important it is desirable to talk about the absolute value of the error defined as follows:

$$\text{Absolute Error} = |\text{Exact Value} - \text{Computed Value}|$$

The relative error can also be expressed in terms of the absolute error:

$$\text{Absolute Relative Error} = \frac{\text{Absolute Error}}{|\text{Exact Value}|}$$

Sometimes it is only possible to obtain an estimate of the maximum possible error that may occur in the computed value due to approximation. This estimate is called the *error bound*. Error bounds are useful in establishing certain facts about how errors are accumulated as a result of mathematical calculations.

Errors Introduced by Arithmetic Operations

The presence of truncation or roundoff errors in representing numbers would not be very serious if they were the only source of error in numerical computation. This is the case because once we know that the errors come from finite-length representation we can try to minimize these errors by either allowing more significant digits in our precision specification or by adjusting the computed result according to the size of error detected. Unfortunately, there are additional sources of error that occur as a result of the rounding or truncation process associated with individual numbers. This is the error that is caused by arithmetic operations such as addition, subtraction, multiplication, and division, performed on the individual numbers which themselves are in error. As we shall demonstrate shortly, the presence of these errors makes it more difficult to predict the behavior of the overall errors in the computation and consequently the quality of the computed results.

Errors in Integer Arithmetic Operations

Whenever we perform addition, subtraction, or multiplication on integers, the result is an integer. Thus, the only difficulty that may occur is that of overflow. If we are careful in planning our program, it is usually possible to select the precision of all integer identifiers so that the value of any computation will fall in the allowable range.

The division of two integers may or may not produce another integer. For example, 107/42 has the value 2.0504. . . . In most computers this result would be truncated to 2 and an error message might be produced. Thus, we see that integer division may lead to truncation or rounding errors.

For most applications, numerical computations involving integers are used in such a manner that we do not have to consider roundoff or truncation errors. Errors become important in computations involving fixed-point and floating-point variables. For the rest of this chapter we concentrate upon this class of numerical information.

Arithmetic Errors

The following examples illustrate the types of errors that can occur under a single addition, subtraction, multiplication, or division. In most computers, numerical information is usually represented with a precision of at least six to twelve (or even more) decimal digits. For pedagogical reasons we assume that all operations in the following discussion are carried out on a hypothetical computer with a precision of three decimal digits. It is also assumed that truncation is used before and after each arithmetic operation, as necessary, to make the results fit into this form.

The examples given below illustrate the effect on the computed result of various operations when truncation must be carried out before and after each operation to fit the three-digit floating-point computation. The digit positions that have been subjected to truncation are underlined.

Addition

Example 1. 4.52 + 3.17 is computed as follows:

$$
\begin{array}{r}
4.52 \\
+3.17 \\
\hline
7.69 \\
\end{array}
\quad \text{no truncation needed}
$$

The exact sum = 7.69.
The computed sum = 7.69 is stored as .769E1.
There is no error.

Example 2. 4.52 + .378 is computed as follows:

$$
\begin{array}{r}
4.52 \\
+ \ .378 \\
\hline
4.898 \\
\end{array}
\quad \text{truncation}
$$

The exact sum $= 4.898$
The computed sum $= 4.89$ is stored as .489E1
The actual error $= 4.898 - 4.89 = 0.008$
    The truncation in addition occurs when the resulting sum has more digits than the allowed precision. When we carry out subtraction, the result may contain fewer digits than either of the two numbers that were used to form the difference. When this happens, zeros are introduced on the right in a floating-point number to make the mantissa have the required number of digits. Truncation introduces errors when one or both of the operands are truncated before the subtraction takes place.

Subtraction

Example 1. $7.92 - 5.48$ is computed as follows:

$$
\begin{array}{r}
7.92 \\
-5.48 \\
\hline
2.44
\end{array}
$$

    The exact difference $= 2.44$.
    The computed difference $= 2.44$ is stored as .244E1.
    There is no error.
Example 2. $10.35 - 9.44$ is computed as follows:

$$
\begin{array}{r}
10.3\underline{5} \\
- \ 9.4\overline{4} \\
\hline
.86
\end{array}
$$
      truncation here; 10.35 is stored as .103E2 or 10.30

    The exact difference $= 0.91$.
    The computed difference $= .86$ is stored as .860E0.
    The actual error $= .91 - .86 = .05$.
Note that in this case the error is approximately 6 percent of the answer and occurs because one of the operands had to be truncated to a precision of 3.

Multiplication

Example 1. $2.06 * 3.12$ is computed as follows:

$$
\begin{array}{r}
2.06 \\
* 3.12 \\
\hline
412 \\
206 \ \ \\
618 \ \ \ \\
\hline
6.42\underline{72}
\end{array}
$$
      truncation

    The exact product $= 6.4272$.
    The computed product $= 6.42$ is stored as .642E1.
    The actual error $= 6.4272 - 6.42 = 0.00720$.
    Example 2. $4.27 * .315$ is computed as follows:

```
      4.27
   *   .315
      2135  ⎫
       427  ⎬   assume no truncation here
      1281  ⎭
     1.34505      truncation
```

The exact product = 1.34505.
The computed product = 1.34 is stored as .134E1.
The actual error = 1.34505 − 1.34 = 0.00505.
Notice that we have assumed that in the multiplication process no truncation will occur during the intermediate steps.

Division

Example 1.   227/33:
   The exact quotient = 6.8787. . . .
   The computed result = 6.87 is stored as .687E1.
   The actual error = 0.008787. . . .
Example 2.   5.72/.83:
   The exact quotient = 6.8915. . . .
   The computed quotient = 6.89 is stored as .689E1.
   The actual error = 6.8915 . . . − 6.89 = 0.0015. . . .

Error Accumulation

In the above examples, the errors resulting from a single arithmetic operation do not appear to be very serious in terms of their size relative to the numbers that are being operated upon. The problem of error, however, becomes much more serious when the problem to be solved involves a very large number of operations, each of which may introduce errors in the result. The fact that errors due to truncation can accumulate in the computational process is one of the important computer limitations affecting numerical computation. Let us look at the effect of error accumulation by again working with three-digit floating-point arithmetic in the following example.

Suppose we wish to form the sum of ten numbers all having the same value 4.56. The sum is to be obtained by successively adding 4.56 ten times to a variable Y initially set to zero. All intermediate results will be stored with a precision of 3 in floating-point form. Carrying out the summation process, we have the computational steps, along with the stored intermediate results, as shown on p. 220.

The computed sum therefore is .451E2, which in fixed-point notation is 45.1. Clearly errors have been introduced in the computational process, since we would expect the actual sum to be $10 \times 4.56 = 45.6$, differing from the computed sum by 0.5. This overall error has resulted from the necessary truncations in performing the summation with finite-length (three-digit, in this

Summation process		Stored result in Y
4.56		.456E1
+ 4.56		
9.12		.912E1
+ 4.56		
13.68	truncation	.136E1
+ 4.56		
18.16	truncation	.181E2
+ 4.56		
22.66	truncation	.226E2
+ 4.56		
27.16	truncation	.271E2
+ 4.56		
31.66	truncation	.316E2
+ 4.56		
36.16	truncation	.361E2
+ 4.56		
40.66	truncation	.406E2
+ 4.56		
45.16	truncation	.451E2

case) storage. Although the overall error produced in this example is not large, it is not difficult to see that small errors can easily accumulate where hundreds or thousands of operations are involved in the computation. With a little more computation, we can show that if the above summation were carried out 100 times, the computed sum would be 427, instead of the expected 456, a difference of $456 - 427 = 29$. In fact, with three-digit precision, it is not possible to keep adding 4.56 and expect the sum to increase after a fixed number of successive additions. If we were to keep adding 4.56 after this fixed number of additions, not only would we waste our valuable computer time, but the answer we obtain would be hopelessly wrong.

Estimating the Error Size

When individual numbers are in error, these errors accumulate as we carry out a computation. The overall error in the computed result is difficult to predict. Thus, we may not be able to use our computed values in any meaningful way if we cannot be sure that the errors associated with our computation are within a reasonable bound. To demonstrate how errors influence our results, consider the following elementary example of adding and multiplying numbers in fixed-point notation.

Let X and Y denote the exact values for the two numbers $\sqrt{11}$ and $\sqrt{29}$, respectively. Suppose that both X and Y and all intermediate values are stored as fixed-point numbers with the form d.dd. Let the computed value $\bar{X}$ for X be

3.31 and the computed value $\overline{Y}$ for Y be 5.38. We wish to compute

$$\overline{X} + \overline{Y} \qquad \overline{X} + (0.1)\overline{Y} \qquad \overline{X} + (0.01)\overline{Y}$$

and determine their errors. In carrying out these operations with the specified precision, there is first the error resulting from the intermediate multiplication followed by truncation:

$$(0.1)\overline{Y} = (0.1)(5.38) = 0.53 \text{ instead of } 0.538$$
$$(0.01)\overline{Y} = (0.01)(5.38) = 0.05 \text{ instead of } 0.0538$$

The additions are then performed as follows:

$$
\begin{array}{ccc}
3.31 & 3.31 & 3.31 \\
\underline{+5.38} & \underline{+0.53} & \underline{+0.05} \\
\overline{X} + \overline{Y} = 8.69 & \overline{X} + (0.1)\,\overline{Y} = 3.84 & \overline{X} + (0.01)\,\overline{Y} = 3.36
\end{array}
$$

Let us now point out the sources of error and estimate their size. First of all, $\overline{X}$ and $\overline{Y}$ are computed values for $\sqrt{11}$ and $\sqrt{29}$, respectively, correct to two decimal places, in accordance with our precision and resolution specification. With X and Y representing their (unknown) exact values, the actual errors in $\overline{X}$ and $\overline{Y}$ are

$$\epsilon_X = X - \overline{X} = X - 3.31$$
$$\epsilon_Y = Y - \overline{Y} = Y - 5.38$$

and, considering the assumed resolution, neither error exceeds 0.01. There are also computational errors introduced in the multiplication operation. In storing the intermediate results, $(0.1)\overline{Y}$ of the multiplication operation, right truncation occurs and 0.538 is stored as 0.53. Similarly, $(0.01)\overline{Y}$ is stored as 0.05 which is the truncated value of .0538. The maximum errors in both cases are limited to 0.01.

Given the error sources and their sizes indicated above, let us try to determine the overall errors after the additions are performed in the three cases. Take the case $\overline{X} + \overline{Y}$ first. The difference between the (unknown) exact value of X + Y and its computed value is

$$(X + Y) - (\overline{X} + \overline{Y})$$
$$= (X - \overline{X}) + (Y - \overline{Y}) = (X - 3.31) + (Y - 5.38)$$
$$= \epsilon_X + \epsilon_Y = (X + Y) - 8.69$$

Since neither of the two errors ϵ_X and ϵ_Y exceeds 0.01, we can give a maximum possible error (absolute value) for the overall error resulting from the addition:

$$|(X + Y) - 8.69| \le 0.01 + 0.01 = 0.02$$

In other words, as a result of adding two numbers with maximum absolute error 0.01, the maximum absolute error for their sum is 0.02, which is twice the individual error. Notice that the addition process in this case has not introduced any additional error into our computed result. The only new element here is that the third digit in the computed sum 8.69 is open to slight suspicion; that is, the actual sum could be between $8.69 - 0.02$ and $8.69 + 0.02$.

Now consider the case $X + (0.1)Y$. Again, we are interested in finding the overall error after the multiplication and addition process. Since $\epsilon_Y = Y - \overline{Y}$, we can write $Y = \epsilon_Y + \overline{Y} = \epsilon_Y + 5.38$ and

$$\begin{aligned}(0.1)Y &= (0.1)(\epsilon_Y + 5.38) \\ &= (0.1)\epsilon_Y + 0.538\end{aligned}$$

To determine the overall error, we are interested in the difference between the (unknown) exact value of $X + (0.1)Y$ and the computed sum $\overline{X} + (0.1)\overline{Y} = 3.84$. This difference is

$$\begin{aligned}X + (0.1)Y - 3.84 &= \epsilon_X + 3.31 + (0.1)\epsilon_Y + 0.538 - 3.84 \\ &= \epsilon_X + (0.1)\epsilon_Y + 0.008\end{aligned}$$

where X has been replaced by $\epsilon_X + 3.31$. The maximum absolute error is bounded by

$$\begin{aligned}|X + (0.1)Y - 3.84| &\le |\epsilon_X| + |(0.1)\epsilon_Y| + 0.008 \\ &\le 0.01 + 0.001 + 0.008\end{aligned}$$

which does not exceed 0.019. Notice that in the maximum absolute error the 0.01 is the error of $\overline{X}$, the 0.001 is associated with the error of $\overline{Y}$, which has been multiplied by 0.1 as the computation proceeds, and the last term 0.008 is due to the truncation process needed in the computation. In a similar way, we can determine the overall error for the case $\overline{X} + (0.01)\overline{Y}$. The difference between the exact value and the computed value is

$$\begin{aligned}X + (0.01)Y - 3.36 &= \epsilon_X + 3.31 + (0.01)\epsilon_Y + 0.0538 - 3.36 \\ &= \epsilon_X + (0.01)\epsilon_Y + 0.0038\end{aligned}$$

And the maximum absolute error is bounded by

$$\begin{aligned}|X + (0.01)Y - 3.36| &\le |\epsilon_X| + |(0.01)\epsilon_Y| + 0.0038 \\ &\le 0.01 + 0.0001 + 0.0038\end{aligned}$$

which does not exceed 0.0139. Examining the overall error estimates obtained in the three cases, we see that the second decimal place in the computed result appears to be open to suspicion. More important, what this example has demonstrated is that even in simple computations involving a single addition and multiplication on two numbers, the question of error is not so easily resolved. We have only been able to establish an error bound on the computed results. When a large number of operations are required, it is even more difficult to predict the quality of our computed result, since the uncertainty in the estimated error itself tends to increase. Let us give an example demonstrating this effect.

Suppose the following sum is to be computed

$$\sqrt{1} + \sqrt{2} + \sqrt{3} + \sqrt{4} + \sqrt{5} + \sqrt{6} + \sqrt{7} + \sqrt{8} + \sqrt{9} + \sqrt{10} = \sum_{n=1}^{10} \sqrt{n}$$

Assume that these square roots have been obtained from some computational procedure and their computed values (truncated to two decimal places) are given below:

n	Computed $\sqrt{n}$	n	Computed $\sqrt{n}$
1	1.00	6	2.44
2	1.41	7	2.64
3	1.73	8	2.82
4	2.00	9	3.00
5	2.23	10	3.16

Assuming that we work with fixed-point notation, the computed sum is 22.43. Notice that such a sum requires at least four digits for its computation and we need two positions to the right of the decimal point in order to avoid improper truncation. Ten numbers are involved in the computation and each has a possible maximum error of 0.01. We wish to determine an error bound for the computed sum 22.43.

To analyze this situation, let the ten exact square roots be denoted by X_1, $X_2, \ldots, X_{10}$; that is $X_1 = \sqrt{1}$, $X_2 = \sqrt{2}$, etc. Let the computed square roots be denoted by $\overline{X}_1 = 1.00$, $\overline{X}_2 = 1.41, \ldots, \overline{X}_{10} = 3.16$. In each square root, the maximum possible error is denoted by $\epsilon = 0.01$. That is, we have the following ten relations.

$$X_1 \leq \overline{X}_1 + \epsilon$$
$$X_2 \leq \overline{X}_2 + \epsilon$$
$$\cdot$$
$$\cdot$$
$$\cdot$$
$$X_{10} \leq \overline{X}_{10} + \epsilon$$

To determine the overall error bound, we are interested in the difference between the exact sum

$$X_1 + X_2 + \cdots + X_{10} = \sum_{i=1}^{10} X_i$$

and the computed sum

$$\overline{X}_1 + \overline{X}_2 + \cdots + \overline{X}_{10} = \sum_{i=1}^{10} \overline{X}_i$$

that is

$$\sum_{i=1}^{10} X_i - \sum_{i=1}^{10} \overline{X}_i = \epsilon_T$$

A bound can be established for ϵ_T by adding the ten inequalities:

$$\sum_{i=1}^{10} X_i \leq \sum_{i=1}^{10} \overline{X}_i + 10\epsilon$$

which simply means

$$\sum_{i=1}^{10} X_i - \sum_{i=1}^{10} \overline{X}_i \leq 10\epsilon$$

or

$$\epsilon_T \leq 10\epsilon$$

That is, the maximum possible error in the computed sum 22.43 is 10ϵ. Applying the error value $\epsilon = 0.01$, the computed sum 22.43 has an error bound $10 \times 0.01 = 0.1$. This suggests that *the sum may not be correct to even one decimal place*, even though each of the ten square roots was correct to two decimal places.

Extending these results, it is not difficult to show that if the sum of N number $X_1, X_2, \ldots, X_N$ is computed on the basis of their approximate values $\overline{X}_1, \overline{X}_2, \ldots, \overline{X}_N$, each with a maximum possible error ϵ, then the error bound for the computed sum $\sum_{i=1}^{N} \overline{X}_i$ is $N\epsilon$.

Exercises

1. Work each of the following problems using a decimal floating-point notation with a precision of 3. Perform necessary truncations before and after each operation in the expression. Determine for each case whether an error has been introduced in the computed result.
  (a) $2.71 + 3.94$ (e) $32.7/4.551$
  (b) $4.52 + .558$ (f) $(14.6 + .476)/12.78$
  (c) $52.436 - 7.71$ (g) $18.34 + 2.96 + 25.0$
  (d) $6.38 * 2.17$ (h) $19.03 + 1.007 - 10.3$

2. (a) Add $\frac{1}{3}$ three times using a floating-point computation with a precision of 3. What is the error in the computed result?
  (b) Add $\frac{1}{3}$ ten times and determine the error in the computed result.
  (c) What would be the error when you have added $\frac{1}{3}$ 100 times? 300 times?
  (d) Show that when you have added $\frac{1}{3}$ 331 times you would always get the value 100 no matter how often you add $\frac{1}{3}$ to 100 thereafter.

3. If $\overline{X} = 3.22$ and $\overline{Y} = 5.39$ are the approximate values for X and Y, respectively, correct to two decimal places due to truncation, can you estimate how large $X * Y$ and $X + Y$ could be? Compare $\overline{X} * \overline{Y}$ and $\overline{X} + \overline{Y}$ with the estimated bounds.

4. Assume the following sum

$$\text{SUM} = \sum_{n=1}^{10} \sqrt{n}$$

is to be computed by successively adding $\sqrt{n}$ to SUM (initially set to zero). Each approximate value for $\sqrt{n}$ is obtained from the table shown on page 223. Determine the computed value of SUM using a floating-point notation with a precision of 3. Compare your result with the expected sum 22.43 which has a maximum possible error 0.1.

4 ■ Errors in Evaluating Arithmetic Expressions

The finite-precision representation of numbers has been shown to be the principle source of computational errors in numerical computation. We have also demonstrated that these errors tend to accumulate during a computation. In this section, we show that the computer has other peculiar characteristics which place a limitation on the accuracy of evaluating numerical expressions under various conditions.

The Equality Relation

One of the common tasks performed in a computation is to test the equality of two numbers. Computational errors can lead to particular difficulty in this situation. Consider the flowchart shown in Fig. 8-5. In this calculation we continue to add $\frac{1}{3}$ to SUM until SUM is equal to 2. Let us assume that all the calculations are done with floating-point numbers with a precision of 3. Under this situation the first ten values for SUM are:

I	SUM	I	SUM
1	.333	6	1.99
2	.666	7	2.32
3	.999	8	2.65
4	1.33	9	2.98
5	1.66	10	3.31

Examining this result we see that SUM is never equal to 2. Thus, in an actual computer program this innocent looking loop that should terminate after six summations is actually an infinite loop.

Nonassociativity of Computer Arithmetic

The evaluation of mathematical expressions forms an essential part in carrying out any numerical computation. It is quite common to find that a single arithmetic expression may include a number of arithmetic operations. The order in which these operations are carried out is determined by the precedence relations of the language used to describe the calculations. It is

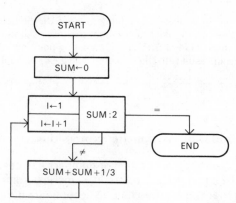

FIGURE 8-5 ■ A simple summation process.

particularly important that we keep these precedence rules in mind when we carry out numerical calculations using a computer, because the associative law does not hold in general for finite-length computer arithmetic. What this means is that the order in which an arithmetic expression is evaluated will have an effect on the result of evaluation. For example, in elementary mathematics, we say that addition and multiplication have the associative property, i.e.,

$$A + (B + C) = (A + B) + C = A + B + C$$

and

$$A * (B * C) = (A * B) * C = A * B * C$$

Because of associativity, we can carry out the sum or product of A, B, and C in each of the two ways, and each will give the same result. When expressions involving addition and multiplication are evaluated on a computer, this associativity property may not be valid. The following example illustrates the nonassociativity of computer arithmetic. For this discussion we limit ourselves to positive numbers.

Suppose we are to evaluate the expression

$$A + B + C$$

with A = 78.9, B = 34.5, and C = 1.9. Let us carry out the evaluation using floating-point notation with a precision of 3 and compare the results when we compute the sum in two different ways.

Method 1

A + B + C is evaluated from left to right as (A + B) + C. The process of evaluation is shown on the following page:

$$
\begin{array}{r}
78.9 \\
+\ \ 34.5 \\
\hline
113.4 \\
+\ \ \ 1.9 \\
\hline
114.9 \\
\end{array}
$$

	stored intermediate value
truncation	$.113E3 = 113$
truncation	$.114E3 = 114$

The computed value for A + B + C is 114.

Method 2

A + B + C is evaluated from right to left as A + (B + C).

B + C:

$$
\begin{array}{r}
34.5 \\
+\ \ 1.9 \\
\hline
36.4 \\
\end{array}
$$

stored intermediate value
$.364E2 = 36.4$

A + (B + C):

$$
\begin{array}{r}
78.9 \\
+\ \ 36.4 \\
\hline
115.3 \\
\end{array}
$$

truncation $.115E3 = 115$

The computed value for A + B + C = 115.

The actual value for A + B + C in exact arithmetic would be 115.3. It can be seen that both computations are in error, but the second method seems to give a better result. The reason for nonassociativity of the addition operation is again the truncation process that occurs as part of the intermediate computation. Furthermore, it can also be seen that adding the two smaller numbers (34.5 and 1.9) first in the second method resulted in better accuracy. This suggests a general way of handling the addition process when a large number of positive numbers must be summed.

There are many situations where it is necessary to add a collection of positive numbers. The minimum summation error may be obtained by operating on the numbers in the order of increasing magnitude. We demon-

n	1/n	Three-digit value
1	$\frac{1}{1}$	1.00
2	$\frac{1}{2}$	0.500
3	$\frac{1}{3}$	0.333
4	$\frac{1}{4}$	0.250
5	$\frac{1}{5}$	0.200
6	$\frac{1}{6}$	0.166
7	$\frac{1}{7}$	0.142
8	$\frac{1}{8}$	0.125
9	$\frac{1}{9}$	0.111
10	$\frac{1}{10}$	0.100
	Total	2.927

strate this idea with an example of evaluating the expression

$$1 + \frac{1}{2} + \frac{1}{3} + \frac{1}{4} + \frac{1}{5} + \frac{1}{6} + \frac{1}{7} + \frac{1}{8} + \frac{1}{9} + \frac{1}{10} = \sum_{n=1}^{10} \frac{1}{n}$$

Let us first evaluate this expression in the order written (decreasing magnitude) again using three-digit floating-point notation. The ten numbers, their represention, and the total are shown on p. 227.

Now let us carry out this same calculation but include truncation of the intermediate results. The results are shown below:

Successive addition		Floating-point representation
1.00 + 0.500 = 1.50		.150E1
1.50 + 0.333 = 1.83	truncation	.183E1
1.83 + 0.250 = 2.08		.208E1
2.08 + 0.200 = 2.28		.228E1
2.28 + 0.166 = 2.44	truncation	.244E1
2.44 + 0.142 = 2.58	truncation	.258E1
2.58 + 0.125 = 2.70	truncation	.270E1
2.70 + 0.111 = 2.81	truncation	.281E1
2.81 + 0.100 = 2.91		.291E1

The computed sum is 2.91, compared with the expected value of 2.927 if no intermediate truncation occurred. The actual error in this case is $2.927 - 2.910 = 0.017$.

Now let us evaluate the sum in the order of increasing magnitude. The intermediate results of this computation process are shown below:

Successive addition		Floating-point representation
0.100 + 0.111 = 0.211		.211E0
0.211 + 0.125 = 0.336		.336E0
0.336 + 0.142 = 0.478		.478E0
0.478 + 0.166 = 0.644		.644E0
0.644 + 0.200 = 0.844		.844E0
0.844 + 0.250 = 1.09	truncation	.109E1
1.09 + 0.333 = 1.42	truncation	.142E1
1.42 + 0.500 = 1.92		.192E1
1.92 + 1.00 = 2.92		.292E1

The computed sum in this case is 2.92. Compared with the exact value 2.927, accurate to three decimal places, the error now is $2.927 - 2.92 = 0.007$, less than one-half of the previous error. The reduction of error in the second case occurred because the addition process has fewer truncations since the smaller numbers are added first (only two truncations, rather than five, were needed in the case of adding numbers of increasing magnitude). For the smallest error, the computer addition of a sequence of positive numbers should be performed in order of increasing magnitude. This will give a better chance for the smaller numbers to accumulate in the final sum.

Grouping Terms to Reduce Errors

There are two general methods that can be used to reduce error in the computer evaluation of arithmetic expressions. The first method can be described as a grouping process. The idea is to group the terms in the expression in such a way that the computed value of the terms in each group would be approximately of similar magnitude. The groups are then operated upon to give the final result. Notice that the effect of this grouping is to make each group of terms felt in the final result, which generally would not be possible if individual terms were to be operated upon. In the problems at the end of this chapter, you will be asked to develop an algorithm that can be implemented to carry out this grouping for adding a sequence of numbers. To illustrate the idea of grouping and to see how it can reduce error in evaluating expressions, let us consider the following example.

The exact value of $\pi/4$ is given by the infinite series:

$$\frac{\pi}{4} = 1 - \frac{1}{3} + \frac{1}{5} - \frac{1}{7} + \frac{1}{9} - \frac{1}{11} \cdots$$

As an approximation, let us evaluate $\pi/4$ by terminating the infinite series at the tenth term and evaluate the expression with three-digit floating-point arithmetic in two ways:

Method 1: Direct calculation.

$$\frac{\pi}{4} \approx 1 - \frac{1}{3} + \frac{1}{5} - \frac{1}{7} + \frac{1}{9} - \frac{1}{11} + \frac{1}{13} - \frac{1}{15} + \frac{1}{17} - \frac{1}{19}$$

Method 2: Grouping

$$\frac{\pi}{4} \approx \left(1 - \frac{1}{3}\right) + \left(\frac{1}{5} - \frac{1}{7}\right) + \left(\frac{1}{9} - \frac{1}{11}\right) + \left(\frac{1}{13} - \frac{1}{15}\right) + \left(\frac{1}{17} - \frac{1}{19}\right)$$

Group 1   Group 2   Group 3   Group 4   Group 5

The computed result from Method 1 can be shown to be

$$\frac{\pi}{4} \approx 1.00 - .333 + .200 - .142 + .111 - .0909$$
$$+ .0769 - .0666 + .0588 - .0526 = .759$$

The approximated value for π is $4(.759) = 3.036$.

For method 2, where grouping of terms is used, the computational process is shown as follows:

Group 1: $1 - \dfrac{1}{3} = 1.00 - .333 = .667$

Group 2: $\dfrac{1}{5} - \dfrac{1}{7} = .200 - .142 = .058$

Group 3: $\dfrac{1}{9} - \dfrac{1}{11} = .111 - .0909 = .0201$

Group 4: $\dfrac{1}{13} - \dfrac{1}{15} = .0769 - .0666 = .0103$

Group 5: $\dfrac{1}{17} - \dfrac{1}{19} = .0588 - .0526 = .0062$

$$\dfrac{\pi}{4} \approx \text{Group 1} + \text{Group 2} + \text{Group 3} + \text{Group 4} + \text{Group 5}$$
$$= .667 + .058 + .0201 + .0103 + .0062$$
$$= .761$$

The approximated value for π in this case is $4(.761) = 3.044$. Examining the above results we see a slight improvement in the grouping method.

Higher Precision to Reduce Errors

The second general method that we can use to reduce the error in evaluating expressions is to carry more significant digits in the precision specification. By carrying more digits in our computation, more accurate results can be achieved at the expense of computation time. This *trade-off is often desirable, because if a sufficient number of digits are carried in the computation, the error accumulated in the computation can be made sufficiently smaller than the errors associated with numbers being operated upon so that the effect of the computational error is negligible.*

Let us illustrate this idea with the example of computing the sum

$$1 + \dfrac{1}{2} + \dfrac{1}{3} + \dfrac{1}{4} + \dfrac{1}{5} + \dfrac{1}{6} + \dfrac{1}{7} + \dfrac{1}{8} + \dfrac{1}{9} + \dfrac{1}{10}$$

by successive additions. Suppose that each number is still represented in decimal floating-point form with a precision of 3, but our computations are carried out and all intermediate results are stored with a precision of 4. The addition process is shown on p. 231.

The actual sum is 2.928, if represented with a precision of four digits. Notice that even though our individual numbers were correct to only three significant digits, our computed sum 2.928 was accurate to four significant digits when we used four-digit precision in the calculation. When we used three-digit precision our result was 2.91 which is only accurate to two significant digits.

Using a precision of 4	Using a precision of 3
$1.00 + .500 = 1.500$	$1.00 + .500 = 1.50$
$1.500 + .333 = 1.833$	$1.50 + .333 = 1.83$
$1.833 + .250 = 2.083$	$1.83 + .250 = 2.08$
$2.083 + .200 = 2.283$	$2.08 + .200 = 2.28$
$2.283 + .166 = 2.449$	$2.28 + .166 = 2.44$
$2.449 + .142 = 2.591$	$2.44 + .142 = 2.58$
$2.591 + .125 = 2.716$	$2.58 + .125 = 2.70$
$2.716 + .111 = 2.828$	$2.70 + .111 = 2.81$
$2.828 + .100 = 2.928$	$2.81 + .100 = 2.91$

This achievement is not an isolated result but rather is close to a general rule for improving the accuracy of computations by carrying more significant digits.

The accuracy of many calculations can be improved if we use a greater precision to store intermediate results in a calculation and only truncate after the final result has been obtained. Many programming languages actually carry out internal calculations with a higher precision than that requested by the programmer. After the calculations are completed the printed results are then truncated to the original precision specifications given in the program.

Catastrophic Subtraction

Of all the basic mathematical operations, subtraction can cause the greatest difficulty in carrying out numerical calculations. Let x_1 and x_2 be the exact value of two numbers and ϵ_1 and ϵ_2 be the errors associated with these numbers. Let the relative errors associated with these two numbers be

$$r_1 = \frac{\epsilon_1}{x_1} \qquad r_2 = \frac{\epsilon_2}{x_2}$$

The relative error associated with the difference $x_1 - x_2$ is

$$r_d = \frac{\epsilon_1 + \epsilon_2}{x_1 - x_2} = \frac{x_1}{x_1 - x_2} r_1 + \frac{x_2}{x_1 - x_2} r_2$$

$$= \frac{x_1 + x_2}{x_1 - x_2} \left(\frac{x_1}{x_1 + x_2} r_1 + \frac{x_2}{x_1 + x_2} r_2 \right)$$

The term within the parentheses represents a value that lies somewhere between r_1 and r_2. The problem arises from the term in front of the bracket. This is always greater than 1. In particular, if x_1 is nearly equal to x_2, the relative error can become extremely large.

As an example of how subtraction may cause trouble, let us try to evaluate

$$f(x) = x^2 - 2.01$$

for $x = \sqrt{2}$. Assume that $\sqrt{2}$ is represented with a precision of three digits. Then

$$\sqrt{2} \approx 1.41$$

The error in the representation of $\sqrt{2}$ is bounded by

$$\epsilon < .01$$

Now the true value

$$f(\sqrt{2}) = 2 - 2.01 = -0.01$$

and the approximate value for $x = 1.41$ is obtained as follows

$$x^2 = (1.41)^2 = 1.98\underline{81} \qquad \text{truncated to } 1.98$$

$$\begin{array}{r} -2.01 \\ 1.98 \\ \hline -0.03 \end{array}$$

The magnitude of the error is .02 which is 200 percent larger than the true value of $f(\sqrt{2})$. The reason, of course, for this large percentage error is that the true value is very small.

As another example let us assume that we wish to compute

$$X - Y + Z$$

where the variables are floating-point numbers with a precision of 7. Let

$$\begin{array}{l} X = 1.176245E16 \\ Y = 1.176231E16 \\ Z = 2.134215E12 \end{array}$$

This desired calculation can be carried out as either $(X - Y) + Z$:

$$\begin{array}{lll} X & 1.176245E16 & \\ -\quad Y & -1.176231E16 & \\ \hline X - Y & .000014E16 & = 1.400000E11 \end{array}$$

$$\begin{array}{lll} X - Y & 1.400000E11 \\ +\quad Z & 21.34215\ E11 \\ \hline & 22.74215\ E11 \\ \text{Answer} & 2.274215E12 \end{array}$$

or as $X + (-Y + Z)$:

$$\begin{array}{lll} -Y & -1.176231E16 & \\ +Z & .0002134215E16 & \\ \hline -Y + Z & -1.176018E16 & \text{truncated} \end{array}$$

$$\begin{array}{lr} X & 1.176245E16 \\ -Y + Z & -1.176018E16 \\ \hline & 0.000227E16 \\ \text{Answer} & 2.270000E12 \end{array}$$

As can be seen these two answers differ by

$$|2.274215 - 2.270000|E12 = 4.215E9$$

This difference corresponds to a very large number, even though it is only approximately 0.2 percent of the value of the answer.

The reason for this large discrepancy is that in the first calculation we form $X - Y$, which turns out to be the difference of two nearly equal numbers which would cause large relative errors. Although the values of X and Y are given with a precision of seven digits, the difference 1.400000E11 really has a precision of only 2 since the five zeros on the right are added to fill out the required number of digits but have no significance.

From the above discussion we see that subtraction of two nearly equal numbers is often the greatest source of inaccuracy in most calculations and can lead to completely meaningless results if the situation occurs in a critical part of the calculation. A programmer must be continually on the alert to avoid problems of this type or at least be aware that such a dangerous situation is possible in a given calculation.

Exercises

1. Compute the following polynomial f(x) for x = 5.31 in two different ways: first from left to right, then from right to left. Compare the two computed values and determine which value is more accurate. Use decimal floating-point arithmetic with a precision of 3 for all computations.

$$f(x) = 15.9 + x + x^2 + x^3$$

2. Compute the following SUM by successive addition in two different ways as in exercise 1. Compare the errors of the two computed values and determine which value is more accurate.

$$\text{SUM} = \frac{1}{2} + \frac{1}{4} + \frac{1}{8} + \frac{1}{16} + \frac{1}{32} + \frac{1}{64} + \frac{1}{128} + \frac{1}{256} + \frac{1}{512} + \frac{1}{1024}$$

$$= \sum_{n=1}^{10} \frac{1}{2^n}$$

3. Let x = 1000, y = 1000.5, and z = 10. Determine the result of the calculation of z/(x − y) using:
(a) Decimal floating-point arithmetic with a precision of 3
(b) Decimal floating-point arithmetic with a precision of 6

4. Let $A = 111113$, $B = -111112$, and $C = 9.50000$. Compute the expression $A + B + C$ in two different orders as indicated by the parentheses in (a) and (b) and compare the results.

(a) $(A + B) + C$ (b) $A + (B + C)$

Use decimal floating-point arithmetic with a precision of 6. Assume that truncation takes place only after each operation is completed.

5. Do exercise 4, but with $A = 113$, $B = -111$, and $C = 7.51$. What happens if a three-digit decimal floating-point arithmetic is used?

6. A statistician wishes to use a computer to carry out the following computation

$$\text{Sigma} = \sqrt{5\left(\sum_{i=1}^{5} x_i^2\right) - \left(\sum_{i=1}^{5} x_i\right)^2}$$

in which $x_1 = 109$, $x_2 = 107$, $x_3 = 105$, $x_4 = 103$, $x_5 = 101$.

(a) He uses three-digit decimal floating-point arithmetic and expects the computer to return a positive value for Sigma. Show that the statistician will be disappointed as the computer will return the value 0 as the computed result for Sigma.

(b) Can you suggest a method of computation so that the statistician could avoid the error? Explain your answer.

5 ▌ Errors in the Evaluation of Functions

In algebra or calculus we define a mathematical function as being a relationship between a set of x-values (associated with the independent variable x) and a set of y-values (associated with the dependent variable y). Symbolically, we describe this mathematical relationship by

$$y = f(x)$$

The function can be displayed by a graph depicting the set of pairs (x,y).

In some cases the function is represented in terms of a mathematical expression such as

$$y = x^2$$

which can easily be evaluated. There are many functions that are represented by infinite series, for example,

$$e^x = 1 + x + \frac{x^2}{2!} + \frac{x^3}{3!} + \cdots \qquad \text{(all real values of x)}$$

$$\sin(x) = x - \frac{x^3}{3!} + \frac{x^5}{5!} - \frac{x^7}{7!} + \cdots \qquad \text{(all real values of x)}$$

$$\log(1+x) = x - \frac{1}{2}x^2 + \frac{1}{3}x^3 - \cdots \qquad (-1 < x < 1)$$

$$\frac{1}{1 \pm x} = 1 \mp x + x^2 \mp x^3 + x^4 \mp \cdots \qquad (x^2 < 1)$$

The above polynomial representations for some of the common functions are those that are usually encountered in introductory calculus courses. There are other possible polynomials that give better representations for these functions in some situations. Since these more advanced representations introduce the same problems that occur when we use the above formulas, we will use the more commonly known infinite-series forms for the rest of the discussion in this Chapter.

Approximation of Polynomials by Series Truncation

Whenever the function of interest, $f(x)$, is represented by an infinite series, we must find an approximate polynomial with a finite number of terms that will give us a good approximation for $f(x)$ over a specified interval of x. This approximation process is commonly achieved by truncating the infinite series into a finite one. The truncation process of course results in error, and our objective is to include a sufficient number of terms in the truncated series in order to minimize that error. In the study of numerical analysis, it has been found that for any function that can be represented as an infinite series, there is always a polynomial with a finite number of terms that will approximate the function to any desired accuracy provided that a sufficiently high degree of polynomial is allowed. We shall only give an example here to show, by way of illustration, the behavior of approximation errors resulting from the truncation process in computing mathematical functions on a computer.

To compute the function $\sin(x)$, the following approximate polynomials can be used:

$$P_1(x) = x$$

$$P_2(x) = x - \frac{x^3}{3!}$$

$$P_3(x) = x - \frac{x^3}{3!} + \frac{x^5}{5!}$$

$$P_4(x) = x - \frac{x^3}{3!} + \frac{x^5}{5!} - \frac{x^7}{7!}$$

$P_1(x)$ is called a linear approximation for $\sin(x)$ between the two points x_1 and x_2; $P_2(x)$ is the cubic approximation (polynomial of degree three); and so on. Suppose we are interested in the values of $\sin(x)$ between $x_1 = 0.5$ and $x_2 = 2.5$. Consider the value of $\sin(x)$ at $x = 1$. The exact value for $\sin(1)$, accurate to three decimal places is known to be .841. The computed values from the approximate polynomials and their corresponding absolute errors are shown on the following page:

$$P_1(1) = 1.00 \qquad\qquad \text{absolute error} = 0.159$$

$$P_2(1) = 1 - \frac{1}{6} = 0.834 \qquad\qquad \text{absolute error} = 0.007$$

$$P_3(1) = 1 - \frac{1}{6} + \frac{1}{120} = 0.842 \qquad\qquad \text{absolute error} = 0.001$$

$$P_4(1) = 1 - \frac{1}{6} + \frac{1}{120} - \frac{1}{5040} = 0.841 \qquad \text{absolute error} = 0$$

All computations have been done using floating-point numbers with a precision of 3. It should be apparent that as more terms are included in the approximation polynomial, the difference between the exact value (accurate to a specified precision) and the computed value becomes smaller. For $P_4(x)$ in our example, this difference has been reduced to zero. This means that if we require that our computation of sin(1) be accurate to three decimal places, it is only necessary to use four terms in the series of sin(x).

Now consider the case where $x = 2$. The exact value of sin(2) is known to be .909, again expressed with a precision of 3. The computed values from the four approximations and their corresponding absolute errors are shown below:

$$P_1(2) = 2 \qquad\qquad \text{absolute error} = 1.091$$

$$P_2(2) = 2 - \frac{2^3}{6} = 0.670 \qquad\qquad \text{absolute error} = 0.239$$

$$P_3(2) = 2 - \frac{2^3}{6} + \frac{2^5}{120} = 0.936 \qquad\qquad \text{absolute error} = 0.027$$

$$P_4(2) = 2 - \frac{2^3}{6} + \frac{2^5}{120} - \frac{2^7}{5040} = 0.910 \qquad \text{absolute error} = 0.001$$

Examining the error behavior in this example, we can discover that the way error decreases as more terms are included in the approximation depends on the value of x under consideration. For $x = 2$ in our example, the error in $P_4(x)$ is 0.001 instead of 0 as was in the case of $x = 1$. It is clear that for $x = 2$ we need to include more terms in the approximate polynomial in order to achieve the same error size as in the case for $x = 1$. This error behavior is not an isolated situation but rather is close to the general rule in computing mathematical functions with approximations. Therefore, in developing algorithms for computing such functions, it is very important to realize the error behavior inherent in the approximation process associated with each problem and to handle it properly.

Exercise

1. The cosine function cos x can be expressed in terms of the following polynomial

$$\cos(x) = 1 - \frac{x^2}{2!} + \frac{x^4}{4!} - \frac{x^6}{6!} + \cdots \qquad \text{(all real values of x)}$$

(a) Determine the number of terms that is necessary in the approximate polynomial P(x) in order that the computed value for cos x when $x = 1$ be accurate to three decimal places. Use floating-point numbers with a precision of 3.

(b) Repeat part (a) with $x = 2$.

6 ∎ Summary

This chapter has been concerned with identifying the principle sources of computational error that can be introduced into a numerical calculation because of the way numerical values are stored and processed in a digital computer. Our presentation has purposely exaggerated the errors and their effect on computed results. In a normal situation, calculations will be carried out with greater precision. Consequently, there are many calculations that may be performed where the resulting errors are so small that they will be unimportant. There are, however, many situations where errors will still introduce an important limitation upon the accuracy of computed results.

The discussion in this chapter should be considered as introductory in nature. It is intended to serve as a warning that just because a number is computed on a computer there is no guarantee that it is correct. Once we realize the fact that errors can occur, we can plan our programs in such a way that these errors will be eliminated if possible, or at least minimized. A much more comprehensive discussion of sources of errors in different types of calculations can be found in books dealing with numerical analysis.

References

A very extensive discussion of computational errors can be found in [1], [3], [4], and [5]. The use of series methods to approximate functions is treated in [2], [3], and [6]. [2] gives other formulas which may be used to approximate a number of functions. In many cases these formulas are easier to use than a truncated series approximation.

1. Hamming, R. W. (1973) *Numerical Methods for Scientists and Engineers, 2nd ed.,* McGraw-Hill, New York.
2. Hastings, C., Jr. (1955) *Approximations for Digital Computers,* Princeton University Press, Princeton, N.J.
3. Knuth, D. E. (1969) *The Art of Computer Programming, Vol. 2, Seminumerical Algorithms,* Addison-Wesley, Reading, Mass.
4. McCracken, D., and Dorn, W. (1964) *Numerical Methods and FORTRAN Programming,* John Wiley & Sons, New York.
5. Pennington, R. E. (1970) *Introductory Computer Methods and Numerical Analysis,* 2nd ed. MacMillan, New York.
6. Ralston, A. (1965) *A First Course in Numerical Analysis,* McGraw-Hill, New York.

Home Problems

If possible, the algorithms developed to solve the following problems should be programmed and tested on a computer.

1. For the programming language or languages being used, determine how the precision attribute for identifiers representating numerical values are defined. How much control does the programmer have over the selection of the precision attributes?

The following comments refer to problems 2, 3, and 4: In most programming languages the range of values which may be assigned to integer identifiers is much smaller than the range of values which may be assigned to floating-point identifiers. In some special types of calculations the truncation errors associated with floating-point arithmetic cannot be tolerated. Integer addition, multiplication, and subtraction generate exact values as long as the result of a computation does not exceed the allowable range.

2. Develop a flowchart of a special algorithm that can be used to add any two integers irrespective of their value. Provision must be made to use two or more identifiers to represent integers which exceed the range of integers that can be assigned to a single identifier.

3. Develop a flowchart of a special algorithm which can be used to subtract any two integers irrespective of their value.

4. Develop a flowchart of a special algorithm which can be used to multiply any two integers irrespective of their value.

5. Develop a flowchart of an algorithm that will add a sequence of 10,000 numbers by the grouping method described in this chapter to reduce errors. Numbers are first added up in groups of ten. These groups of ten are then summed to form groups of 100. This process is continued until the total of 10,000 numbers has been formed.

6. Hastings (reference [2]) gives the following approximate formula for $\sin[(\pi/2)x]$:

$$\sin[(\pi/2)x] = ax + bx^3 + cx^5$$

where $a = 1.5706268$, $b = -.6432292$, $c = 0.0727102$, and $-1 \leqslant x \leqslant 1$.

(a) Compute a table of $\sin[(\pi/2)x]$ for steps of .05 using the above formula, the $\sin[(\pi/2)x]$ function in the local programming language, and the infinite-series approximation for $\sin[(\pi/2)x]$ given in Chapter 5, Section II. The table entries should have a precision of 12.

(b) Compare the results of the above calculations.

7. In many scientific studies the solution to a problem is often expressed by using an infinite series of the form

$$f(x) = \sum_{n=0}^{\infty} g(n,x)$$

where $g(n,x)$ is a given function. To evaluate $f(x)$ on a computer we must truncate the series to a form such as

$$f(x) = \sum_{n=0}^{N\max} g(n,x)$$

This, of course, introduces errors. In addition, the computation of $g(n,x)$ introduces additional error.

Assume $g(n,x) = (-1)^n x^n$

Define

$$f(x) = \sum_{n=0}^{\infty} (-1)^n x^n \qquad 0 \leq x \leq 1$$

Note that the true value of $f(x)$ is given by

$$f(x) = \frac{1}{1+x}$$

Study how the value of

$$f'(x) = \sum_{n=0}^{N\max} (-1)^n x^n$$

approach the true value of $f(x)$ as N_{max} increases and as the precision of computation increases.

8. In most computer languages there is a way for the programmer to control the precision of the numbers used in a calculation. Truncation errors may be reduced or eliminated by using a higher precision. The price we pay for the increased precision, and hence reduced error, is the increase of memory space to store the numbers with higher precision and the increase of computer time required to carry out operations on these numbers. For the local computer language you are to discuss the trade off between these factors—precision, storage, and execution time—affecting the design of an algorithm involving a large number of numerical calculations.

searching and sorting

1 ∎ Introduction

One of the major characteristics of a computer is that it can tirelessly carry out routine, repetitive tasks without error. This ability provides a very powerful tool to a large number of computer users who are faced with the problem of manipulating data rather than of making extensive and involved calculations. In fact, the largest single application of computers is not the carrying out of numerical calculations, but the carrying out of business data-processing tasks such as maintaining inventory records, preparing payrolls, keeping subscription records, or making up mailing lists.

But these business data-processing tasks are not the only ones which require the manipulation of data. There are many instances in scientific research where it is necessary first to collect an extensive amount of factual data and then to process it to prove or disprove a given hypothesis. A considerable amount of the required data processing involves tedious tasks such as sorting data into classes, searching for the occurrence of particular data patterns, or establishing cause–effect relationships between a change in one experimental parameter and an observed change in a second observed parameter. Before computers, a large portion of many research programs consisted of doing these data-processing tasks by hand or with mechanical processing aids. Computers can now do in seconds what used to require days, weeks, or even months to do by hand. The computer has not only speeded up the data-analysis process, it has made it possible to carry out scientific investigations that would be impossible to do with noncomputerized techniques.

The programs needed to carry out the standard data-processing tasks are quite simple and straightforward. In this chapter we investigate some of the standard techniques that can be used to sort data or search for patterns in collections of data. The data itself may come in a number of different forms since the algorithms do not depend upon any other property than that of being able to compare two data items and determine if the two items are equivalent or if one item comes before or after the other item according to some ordering principle.

The techniques discussed in this chapter, and the more advanced data-processing techniques presented in the references, have such widespread applicability that several standard subroutine packages and special programming languages have been developed to carry out these tasks. Thus, before one attempts to develop a program to handle a given data-processing problem, it is often advantageous to check the program library at the local computer center to see if a standard program is already available to carry out the desired task.

2 ∎ Sorting of Data

Data comes in many forms. For our purpose, assume that we are given a collection of data made up of items using the methods of Chapter IV. Each item is represented by a record with one or more information fields. The records are collected in a file which contains all the data making up the information base upon which our processing tasks are to be performed. The organization and manipulation of a large number of data items in a file is the primary concern of this Chapter.

There are two basic tasks that are of fundamental importance to almost all data-processing work. The first deals with the question of how to put the data items in a data file in order. This is the task of *sorting*. The second task concerns the problem of looking up, or searching, for a particular data item or other information in the data file. This is the problem of *searching*. Both of these tasks are so frequently performed in various types of information-processing applications that a number of sorting and search algorithms have been developed, and many, when properly used, can result in savings of computer time and other computing resources.

File Structures

Each data item in a data set is assumed to be represented by a record with K fields. Each field may contain either numeric or character information. The organization of each record depends upon the particular problem being considered and has no influence upon the data-processing algorithms to be considered.

A file is assumed to be formed as an ordered collection of N records. Although a file may be retained in memory while it is being processed, we often find that the data set is so large that it must be stored on some auxiliary device such as a magnetic tape unit. In that case, we usually wish to process the file without loading the whole file into the computer's main memory. When working with a file, there is usually a particular field in each record on which a processing task is to be performed. This field is called the *key* of the record. For example, each record might correspond to the information associated with an individual magazine subscription. The key field in this case might be the field used to store the subscriber's name.

To carry out a given processing task on a file, it is not necessary to manipulate the complete file or even to have the file in the computer's main memory. We can instead form a *key file*.† This file is stored in main memory and is used for most of the steps of a given data-processing operation. Each record in the key file consists of two fields. The first field contains the key and the second field contains the record number of the record associated with the

---

† If a file is made up of records with only a single field, there is no need to use a key file. We can, instead, think of the file as a simple one-dimensional array.

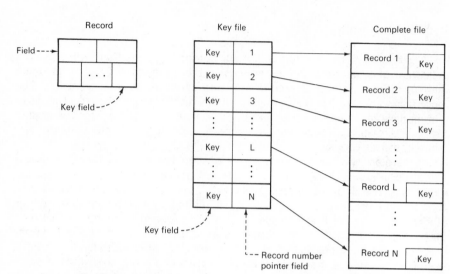

FIGURE 9-1 ▪ Illustration of the organization of a data set into files.

key. This field thus serves as a pointer to the complete record in the complete file. The relationship between records, files, keys, and key files is illustrated in Fig. 9-1.

Both the complete file and the key file may be stored in a number of different ways. Those files that are actually placed in the computer's main memory will usually be represented by either some type of array structure or, as will be discussed in the next chapter, a linked list. In order to avoid unnecessary complications in discussing the algorithms used to carry out the tasks to be discussed, we make the following simplifying assumptions. All the processing algorithms discussed operate on key files and each key file is stored in two one-dimensional arrays. The keys for each record in the complete file are

Key file address I	Key array A_I	Record number array RN_I
1	78	1
2	92	2
3	65	3
4	88	4
5	45	5
6	96	6
7	80	7
8	75	8
9	58	9
10	85	10

FIGURE 9-2 ▪ An illustration of a key file.

TABLE 9-1 ■ A file of student records

Record number	Student name	Student number	Semester standing	Examination score
1	ALAN, A.	028 362 808	4	78
2	BAYLOR, M.	041 425 766	4	92
3	COOPER, G.	078 280 108	5	65
4	FINCH, B.	047 465 261	6	88
5	IVES, K.	012 484 783	5	45
6	MORRIS, R.	213 448 950	4	96
7	NELSON, H.	043 422 544	4	80
8	SMITH, F.	015 560 480	5	75
9	TEED, S.	143 321 766	4	58
10	WALTER, D.	071 406 659	4	85

stored in a one-dimensional array, $[A_I]$, $I = 1, 2, \ldots, N$. The record-number pointer associated with each key is stored in a one-dimensional array, $[RN_I]$, $I = 1, 2, \ldots, N$. The value of I associated with a given element of either array is called the address of the item in the array.

To illustrate these ideas, assume that we are given the file of Table 9-1. Assume that we wish to process this file in terms of examination scores. The key in each record would thus be the examination score. Using this key, we can generate the key file as shown in Fig. 9-2.

Sorting

Sorting is the process of arranging data records into a sequential order according to some predetermined criterion. Records are sorted by identifying a particular field in the record, namely the key. Depending on the characteristics of the key, records may be sorted either numerically or alphabetically. In numerical sorting, we arrange the records in ascending (or descending) order according to the numeric value contained in the key. An example of this would be the sorting of the student records (Table 9-1) according to their examination scores.

We may also sort alphabetically when the key is a character sequence. As discussed in Chapter III, a dictionary ordering is established according to the collating sequence associated with the particular character set being used. For our discussion, we use the collating sequence

$$\sqcup < A < \cdots < Y < Z < 0 < 1 < \cdots < 8 < 9$$

which is the same as that presented in Chapter III.

For convenience, it is assumed in the following discussion that the key upon which the sorting is performed is numeric. This is not a restrictive as-

Key file address I	Key A_I	Record number RN_I
1	78	1
2	92	2
3	65	3
4	88	4
5	45	5
6	96	6
7	80	7
8	75	8
9	58	9
10	85	10

(a)

Key file address I	Key A_I	Record number RN_I
1	96	6
2	92	2
3	88	4
4	85	10
5	80	7
6	78	1
7	75	8
8	65	3
9	58	9
10	45	5

(b)

FIGURE 9-3 ■ Use of pointers in sorting a key file. (a) Key file before sorting. (b) Key file after sorting.

sumption because all the sorting algorithms to be discussed apply equally well to alphanumeric data if we use the ordering convention just discussed.

Most sorting algorithms involve moving the data elements to be sorted from one place to another in the file. By using the idea of a key, we can carry out the sorting merely by moving the key and the corresponding pointer element in the key file. After the sorting algorithm has completed the sorting task, the key file can be used to transfer the records of the complete file into the proper order. This approach provides a major saving of computer time since a large number of unnecessary information transfers are eliminated.

As an illustration, let us assume that we wish to sort the student record file given in Table 9-1 according to grades. The key file for this sorting task is given in Fig. 9-3(a).

Before the sorting begins, the ten keys and their corresponding record-number pointers are stored in the key file in the order in which the records are stored in the main file. After sorting, the key file takes the form shown in Fig. 9-3(b). Since the record-number pointers were moved along with the keys, they indicate the original position of each record in the main file. This information can then be used to move the records in the main file into the proper ordering as indicated by the sorted key file. Before proceeding, we summarize the assumptions we make about the sorting algorithms to be described:

1. The keys to be sorted are stored in a one-dimensional array $[A_I]$.
2. The record-number pointers are stored in a one-dimensional array $[RN_I]$.
3. The keys are numeric. (The same general techniques can be used for nonnumeric keys.)
4. Only the keys and pointers are manipulated during the sorting process.
5. The keys are to be sorted in ascending or increasing order. (The same general techniques can be used to sort the keys in decreasing order.)

For each sorting algorithm we will pay special attention to how well it performs the sort in terms of the computer resources necessary to accomplish this task. This includes such performance measures as the storage requirements, the number of data comparisons, and the number of data movements needed to perform the sorting task. Performance measures of this kind enable us to estimate the cost of a particular sorting method and compare the relative merits of the different sorting algorithms.

Selection Sort

One of the simplest sorting algorithms is the selection sort. By the above assumptions, the N key elements are stored in a one-dimensional array, $[A_I]$, $I = 1, 2, \ldots, N$, and that the N record-number pointers are in the one-dimensional array, $[RN_I]$, $I = 1, 2, \ldots, N$. Beginning with the first element A_1, the array A is searched for the smallest data element. When the smallest element is selected, it and its pointer are interchanged with the first key and pointer elements of the array. This interchange places the smallest element in the first position of the entire array. The search process for the smallest key element is now repeated for the array, beginning this time with the second key elements A_2 (since A_1 already contains the smallest element). This element is now interchanged with the second data element A_2 and the result of this interchange places the second smallest element of the entire array in its proper location. The next search for the smallest element begins with the third data element A_3, which is interchanged with the smallest element found in this search. This process of searching for the smallest element and making interchanges continues until all the elements in the array are placed in their proper location (i.e., in ascending order).

I	A₁	Step number for the sort process								Sorted array
	Unsorted array	1	2	3	4	5	6	7	8	9
1	4	1	1	1	1	1	1	1	1	1
2	2	②	2	2	2	2	2	2	2	2
3	7	7	7	3	3	3	3	3	3	3
4	①	4	4	④	4	4	4	4	4	4
5	6	6	6	6	6	5	5	5	5	5
6	5	5	5	5	⑤	⑥	6	6	6	6
7	8	8	8	8	8	8	8	7	7	7
8	3	3	③	7	7	7	⑦	⑧	8	8
9	10	10	10	10	10	10	10	10	10	9
10	9	9	9	9	9	9	9	9	⑨	10

FIGURE 9-4 ■ Sorting of ten data elements using selection method; =, data elements sorted above this point; ○, smallest element selected; ⟩, interchange performed on the two elements pointed at.

An example of the selection sort process is shown in Fig. 9-4. For simplicity, the movement of the pointers is not indicated. From this example, we see that the number of search steps required to sort the entire array is equal to $N - 1$. This is because each search step places one element into its proper location. When the first $N - 1$ elements have been put in their proper position, the Nth element (the data element 10 in the example) must be the largest element and therefore is automatically in its proper location.

It is also of interest to determine how many data comparisons and data interchanges are required to complete the sort. Upon examining the example, we see that in the first step of the search for the smallest element a series of $N - 1$ data elements must be looked at and compared. For the second step of the search, only $N - 2$ data elements must be compared. In general, for the ith step of the search, $i = 1, 2, \ldots, N - 1$, a series of $N - i$ comparisons are required. The total number of comparisons is therefore the sum

$$(N - 1) + (N - 2) + \cdots + 2 + 1 = \sum_{i=1}^{N-1} (N - i) = \frac{1}{2} N(N - 1)$$

Thus, in the example shown in Fig. 9-4, the total number of comparisons needed to sort the ten elements is $(10 \times 9)/2 = 45$.

The number of data interchanges depends upon how badly out of order the data elements are. Since, during each step of the search, at most one interchange is needed, the maximum number of interchanges for this sort algorithm is $N - 1$.

A flowchart for the selection sort algorithm is given in Fig. 9-5. Examining this flowchart, we conclude that 2N memory locations are needed to store the key file to be sorted and the only additional storage required is the two temporary locations, TEMPA and TEMPP, that are used to carry out the interchange operation.

For small arrays, selection sorting is easy to carry out and not particularly time consuming. However, assume that $N = 1000$ or $N = 10,000$, which are typical of some large data-processing applications. For this case, we would need

$$\frac{1000 \times 999}{2} = 499,500 \qquad \text{or} \qquad \frac{10,000 \times 9,999}{2} = 4,995,000$$

comparisons, respectively. For large files this is thus a very inefficient sorting method.

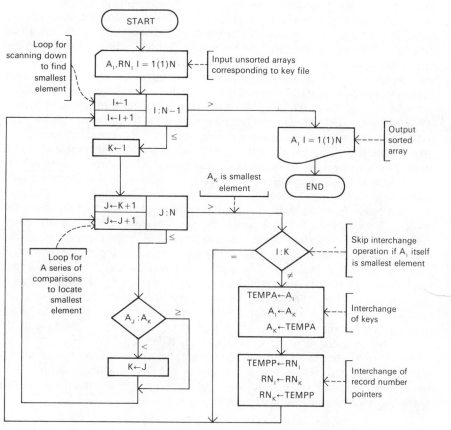

FIGURE 9-5 ■ A flowchart for the selection sort algorithm.

Bubble Sort

Another well-known comparative sort algorithm is the bubble sort. It differs from the selection sort in that, instead of finding the smallest element for interchange purposes, an exchange takes place as soon as the comparison of two data elements reveals that they are in reverse order. This sort algorithm has been found very easy to remember and simple to program. It is very fast for small numbers of data elements (say 15 or less) and therefore can be used efficiently for sorting small data files or in conjunction with other sorting methods (such as the partition sort to be described later).

To describe the sorting algorithm, it is again assumed that the N key elements are stored in an array A and the N record-number pointers are in an array RN. The first two elements A_1 and A_2 in the array are compared. If the second element is smaller than the first (i.e., A_1 and A_2 are in reverse order), then the two elements and the corresponding pointers are exchanged. Otherwise, no exchange is made. The second and third elements are then compared and an exchange of these two elements is made if the third element is found to be smaller than the second. If the interchange takes place, the third element is in the second position. This element is compared to the element in the first position. If the element now in the second position is smaller than the element in the first position, an exchange is made. Otherwise, the sorting process continues by comparing the element in the fourth position with that in the third.

As we work down the array, we encounter elements that are out of order. When we reach such an element, we then work it up to its proper place in the list by interchanging it with the preceding element until it reaches the proper array position. This action is similar to the behavior of an air bubble in water. Thus, this process is referred to as "bubbling up." The sorting process continues with this exchange and bubbling-up process until the entire array is sorted.

An example of the bubble sort process applied to a set of ten data elements is shown in Fig. 9-6. For simplicity, the movements of the pointers are not indicated. From this figure, we see that it is only necessary for the algorithm to scan through the data array once from the top to the bottom in order to complete the sort. The number of comparisons and exchanges required to sort N data elements depends on how badly out of order these N elements are before the sorting process begins. If the data elements are already in order, only $N - 1$ comparisons are required but no exchange is required. The maximum number of exchanges occurs when the data elements are in reverse order in which case a total of $N(N - 1)/2$ exchanges must be made. (This number is the binomial coefficient which gives the number of distinct pairs that can be formed out of N elements.) On the average, therefore, if we assume that the set of data elements is originally arranged in random order, the average number of exchanges expected is

$$\frac{0 + N(N - 1)/2}{2} = \frac{N(N - 1)}{4}$$

Unsorted array		Step number																			Sorted Array
I	A_I	1	2	3	4	5	6	7	8	9	10	11	12	13	14	15	16	17	18	19	20
1	4	✓4	2	2	2	✓2	1	1	1	1	1	1	1	1	1	1	1	1	1	1	1
3	2	✓2=	✓4	4	✓4	✓1	2	2	2	2	2	2	2	2	2	2	2	✓2	2	2	2
3	7		✓7=	✓7	✓1	4	4	✓4	4	4	✓4	4	4	4	4	4	✓4	✓3	3	3	3
4	1			✓1=	7=	7=	✓7	✓6	6	✓6	✓5	5	5	5	5	✓5	✓3	4	4	4	4
5	6						✓6	7=	✓7	✓5	6	6	6	6	✓6	✓3	5	5	5	5	5
6	5								✓5=	7=	7=	✓7	7	✓7	✓3	6	6	6	6	6	6
7	8											✓8=	✓8	✓3	7	7	7	7	7	7	7
8	3												✓3=	8=	8=	8=	8=	8=	✓8	8	8
9	10																		✓10=	✓10	9
10	9																			✓9=	10=

FIGURE 9-6 ■ Step-by-step bubble sort of ten data elements; =, data elements scanned above this point; ✓, indicate the two elements being compared; ⤸, point to the two elements being exchanged, ----→, data element being bubbled up.

In the above example, the number of exchanges is found to be 13, compared to the expected average value $N(N-1)/4 = (10 \times 9)/4 = 22.5$.

There will be at most $N-1$ more comparisons than exchanges. This is because we must make $N-1$ comparisons even if the original data elements are in order. Since the average number of exchanges is proportional to N^2, as shown above, we expect the same behavior for the average number of comparisons.

A flowchart for the bubble sort algorithm is shown in Fig. 9-7. From this flowchart, we see again that the only additional storage required to sort the N data elements is the two temporary locations, TEMPA and TEMPP, used to carry out the exchange operation.

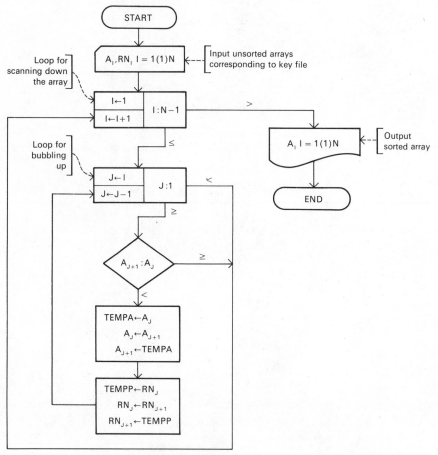

FIGURE 9-7 ■ A flowchart for the bubble sort algorithm.

There are a number of possible variations of the bubble sort algorithm. One variation is that the exchange of data elements during the bubbling up process is delayed until the last. This is accomplished by first picking up the position of the element to be bubbled and the resulting position is propagated toward the top of the array as far as possible by moving the series of elements above that position one position down. The element to be bubbled is then placed back on the top of the series of elements that have just been moved down as the final step of the bubble-up operation. This variation eliminates the need for the series of exchanges of data elements and consequently will result in a slightly faster program. A simple modification of the flowchart given in Fig. 9-7 can be made to implement this variation. This modification is left as an exercise.

In another popular variation of the bubble sort algorithm, several passes of the array are made. On each pass, the first element of the array is compared with the second and an exchange is made to place the smaller of the two in the first position. The second element of the array is then compared with the third element and the smaller is placed in the second position. This comparison and exchange process continues throughout the array until the last element has been compared. This completes the first pass. The array is then processed in this manner until no exchanges are required in a pass through the array. The data elements are then sorted. It is not difficult to see that in this variation of the bubble sort, the first pass puts the largest element of the entire array in position N. On second pass, the next largest element is placed in position $N - 1$, and so on.

Partition Sort

The partition sort, also known as the quicksort, is also a comparative, interchange sort that determines data movement by a series of comparisons and exchanges of elements within the file. In addition to being a comparative, interchange sort, however, partition sort is a typical example of what is known as a *distributive sort*. The major function of a distributive sort consists of rearranging the data elements so that they are partitioned into two or more disjoint subsets of elements. These subsets are then further partitioned into smaller subsets and this partition process continues until the file is divided into subsets, all consisting of only a single element, arranged in the specified order.

In order to see how the partition process is repeatedly used in the sort algorithm, let us assume that a set of unsorted elements is stored in a subarray $[A_I]$, $I = M, M + 1, \ldots, N$.[†] of the array A. The first partition starts by taking an arbitrary element, say A_F, from the subarray $[A_I]$ as an estimate of the

---

† We omit the array RN corresponding to the record-number pointers from the discussion for simplicity. It should be remembered that every time an interchange takes place, the pointer as well as the key elements must be changed.

median value of the $N - M + 1$ data elements.[†] Next, the entire subarray is rearranged in such a way that two integers I and J satisfying

$$M \leqslant J < I \leqslant N$$

are selected. Then the entire subarray is arranged into three subsets with the following properties:

$$\text{Subset } 1 = \{\text{All } A_K \text{ such that } A_K \leqslant A_F \text{ for } M \leqslant K \leqslant J\}$$
$$\text{Subset } 2 = \{\text{All } A_K \text{ such that } A_K = A_F \text{ for } J < K < I\}$$
$$\text{Subset } 3 = \{\text{All } A_K \text{ such that } A_K \geqslant A_F \text{ for } I \leqslant K \leqslant N\}$$

That is, the subarray $[A_I]$ is now divided into two or three subsets, each of which is smaller than the original subarray. Subset 1 contains all the elements that are less than or equal to the estimated median A_F, and Subset 3 contains all the elements greater than or equal to A_F. All the elements in Subset 2, when it exists, are equal to A_F.

The above partition process can be accomplished by carrying out a scanning procedure to be followed by a series of data comparisons and exchanges. Starting at the top (first element, A_M) of the subarray, the procedure scans down until an element greater than A_F is found. Let this element be denoted by A_I. Then starting at the bottom (last element, A_N) of the subarray, the procedure scans up until an element less than A_F is found. Let this element be denoted by A_J. These two elements A_I and A_J are then exchanged. Continuing this scanning procedure, up and then down, the second element greater than A_F and the second element less than A_F are found and exchanged. This process continues until the scan coming down from the top meets the scan coming up from the bottom and at this point the partition process knows that all the elements less than A_F have been placed above all the elements greater than A_F. The final step of the partition process is to place the element A_F in its proper position by exchanging A_F with the last element A_I (or A_J depending upon the position of A_F) at which the scan terminated. A complete flowchart showing the partition process in the form of a subroutine is given in Fig. 9-8.

Examining this flowchart, we see that the partition subroutine divides the input subarray $[A_I]$, $I = M, \ldots, N$, into three subsets. One of the subsets contains elements which have the same value as A_F. The other two subsets (Subset 1 and Subset 3) must be further sorted in turn. This is achieved by considering each one of the two subsets as a new file and calling the partition subroutine to perform the partition on the new file. This subroutine can be called upon by a main procedure as many times as needed until finally only subsets of one element remain and the elements in the original array are sorted.

An example of the partition process is shown in Fig. 9-9. In this example,

---

† This could be a very poor estimate and the sort algorithm can be improved by making better estimates for the median. The discussion of the estimation procedures can be found in the references listed at the end of this chapter.

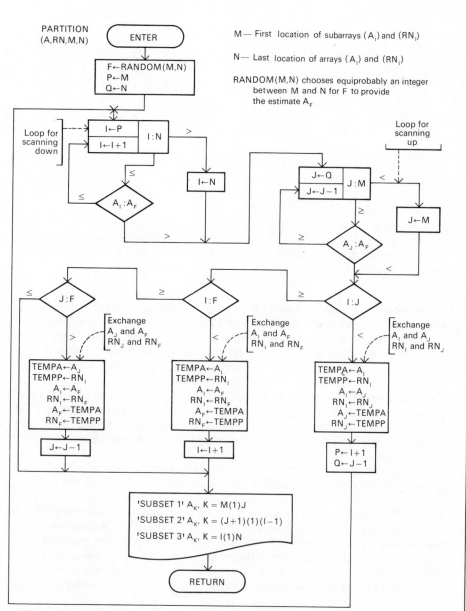

FIGURE 9-8 ■ A subroutine flowchart for the partition sort algorithm.

Unsorted Array						Step number									
I	A_I	1	2	3	4	5	6	7	8	9	10	11	12		
M←1	4	④	④	④	④	④	④	④	④	④	④	④		1	M
2	2	2	2	2	2	2	2	2	2	2	2	2		2	
3	7	7	7	7	7	7	3	3	3	3	3	3		3	J
4	1	1	1	1	1	1	1	1	1	1	1	1		4	
5	6	6	6	6	6	6	6	6	6	6	6	6		6	I
6	5	5	5	5	5	5	5	5	5	5	5	5		5	
7	8	8	8	8	8	8	8	8	8	8	8	8		8	
8	3	3	3	3	3	3	7	7	7	7	7	7		7	
9	10	10	10	10	10	10	10	10	10	10	10	10		10	
N←10	9	9	9	9	9	9	9	9	9	9	9	9		9	N

FIGURE 9-9 ■ Steps of the first partition of ten data elements; subset $1 = \{A_K, 1 \leq K \leq 3\}$; subset $2 = \{A_K, 3 < K < 5\}$; subset $3 = \{A_K, 5 \leq K \leq 10\}$; ○, A_F;), data elements to be exchanged; ✔, data elements being compared; □, subset of elements after partition.

the estimate A_F of the median is taken to be the first element (top element) in the array. As shown in the figure, the first partition divides the array into three subsets: Subset 1 contains all the elements smaller than $A_F = 4$, Subset 2 contains the element A_F, and Subset 3 contains all the elements greater than 4. Subset 1 and Subset 3 must be further sorted using the same partition process. Since a computer can only sort one of the two subsets at a time, it must remember where the second one is while it is sorting the first. A subset of data elements can be remembered by placing the locations of the first and last elements in temporary storage to be passed on as parameters M and N in the subroutine PARTITION. Because of the need for bookkeeping, a small amount of additional computer storage is required.

The number of data comparisons and movements for the partition sort depends on the original unsorted data. It has been found that, on the average, $2M\log_2(N)$ comparisons are required. Since the average number of comparisons for the bubble set is proportional to N^2, one would expect the partition sort to be faster than the bubble sort when the number of data elements in the file is relatively large. When the number is small, however, the bubble sort is expected to be faster than the partition sort. This relationship suggests that, when sorting a large file, one may gain speed by switching to a bubble sort whenever partition sort has sorted the large file down to small subsets of data elements.

One of the potential advantages of the partition sort algorithm is that the subsets of data elements generated in each iteration may be best suited for sorting large files on a computer that is capable of performing several computational tasks in parallel. The term "parallel computation" refers to the situation where more than one computational task can be carried out independently of other tasks. Some of the larger currently available computers are designed to carry out parallel computations. The increasing availability of such computers will mean that the possibility of parallel processing will soon become an important consideration in the development of all problem-solving methods.

Exercises

1. Using the bubble sort algorithm discussed in this section, sort the following array of data elements in ascending order:

I	A_I
1	9
2	6
3	3
4	5
5	10
6	2
7	7
8	4

(a) Show the detailed steps of the sort process.
(b) Determine the number of data comparisons and exchanges required to complete the sort.

2. Modify the bubble sort flowchart shown in Fig. 9-7 so that the bubble-up process delays the series of exchanges until the last step (See p. 253). Do exercise 1 using this modified algorithm.

3. Show the detailed steps of partition sort performed on the data elements given in exercise 1. Use the bottom element in the subarray (or the subsets) as the estimate of the median for each partition. Determine the number of data comparisons and exchanges.

3 ■ Search Techniques

Searching for some information in a file is another of the most frequently performed tasks in information-processing applications. These applications include such tasks as searching for a part number in an inventory file, searching for the flight number in an airline reservation system, or in computer-science applications involved with the compilation and interpretation of programs. There are many techniques that may be used in searching a file. In this discussion we concentrate upon some of the simplest techniques and their related problems. More elaborate discussions on various search techniques aiming at specific tasks may be found in advanced texts or the references listed at the end of this chapter.

To simplify our present discussion, it will be assumed that the record key along with the record-number pointer are stored in arrays in which all key positions are equally available to the programmer. Furthermore, the file to be searched will be assumed fixed during the entire search process; that is, it will not be altered, or updated (records to be deleted, added, or otherwise revised) dynamically. In a general situation, we would search the key file to locate the desired key and then use the record-number pointer to locate the desired record in the main file. To simplify the following discussion, we concentrate only on the problem of searching for the record key.

Sequential Search

Sequential search is the most straightforward and simplest of all search techniques. It is also easy to program on a computer in any programming language. To describe the search procedure, assume that the keys associated with the records of a file are stored in a one-dimensional array, $[A_I]$, $I = 1$, 2, . . . , N.

Suppose that the requested key, which specifies the desired information to be located in the file, is denoted by R. The sequential search algorithm consists simply of starting at the first position ($I = 1$) of the key file and comparing the requested key R with each record key in the array A, one at a time, until either a match is found or all the key positions have been searched. A flowchart for the sequential search algorithm that will process all the requested keys is shown in Fig. 9-10.

The sequential search technique does not require the keys to be sorted in order. Thus, if the requested key R happens to be the key stored in the top (first) element of the array, only one comparison is needed to find a match. On the other hand, if the requested key is the key stored at the bottom, the maximum number, N, of comparisons must be made before a match is found. Therefore, the number of comparisons required in processing a requested key depends upon how the keys are arranged in the file and the value of the requested key. If we assume the value of the requested key is equally likely to be any key in the file (i.e., the probability of any of the N keys being requested is the same for all keys and is equal to 1/N), then, if a large number of requests are processed, each key in the file will be requested approximately the same number of times. Based upon this assumption, we can compute the average number of comparisons needed to find a requested key in the following way.

Let M be the total number of requests. Each key in the file is therefore requested, on the average, M/N times. Since the number of comparisons needed to locate the Jth key (A_J) is J, the total number of comparisons is the sum

$$1\left(\frac{M}{N}\right) + 2\left(\frac{M}{N}\right) + \cdots + J\left(\frac{M}{N}\right) + \cdots + N\left(\frac{M}{N}\right) = \frac{M}{N} \sum_{i=1}^{N} i = \frac{M}{N} \frac{N(N+1)}{2} = \frac{M(N+1)}{2}$$

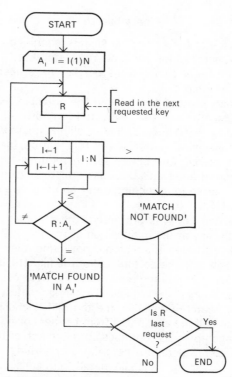

FIGURE 9-10 ■ A flowchart for sequential search.

The average number of comparisons per request is therefore

$$\left[\frac{M(N+1)}{2}\right]\Big/M = \frac{N+1}{2}$$

From this equation we see that, if all the keys in the file are requested with equal probability, the average number of comparisons for each request is proportional to the number of keys N in the file. Clearly, if N is large, the average number of comparisons needed is also large.

    If the file is already sorted on the key (for example, using any of the methods discussed previously), a number of variations of sequential search can be used to speed up the search. For example, the key in every tenth key position could be compared, starting with the first position, until a key greater than the requested key is found, at which point a sequential search could be performed in reverse on each position until a match is found. Other variations are possible if the requested keys are known to have certain characteristics that can be used to rearrange the keys to our advantage. These improved methods are further explored in the exercises.

Binary Search

We have shown that the sequential search technique can be very costly when a large file is searched for randomly requested keys. Fortunately, other methods that require fewer comparisons per key have been developed. One such method is *binary search*.

The term "binary search" comes from the principal feature of the technique that each comparison of the requested key with a key in the file will result in either finding the requested key or eliminating *half* of the key positions from further consideration. Because of this feature, the technique is also called *dichotomous search*. The binary search requires that the key file be sorted in order before the search takes place. In this discussion, we assume that the N keys are sorted in ascending order and they are stored in an array [A_I], I = 1, 2, . . . , N.

When a requested key R is presented, the search algorithm begins by comparing R with the key at the midposition of the file. If the key at the midposition is R, a match is found. If a match is not found, then the requested key is either in the top half or in the bottom half of the file. The half chosen for the next comparison depends upon the result of the current comparison of R with the key at the midposition. If the requested key R is greater, the bottom half is chosen for the next search; otherwise, the top half is chosen. In either case, the keys in the other half are eliminated from further consideration. This comparison and elimination process continues until a match of the key is found, or until the halves to be considered further reduce to nothing. Each time a match is tried, half of the remaining file is eliminated from consideration.

A flowchart of the binary search algorithm is shown in Fig. 9-11. In this flowchart two tests are provided at the beginning of each search to prevent the search algorithm from proceeding further if the requested key will not be found in the file. This may save computer time if such requests are frequently encountered. The variables TOP, BOT, and AVE are defined to control the key positions to be searched after each elimination. The flowchart as shown

TABLE 9-2 ■ A telephone area code file

Position I	Area code A_I	Other information
1	202	Washington, D.C.
2	203	Connecticut
3	401	Rhode Island
4	413	Massachusetts
5	516	Long Island
6	607	New York State
7	609	New Jersey
8	717	Pennsylvania
9	802	Vermont

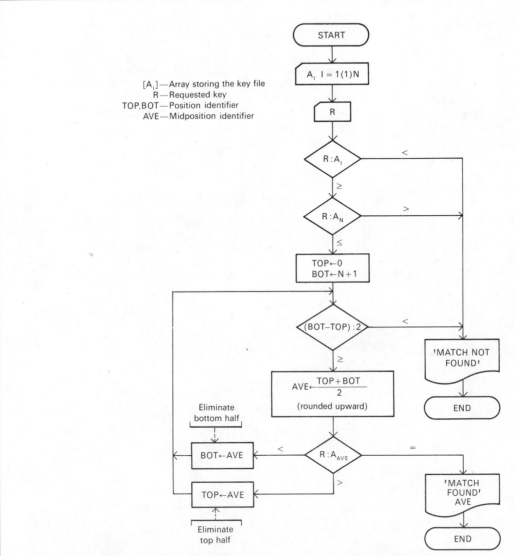

FIGURE 9-11 ■ A flowchart for the binary search algorithm.

handles only a single request. It can be easily modified to handle a sequence of requests without difficulty.

The following example illustrates the binary search algorithm. A record file containing the telephone area codes of nine northeastern districts of the country is shown. The file of Table 9-2 which is sorted on the area code (key) is given. Figure 9-12 shows the operation of the binary search algorithm by finding the area codes 203 and 609 in the file.

Key file		Search pattern				
I	A_I	First comparison	Keys for consideration	Second comparison	Keys for consideration	Third comparison
1	202		202		202	
2	203		203		(203) ⟵	midposition a match
3	401		401 ⟵	midposition	401	
4	413		413			
5	516 ⟵	midposition	516			
6	607					
7	609	$AVE = \frac{TOP + BOT}{2}$		$AVE = \frac{0+5}{2}$		$AVE = \frac{0+3}{2}$
8	717	$= \frac{0+10}{2}$		$= 3$		$= 2$
9	802	$= 5$		(rounded upward)		(rounded upward)

(a)

Key file		Search pattern				
I	A_I	First comparison	Keys for consideration	Second comparison	Keys for consideration	Third comparison
1	202					
2	203					
3	401					
4	413					
5	516 ⟵	midposition	516		516	
6	607		607		607	
7	609		609		(609) ⟵	midposition
8	717	$AVE = \frac{0+10}{2}$	717 ⟵	midposition	717	a match
9	802	$= 5$	802			
				$AVE = \frac{5+10}{2}$		$AVE = \frac{5+8}{2}$
				$= 8$ (rounded upward)		$= 7$ (rounded upward)

(b)

FIGURE 9-12 ■ Illustration of the binary search process. (a) Search for $R = 203$. (b) Search for $R = 609$.

TABLE 9-3 ▇ A comparison between binary and sequential search

| Number of keys N | | Number of comparisons required | | | |
| | | Sequential | | Binary | |
N = 2^M	M	Maximum	Average	Maximum	Average
16	4	16	8	4	3
32	5	32	16	5	4
64	6	64	32	6	5
128	7	128	64	7	6
256	8	256	128	8	7
512	9	512	256	9	8
1024	10	1024	512	10	9
2048	11	2048	1024	11	10
4096	12	4096	2048	12	11

Since the number of items left is always halved after each comparison, we see that the maximum number of comparisons necessary to either find the requested key or to declare a "match not found" is the smallest integer, L, satisfying the relation

$$2^L \geqslant N + 1$$

where L is the number of comparisons needed and N is the number of keys in the file. The above relation can also be written in the form

$$L \geqslant \log_2(N + 1)$$

This equation suggests that in a binary search the maximum number of comparisons required is a logarithmic function of the number of keys in the file. Clearly, the average number of comparisons is smaller than that required in a sequential search. If we again assume that the requested keys are uniformly distributed, it has been found that for a file with $N = 2^M$ keys, M = 1, 2, . . . , the average number of comparisons is computed by the formula[†]

$$\text{Average number of comparisons} = \frac{(M - 1)2^M + M + 2}{2^M}$$

Note that as M increases this formula is approximately equal to (M − 1). Table 9-3 shows a comparison between the binary search and the sequential search on the basis of the maximum and average numbers of comparisons per requested key.

† For a detailed discussion of this formula, see Reference (2) at the end of this chapter.

Direct Lookup and Key Transformation

In the sequential and binary search techniques, the position of the keys to be compared with the requested key is essentially predetermined. It is either the next position or the midposition in the remaining key positions. Other types of search techniques involve the establishment of a relationship between the value of the keys in the file and the position of these keys. This relationship is usually in the form of an exact formula or an approximate formula that can be used to compute the key positions to be compared in the search process. We will describe a simple algorithm of this type, the *direct lookup technique,* and discuss some of its related problems.

The direct lookup technique establishes an *exact* relation between the key value and the position of the key. This relation must be determined or given in advance so that the keys of the file are created and stored in the computer memory according to this relation.

Let us consider an example in which the keys are numeric and are four-digit part numbers of an inventory file ranging from the allowable values of 0001 to 9999. Since there are 9999 possible keys, we could use an array $[A_I]$, $I = 1, 2, \ldots, 9999$ to store the keys. The simplest formula relating the key values to their key positions in the array would be a direct one-to-one relationship so that part number 0001 is stored in the first position, part number 0002 is stored in the second position, part number 0512 is stored in the 512th position of the array $[A_I]$, etc. This is a straight-line relation as depicted in Fig. 9-13(a). Other straightforward variations are possible. Figure 9-13(b) shows another straight-line relationship in which the first key is stored in an arbitrary position ($a \neq 0$) and each record is b units long. The key value is related to key position by the formula

$$\text{Key Value } = a + b * (\text{Key Position})$$

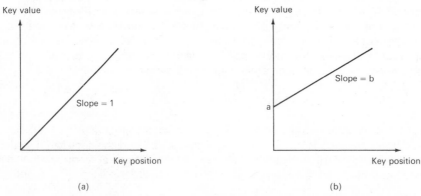

(a)   (b)

FIGURE 9-13 ∎ Straight lines showing relation between the keys and their positions.

or

$$\text{Key Position} = \frac{(\text{Key Value}) - a}{b}$$

Note that because of this one-to-one relationship between the key values and their positions, it is not necessary to store the keys in the computer memory as the key values are implied by the key positions. Thus, as a requested key R is presented, the search algorithm simply needs to compute the position indicated by R to find the associated information in the main file. This search technique is therefore called direct lookup.

For example, if the straight-line relation in Fig. 9-13(a) is used, the information associated with a requested part number 512 would have been found in the position 512 of the record file. That is, if a key file [A_1] is created, A_{512} would contain the desired key. If, on the other hand, the straight line in Fig. 9-13(b) is used in storing the data file, a simple computation of the formula relating the key position to the key value reveals the desired key position and its associated information.

The direct lookup method discussed above is perhaps the fastest search algorithm when it can be used. However, an obvious waste of computer memory occurs if the array storing the keys has too many empty entries. For example, if only 3000 part numbers of the possible 9999 positions are actually created and stored in the array [A_1], then there are 6999 wasted positions. This shortcoming can be remedied by the technique known as *key transformation*.

When the keys of a file are not directly suitable for use as key positions, a transformation of the keys from their natural form to a different representation may be desirable. This transformation is often called *hashing*. Hashing addresses are the transformed keys created by some routine operation performed on the original keys. The main objective of key transformation is that the resulting hash addresses can be more efficiently used to store the data file in a direct lookup search.

To further illustrate the rationale for key transformation, consider the following example. Suppose there is a file of part numbers consisting of seven-digit decimal numerals. Since there are 10^7 possible different part numbers to be stored, an array of 10^7 positions must be used. Assuming that in practice there may be no more than 1000 unique part numbers in the file, the array of 10^7 positions to store only 1000 part numbers will obviously represent a waste of memory.

There are many possible techniques for key transformation. The simplest and perhaps the most popular one is the division-remainder method. This method chooses a number D close to the actual number of positions needed in a given file. Next the number D is used as a divisor to extract a quotient and a remainder from the original key, the dividend. The remainder so obtained is the new, transformed key.

Table 9-4 shows an example of two different transformations performed on a set of seven-digit keys. Both transformations used the division–remainder

TABLE 9-4 ■ Two different transformations of keys

Original keys (part number)	Transformation I (D = 1000)	Transformation II (D = 2000)
0 0000 0001	1	1
0 0000 0112	112	112
0 0000 1044	44 ⎱ Hash clash	1044
0 0002 0044	44 ⎰	44
1 0001 0234	234	234
1 0024 1072	72	1072
1 1000 0345	345	345
1 1111 1111	111	1111

method. In the first transformation, the divisor was chosen to be 1000 and the divisor for the second transformation was 2000. Ideally, the transformation scheme should convert the original keys into a set of distinct new keys with no duplicates. This is the case of the second transformation. When this ideal situation is not achieved, such as the case in the first transformation, *"hash clash"* occurs. Many advanced search techniques have been developed to deal with these hash clashes so that the occurrence of duplicates is either eliminated or minimized. The discussion of these techniques may be found in advanced texts and in the references listed at the end of this chapter.

Exercises

1. A data file containing nonnumeric keys (not all distinct) is shown below. Assume that the keys are requested randomly.

I	A_I (key)	Other information
1	A2	
2	B1	
3	B5	
4	C3	
5	D4	
6	MS	
7	MS	
8	P3	
9	P9	

Assume the collating sequence

$$\sqcup < A < \cdots < Z < 0 < 1 \cdots < 9$$

(a) How does the presence of duplicate keys influence both the sequential and binary search process?

(b) Compute the average number of comparisons per request in a sequential search.

(c) Determine the average number of comparisons per request in a binary search by searching for each and every key in the file.

2. Assume that a file contains ten keyed records stored in an array $[A_I]$. If the distribution of requests for each key is as shown in the table, determine the average number of comparisons in a sequential search.

I	A_I	Requests (%)
1	A_1	5
2	A_2	10
3	A_3	5
4	A_4	25
5	A_5	20
6	A_6	5
7	A_7	10
8	A_8	10
9	A_9	5
10	A_{10}	5

Can you suggest a better arrangement for the ten data elements?

3. Develop a flowchart that will carry out the following modified sequential search on N numeric keys stored in an array $[A_I]$, $I = 1(1)N$. The keys are sorted in ascending order. The algorithm compares the requested key R with every Kth key position, starting with the Kth position, until a key greater than R is found at which point a backward sequential search is performed on each key position, one at a time, until a match is found. Assume that N is a multiple of K. Determine the number of comparisons needed to locate R if R is stored in:

(a) A_1 (b) A_N (c) A_K

4. One method of key transformation is called *folding*. Folding consists of splitting the original key (assumed numeric or coded into a numeric form) into two or more parts. The parts are then added to form a sum. This sum, or some part of it, is then used as the transformed key. For example,

Original key = 20 4152 9365
Splitting and adding = 20 + 4152 + 9365 = 13537
Transformed key I = 13537 (use the entire sum)
Transformed key II = 3537 (discard the highest order digit)
Transformed key III = 1353 (discard the lowest order digit)

Using the folding method, determine the transformed key for the following set of original keys by:

(a) discarding the highest-order digit,
(b) discarding the lowest-order digit,
(c) taking every other digit starting from the highest order digit,
(d) taking the two least significant digits.

Original three-part keys: 20   0050   0001
                            20   2125   9146
                            30   0182   0004
                            30   0050   0176

Which method gives the best result for the set of keys given?

5. Modify the flowchart of Fig. 9-11 so that it can be used as one of the following:
   (a) a main procedure that handles a sequence of requests,
   (b) a subroutine that searches for any requested key.

4 ■ Summary

This chapter has presented a number of the common techniques that are used to search and sort various types of information. The methods presented are easily implemented and can be successfully used to carry out small to medium size data-processing tasks. When it becomes necessary to work with large data files where each record has a complex form, it becomes very important that the right processing technique be selected if one wishes to carry out the required calculations efficiently.

The problem of searching and sorting large data files has received considerable study since processes of these types are quite common in many business operations. The references at the end of the chapter discuss many of the advanced techniques that can be used to carry out these tasks.

References

There are a large number of books and articles that treat searching and sorting. [1], [2], [3], and [4] are books covering many of the details. [9] illustrates how PL/I can be used to carry out many of these operations. [5], [6], [7], and [8] present a shorter discussion of many of the important topics.

1. Barrodale, I., Roberts, F., and Ehle, B. (1971) *Elementary Computer Applications*, John Wiley & Sons, New York, Chapters 8–10.

2. Brooks, F., and Iverson, K. (1969) *Automatic Data Processing: Systems/360 edition*, John Wiley & Sons, New York.

3. Flores, I. (1969) *Computer Sorting*, Prentice-Hall, Englewood Cliffs, N.J.

4. Knuth, D. (1973) *The Art of Computing Programming, Vol. 3, Sorting and Searching*, Addison-Wesley, Reading, Mass.

5. Lorin, H. (1971) "A Guided Bibliography to Sorting," *IBM Systems Journal*, Vol. 10, No. 3, pp. 244–254.

6. Martin, W. (December 1971) "Sorting," *ACM Computing Surveys*, Vol. 3, No. 4, pp. 147–174.

7. Price, C. E. (June 1971) "Table Lookup Techniques," *ACM Computing Surveys*, Vol. 3, No. 2, pp. 49–66.

8. Papers presented at the 1962 ACM Sort Symposium, Princeton, N.J. Published (May 1963) in the *Communications of the ACM,* Vol. 6, No. 5.

9. Rich, R. P. (1972) *Internal Sorting Methods, Illustrated with PL/I Programs,* Prentice-Hall, Englewood Cliffs, N.J.

10. Salton, G. (1968) *Automatic Information Organization and Retrieval,* McGraw-Hill, New York.

Home Problems

If possible, the algorithms developed to solve the following problems should be programmed and tested on a computer.

1. Assume that a file is to be maintained in a sorted order. It is often necessary to be able to insert and delete records from the file. Develop the flowchart of an algorithm that can be used to either insert or delete a record if the file is organized as shown in Fig. 9-1.

2. Assume that F1 and F2 are two files which have been sorted and which do not contain any common records. Give the flowchart of an algorithm that can be used to create a new ordered file F3 which consists of the merger of F1 and F2.

3. Assume that F1 and F2 are as defined in problem 2 except that a record in F1 may also appear in F2. Give the flowchart of an algorithm that will merge F1 and F2 into a single sorted file F3 so that F3 does not contain any duplicate records.

4. Let F1 be a file that contains records of the following form:

   1. Name
   2. Sex

Give the flowchart of an algorithm which will create two new files, F2 and F3, such that F2 is a file which contains the names of all the males in order and F3 is a file which contains the names of all the females in order.

5. It is desired to develop an information retrieval system for use by the receptionist in a large company. The following information is to be stored about each employee:

   1. Name (last, first, middle initial)
   2. Office number
   3. Position
   4. Telephone number

Develop a simple information retrieval system which has the following capabilities:

   1. can locate and output an employee record if the employee's name is given in any form;
   2. is able to enter the record of a new employee;
   3. is able to remove the record of any employee who leaves the company;
   4. can modify the record of any employee.

6. A file is to be created which represents the inventory records of a company.

Each item in the file is represented by a seven-digit number between 0000000 and 9999999. There will be a maximum of 3000 items entered in the file. The record associated with each item has five fields:

1. Number
2. Quantity in stock
3. Sales price
4. Supplies
5. Reorder level

   Develop a flowchart of an algorithm which will:

1. add or delete an item from the file;
2. update the status of the file every time an item is removed from stock or a new shipment is received;
3. generate an order request when the supply of a given item reaches the reorder level.

Use the key transform technique for file searching. When a hash clash occurs, use the address generated by the key transform as the entry point to the file and use a sequential search from that point to locate the desired record.

7. Assume that a file is made up of records with the following fields:

1. Name
2. Street address (number, street name)
3. Town
4. State

   Develop the flowchart of an algorithm which will order the file alphabetically in the following manner

   State, Town, Street Name, Street Number, Name

The contents of the file are to be printed out in the following format

```
        STATE
                TOWN
                        Street
                                #       Name
                                #       Name
                        Street    ·          ·
                TOWN      ·       ·          ·
                 ·        ·       ·          ·
                 ·        ·
        STATE
          ·
          ·
          ·
```

8. Develop the flowchart of an algorithm which will examine all of the words in a paragraph and generate a table consisting of all the distinct words in the paragraph and the number of times each word occurs. Print out the table in alphabetic order.

9. A master file contains all of the voter registration information about voters in a given county. The county has three separate towns. Develop an algorithm which:

1. will print an alphabetic list of all voters in the county and their address;
2. will print an alphabetic list of all voters in a given town and their address;
3. will allow for the addition or deletion of a voter record from the file;
4. will correct the record of the voter if the voter moves from one town to another or changes address.

10

extended data structures

1 ▮ Introduction

Computers are information-processing devices. Up to this point we have concentrated upon some of the basic numerical and data-processing techniques that have a wide range of applications. As long as our interests are restricted to making massive numerical calculations or to carrying out a standard data processing task, we can use the computational techniques presented in the previous chapters. However, as soon as we become interested in more complex information-processing tasks, such as the manipulation of algebraic equations, information retrieval systems, inventory control systems, language translation systems, or question-answering systems, we find that these techniques have a number of shortcomings.

For a given information-processing task, the way the information is stored and accessed in a computer can have a significant influence upon the complexity of the algorithm required to carry out the task. By selecting the proper way to arrange the information associated with a task, we can often simplify the algorithm needed to process the information. In addition, we may also reduce the overall cost of the calculation by making better use of available memory space or by increasing computational speed.

We have already worked with many of the standard data structures, such as arrays, records, files, and structures. These basic types of data structures serve as a starting point for the more advanced type of data structures that we consider in this chapter. Most of the techniques that we will discuss involve ways that allow us to store complete units of information in a dynamic manner or to represent complex interrelationships among the units.

In the following discussion, we will show how the different information structures to be considered can be realized using arrays and a special algorithm to insert and remove information from the information structure. We do this because many programming languages do not include the ability to represent these complex information structures as an inherent part of the language. Subroutines can easily be developed to handle these advanced methods of information storage and manipulation in any language that does not include these features.

2 ▮ Stacks and Queues

Arrays are used to store a number of elements belonging to a set. Each element has a unique position in the array and the quantity represented by that element can be accessed by giving its array position. This is a very general method of information storage. When using an array, it then becomes important to know the location of each element stored in the array. There are many applications where all we wish is to use the array to temporarily store information and where it is not important to uniquely specify the location in the array where the information is stored. Two special types of one-dimensional arrays,

called stacks and queues, have been developed to solve this type of information-storage problem.

Stacks

A *stack,* often called a *pushdown list,* is a data structure that places a
sequence of elements in the consecutive locations of an array. Elements can
be added or removed from only the top of the array and an element lower down
in the array cannot be utilized until all elements above this particular element
are removed. As soon as the element at the top of the array is used, it is
removed. A stack can be visualized as behaving in a manner similar to a stack
of plates on a shelf.† As each new plate is added to the top of the stack, its
height increases. Whenever a plate is needed, it is removed from the top of the
stack and the stack's height decreases. Storage of this type is referred to as
last-in first-out storage.

Figure 10-1 provides a pictorial representation of a stack. The difference
between a stack and a general array is that we do not have to keep track of the
location of specific items in the stack. All we have to do is make sure that
the information is placed on the stack in proper order and that it is taken
off the stack at the right time.

A stack can easily be realized by using an array and a pointer that points
to the top item of the stack. This representation is illustrated in Fig. 10-2.
(Note that for convenience of visualization the array is represented "upside
down.") As indicated in this figure, we must assign an array of a fixed size to
serve as the stack. (A more general representation that removes this restriction is discussed in Section IV.) For this discussion we assume that the stack

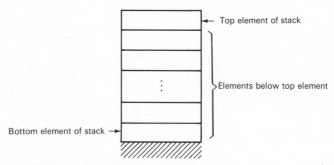

FIGURE 10-1 ■ Pictorial representation of a stack.

† An alternative visualization is to think of the stack as similar to a stack of trays
resting in a holder with a spring loaded false bottom. As each new tray is added to
the stack, the other trays are pushed down into the holder and the new tray is at
the level of the previous tray. The last tray placed on the stack is thus the first one
removed. In this representation, information is pushed down when it is added to
the stack. Thus the name *pushdown list.*

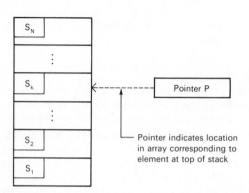

FIGURE 10-2 ■ Representation of a stack as an array and a pointer.

will be realized using an N-element array $S = [S_I]$ and a pointer P. The N locations in the stack are used to store information and the pointer is used to indicate the element that is currently at the top of the stack. The pointer variable is an integer that takes on values between 0 and N. If P has a value of 0, this indicates that the stack is empty and no information is available to be removed from the stack. If P has a value of N, this means that the stack is full and no additional information can be added. When possible, N is selected so that the stack is never full.

Let us assume that we wish to place an item, represented by the identifier X, on the stack. We can do this by using the sequence of operations shown in Fig. 10-3(a), where it is assumed that this operation is realized by a

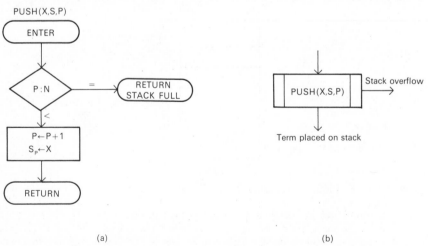

FIGURE 10-3 ■ Representation of the operation of placing an element on a stack. (a) Flowchart of subroutine to place element on stack. (b) Flowchart representation of subroutine PUSH.

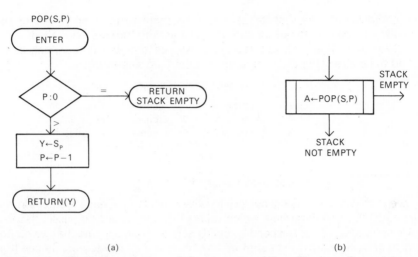

FIGURE 10-4 ■ Representation of the operation of reading an element from a stack. (a) Flowchart of function procedure to read element from stack. (b) Flowchart representation of function POP.

subroutine PUSH(X,S,P). The parameters X, S, and P correspond to the information to be placed on the stack, the stack array, and the stack pointer, respectively. The flowchart representation of this task is shown in Fig. 10-3(b). The operation of placing an element onto a stack is usually called a *push operation,* since initially the term pushdown list was used as the descriptive title of this type of storage technique.

We can remove an item from the stack and assign it to a variable A by using the sequence of operations shown in Fig. 10-4(a). It is assumed that this operation is realized as a function POP(S,P). The parameters S and P again correspond to the stack array and stack pointer, respectively. The flowchart representation of this task is shown in Fig. 10-4(b). The operation of reading a term from a stack is traditionally called a *pop operation.*

Whenever we use a stack as an information-storage device, we must provide for the initialization of the stack pointer to zero before the stack is used. This insures that the stack is "empty" before we start our calculation. The following example illustrates how a stack can be used in a very simple task. In later chapters, we deal with problems that make more complex use of the idea of a stack.

An Illustrative Use of Stacks

Assume that we have two N-element arrays [$NAME_I$] and [$SCORE_I$]. The first array contains student names and the second array contains the score that the student received on an examination. Any student with a grade of 70 or better is considered to have passed the examination while a grade below 70 is considered failure. We wish to develop a program to print out a list of the students who passed the exam followed by a list of students who failed.

Examining this problem statement, we see that the data, which is assumed to be already in the computer, has the following form:

I	NAME$_I$	SCORE$_I$
1	⟨first name⟩	⟨score⟩
2	⟨second name⟩	⟨score⟩
3	⟨third name⟩	⟨score⟩
.	.	.
.	.	.
.	.	.
N	⟨Nth name⟩	⟨score⟩

We see that in order to make our two lists we must look at each element in the array [SCORE$_I$] and determine which values of I correspond to passing scores and which values of I correspond to failing scores. If we assume that we do not start to print our output lists until we have checked all the scores, we see that we must be able to remember temporarily the values of I corresponding to the passing scores and the values of I corresponding to the failing scores. This information can easily be stored on two stacks. Stack 1 will keep a list of those values of I that indicate a passing score, and stack 2 will keep track of the values of I corresponding to a failing score.

Assume that the two stacks are stored in the arrays S1 and S2 and that the respective pointers are P1 and P2. The flowchart of the algorithm necessary to carry out the sorting process is given in Fig. 10-5. The first stack, S1, is used to store the values of I, which correspond to students with a score greater than or equal to 70, while the other stack stores the values of I corresponding to students with a score less than 70. After all the students are processed, we then print out the two lists. To see how this algorithm operates, assume that N = 6 and that the two arrays are as follows:

I	NAME$_I$	SCORE$_I$
1	JOHN	45
2	BILL	59
3	BOB	90
4	MARY	88
5	SUE	68
6	PAULA	70

After the algorithm has completed the first loop, the two stacks would contain:

Stack S1		Stack S2	
6	top of stack	5	top of stack
4		2	
3	bottom of stack	1	bottom of stack

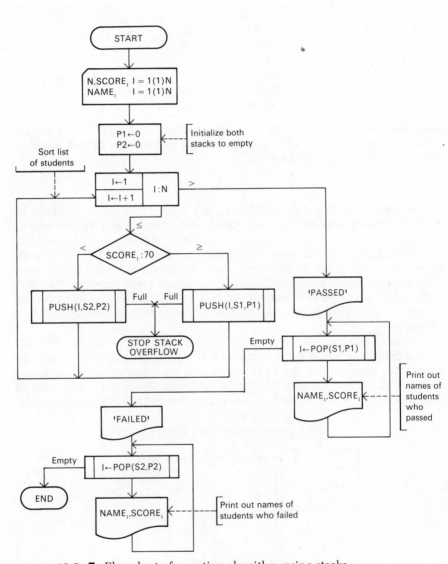

FIGURE 10-5 ■ Flowchart of a sorting algorithm using stacks.

The information in these two stacks are then used to print out the following:

PASSED

PAULA	70
MARY	88
BOB	90

FAILED

SUE	68
BILL	59
JOHN	45

Examining this list, we see that the names appear in an order the reverse of that in the original array. This inversion comes about because of the last-in, first-out characteristics of the stack.

Queues

A *queue* is a data structure that is very similar to a stack. However, instead of allowing elements to be entered and removed at only one end, a queue is similar to a line that forms at a theater box office while waiting to purchase a ticket. The elements that make up a queue are stored in an array. As new elements arrive to be stored, they are placed on "top" of the array while elements which are needed from the array are taken from the "bottom" of the array. This type of storage has a feature that is referred to as *first-in, first-out* service. This is just the type of behavior that we experience in a waiting line.

Figure 10-6 provides a pictorial representation of a queue. The difference between a queue and an array is that we do not keep track of specific items in the queue. All we do is make sure that the information is placed into and taken out of the queue in the proper sequence. There are a large number of applications where a queue is a very useful method of information storage.

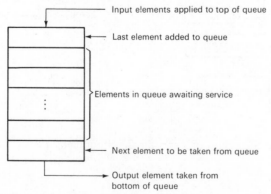

FIGURE 10-6 ■ Pictorial representation of a queue.

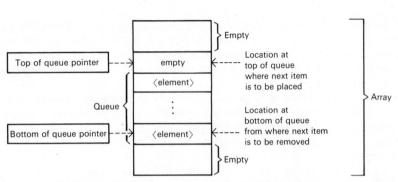

FIGURE 10-7 ■ Illustration of how a queue fits into an array.

The implementation of a queue is somewhat more complex than a stack. For a stack, we only need a single pointer to indicate the element on the top of the stack. For a queue, we need two pointers, one to indicate the top of the queue and one to indicate the bottom of the queue. Another problem that occurs is illustrated in Fig. 10-7. A queue must fit into an array. As elements are added to the queue, the top of the array fills up, while as elements are taken from the bottom of the queue, the bottom of the array becomes empty. Thus, the queue tends to float towards the top of the array. When the queue reaches the top of the array, it must be "folded over" to use the vacated space at the bottom of the array. This *foldover* process is illustrated in Fig. 10-8.

Let us assume that we wish to realize a queue that can store up to N elements. Because of the foldover problem, we must be very careful in defining

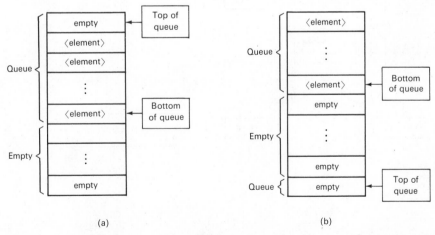

FIGURE 10-8 ■ Illustration of how foldover is used to accommodate a queue in an array. (a) Queue fills top of array. (b) Queue "folded over" to accommodate next item.

how the queue will operate. First, we introduce two pointers, PT and PB, corresponding to the top pointer and bottom pointer, respectively. The pointer PT indicates the next location in the queue where an item is to be entered and the pointer PB indicates the next item to be removed from the queue. The pointers take on integer values.

There are two special situations that must be considered. When no information is stored in the queue, the queue is empty. This situation is indicated by setting the pointer PT to zero. The second problem occurs when the queue is filled. This condition can be detected when both pointers PT and PB have the same value.

Assume that we wish to enter an element, represented by the identifier X, in the queue. We can do this by the sequence of operations shown in Fig. 10-9(a), where it is assumed that this operation is realized by a subroutine LOAD(X,S,PT,PB). The parameters X, S, PT, and PB correspond to the information to be placed in the queue, the queue array, the top pointer, and the

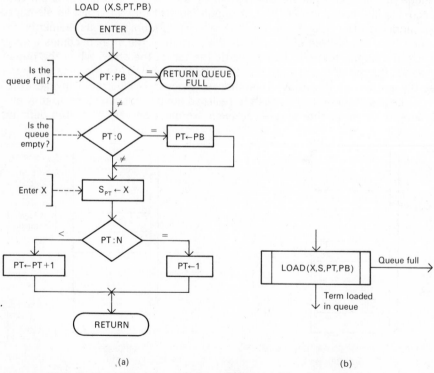

(a)   (b)

FIGURE 10-9 ■ Representation of the operation of loading an element into a queue. (a) Flowchart of subroutine to load an element into a queue. (b) Flowchart representation of subroutine LOAD.

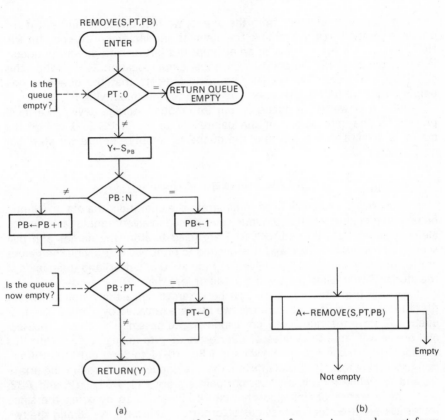

FIGURE 10-10 ■ Representation of the operation of removing an element from a queue. (a) Flowchart of function to remove an element from a queue. (b) Flowchart representation of function REMOVE.

bottom pointer, respectively. The flowchart representation of this task is shown in Fig. 10-9(b).

To enter an item, we first check to see if PT = PB. If this is true, the supposedly empty location on the top of the queue is actually occupied by the element at the bottom of the queue. Thus, the queue is full. Next, we check to see if the queue is empty by testing if PT is zero. If the queue is empty, we set PT to the same value as PB and load the item into the location indicated by PT. The final task is to move the pointer PT to the next empty location.

We can remove an element from the queue and assign it to a variable A by using a sequence of operations shown in Fig. 10-10(a). This operation is realized as a function REMOVE(S,PT,PB), where the parameters S, PT, and PB again correspond to the queue array and the two pointers to the top and bottom of the queue. The flowchart representation of this function is shown in Fig. 10-10(b).

To remove an element from the queue, we first check to find out if the queue is empty. If not, we remove the element and increment the pointer PB. Next, we check if the removal of an element has left us with an empty queue. If this is the case, PB will point to the same empty location as PT. When this condition is detected, we set PT to zero to indicate that the queue is now empty before we return. Otherwise, we return without modifying PT.

Whenever we use a queue as our information-storage device, we must provide for the initialization of the pointer PT to 0 and PB to 1 before the queue is used. This insures that the queue is "empty" before we start our calculations.

An Illustrative Use of Queues

The previous example used to illustrate the operation of a stack will now be repeated to illustrate how a queue can be used in a very simple task. Two N-element arrays [NAME$_I$] and [SCORE$_I$] are used to store the names and test score of the students in a class. It is desired to print two lists giving the names of the students who passed (received a grade of 70 or better) and the names of the students who failed (received a grade of less than 70).

Exactly the same approach can be taken to solve the problem, except that the two stacks used to store the two lists are replaced by queues. The first queue will store the values of I corresponding to passing scores and the second queue will store the values of I corresponding to failing scores. With this modification, we can use the flowchart of Fig. 10-11 to carry out the information-processing task. In this algorithm, the two queues are stored in the arrays Q1 and Q2, while the top and bottom pointers are PT1, PB1, PT2, and PB2.

The operation of this algorithm can be investigated by using the same tables as were used for the previous algorithm. In this case, $N = 6$ and the two tables were

I	NAME$_I$	SCORE$_I$
1	JOHN	45
2	BILL	59
3	BOB	90
4	MARY	88
5	SUE	68
6	PAULA	70

After the algorithm has completed the first loop, the two queues would contain:

	Queue 1		Queue 2
6	top of queue	5	top of queue
4		2	
3	bottom of queue	1	bottom of queue

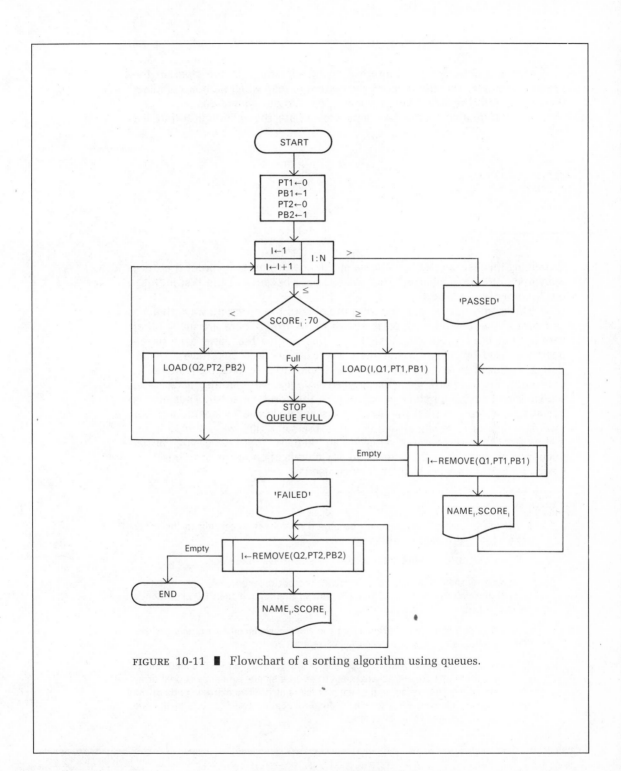

FIGURE 10-11 ■ Flowchart of a sorting algorithm using queues.

This is exactly the same information that is stored in the stack of the previous example. The difference in the system is seen when we now complete the execution of the algorithm and look at the printout generated.

The information in the two queues generate the following output list

PASSED	
BOB	90
MARY	88
PAULA	70
FAILED	
JOHN	45
BILL	59
SUE	68

Examining this list, we see that the names appear in the same order that they appeared in the original array. This comes about because of the first-in, first-out feature of the stack.

Stacks and queues are examples of some of the alternate ways that we can control the way information is stored in an array. There are many other variations of the basic ideas presented in this section that have been developed and used by computer scientists. For example, we could have a queue that is organized so that we can make additions and deletions to the queue at both ends. Such an arrangement is called a *deque*. We can also access the arrays, used to realize a stack or a queue, in the normal manner. Thus, if it is advantageous, we can treat the array as a stack or queue for operations that involve adding or removing elements and at the same time we can read information from the array without removing an element. There is nothing special about any of these data structures and any modification of the structure that leads to a better problem solution may be used.

Exercises

1. Let the following data elements be stored in a stack according to the order (from left to right) they are written below

     'JOHN'   'MARK'   'BOB'   'SUSAN'   'MARY'

(a) What is the top element of the stack? The bottom element?
(b) Determine the top and bottom element of the stack if the POP operation is executed three times consecutively.

2. Do exercise 1 with the difference that the stack is replaced by a queue and the POP operation is replaced by the REMOVE operation.

3. Develop an algorithm that will operate two stacks S1 and S2 concurrently.
     Assume that both stacks are maintained in a single, one-dimensional array with N elements. The bottom end of each stack is at the two extreme ends of the array. This arrangement will allow the storage allocation to either one of the two stacks to vary as requirements change.

(a) Give a flowchart that will implement this algorithm.

(b) Apply this algorithm to the student examination-score example discussed in this section with the following two sets of exam scores:

I	NAME$_I$	Set #1 SCORE$_I$	Set #2 SCORE$_I$
1	JOHN	45	72
2	BILL	59	60
3	BOB	90	95
4	MARY	88	85
5	SUE	68	75
6	PAULA	70	68

4. Develop a flowchart of the LOAD and REMOVE operation of a queue that does not accommodate foldover.

(a) What are the conditions under which an overflow or empty queue would occur?

(b) Compare the performance of this flowchart to the one developed in this section in which the foldover is used.

3 ▌ Pointers, Nodes, and Lists

In our previous discussions, we have developed various techniques based upon the assumption that the data elements we deal with are stored in simple arrays. Data elements stored in arrays are arranged in a sequential manner within the computer memory. There are many situations where this is a poor information-storage technique. For example, suppose we wish to carry out algebraic calculations on polynomials of the form

$$p(x) = a_0 + a_1x + a_2x^2 + \cdots + a_nx^n$$

We are faced with the problem of trying to store a representation of this polynomial in the computer.

One approach would be to use an $(n + 1)$-element array $[A_I]$. The jth element of the array would then store a_{j-1}, the coefficient of x^{j-1}. For example, the polynomial

$$p(x) = 6 + 3x - 2x^2 + 4x^4$$

could be stored in a five-element array as

$$
\begin{array}{ll}
A_1 & 6 \\
A_2 & 3 \\
A_3 & -2 \\
A_4 & 0 \\
A_5 & 4
\end{array}
$$

However, consider the problem of storing the polynomial

$$p(x) = 2 + 3x - 46x^{25}$$

We would need an array with 26 elements to store this polynomial, even though there are only three nonzero coefficients.

In a general situation, we would probably be working with polynomials in which both the degree n of the polynomial and the number of nonzero coefficients would be variable. To use an array to store polynomials would then require that we select a maximum value of n, say N_{max}, and then require that all arrays representing polynomials have $N_{max} + 1$ elements.

Arrays are a wasteful method for storing general polynomials. This suggests that we need a different type of data structure to store information that is not of a sequential nature. We now introduce the idea of a linked list which provides a very flexible way to store a large set of interrelated information items.

Nodes and Links

As a starting point, we assume that the information we wish to represent can be represented as a set of individual units of information. Each unit of information has a fixed number of elements which describe the unit. In addition, because of the characteristics of the information, there is some type of interrelationship that exists between the basic information units that make up the set. We have two problems to solve if we wish to store information in this form. We must standardize how the information associated with each basic unit is to be organized and we must have a standard way to indicate the interrelationships that exist between the units. To solve these problems, we can combine the ideas of records and pointers that we have used in our previous discussions.

A set of information can be arranged as a file and each basic item in the file is represented by a record. Each record consists of one or more fields that store the information associated with the record. In our initial discussion, we assumed that the records that made up a file were stored sequentially. If we wish to increase the flexibility of this storage technique, we can introduce one or more additional fields in each record. These fields, called *link fields,* are used to store pointer information that points to another record in the file.

A record that contains one or more link fields is called a *node.* Associated with each node is a number called the *address* of the node. This number is similar to the subscript associated with the elements of an array and is not stored as part of the record associated with the node. Thus, the essential feature of a node is not only that it can be accessed by a reference to its own address but that it also has the capability of pointing to other nodes by using the link fields to store the address of those nodes. Thus, conceptually we can represent a node with two information fields and two link fields in the manner shown in Fig. 10-12. The number of information fields and link fields needed in

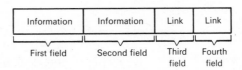

FIGURE 10-12 ■ A graphical representation of a node.

a given situation is determined by the nature of the problem being analyzed and the structure of the information being processed. For the following discussions, we assume that each node has a single information field. This, of course, is not a necessary restriction and a node can contain as many information fields as necessary to store the information associated with each node.

Linked Lists

The introduction of the concept of a link field is the key to the computer representation of complex information structures. The pointer stored in a link field of a node indicates the address of a node that is related to the current node in some predefined manner. A file with nodes linked to one another in this manner is called a *linked list,* or simply a *list.*

For example, consider a list which consists of four nodes, node 1, node 2, node 3, and node 4. It is assumed that each node has one information field and one link field. The information field is used to store character sequences corresponding to student names. If we wish to store the following set of names in the indicated order

                    JOHN
                    PAUL
                    MARY
                    SUE

then we can use the list arrangement shown in Fig. 10-13(a). Linked lists of this type in which each node has only one link field are called *singly linked lists.* In this figure, node 1 contains the first name in the list, node 2 contains the second, node 3 contains the third, and node 4 contains the last name in the list. The node in which a given name is stored is not of importance. The same list in the same order could be stored as shown in Fig. 10-13(b). Although different nodes are used to store the names, the link field information indicates the order in which the names should be considered in a given information-processing task.

The special value "λ" shown in the link field of the node associated with SUE is used to mean a *null link* indicating the end of the list (that is, pointing to no other node). External pointers are used to indicate particular nodes in the list. The pointer FIRST, which is not part of the linked list, contains the address of the node which we use as a point of access to the list. In our example, the pointer contains the address of the node associated with JOHN,

Node address	Information field	Link field	Input pointer	
1	'JOHN'	2	1	FIRST — Input pointer identifier
2	'PAUL'	3		
3	'MARY'	4		
4	'SUE'	λ		

(a)

Node address	Information field	Link field	Input pointer	
1	'MARY'	3	2	FIRST — Input pointer identifier
2	'JOHN'	4		
3	'SUE'	λ		
4	'PAUL'	1		

(b)

FIGURE 10-13 ■ Illustration of a singly linked list. (a) Storage of a linked list. (b) Another arrangement of the same linked list.

since JOHN is the first name on our list. Unique identifiers are associated with each such pointer.

When we are talking about lists, it is of little importance to us if we know the address of each node. All we are interested in is the information stored in the list and the interrelationships that exist between the nodes of the list. Because of this, it is convenient to use a graphical representation of a list such as shown in Fig. 10-14. In this type of representation, the links between the nodes are represented by arrows and no information is included about the address associated with each node. The null link is indicated by the notation ⊥ to indicate the termination of a list.

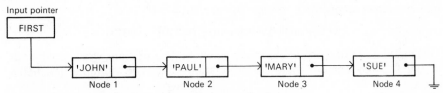

FIGURE 10-14 ■ Graphical representation of a list.

Referencing Information in a List

To use a linked list, we must have a means of referring to a node and the fields within a node. We can use the address of a node to reference the node. However, one of the advantages of a linked list is that we can work with the list and reference elements of the list without keeping track of the numerical addresses of the particular nodes in the list.

All of the fields associated with a node are given a name. To indicate the value of any field of a node, all that we have to do is give the name of the field followed by the pointer, in parentheses, that points to the node. The pointer may be indicated as an identifier or as a constant.

For example, consider the list illustrated in Fig. 10-14. Each node has two fields. Denote these fields by the names INFOR and LINK, corresponding to the information field and the link field. The input pointer is indicated by the identifier FIRST. Using these names, we can access the information contained in each node. For example,

$$\text{INFOR (FIRST)} = \text{'JOHN'}$$
$$\text{INFOR(LINK(FIRST))} = \text{'PAUL'}$$

The address of any node depends upon the particular way that the information is stored. Figure 10-13 shows two different ways that the list of Fig. 10-14 can be stored. Thus, corresponding to Figs. 10-13(a) or (b), we have

FIRST has a value of either 1 or 2
LINK (FIRST) has a value of either 2 or 4
LINK (LINK(FIRST)) has a value of either 3 or 1

Similarly, we can refer to a node directly by address. However, the address of a node depends upon how it is stored. Thus,

LINK (3) has a value of either 4 or λ
INFOR (3) has a value of either 'MARY' or 'SUE'

When we wish to avoid any confusion, it is always better to refer to a node by giving a symbolic representation of the link rather than trying to indicate the numerical address of the node. Thus,

$$\text{LINK(LINK(LINK(FIRST)))}$$

indicates the link of the third node in Fig. 10-14 and

$$\text{INFOR(LINK(LINK(LINK(FIRST)))) = 'SUE'}$$

This method of notation can be easily extended to situations where each node in the list may contain multiple information fields and multiple link fields.

Disadvantages of Linked Lists

Although linked lists are very useful data structures, their use has a price that must be considered whenever they are employed. The main cost of a linked list is in the increased storage space needed for the link fields associated with each node. In some cases, this increased storage requirement is compensated for by a reduction in the space required to store the information in the list. In other cases, the increased flexibility of storage is the important consideration.

The use of linked lists also may require more computer time to carry out a given task, since it may take longer to locate a particular item in a list. Here again, a trade-off evaluation must be made between increased cost and increased flexibility. Linked lists are powerful computational tools when used in the proper situation. They should, however, be used only when they have a clear advantage over the other types of data structures.

Exercises

1. Assume that each student record containing four fields is represented by a node as follows:

NAME	SCHOOL
SCORE	LINK

A list of five nodes is shown below:

		Content of node			
Input pointer	Address	NAME	SCHOOL	SCORE	LINK
FIRST →	1	'ALAN'	'ART'	78	5
	2	'IVES'	'ENG'	88	4
	3	'TERRY'	'AGR'	75	λ
	4	'SMITH'	'BUS'	95	3
	5	'COOPER'	'EDU'	60	2

Determine the following values:
   (a) SCHOOL (FIRST)
   (b) NAME (LINK(FIRST))
   (c) SCORE (LINK(LINK(FIRST)))

(d) LINK (5)

(e) NAME (LINK(LINK(LINK(LINK(FIRST)))))

2. Give a graphical representation of the linked list of the five student records shown in Exercise 1.

4 ■ Linear Linked Lists and List Operations

Some programming languages are designed so that linked lists are one of the data structures that are directly realized by the language. However, we can easily use arrays to realize linked lists in those languages that do not contain this feature. In this section, we consider some of the standard ways that linked lists can be realized and show how linked lists are used. To do this, we concentrate upon the simpler type of information structures in which the information nodes are related in a linear manner. Linked lists which represent complex information structures with nonlinear relationships are discussed in the next chapter.

A *linear list* is a set of nodes with the structural property that the nodes are arranged in a sequential order. Given a set of n nodes, say N_1, N_2, ..., N_n, we can always set up an ordering so that we can decide if one node comes before or after another node. For example, a natural linear ordering would be: N_1 is the first node, N_2 is the second, N_i is the ith node preceded by N_{i-1} and followed by N_{i+1}, and N_n is the last node. Other orderings are, of course, also possible.

Any information stored in a one-dimensional array corresponds to a linear list. A stack is also a linear list in which all insertions and deletions of nodes are made at one end of the list. Similarly, a queue is a linear list for which all insertions are made at one end of the list and all deletions are made at the other end of the list. We now show how these ideas can be generalized if we use a linear linked list to realize these same data structures instead of arrays.

Array Realization of Linked Lists

Assume that we wish to realize the linear linked list shown in Fig. 10-15(a). Each node consists of two fields: an information field and a link field. We could store this list in two one-dimensional, four-element arrays as shown in Fig. 10-15(b). This approach is inflexible, however, since it would be impossible to add additional nodes to the list.

To provide the flexibility needed to effectively use a linked list, we can use two one-dimensional, N-element arrays as shown in Fig. 10-15(c). In this arrangement we actually realize two linked lists in the same array. The first list, called the *main list,* is the list that we are working with. The second list, called the *free list,* is a linked list of unused nodes. Two pointers are used in this case. The pointer FIRST points to the beginning of the main list while the

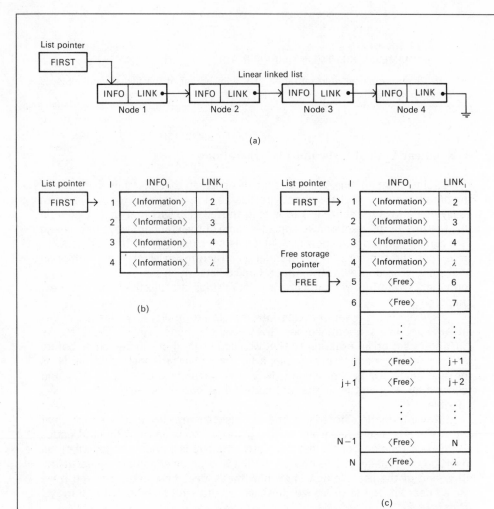

FIGURE 10-15 ■ Array representation of a linear linked list. (a) Representation of simple linear linked list. (b) Array representation of a linear linked list with any four elements. (c) Array representation of linear linked list in an N-element array, N > 4.

pointer FREE points to the beginning of the list of free nodes. A free list is often called a *list of available space*.

Deletion and Insertion Operations on a List

Perhaps the most important flexibility provided by the linked storage is the fact that it lends itself immediately to easier alteration of lists. It is very simple to delete a node from a linked list without having to "close up" the resulting gap created by the deletion. It is equally simple to "open up" a linked list to insert a new node without requiring the movement of other nodes in the list. Many types of sorting and search tasks can also be performed more efficiently on linked lists.

To illustrate the above ideas, let us first consider how a node is deleted from a linked list. Suppose that the second node in a singly-linked list of four nodes is to be deleted. This deletion can be achieved by changing the pointer in the link field of the node preceding the second node so that it will point to the third node. Graphically, the deletion operation is shown in Fig. 10-16. When a node is deleted, we have two alternatives. We can transfer the deleted node to the free list, in which case the node is available for later use, or we can disregard the deleted node, in which case it is no longer available for use. Retaining the node in the free list requires extra programming effort but saves memory space. The decision to retain or not to retain the deleted node for later use depends upon the particular problem being considered.

If we examine Fig. 10-16, we see that the deletion of a node is a simple task. If the same information were stored sequentially in an array, the deletion

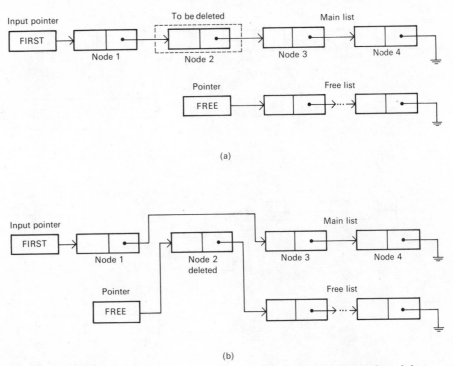

(a)

(b)

FIGURE 10-16 ■ Deletion of a node from a single linked list. (a) Before deletion. (b) After deletion.

process would imply that all of the elements below the deleted element in the array would have to be moved up one location to close the gap created by the deletion. This is a very time-consuming operation if a large number of nodes must be removed.

The insertion of a new node into a linked list is also very straightforward. Suppose that a node, called node $2\frac{1}{2}$ is to be inserted into a position between node 2 and node 3 in the above list with four nodes. This insertion operation is achieved by changing the pointer of node 2 so that it will point to the address of the new node, node $2\frac{1}{2}$, and by making the link field of node $2\frac{1}{2}$ point to node 3. This insertion operation would be extremely time consuming if the same information were stored sequentially in an array, since it involves moving a large number of the array elements to the next higher array location. Figure 10-17 shows graphically how the insertion of node $2\frac{1}{2}$ is achieved with a linked list.

From the above discussion, we see that the linked list structure frees us from any constraints that might be imposed by the sequential nature of the computer memory. Our next task is to develop algorithms that can be used to

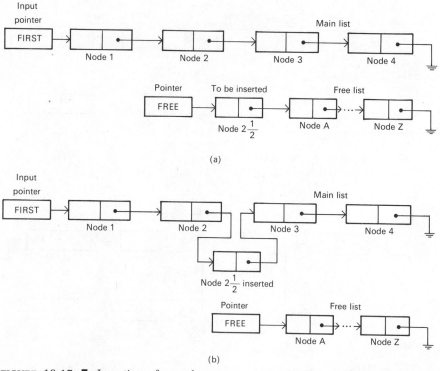

FIGURE 10-17 ■ Insertion of a node into a singly linked list. (a) Before insertion. (b) After insertion.

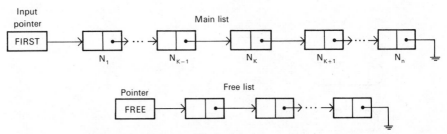

FIGURE 10-18 ■ Assumed form of linked list.

carry out the insertion, deletion, and other operations on linked lists. The application of these algorithms are discussed in the next section.

Deletion Algorithm

We assume in this discussion that a singly linked list consisting of n nodes, $N_1, N_2, \ldots, N_n$, is represented as shown in Fig. 10-18. Each node is assumed to have an information field and a link field as follows

| INFOR | LINK | A node |

To delete the Kth node (K arbitrary), N_K, from the main list and place it on the free list, the graphical representation in Fig. 10-16 suggests the following steps of operations:

1. Determine the address of the $(K - 1)$st node.
2. Set a pointer variable Q to the address of the Kth node.
3. Set the link field of the $(K - 1)$st node to the address of the $(K + 1)$st node (which is contained in the linked field of the Kth node to be deleted).
4. Set the link field of the Kth node to the address indicated by the pointer FREE.
5. Set the pointer FREE to the address indicated by Q.

A flowchart of an algorithm for deleting the Kth node from a singly linked list is shown in Fig. 10-19. The test included in the deletion algorithm is intended to take into account the possibility of an empty list. This situation may occur if the above algorithm is used as a subroutine. The inclusion of such a test makes certain that the algorithm works for all cases. Steps 4 and 5 of the algorithm can be omitted if we do not wish to retain the deleted node on a free list.

Insertion Algorithm

A similar algorithm may be developed to insert a new node from the free list into the singly linked main list between two specified nodes, say, the Kth and the $(K + 1)$st node. If $K = 0$, then the new node is to be inserted at the

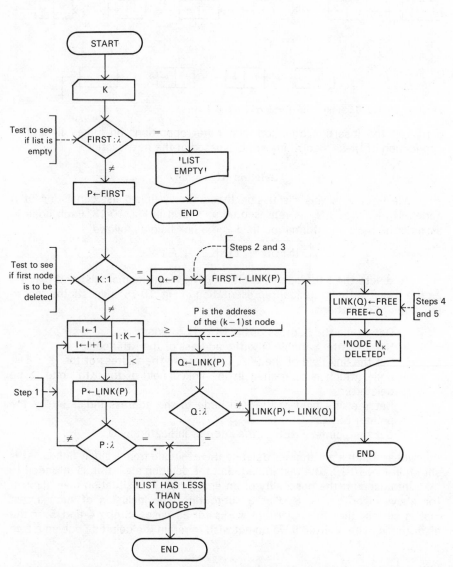

FIGURE 10-19 ■ Flowchart for deleting the Kth node from a singly linked list.

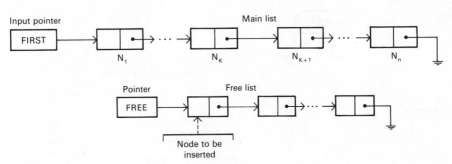

FIGURE 10-20 ■ Assumed form of linked list.

beginning of the list. After we insert the node, a value is assigned to the information field of the new node. Figure 10-20 is a representation of the lists before insertion takes place. The pointer FREE points to the new node to be inserted. Examining Fig. 10-17 leads to the following steps necessary to insert a new node:

1. Locate and temporarily store the address of the new node to be taken from the free list.
2. Set the pointer FREE to point to the next node on the free list.
3. Determine the address of the Kth node.
4. Set the link field of the new node to the address of the (K + 1)st node.
5. Set the link field of the Kth node to the address of the new node.
6. Store information in added node.

A flowchart for the insertion algorithm is shown in Fig. 10-21.

Search Algorithm

In addition to deletion and insertion, another basic operation is to search for a particular node in a linked list. In order to use an appropriate method in the search for a node, it is necessary to know exactly how the nodes in the list are linked together. The simplest method to locate a particular node in a linear linked list is a sequential search.

Consider the linked list illustrated in Fig. 10-22, where we wish to locate the node whose information field contains the data represented by the identifier X.

To search for the unknown node, we set up a special search pointer TEST that points to the address of the successive nodes in the list, starting with the value FIRST. Each time TEST is assigned a new value (points to the next node in the list), a comparison is made between the information field of the node pointed to by TEST and the information represented by X. If the comparison succeeds, the program reports that the node is located and the value in TEST is the address of the desired node. If the comparison does not succeed, then TEST is updated by assigning it a value corresponding to the contents of the

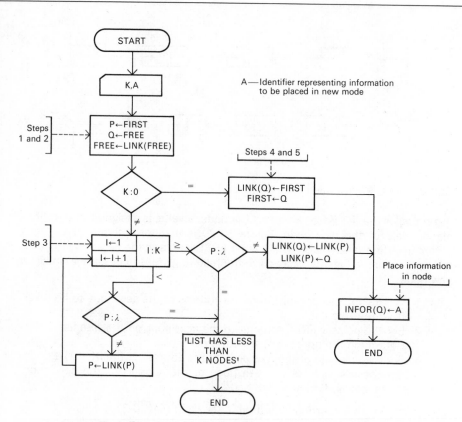

FIGURE 10-21 ■ A flowchart for the insertion of a new node after the Kth node and inserting information.

link field of the current node. TEST then points to the next node in the list and we repeat the search process. This process continues until either a match of the node is found or TEST has reached the end of the list. A flowchart describing this search process is shown in Fig. 10-23.

The linearly linked lists we have been considering are simple to realize and easy to work with. They require more storage space to store a given list,

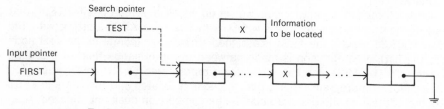

FIGURE 10-22 ■ Organization of a list to carry out a sequential search.

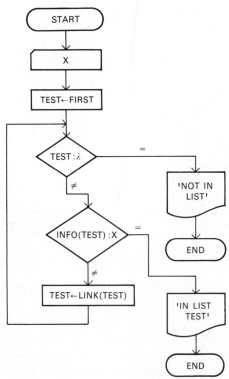

FIGURE 10-23 ■ A flowchart of the sequential search of a singly linked list.

but they are much more flexible than arrays. There is no reason, however, to limit the structure of our list to the simple types that we have been considering. We now consider some of the ways that the idea of a linked list can be expanded to accommodate different information-processing requirements.

Circularly Linked Lists

A *circularly linked list* (or *circular list,* or *ring*) is a linked list in which its last node points back to the first node instead of to λ. An obvious consequence of this linking method is that it is then possible to access all the nodes in the list starting at any given node. In effect, we need not think of the linear list as having a first node and a last node. Figure 10-24 shows a circular list and its graphical representation. When we work with a circular list, we use a pointer to indicate the node with which we are currently dealing. For example, the pointer PLACE in Fig. 10-24(b) indicates the second node. We can perform the same types of operations on circular lists as on linear lists. One problem which we

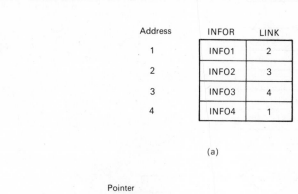

(a)

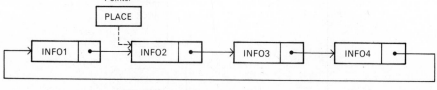

Pointer

(b)

FIGURE 10-24 ▪ A circular list. (a) The linking scheme. (b) The graphical representation.

must consider in these operations is that of knowing when we have processed the whole list or have reached a stopping point. Since the list has no end elements, we may introduce a special *marker node* in the list that can be detected. This marker node then serves to indicate a special location in the list.

The marker node can be produced in a number of ways. A special marker field can be introduced as shown in Fig. 10-25(a). If MARK is 0, then the node is a regular node while a MARK value of 1 would indicate a marker node. If more than one type of marker is needed, the value of MARK can be assigned additional numbers to indicate these conditions. Another way to indicate a marker node is to assign a value to the information field that can be recognized as being a special value. For example, if the information field is used to store names, the symbol 'XXXX', which is clearly not a name, could be used as a marker value. Figure 10-25(b) shows this type of marker.

A marker node can be inserted in a circular list as shown in Fig. 10-26.

(a)   (b)

FIGURE 10-25 ▪ Two ways to represent a marker node. (a) A node with a marker field MARK. (b) A node with a special symbol to indicate a marker.

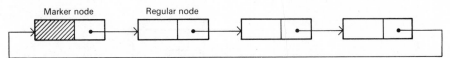

FIGURE 10-26 ■ A marker node inserted in a circular list.

Doubly Linked Lists

A more flexible linking scheme for the manipulation of linear lists can be obtained by including two link fields in each node: one pointing to the address of the preceding node and the other pointing to the address of the next node. This is commonly referred to as a *doubly linked list.* If we denote the two link fields by LINKP and LINKN, a typical node of a doubly linked list can be represented as shown in Fig. 10-27. A typical doubly linked list together with its graphical representation is shown in Fig. 10-28.

The main advantage of a doubly linked list is the fact that we can move either up or down the list. Not only do we know which node is the next node on the list, we also know which node is the previous node.

All the list operations just discussed can be just as easily performed on a doubly linked list. The difference is that more pointer values must be changed. An example of deleting a node from a doubly linked list is shown in Fig. 10-29. Examining this figure, it is clear that the deletion operation is essentially the same as that in singly linked lists except that two additional pointers must be changed. There is, however, one important feature that the doubly linked list has which permits us to perform deletion and insertion more easily. In a singly linked list, we cannot delete an arbitrary node unless the knowledge about the address of the node to be deleted is given, since the link field of the preceding node must be changed as part of the deletion process. To locate this node requires a sequential search. For a doubly linked list, this knowledge is always provided in the link field of the node to be deleted. For this reason, doubly linked lists are often used in data-processing work where deletions and insertions are frequently performed and it is necessary to move both ways along the list. The derivation of the deletion and insertion algorithm is left as an exercise. More applications of doubly linked lists will be discussed in the next chapter.

The desirability of using a linked list in a given information-processing task will depend upon the structure of the information involved in the task and the type of operations that must be performed. The techniques presented in this section are of an introductory nature and are intended to illustrate how

INFOR	LINKP	LINKN

FIGURE 10-27 ■ Node with two link fields.

	Content of node		
Address	INFOR	LINKP	LINKN
1	INFO1	λ	2
2	INFO2	1	3
3	INFO3	2	4
4	INFO4	3	λ

(a)

Input pointer

FIRST → INFO1 → INFO2 → INFO3 → INFO4

(b)

FIGURE 10-28 ■ A doubly linked list. (a) The linking scheme. (b) The graphical representation.

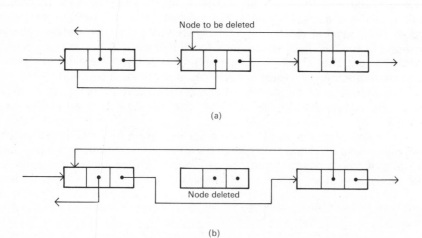

Node to be deleted

(a)

Node deleted

(b)

FIGURE 10-29 ■ Deletion of a node from a doubly linked list. (a) Before deletion. (b) After deletion.

lists are represented and operated on. Every programmer should feel free to use these ideas or modifications of these ideas whenever they will simplify the algorithm necessary to carry out a given task.

Exercises

1. For the singly linked list shown below:

Address	Content of node INFOR	LINK
1	'I'	3
2	'L'	1
3	'S'	4
4	'T'	λ

FIRST → 2

(a) give the graphical representation of the list;
(b) give the graphical representation of the list after the third node (containing the letter 'S') has been deleted. Show the contents of the list after the deletion.

2. Show the contents of the list in exercise 1 if the list is doubly linked.

3. The "POP" and "PUSH" operation of a stack can be considered as the deletion and insertion of the first (top) node in a singly linked list.

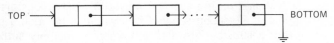

FIGURE E10-1

Modify the flowcharts in Figs. 10-19 and 10-20 so that they will only carry out the POP and PUSH operations, respectively, on a linked stack.

4. Show how a queue can be realized as a singly linked list.

5. Develop the delete and insert algorithms for a doubly linked list. The node in the list is assumed to have two link fields in addition to the information field.

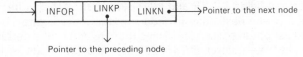

FIGURE E10-2

6. Show how two different lists can be created using nodes stored in the same free list. Use a figure such as Fig. 10-15 to explain how this is accomplished.

5 ∎ Application of Linked Lists

We now investigate some of the applications of linked-list concepts to problem-solving tasks. This section illustrates how we can apply linked lists to the solution of the following problems:

1. Information retrieval systems in which all or portions of a list must be frequently searched, altered, etc. A linked list provides an efficient way of performing these tasks and often requires a minimum of memory space.
2. Formula manipulation problems in which numerical calculation of mathematical formulas can be better carried out by nonnumerical techniques. A linked list in this case often makes this alternative method of numerical computing more efficient by using more flexible computer representation of formulas.
3. Efficient Data Storage.—A linked list may actually save memory space for a class of problems in which a large portion of the data file is not actively needed in the computing process.

Information Retrieval System

An airline wishes to have a system for handling passenger reservations for a daily flight. The system must be able to keep an alphabetically ordered list of all passengers that have a reservation for the flight. Since both reservations and cancellation requests must be handled, the system must be able to perform search, delete, and insert operations on the passenger list as requests come in. Assume that the maximum number of passengers that the flight can accommodate is 200, and on the average, only 100 reservations are filled on any flight. A sequential allocation scheme for manipulating such a passenger list would represent a substantial waste of computer memory since, on the average, half the memory space allocated is never used. We now demonstrate that a linked list is an efficient way to keep such a list of passengers.

Each passenger is represented in the computer by a node consisting of three fields:

| INFOR | LINKP | LINKN | A passenger node

The INFOR field contains the name of the passenger requesting a reservation. There are two link fields, LINKP and LINKN, indicating the address of the preceding node and the next node in order, respectively. Figure 10-30 shows a doubly linked list of ten passenger names that are active at a certain time for a particular flight. The pointer FIRST indicates the first node in the list. The names on the list are to be stored in alphabetical order. The null link λ again signifies the end of the list in either direction. A free list of available nodes is maintained. The pointer FREE indicates the address of the first node of this free list.

To see how this passenger list is dynamically altered as requests come in, assume that a passenger named FRANK requests a cancellation. The list in Fig. 10-30 can be altered to reflect this request by the following operations:

1. Use the search algorithm to locate the node representing passenger 'FRANK' (X is 'FRANK' in the search flowchart of Fig. 10-23).

Doubly linked list

Address	INFOR	LINKP	LINKN
1	'HALL'	6	10
2	'CARTER'	4	9
3	'MOORE'	5	7
4	'ALBERT'	λ	2
5	'LEWIS'	10	3
6	'GRANT'	8	1
7	'TERRY'	3	λ
8	'FRANK'	9	6
9	'ERICK'	2	8
10	'JAMES'	1	5

Input pointers

FIRST 4

FREE 20

FIGURE 10-30 ■ A doubly linked list of passengers before alteration.

2. Delete this node using a delete algorithm similar to that shown in Fig. 10-19.

The result of these operations is shown in Fig. 10-31. Note that the effect of deleting 'FRANK' is to change the value of LINKN in the node 'ERICK' preceding 'FRANK' and the value of LINKP in the node 'GRANT' following 'FRANK' The address of the node corresponding to 'FRANK' is placed on the free list. The address, 20, of the next node on the free list is placed in LINKN(8).

Now consider the case where a request for a reservation is made by a

Doubly linked list

Address	INFOR	LINKP	LINKN
1	'HALL'	6	10
2	'CARTER'	4	9
3	'MOORE'	5	7
4	'ALBERT'	λ	2
5	'LEWIS'	10	3
6	'GRANT'	9	1
7	'TERRY'	3	λ
8	'FRANK'	λ	20	←— Node deleted
9	'ERICK'	2	6
10	'JAMES'	1	5

Input pointers

FIRST 4

FREE 8

Denotes link changed

FIGURE 10-31 ■ Passenger list after cancellation of FRANK.

passenger named 'JONES'. To add this name to the passenger list shown in Fig. 10-31, we obtain a new node, if one is available, from the free list. In this example, the node would be the one just vacated by the cancellation of 'FRANK'. The address of this location is indicated by the pointer FREE. The list is changed to reflect the new addition by the following operations:

1. Perform a search to determine the position where the new node is to be inserted. This is achieved by sequentially comparing the name 'JONES' with the contents of the INFOR fields of the nodes in the list until 'JONES' is found to follow 'JAMES' and to precede 'LEWIS'. That is, the comparison continues until

$$\text{'JAMES'} < \text{'JONES'} < \text{'LEWIS'}$$

2. Insert the name 'JONES' into the list by using a node from the free list and an insertion algorithm similar to that shown in Fig. 10-21.

The result of these operations is shown in Fig. 10-32. In this figure, we see that LINKP of 'LEWIS' and LINKN of 'JAMES' must be changed to the address of 'JONES' in order to insert the new passenger into the list. Also, the two link fields of 'JONES' must be assigned to indicate its relation to 'JAMES' and 'LEWIS'.

It should be clear that the use of a linked list in this information retrieval system implies that whenever a new passenger's name is to be added to the list in its proper place, there is always an available memory location to store the name and its related information. Since it is our objective not to allocate memory space in advance and to use only the amount of storage needed for the list at any given time, we have made use of the free list to store nodes

| | Address | Doubly linked list | | |
		INFOR	LINKP	LINKN
	1	'HALL'	6	10
	2	'CARTER'	4	9
Input pointers	3	'MOORE'	5	7
FIRST 4	4	'ALBERT'	λ	2
	5	'LEWIS'	8	3
FREE 20	6	'GRANT'	9	1
	7	'TERRY'	3	λ
Node inserted →	8	'JONES'	10	5
	9	'ERICK'	2	6
	10	'JAMES'	1	8

Denotes link changed

FIGURE 10-32 ■ Passenger list after addition of JONES.

removed from the main list or to provide nodes when additional information must be added to the main list. Other lists may also draw on this free list. Thus, we are assured that memory area is allocated as needed. This method of adding nodes released from a main list to a free list is referred to as *garbage collection*.

Formula Manipulation

There are many problems in which an engineer or a scientist wishes to manipulate polynomials in one or more variables. For example, one might like to add the polynomial

$$P_1(x) = x^4 + 5x^3 - 4x^2 + x + 1$$

to the polynomial

$$P_2(x) = x^3 + 4x^2 + 7x + 2$$

to get the polynomial

$$P(x) = P_1(x) + P_2(x) = x^4 + 6x^3 + 8x + 3$$

Or, one might want to multiply the polynomial

$$P_3(x) = x^3 + x^2 + x + 1$$

by the polynomial

$$P_4(x) = x - 1$$

to obtain the polynomial

$$Q(x) = P_3(x) * P_4(x) = x^4 - 1$$

Since these operations are performed on symbols and formulas, they are often referred to as *Formula Manipulation*.

Ordinarily, the representation of polynomials in a computer can be very cumbersome, since polynomials can grow to large sizes or shrink to small sizes which make the storage difficult. However, a linked list provides a natural tool for the representation as well as the manipulation of polynomials. A polynomial $P(x)$ has the mathematical form

$$P(x) = a_n x^n + a_{n-1} x^{n-1} + \cdots + a_i x^i + \cdots + a_1 x + a_0$$

The term $a_n x^n$ is called the leading term of the polynomial. This polynomial may be represented by a singly linked list where each node stands for a nonzero term $a_i x^i$ ($a_i \neq 0$) of the polynomial. A node has the following form:

EXPT	
COEF	LINK

A node representing a term in the polynomial

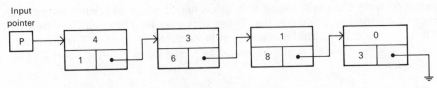

FIGURE 10-33 ■ Linked-list representation of the polynomial $X^4 + 6X^3 + 8X + 3$.

There are three fields: EXPT, COEF, and LINK. The EXPT and COEF fields correspond to the exponent i and coefficient a_i of the term $a_i x^i$, respectively. The LINK field points to the node representing the next term of the polynomial.

We assume that the nodes in the list appear in decreasing order of the EXPT field and the last node is terminated by a null link. Thus, the polynomial $x^4 + 6x^3 + 8x + 3$ would be represented as shown in Fig. 10-33. The pointer P indicates the leading term of the polynomial.

Addition of Polynomials

Two polynomials are added by adding the coefficients of their corresponding terms (terms with the same exponent). When the two polynomials are represented by linked lists, this addition process can be achieved by carrying out the following operations:

1. Set up pointers to the polynomial lists.
2. Compare the EXPT fields of the two polynomials term by term to locate the corresponding terms.
3. Add coefficients of the corresponding terms.

A flowchart for the addition of two polynomials, P and Q, is shown in Fig. 10-34. The operation of this flowchart can be understood by considering the schematic representation of the problem illustrated in Fig. 10-35. The two polynomials are represented by linked lists and the head of both lists are indicated by the pointers P and Q, respectively. In this flowchart the sum polynomial is retained in polynomial Q. Thus, the polynomial P is unchanged but the polynomial Q is modified according to the relationship

Polynomial Q ← Polynomial P + Polynomial Q

Two search pointers SP and SQ are used. We scan through the P list and the Q list node by node. When the exponent of a P-list node is greater than the corresponding Q-list node, a copy of the P-list node is added to the Q list. When the two nodes correspond to the same exponent, the coefficients are added and the new value becomes the coefficient of the Q-list node. If this new coefficient is zero, then the Q-list node is deleted. When the exponent of the P-list node is less than the exponent of the Q-list node, we simply move the SQ pointer to the next node on the Q list. When we reach the last node on the P

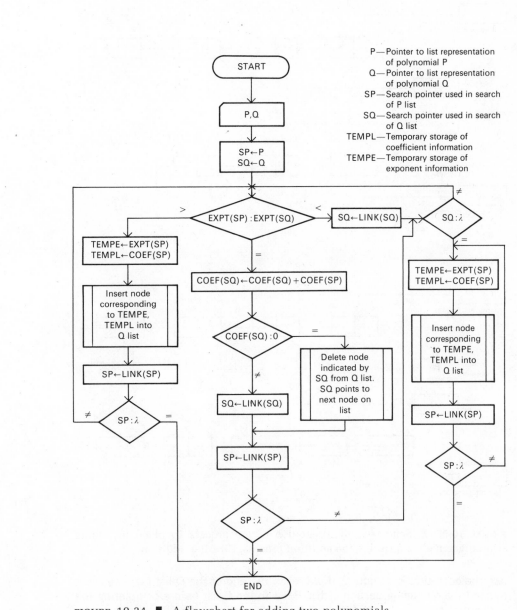

FIGURE 10-34 ■ A flowchart for adding two polynomials.

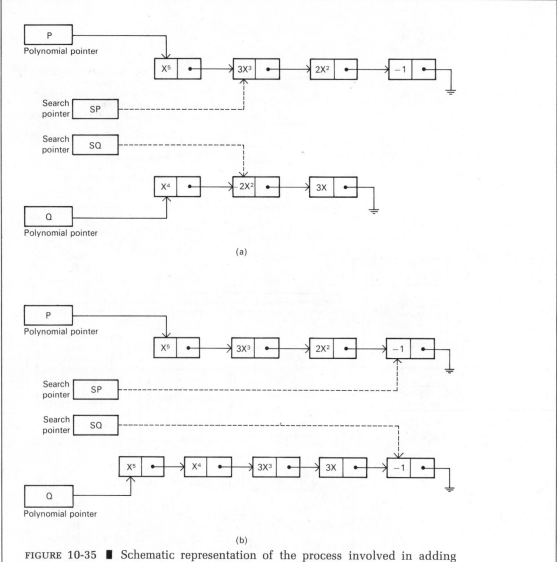

FIGURE 10-35 ■ Schematic representation of the process involved in adding two polynomials. (a) During the addition process. (b) After addition.

list, the operation is complete. If we reach the end of the Q list first, we must append the remaining portion of the P list to the Q list before completing the summation task.

The actual operation of adding and deleting nodes from the Q list is carried out in the manner described previously and is not presented in detail. The insertion and deletion operation maintains the ordering of the Q list.

Multiplication of Polynomials

Given the algorithm for polynomial addition, the multiplication of two polynomials is easy to carry out. This is because multiplication can be achieved by a series of addition operations. For example, for the polynomials

P: $3X + 1$
R: $X^2 + 2X + 5$

the polynomial corresponding to the product of P and R can be considered as the sum of the three following polynomials:

P1: $X^2(3X + 1) = 3X^3 + X^2$
P2: $2X(3X + 1) = 6X^2 + 2X$
P3: $5(3X + 1) = 15X + 5$

Assume that the product is represented by

Polynomial Q ← (Polynomial P) ∗ (Polynomial R)

Then this product is formed by executing the following

Polynomial Q ← 0
Polynomial Q ← Polynomial Q + Polynomial P1
Polynomial Q ← Polynomial Q + Polynomial P2
Polynomial Q ← Polynomial Q + Polynomial P3

The detailed steps of the multiplication algorithm using the addition algorithm are left as an exercise.

In addition to polynomial arithmetic such as addition and multiplication discussed above, linked lists also prove to be a convenient data structure for carrying out differentiations and integrations of polynomials. For readers who are familiar with the differential and integral calculus, these polynomial operations are explored in the exercises.

Arrays and Linked Lists

One of the most frequently used data forms for computer algorithms is the two- or higher-dimensional array. For example, consider the case of an $M \times N$ array.

$$[A_{I,J}] = \begin{bmatrix} A_{1,1} & A_{1,2} & \cdots & A_{1,N} \\ A_{2,1} & A_{2,2} & \cdots & A_{2,N} \\ \cdot & \cdot & & \cdot \\ \cdot & \cdot & & \cdot \\ \cdot & \cdot & & \cdot \\ A_{M,1} & A_{M,2} & \cdots & A_{M,N} \end{bmatrix}$$

The information represented by this array can be stored in a computer in the normal manner. To do so requires that the $(M) \cdot (N)$ locations be allocated in advance. These locations, once allocated, are no longer available for other uses. If only a few of the elements have assigned values, this approach can be a very wasteful to store the array.

To illustrate how linked lists are of use in this problem, let us consider the situation where the array is a matrix (i.e., the elements of the array are numbers). A *sparse matrix* is a two-dimensional array of numbers in which a large number of the elements are zero. For example, the following array is a sparse matrix.

$$\begin{bmatrix} 5 & 0 & 0 & 0 \\ 1 & -2 & 0 & 0 \\ 0 & 0 & 4 & 0 \\ -3 & 0 & 0 & 7 \end{bmatrix}$$

Since in many matrix operations the zero elements are not of importance, their presence in the matrix represents a waste of computer memory. Our goal is therefore to develop a method for representing sparse matrices so that they can be operated upon as though the entire matrix were present but without actually storing the zero elements. There are many ways to achieve this goal. The method of two-dimensional linked lists to be discussed is often preferable because it reflects the matrix structure in a natural way.

To represent a sparse matrix by a linked list, we first represent each nonzero element of the matrix by a node with five fields arranged in the following manner:

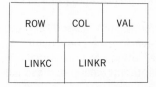

A node representing a
nonzero element

The fields ROW and COL contain the row and column indices of the matrix element represented by the node and the field VAL is the value of that element. There are two link fields, LINKC and LINKR, that contain pointers to link up all the nonzero elements of the matrix. LINKC contains the pointer to the next nonzero element in the column dimension and LINKR is the link to the next nonzero element in the row dimension. Thus, for example, the element $A_{2,1}$ in the above matrix is represented by the node

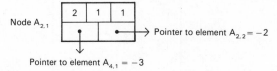

A matrix whose elements are represented in this manner is said to have a two-dimensional linked list representation. We can think of a nonzero element of

the matrix as belonging to two linked lists: the row list and the column list corresponding to the row and column indices specified in the ROW and COL fields.

In order to perform matrix operations, we must have a convenient way of accessing the row lists and column lists in which the matrix elements are stored. This is achieved by providing an access node, called ACCESS, for each row and column of the matrix. Thus, the access node for Row I is represented by

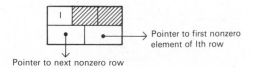

and similarly, the access node for column J is represented by

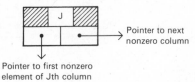

For the access nodes, only the row or column field and the two link fields are used; the other two fields contain no information and are cross-shaded as shown.

Entry to the array is indicated by two pointers ROWA and COLA which point to the first row-access node and column-access node, respectively. Using this method of representation, the sparse matrix given above would have the form shown in Fig. 10-36.

Note that in Fig. 10-36, the access nodes appear at the left (row access) and the top (column access). The successive row elements are then reached by linking the row pointers to the right and the successive column elements are reached by linking the column pointers downward. The last nonzero element in each row and column is indicated by the null symbol λ in the corresponding link field.

With the linked list representation, we can save computer memory whenever a large number of zero elements appear in the matrix. For example, a 100×100 matrix would normally take 10,000 sequential memory locations, which represents a large portion of the memory space available in most computers. Assume that this matrix is suitably sparse with 90 percent of the elements being zero. If each node requires two memory locations to represent, then the linked representation needs only

$$2[.1 \times 100 \times 100 + 2 \times 100] = 2,000 + 400 = 2,400$$

locations. The 400 locations in the above calculation correspond to the access nodes needed for accessing the rows and columns of the matrix. The amount

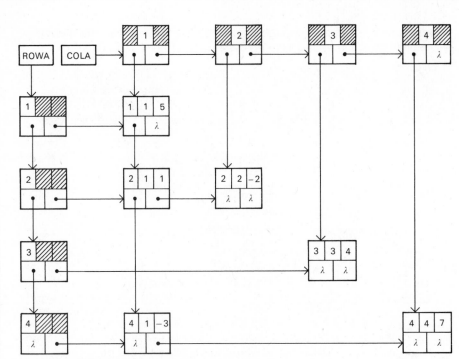

FIGURE 10-36 ■ Linked representation of a sparse matrix.

of time needed to access a particular node is generally greater than that needed in sequential allocation. Since many matrix operations proceed by walking sequentially through the elements of the matrix anyway, the total time required to perform the complete matrix operation may be comparable for both storage methods. Any saving, in time and in memory, depends upon the nature of the matrix and also upon the types of operations to be performed on the matrix.

Various algorithms dealing with sparse matrices represented as two-dimensional linked lists can easily be developed. As an example, consider the addition of two $M \times N$ sparse matrices, $[A_{I,J}]$ and $[B_{I,J}]$, represented in linked list form. This is accomplished by

$$[C_{I,J}] \leftarrow [A_{I,J}] + [B_{I,J}]$$

The element $C_{I,J}$ of the sum matrix $[C_{I,J}]$ is obtained by adding the element $A_{I,J}$ of $[A_{I,J}]$ to the element $B_{I,J}$ of $[B_{I,J}]$ and storing the sum in location $C_{I,J}$. This addition operation can be more economically achieved by the following assignment

$$[B_{I,J}] \leftarrow [A_{I,J}] + [B_{I,J}]$$

for appropriate values of I and J. Detailed steps for carrying out this addition process are summarized below:

1. Determine the first nonzero element of $[A_{I,J}]$ starting with the first row.
2. Add this element to the corresponding element in $[B_{I,J}]$ (i.e., the element with the same row and column indices). If there is no such element in $[B_{I,J}]$, insert this element in $[B_{I,J}]$. If the sum element is zero after adding the corresponding elements, delete the sum element from $[B_{I,J}]$.
3. Determine the next nonzero element of $[A_{I,J}]$ in the same row and perform step 2 until the last element in that row is processed.
4. Determine the first nonzero element of the next row that has at least one nonzero element and perform steps 2 and 3 above.
5. Repeat the above steps until the last row containing at least one nonzero element has been processed.

The matrix addition algorithm described above is in many ways similar to the addition algorithm we have developed for two polynomials. Instead of adding terms of the same exponent by traversing through the one-dimensional linked list, we now add elements of the same row and column indices with two-dimensional linked lists. There are two major differences in the algorithms, however. The first difference is that the matrix algorithm must be able to determine the new row with at least one nonzero element after each row has been processed. This is achieved by using the pointers of the row access and column access nodes. When either one of the pointers has the value λ, we know that we have come to the end of the row access list or the column access list.

The second difference concerns the insertion and deletion of elements in the sum matrix. These operations are slightly more complicated in two-dimensional lists than those performed on one-dimensional lists. The reason for this complication is that we must be able to determine which links, in both dimensions, are involved with the node being inserted or deleted. We need two auxiliary pointer variables, one for each dimension, that are always one node "ahead" of the node being processed. These pointer variables then contain the links that must be changed for deletion or insertion purposes.

Exercises

1. For the information retrieval system discussed in this section, show the resulting contents of the information and linked fields in the passenger list shown in Fig. 10-30 after each of the following requests. Assume that the four requests are processed in the order given. Nodes that are deleted from the list are to be stored in a stack serving as a FREE list. The address of the top node in the FREE list is initially 20.

(a)	GRANT	Cancellation
(b)	MOORE	Cancellation
(c)	ALBERT	Cancellation
(d)	ALDER	Reservation

2. Assume that a set of nodes representing the terms of a polynomial are read into a computer in random order. Develop an algorithm that will put each term in its proper place when it is read in so that the polynomial is always in descending order. Example:

Input	Desired form of polynomial
$2X$	$2X$
$3X^2$	$3X^2 + 2X$
5	$3X^2 + 2X + 5$

3. Develop a flowchart for the multiplication of two polynomials using the addition algorithm discussed in this section.

4. The derivative (first derivative) of a term AX^B with respect to X is

$$A \cdot BX^{B-1}$$

and the integral of AX^B is

$$\frac{A}{B+1} X^{B+1}$$

Thus, the nodes representing the term AX^B, its derivative, and its integral are

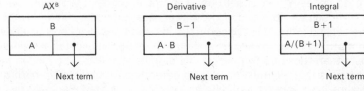

Develop an algorithm that will compute the derivative and the integral of a polynomial

$$P(X) = a_n X^n + \cdots + a_i X^i + \cdots + a_1 X + a_0$$

It is assumed that the derivative (integral) of P(X) is the sum of the derivatives (integrals) of the individual terms.

5. Given a 200×200 matrix in which there are at most four nonzero elements per row, determine the storage requirement (number of memory locations) if:
   (a) the matrix is stored in sequential memory locations;
   (b) the matrix is stored in two-dimensional linked lists. Assume each node requires two memory locations of storage space.

6. Let $[A_{I,J}]$ and $[B_{I,J}]$ be two sparse matrices:

$$[A_{I,J}] = \begin{bmatrix} 1 & 0 & 0 \\ 0 & -2 & 1 \\ 5 & 0 & 0 \end{bmatrix} \quad [B_{I,J}] = \begin{bmatrix} 0 & 0 & 1 \\ 0 & 2 & 0 \\ 0 & 3 & 0 \end{bmatrix}$$

(a) Show the linked representation of these two matrices.

(b) Show the linked representation of $[B_{I,J}]$ after the following operation:

$$[B_{I,J}] \leftarrow [B_{I,J}] + [A_{I,J}]$$

6 ■ Summary

Several important data structures are introduced in this chapter. Many of these structures are most conveniently represented within a computer by the use of linked lists. A linked list representation often makes it possible for the computer to store and process information more efficiently than the sequential scheme whenever the information structure is subject to frequent dynamic changes.

The use of these data structures, however, does not necessarily increase the complexity of our programming tasks. Most of the programming techniques we discussed before remain applicable without modification. Only a slight change of notation is occasionally needed to allow us to use pointers as an integral part of the data nodes. Perhaps a brief summary of the typical iteration process in a loop that was used in many of the list algorithms will help to clarify this point.

As was discussed in our previous chapters, a typical iteration process involves four essential elements of operation: initialization, test, computation, and update. In a linked list representation, the data nodes are accessed by successively following the pointers in the LINK fields associated with the nodes, starting with the first node. For the computer to reach the next node from the present node, the pointer variable P containing the address of the present node is updated to contain the address of the next node. This is achieved by the following assignment operation:

$$P \leftarrow LINK(P)$$

Thus, a typical iteration process can be characterized as shown in Fig. 10-37.

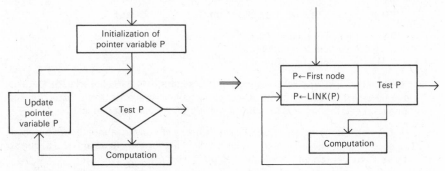

FIGURE 10-37 ■ General flowchart representation of an iteration process involving linked lists.

From that illustration, we see that the iteration process that is typically carried out by many list algorithms is identical to that used in algorithms with sequential schemes. The only difference is that counter variables are now replaced by the pointer-linking operations.

References

[4] and [5] present a very comprehensive treatment of all types of linked lists. [1] and [2] also treat the general properties of stacks, queues, and lists. [3] discusses how many of these data structures can be realized using FORTRAN. [6] considers how different matrix operations can be performed on sparse matrices.

1. Barrodale, I., Roberts, F., and Ehle, B. (1971) *Elementary Computer Applications,* John Wiley & Sons, New York.
2. Brooks, F. P., and Iverson, K. E. (1969) *Automatic Data Processing, System/360 Edition,* 2nd ed., John Wiley & Sons, New York.
3. Day, A. C. (1972) *FORTRAN Techniques; with Special Reference To Non-Numerical Applications,* Cambridge University Press, London.
4. Foster, J. M. (1967) *List Processing,* Computer Monograph Series, American Elsevier, New York.
5. Knuth, D. (1968) *The Art of Computer Programming, Vol. 1, Fundamental Algorithms,* Addison-Wesley, Reading, Mass.
6. McNamee, J. (April 1971) "Algorithm 408—A Sparse Matrix Package (Part I)," *Communications of the ACM,*Vol. 14, No. 4, pp. 265–273.

Home Problems

If possible, the algorithms developed to solve the following problems should be programmed and tested on a computer.

1. Develop the flowchart of an algorithm which can be used to merge two sorted linearly linked lists.

2. Develop the flowchart of an algorithm which can be used to:

    1. insert a node in a circular list;
    2. locate an item in a circular list;
    3. delete a node from a circular list.

3. Two stacks S1 and S2 are stored in two separate, linearly linked lists. Develop the flowchart of an algorithm for combining the two stacks where S1 is stacked upon S2, i.e., the top of S1 becomes the top of the combined stack.

4. Develop the flowchart of an algorithm that will convert a queue into a deque. Choose an appropriate form of a doubly linked list for the queue and the deque so that the conversion can be easily accomplished.

5. Consider the problem where the end part of a large linked list must be altered a large number of times. Instead of working with such a list directly, we may save

time by first reversing the order of the nodes in the list before the alterations take place. When the alterations are completed, the list is put back in its original order by a second reversion. Develop the flowchart of an algorithm to perform the reversion process on a linked list.

6. A program is to be developed to register students for a course with a maximum of N openings. Students are registered on a first-come, first-served basis except that all seniors have priority over all lower class students, all juniors have priority over all freshmen and sophomores, and all sophomores have priority over all freshmen. Develop the flowchart of an algorithm that will assign N students to a given class according to the above ordering relationships. Use queues to store the student request information as it is received. Print out an alphabetic class list and a list in order of admission priority, of all students not admitted to the class.

7. Develop the flowchart for an algorithm which will add two sparse matrices $[A_{I,J}]$ and $[B_{I,J}]$ which are stored in linked-list form. The result is to be stored in the sparse matrix $[A_{I,J}]$.

8. Develop the flowchart of an algorithm which can be used to divide a polynomial $f(x)$ by a polynomial $g(x)$. The result is to be a quotient polynomial $q(x)$ and a remainder $r(x)$. For example, let

$$f(x) = x^7 + x^5 + x^4 + x^3 + 2x + 2$$
$$g(x) = x^4 + 1$$

then

$$q(x) = x^3 + x + 1 \qquad r(x) = x + 1$$

9. A computer can be used to edit textual material. Assume that a linked-list is used to store the individual words in a sentence. Develop the flowchart of an algorithm which can be used to carry out the following editing tasks:

1. delete a particular word or a particular sequence of words;
2. insert a word or a sequence of words;
3. change a word or a sequence of words to another word or sequence of words.

10. Develop the flowchart of an algorithm that can be used to sort a linearly linked list. Compare this method of sorting information to the methods used in Chapter IX for sorting information stored in array form.

**tree algorithms
and applications**

1 ■ Introduction

The organization of any computer program is very strongly influenced by the way we organize the information it uses. As long as we deal with numerical calculations, the needed numerical information can be represented in a form that closely parallels standard mathematical notation.

Computers are now used to perform a wide variety of tasks which do not involve complex mathematical calculations. We have seen that we can carry out a wide range of symbolic information-processing tasks, such as carrying out arithmetic operations on polynomials or maintaining a list of names in alphabetic order. The algorithms used to describe these computations are very strongly dependent upon the methods used to store the data required during the computation. We use the term "nonnumerical information processing" to describe the class of computations which are primarily concerned with symbol manipulation rather than with standard mathematical calculations on numeric information.

In this chapter, we extend the concepts of linked lists to handle a number of the standard information representations and processing problems encountered in nonnumerical information processing. Our task is to identify the basic structural properties inherent in the tasks to be performed and then to develop methods which can be used to represent these structural features. These methods will usually involve extending the data-structure concepts treated in the previous chapters to handle slightly more complex interrelationships.

While we are dealing with nonnumeric data, it is important to realize that we do not exclude the possibility of having to perform numerical calculations or mathematical operations as part of a nonnumerical information-processing task. The term "nonnumerical" is therefore not to be taken too literally. Quite often we find that the concept of numbers plays such an important role in automatic computing that we cannot get away from it even if we are primarily concerned with characters and symbols.

2 ■ Trees

Many nonnumerical information-processing tasks involve the processing of very large collections of data. Inherent in these tasks is the need to order the data in some manner, say alphabetically, so that we can search the data for the occurrence of a given item, remove an element from the collection, or add an element to the collection. The linked-list information structure presented in Chapter X is a very convenient way to represent information of this type if the number of elements is small. However, as the number of data items increases, linear linked lists become less attractive for many applications, particularly if the list must be operated upon a large number of times. One way to overcome these problems is to introduce a nonlinear data structure which represents a generalization of simple linked lists.

Binary Trees

Assume that we have the list of cities given in Table 11-1 that we wish to use in some information-processing task. To carry out the task we must store this list in such a way that it is easy to determine if a given city is or is not on the list. There are a number of ways that this could be represented. Two methods, which we have already considered, are arrays and linear linked lists. Another method is to use a binary tree. These three methods are compared in Fig. 11-1.

As illustrated in Fig. 11-1, *binary trees* are a generalization of linear linked lists. Every node in the tree has one or more fields which contain information and two link fields. The left link field, denoted by LINKL, points to the part of the tree that is to the left of the current node, and the right link field, denoted by LINKR, points to the part of the tree that is to the right of the current node.

Binary trees are very useful if we wish to perform a binary search on data. To see how such a search is carried out, assume that we wish to determine if 'HARTFORD' is in the data represented by the tree of Fig. 11-1(c). We enter the tree at the point indicated by the pointer ENTER. 'HARTFORD' is then compared to the name in the information field of that node. If the two were equal, we would know that we had located 'HARTFORD' in the list and we would stop our search. However, 'MIAMI' is in the name field. Since we have the relation

$$\text{'HARTFORD'} < \text{'MIAMI'}$$

we then go to the node pointed to by the left link field. This node represents the name 'CHICAGO'. Since

$$\text{'HARTFORD'} > \text{'CHICAGO'}$$

we then follow the right link pointer to the node representing 'DENVER'. Here again, we find no match. Instead, we have

$$\text{'HARTFORD'} > \text{'DENVER'}$$

TABLE 11-1 ∎ List of city names

1.	AKRON	6.	MOSCOW
2.	ALBANY	7.	MIAMI
3.	CHICAGO	8.	PARIS
4.	DENVER	9.	SALEM
5.	HARTFORD	10.	YUKON

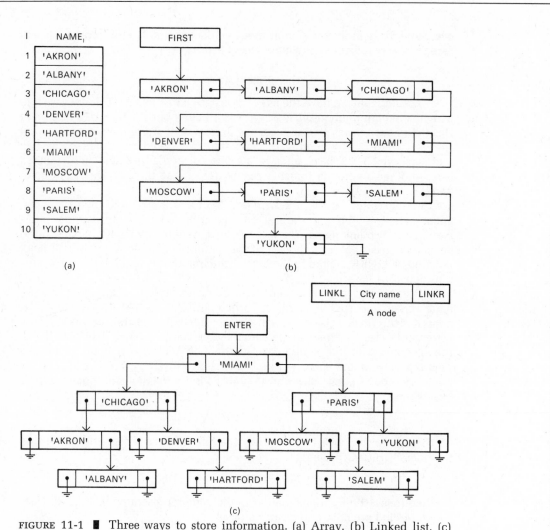

FIGURE 11-1 ■ Three ways to store information. (a) Array. (b) Linked list. (c) Binary tree.

Thus, we follow the right link to the node representing 'HARTFORD', where we finally obtain a match.

Now that we have a general idea of the form that a tree takes, we introduce some of the standard terminology used to describe and discuss trees.

Notations and Terminology

A tree consists of a set of nodes, denoted by $\{N_i\}$, and a set of unidirectional associations between pairs of nodes. We will call these associations *branches.* There are several important features that characterize a tree. Each tree has a *root* which is a node that has no branches entering it. A node which has no branch leaving it is called a *terminal node.* Any node that is not a root or a terminal node is called a *branch node,* or a *nonterminal node.* A *path* between two nodes N_i and N_j of a tree is the sequence of branches leading from N_i to N_j. The number of branches in a path is called the *length* of the path. A tree is a *binary tree* if at most two branches leave any node. When a nonterminal node of a binary tree has exactly two branches, we distinguish between the left branch and right branch of that node.

The hiearchical relationship in a tree is specified by the *level* associated with each node. The root of a tree is defined to lie on the *first level* and any other nodes that lie at the end of a path of length $j - 1$ from the root is on the *jth level.* To talk about trees and tree algorithms, it is useful to refer to the set of nodes that lie at the end of a path of length one from a particular node N_i. This set of nodes is called the *filial set of node* N_i and N_i is called the *parent node* of that set. Nodes in the filial set have the same level number.

Many methods are used to represent tree structures graphically. Figure 11-2 shows a conventional representation of a general tree with an illustration of the notation and terminology used to describe a tree. In this conventional representation of a general tree, the root A is drawn at the top of the tree and terminal nodes are at the bottom (contrary to the way trees grow in nature).

Array Representation of Trees

The actual representation of a tree in a computer can easily be accomplished once we define the information to be represented by each node.

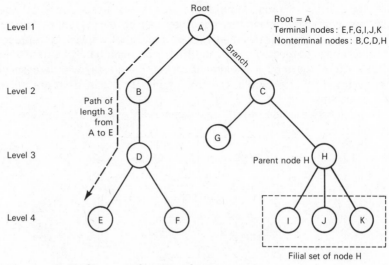

FIGURE 11-2 ■ A diagram of a general tree.

TABLE 11-2 ■ Test record of a class

Student	Test 1	Test 2	Test 3	Grade
ABEL	67	74	70	C
ASH	76	39	87	C
BAKER	100	92	99	A
DAVIS	60	25	40	F
MILLS	87	90	60	B
SMITH	77	70	81	C

First, we define the structure of binary trees and then we show how a general tree can be represented as a binary tree.

Every node in a binary tree is made up of at least three fields. Two of the fields are used as link fields while the remaining fields are used to hold the information associated with the node. One of the information fields is selected to represent the *key field* of the node. Whenever a comparison is made, it is carried out on the information in the key field, and all discussions of ordering are understood to mean an ordering according to the value of the key information.

To illustrate these ideas, assume that we wish to store the information given by Table 11-2 using a tree structure. Each node has seven fields, as shown in Fig. 11-3. The key field is NAME. Using this organization, one tree corresponding to Table 11-2 is shown in Fig. 11-4. Note that the form of the tree is not unique and that other tree organizations can also be used to store the same information.

If the particular programming language being used does not have a special method for representing trees, they can be easily realized using arrays just as we did for linear linked lists. Assume that we wish to represent a tree that will have at most N nodes and that each node has K fields. To represent such a tree, we need K N-element arrays. Each array will be associated with a given field. For example, the tree of Fig. 11-4 can be represented in array form as shown in Fig. 11-5.

Two pointers are used to indicate special entry points to the array. The

FIGURE 11-3 ■ Field arrangement to store the information of Table 11-2.

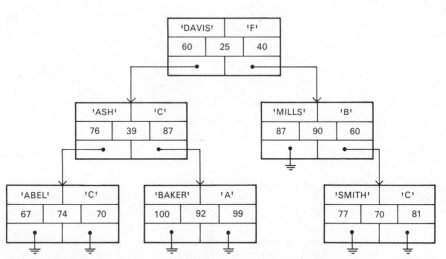

FIGURE 11-4 ■ Tree representation of the information in Table 11-2.

pointer ENTER is used to indicate the root node of the tree. The unused nodes of the array are kept on a *free list* of nodes which are available for use at a later time. The free list is organized as a linear linked list and the pointer FREE indicates the first node on the list.

General Trees

So far our discussion has concentrated on the structure of binary trees. There are many other types of trees that are of use in particular situations.

Input pointer	ENTER			FREE		Free list pointer
	1			7		

I	NAME	GRADE	TEST 1	TEST 2	TEST 3	LINKL	LINKR
1	'DAVIS'	'F'	60	25	40	3	2
2	'MILLS'	'B'	87	90	60	λ	5
3	'ASH'	'C'	76	39	87	4	6
4	'ABEL'	'C'	67	74	70	λ	λ
5	'SMITH'	'C'	77	70	81	λ	λ
6	'BAKER'	'A'	100	92	99	λ	λ
7						λ	8
8						λ	9
9						λ	λ

FIGURE 11-5 ■ Array representation of the tree of Fig. 11-4.

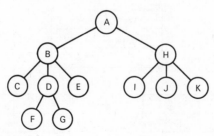

FIGURE 11-6 ■ A general tree.

Whenever such a tree is encountered, we can restructure the tree so that it has the same general form as a binary tree, and it can thus be represented in a computer as a binary tree. The following example illustrates how this can be done.

Assume that we are given the tree shown in Fig. 11-6 and we wish to represent this tree in the form of a binary tree. One way we do this is illustrated in Fig. 11-7. Examining this figure, we see that the left link is used to point to the nodes of a higher level number and the right link is used to point at all of the nodes on the same level which have the same parent node.

When we deal with general trees, we no longer retain the ordering property usually present in binary trees. When we transform a general tree into a binary tree, there is usually no implied ordering. For the rest of this chapter, in discussing tree operations and algorithms, we concentrate most of our attention on binary trees.

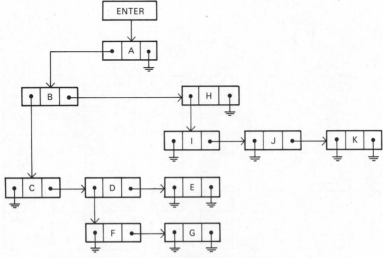

FIGURE 11-7 ■ Binary-tree representation of a general tree.

Cost of Using Tree Structures

Tree structures have many advantages, but they also have disadvantages which must be considered. For large trees, a considerable amount of memory space must be devoted to the storage of link information. In some situations, the flexibility of a tree representation is not needed and the information can be just as conveniently stored in a simple array. This would reduce the amount of storage space required.

When using a tree structure, we never know the exact location of any particular node of the tree. If we must keep track of particular nodes, we must use a separate external pointer to indicate that location.

In the next section, we investigate many of the basic operations which are often necessary to manipulate an ordered binary tree. These operations often require a much more complex algorithm than would be required if the information were stored in a simple array.

The final decision, concerning whether a tree structure should be used instead of an array or a linear linked list, must be made after the requirements of the computation have been fully analyzed. In any event, a proper decision cannot be made unless we fully appreciate the characteristics of all types of information storage.

Exercises

1. For the following general tree

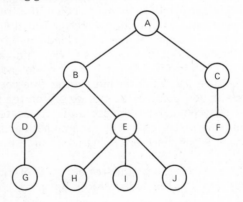

FIGURE E11-1

  (a) determine all the terminal and nonterminal nodes;
  (b) determine the filial set for each of the nonterminal nodes;
  (c) convert the tree to a binary tree.

2. Give a binary tree similar to that shown in Fig. 11-1 for the list of city names given in Table 11-1. Let the root of the binary tree be 'HARTFORD'.

3 ■ Operations on Binary Trees

In Chapter X, we introduced a number of standard list-processing operations that are required to manipulate information stored in the form of a linear linked list. We now introduce equivalent operations for binary trees. This section gives the algorithms which are used to carry out the following tree operations:

1. Search for a particular node
2. Insert a node
3. Traverse a tree in order
4. Delete a node

For this discussion, it is assumed that each node has the form shown in Fig. 11-8. The information contained in the node may occupy one or more fields. However, INFOR represents the *key field* of the node. Whenever a comparison is made, it is carried out on the information in the key field and all discussion of ordering is understood to mean an ordering according to the value of the key information.

Search of a Sorted Binary Tree

Assume that we are given a binary tree such as that illustrated in Fig. 11-9. The nodes of the tree are sorted so that nodes in the portion of the tree to the left of any node have keys which are less than the key of the node and the keys in the portion of the tree to the right of any node have keys which are larger. The pointer ENTER points to the root node of the tree and the pointer TEST is used to keep track of our current position in the tree as we move through the tree. The item being searched for is indicated by the identifier X.

The search process is a binary search. We enter at the root node and compare X to INFOR(ENTER). If the two do not match and if X < INFOR(ENTER), then we search the left subtree (the portion of the tree to the left of the node in question). Otherwise, we search the right subtree. We continually repeat this comparison process until we locate the node corresponding to X or until we reach the end of a search path and find that X is not contained in the tree. A flowchart describing this search process is shown in Fig. 11-10.

Assume that we wish to search the tree of Fig. 11-9 and that the input X is 'MARY'. The first stop is at the node 'MARK'. Since

$$\text{'MARY'} > \text{'MARK'}$$

LINKL	INFOR	LINKR

FIGURE 11-8 ■ Assumed form of node.

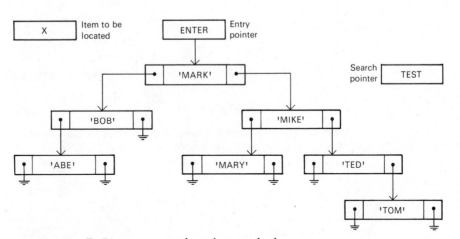

FIGURE 11-9 ■ Binary tree ready to be searched.

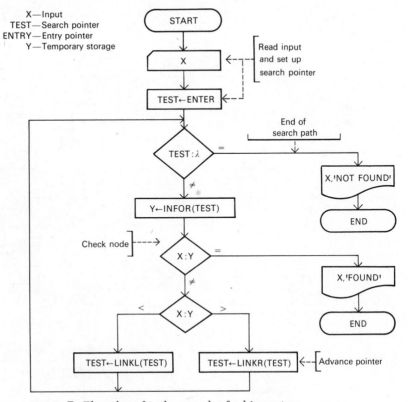

FIGURE 11-10 ■ Flowchart for the search of a binary tree.

we go down the right path to the node 'MIKE'. Since

$$\text{'MARY'} < \text{'MIKE'}$$

we go down the left path to the node 'MARY' where we find a match. Thus, we report that 'MARY' was found.

Insertion of a Node

Assume that we are given a sorted binary tree such as is illustrated in Fig. 11-11(a) and that we wish to add new information to the tree. To do this,

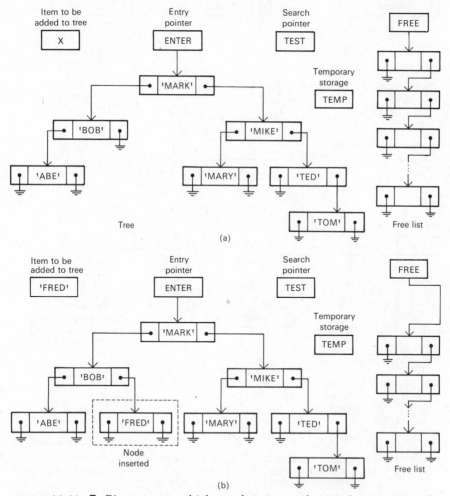

FIGURE 11-11 ■ Binary tree to which a node is inserted. (a) Before insertion. (b) After insertion.

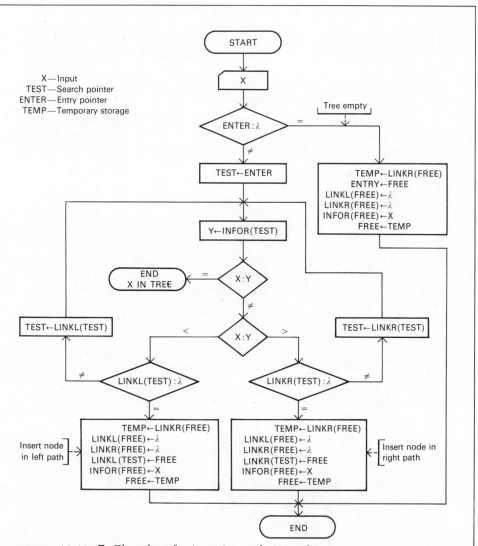

FIGURE 11-12 ■ Flowchart for inserting node into a binary tree.

we must have a list of free nodes which is also shown in Fig. 11-11(a). The pointers ENTER and TEST serve the same function as before and FREE is the pointer associated with the free list. The item to be added to the list is indicated by the identifier X.

The insertion process consists of searching the tree until the end of a path is reached. The item to be inserted is then added to the tree at that location. The node is taken from the free list, inserted into the tree, and then the information represented by X is inserted into the information field of the node.

An example of inserting a node containing the item 'FRED' to a binary tree is shown in Fig. 11-11(b). A flowchart describing the insertion algorithm is shown in Fig. 11-12.

Traversing a Binary Tree

A binary tree represents an ordered collection of information. It is often necessary to examine each node in the tree in a fixed order. For example, consider the tree of Fig. 11-13. If we wish to print the names represented by this

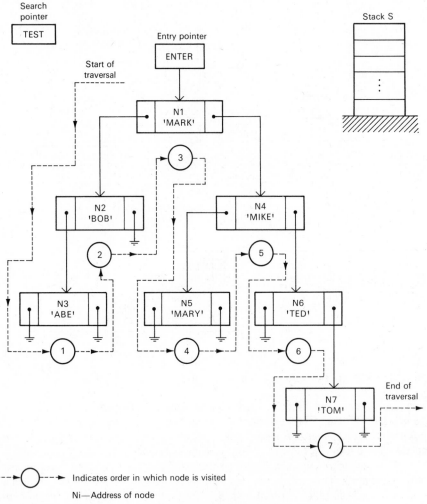

FIGURE 11-13 ■ Illustration of a postorder search of a binary tree.

tree in alphabetical order, it is necessary to read the name represented by each node in the order indicated.

When we work our way through a tree in such a way that we "visit" or "stop" at each node once and only once, we say that we have traversed the tree. The traversal of the tree shown in Fig. 11-13 is said to be a *postorder traversal*. Such a traversal can be accomplished by the repeated execution of the following steps:

1. Traverse the nodes on the left side of the parent node.
2. Visit the parent node.
3. Traverse the nodes on the right side of the parent node.

The example shown in Fig. 11-13 illustrates these traversal steps. Starting at the root of the tree, we move off to the left and proceed down the leftmost path until we reach the end of the path (indicated by ①). We visit this node and carry out the desired computational task on the information repre-

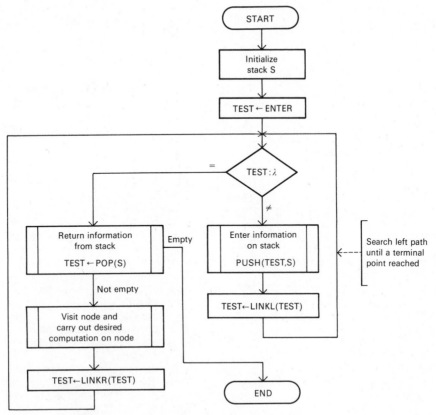

FIGURE 11-14 ■ Flowchart of postorder traversal algorithm.

sented by the node. We then try to move along a right-hand path but find, in this example, that there is no right-hand path. Thus, we backtrack to the parent node (indicated by ②) and visit at that node. Here again there is no right-hand path, so we return to the previous node (indicated by ③) and visit at that node. Next, we start to follow the right-hand path, which takes us to the node indicated by ④. The traversal is completed by visiting the nodes indicated by ⑤, ⑥, and ⑦, in that order.

TABLE 11-3 ■ Execution of postorder traversal algorithm

Step	Contents of search pointer	Contents of stack	Comments
0	N1	λ	Start of traversal
1	N2	N1	Pass through first node N1
2	N3	N2 N1	Pass through node 2
3	λ	N3 N2 N1	Pass through node 3 and detect end of path
4	N3	N2 N1	Visit node N3
5	λ	N2 N1	Try to follow right path from node N3; find END
6	N2	N1	Visit node N2
7	λ	N1	Try to follow right path from node N2; find END
8	N1	λ	Visit node N1
9	N4	λ	Start following right path from N1
10	N5	N4	Pass through node N4
11	λ	N5 N4	Pass through node N5 and detect end of path
12	N5	N4	Visit node N5
13	λ	N4	Try to follow right path from node N5; find END
14	N4	λ	Visit node N4
15	N6	λ	Start following right path from N5
16	λ	N6	Pass through node N6 and detect end of path
17	N6	λ	Visit node N6
18	N7	λ	Start following right path from N6
19	λ	N7	Pass through node N7 and detect end of path
20	N7	λ	Visit node N7
21	λ	λ	Try to follow right path from node N7; detect end of path and empty stack END OF TRAVERSAL

Tracing through this sequence of visits, we see that we visit each node only once and that the nodes are visited according to our ordering convention. Examining the path of the traversal, we see that we "pass through" a number of nodes before we finally return to pay a visit. As we go down a left-hand path, we must remember those nodes that we "pass through" so that we can visit them on our return trip. When we move down the right-hand path, it is not necessary to make a return visit to the parent nodes. Thus, we do not have to remember these nodes.

A simple way of remembering the parent nodes whenever they are needed is to use a stack to keep track of the locations of the parent nodes as they are encountered. The location of these nodes is pushed down in the stack as we scan down from the root. The most recent parent node is later popped up when its location is needed for a visit and we then go on traversing the nodes on the right side of the parent node. The location of a node is added to the stack only when we pass through while following a left path. A flowchart of the postorder traversal algorithm using a stack is shown in Fig. 11-14.

The operation of this algorithm is easily understood if it is applied to the tree shown in Fig. 11-13. Table 11-3 gives the successive contents of the search pointer and the stack S as the various steps of the traversal algorithm are carried out.

Deletion of Nodes from Sorted Binary Trees

The deletion of a node from a sorted binary tree is a much more complex operation than the insertion of a node. When a node is inserted, it is always inserted at the end of a tree path. However, we may be required to delete a node from any position in the tree including the root node.

Figure 11-15 illustrates two possible ways that a deletion may occur. In the first case, Fig. 11-15(a), the deleted node is a terminal node and it is easily deleted without having to reorganize the tree. Next, consider the case illustrated in Fig. 11-15(b). In this case, a nonterminal node is deleted. When this node is removed, it must be replaced with the node which immediately precedes† it according to the ordering represented by the tree.

When we remove a node from a tree, we must keep track of both the location of the node and the location of the node which points to the node being removed. We need both these items of information so that we can reestablish the necessary linkages after the node has been deleted. This means that we must use extra pointers to keep track of this information.

The general steps of the deletion algorithm are shown in Fig. 11-16. The implementation of this algorithm requires four auxiliary pointers, as illustrated in Fig. 11-17. The pointers T1 and T2 are used to locate the node to be removed and the parent node of the node to be removed. The pointers R1 and

† The node could also be replaced with the node which immediately follows it according to the ordering represented by the tree.

R2 are used to locate the replacement node which will replace the node to be removed and the parent node of the replacement node. The complete flow-chart of the replacement algorithm is given in Fig. 11-18.

This section has presented the basic algorithms we need to manipulate information represented by a tree structure. We now use these ideas to illustrate how some standard problem-solving tasks can be carried out using various tree algorithms.

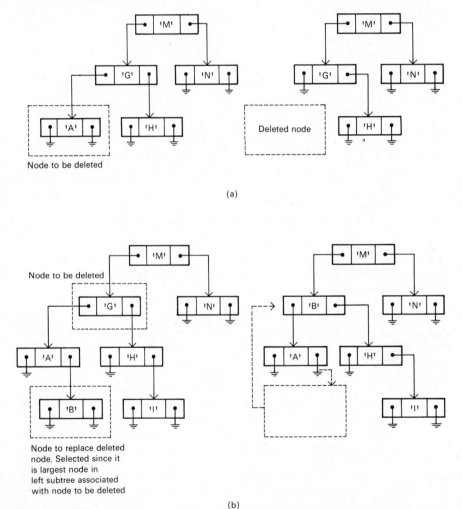

FIGURE 11-15 ■ Illustration of two possible ways that a node can be deleted from a sorted binary tree. (a) Deletion of a terminal node. (b) Deletion of a non-terminal node.

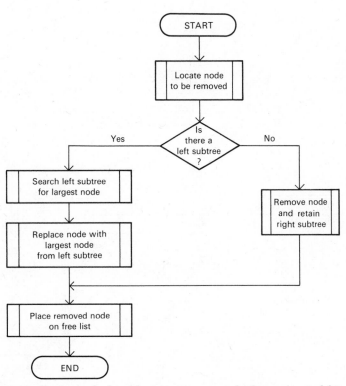

FIGURE 11-16 ■ General algorithm to remove node from a sorted binary tree.

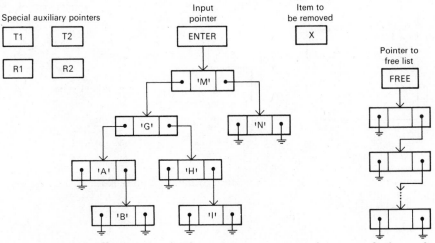

FIGURE 11-17 ■ Illustration of information organization for removal of a node from a sorted binary tree.

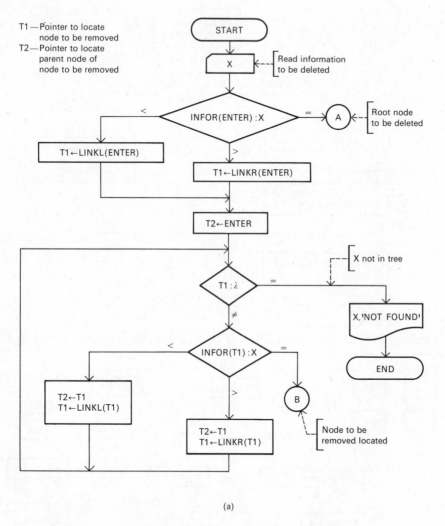

T1 — Pointer to locate
node to be removed
T2 — Pointer to locate
parent node of
node to be removed

START

X ← Read information
to be deleted

INFOR(ENTER) : X

<
= A ← Root node
to be deleted

T1←LINKL(ENTER)

>
T1←LINKR(ENTER)

T2←ENTER

T1 : λ
= X not in tree

X,'NOT FOUND'

≠

INFOR(T1) : X
<
=

END

>
T2←T1
T1←LINKL(T1)

T2←T1
T1←LINKR(T1)

B ← Node to be
removed located

(a)

FIGURE 11-18 ■ Flowchart of algorithm to delete a node from a tree. (a) Location of node to be removed.

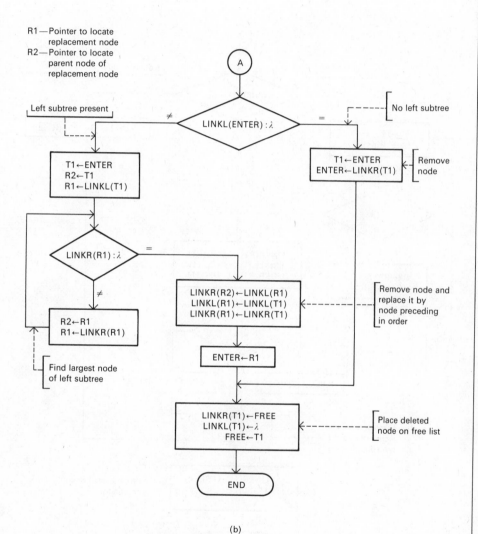

(b)

FIGURE 11-18 ■ (b) Remove root node.

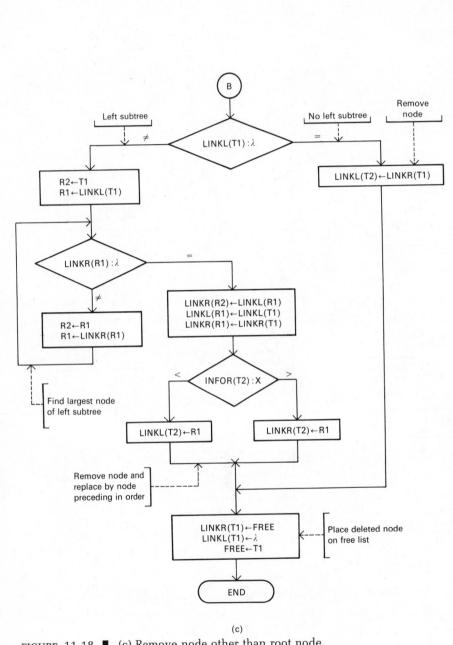

(c)

FIGURE 11-18 ▪ (c) Remove node other than root node.

Exercises

1. The word COMPUTER can be stored in the form of a binary tree. The following figure shows one possible form of this type of storage in which each letter in the word is represented by a node, and the letter 'P' is the root of the tree.

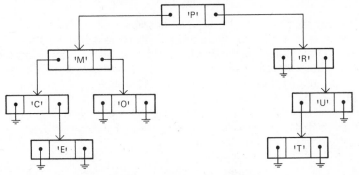

FIGURE E11-2

(a) For the tree shown in the figure, determine the left and right subtrees for each and every one of the nonterminal nodes.

(b) Write out the nodes in the order determined by the postorder traversal algorithm.

(c) Determine the number of different binary trees, sorted according to alphabetical order, that can be created by rearranging the nodes. Assume that the letter 'P' is always used as the root node.

Do these different trees produce different sequence of letters when they are traversed by the postorder algorithm?

2. Given the binary tree shown in the figure in exercise 1, we can obtain the word COMPUTING by performing the following sequence of operations:

1. Delete node containing the letter 'E'.
2. Delete node containing the letter 'R'.
3. Insert node containing the letter 'I'.
4. Insert node containing the letter 'N'.
5. Insert node containing the letter 'G'.

(a) Show the graphical representation of the resulting tree after each and every operation.

(b) Determine the sequence of nodes when the final tree (after all five operations have been completed) is traversed by the postorder algorithm.

4 ▌ Applications of Trees to Problem Solving

There are many problem areas in which tree structures occur quite naturally in computer work. We have already encountered simple structures in Chapter IV where it was necessary to represent a grouping of information with

LAST__NAME	FIRST__NAME	INITIAL
LINKL	SEMESTER	LINKR

FIGURE 11-19 ■ Assumed form of node.

a structural interrelationship. The relationships that exist between the different elements of a structure were graphically represented by a tree. There is no reason to limit ourselves to simple structures. Instead, by using the techniques presented, we can dynamically create, modify, and search tree structures as the solution to a given problem progresses.

In this section we present a number of examples which illustrate some of the ways that tree structures can be used. The examples only suggest the types of tasks that can be performed using trees. The references at the end of this chapter cover many other applications.

Generation of a Sorted Binary Tree

There are a considerable number of problems where we must read information in a random order and then print the information according to a fixed ordering relationship. For example, assume that we are developing a program that will automatically keep track of the registration for a class. When registration is completed, we must produce a class list in alphabetic order. This task can be carried out in the following manner.

Our first task is to identify the information that must be recorded for each student. For our problem, let us assume that we must record the student's full name, with the last name first, and semester standing. Each node in the tree is therefore represented as shown in Fig. 11-19. The key field of the node is taken to be LAST_NAME.

Assume that the students listed in Table 11-4 register for the class in a random order. The flowchart shown in Fig. 11-20 will accept student information in random order until the end of registration and then use a postorder search of the tree to print out the class list in alphabetic order. The exact algorithms needed to carry out the various basic tree operations are given in the previous section.

TABLE 11-4 ■ Students registering for class

	Student	Semester		Student	Semester
1.	BROWN, JOHN S.	6	5.	ALDAY, MILLY B.	8
2.	SMITH, MARY A.	3	6.	HARRIS, FRED M.	1
3.	BLACK, BILL E.	2	7.	OHM, HENRY L.	4
4.	JONES, SUSAN L.	5	8.	ARRON, JOHN M.	2

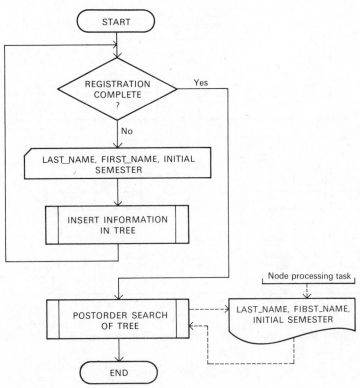

FIGURE 11-20 ■ Flowchart to create a sorted class list.

The tree created by this algorithm is shown in Fig. 11-21 when the input occurs in the order presented in Table 11-4. The postorder search path followed is also indicated. The output produced by this path is

ALDAY MILLY B	8
ARRON JOHN M	2
BLACK BILL E	2
BROWN JOHN S	6
HARRIS FRED M	1
JONES SUSAN L	5
OHM HENRY L	4
SMITH MARY A	3

This example illustrates the fact that the order in which the information is received is of no importance. The tree structure sorts the information as it is received and the postorder traversal allows us to generate the output information in the desired order.

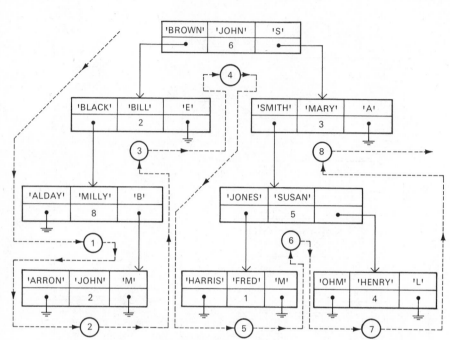

FIGURE 11-21 ■ Sort tree and postorder search path associated with Table 11-4.

Concordance Generation

Recent studies by educational psychologists suggest that there is a relationship between the academic ability of a grade school student and the student's breadth of vocabulary and use of words in written work. To investigate this relationship, it is necessary to determine the number of different words a student uses in a composition and the number of times each word is used. Such a list is called a *concordance*. Since studies of this type must be very flexible and place no artificial limits on the student, a wide range of subjects and words must be accommodated. Tree structures provide a very practical way to collect the desired information.

If it is assumed that the passage to be analyzed is in machine readable form, it is an easy matter to generate a tree which represents the information that makes up the concordance. After all the passage is processed, a postorder search of the tree can be used to print the concordance for the use of the investigator.

The tree structure chosen to represent the concordance has nodes with the field organization shown in Fig. 11-22. The field WORD stores a particular word that has been found in the passage, the field COUNT contains the number of times the word has appeared while LINKL and LINKR are the link pointers.

WORD	COUNT
LINKL	LINKR

FIGURE 11-22 ▮ Node structure for concordance tree.

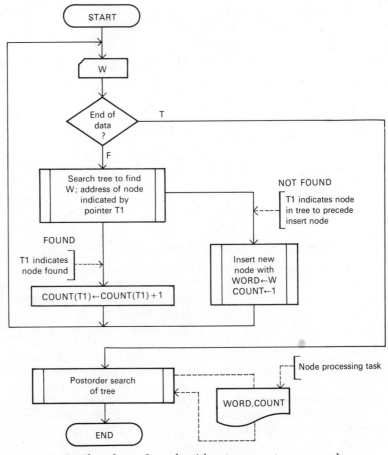

FIGURE 11-23 ▮ Flowchart of an algorithm to generate a concordance.

Initially the concordance tree is empty. We read in words one at a time and search the tree. If the word is not found, a new node is added to the tree. The WORD field of the new node is given a value corresponding to the word which was not found and the COUNT field is set to a value of 1. If the word is found in the tree, the COUNT field corresponding to this node is increased by 1. This processing sequence is continued until all the words from the given passage have been processed. A postorder search is then used to print the final concordance.

Figure 11-23 is a general flowchart describing the above steps. Assume that the input being processed was

MY FELLOW AMERICANS—ASK NOT WHAT YOUR COUNTRY CAN DO FOR YOU—ASK WHAT YOU CAN DO FOR YOUR COUNTRY

The tree resulting from this process, ignoring the punctuations, is shown in Fig. 11-24. The concordance printed out from this tree is:

AMERICANS	1
ASK	2
CAN	2
COUNTRY	2
DO	2
FELLOW	1
FOR	2
MY	1
NOT	1
WHAT	2
YOU	2
YOUR	2

Representation of an Exhaustive Search Process

Since a computer may perform a large number of tasks in a very short time, it is often possible to solve problems by use of exhaustive search or semi-exhaustive search techniques. These techniques essentially generate a large number of possible solutions to a problem and select the best solution out of all those generated. A tree structure can be used to represent all such solutions.

Initially the problem is started with a description of the task to be performed and a set of rules that tell us how to form the possible solutions. Each condidate solution is represented by a path through a solution tree. The rules allow us to generate this tree level by level until all the paths are found. In some cases, we can truncate some paths before we reach the terminal node because we know that the solution represented by that path is not acceptable.

This method of problem solving requires two basic steps. First, we start with an initial description of the problem and a set of rules that tell us the dif-

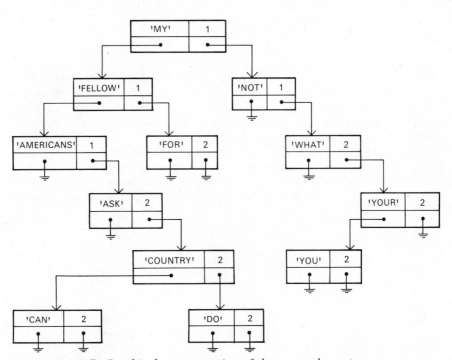

FIGURE 11-24 ■ Graphical representation of the concordance tree.

ferent possible operations which we can carry out to solve the problem. Using this information, we generate a tree which represents all possible solution paths. The nodes of the tree represent the possible intermediate solutions. A path leads from one node N_i to the next N_j whenever there is an operation that will transform the partial solution represented by N_i into the partial solution N_j. The node N_j is a terminal node if either

1. N_j represents a solution to the problem, or
2. N_j represents an unacceptable intermediate solution.

After the tree is completed, a solution path is selected by conducting some sort of search starting from the root through the nonterminal nodes until a terminal node corresponding to an acceptable solution is reached.

When a tree is generated, there may be more than one solution to the original problem. In most situations, not all of these solutions are equally acceptable. This is because all intermediate solutions included in the solution path may have different degrees of complexity. A good problem-solving process should, therefore, always include techniques that will guide the search process so that an optimal (minimum cost) or suboptimal (nearly minimum cost) solution is selected. The following discussion will show how we can use the concept of trees to study the problem-solving process.

Game Trees

Many of the concepts and techniques developed for general problem-solving tasks can be illustrated by finding the playing strategies for certain kinds of games. Games are simple to handle because their rules are explicit and well defined. Although most of the important problems in real life are not necessarily well defined, the method of finding playing strategies of a game provides a good source of examples useful later for developing and testing other methods of general problem solving.

Consider a board game played by two persons who move in turn. We assume that each player knows the current status of the game and all the possible future moves. It is also assumed that the game always results in a win–lose or a draw situation (e.g., checkers, chess, tic-tac-toe, etc.). If we represent

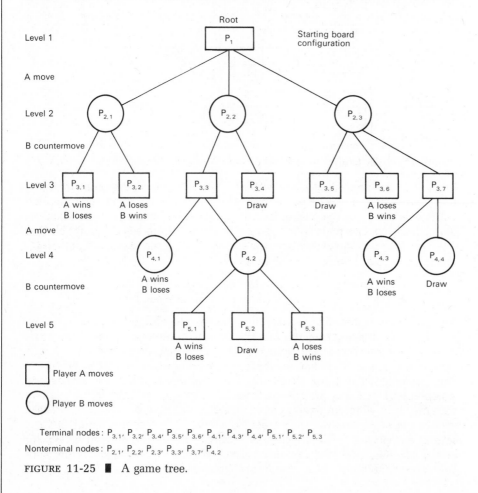

Terminal nodes: $P_{3,1}, P_{3,2}, P_{3,4}, P_{3,5}, P_{3,6}, P_{4,1}, P_{4,3}, P_{4,4}, P_{5,1}, P_{5,2}, P_{5,3}$
Nonterminal nodes: $P_{2,1}, P_{2,2}, P_{2,3}, P_{3,3}, P_{3,7}, P_{4,2}$

FIGURE 11-25 ■ A game tree.

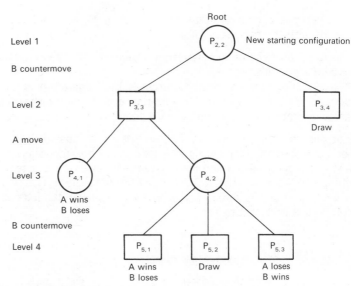

FIGURE 11-26 ■ A partial game tree.

the possible board configurations as nonterminal or terminal nodes and the moves and counter moves as branches, we obtain a *game tree.* Figure 11-25 shows the general form of a game tree with two players A and B after a few moves. In this figure, the root of the game tree is the starting board configuration of the game and the terminal nodes are the possible win–lose–draw consequences, after each player has played the first and second move. The nonterminal nodes are the intermediate board configurations resulting from the possible moves that each player has made without leading to a win–lose–draw situation.

Game trees such as the one shown in Fig. 11-25 are explicit tree structures that display the playing process. These trees tend to become very large as the play goes on. Thus, we may also choose to display a partial tree that displays only certain portions of the game. For example, assume that player A, starting with the initial configuration P_1, has made a move so that the board configuration becomes $P_{2,2}$. Starting with $P_{2,2}$, a new game tree can be generated describing the possible future history of the game from this configuration. Figure 11-26 illustrates this idea. Game trees can be used to describe either the complete or partial outcomes of a game.

A more interesting use of game trees is that they can be systematically generated and searched to help a player look ahead at the possible future moves that may be made and determine the best move to make during the next play. This tree generation and search procedure can be achieved in the following manner.

For a given board configuration as the root node, a game tree is generated, starting with the root, according to:

1. The rules of the game to generate the successor nodes of each parent node (nonterminal node).
2. A termination criterion that terminates the generation of new successors, (i.e., indicates that a condition exists which either ends the game or stops the generation of new successors).

The rules of each game are explicit and determine all the possible legal moves that can be made next by the player given the present board configuration. To avoid generating a game tree which is too large to be of practical use, a termination criterion on the generation process must be established. This usually involves an upper limit on the number of moves that a player can look ahead in the tree to find the best next move.

Evaluation Functions

The object of generating a game tree is to search for a path in the tree that eventually leads to a winning position for the player. To achieve this, it is necessary to set up a numeric measure that can be applied to all board configurations so that their relative "goodness" can be evaluated. This is accomplished by using an evaluation function.

An *evaluation function* is a numeric function which assigns a numeric value for every possible board configuration without generating any of its successors. We assume that the higher the numeric value assigned to a configuration the better its associated configuration is considered to be. A typical evaluation function can be chosen to be a linear function

$$E(P) = C_1 X_1 + C_2 X_2 + \cdots + C_n X_n$$

Where P is the board configuration under evaluation and the X_i are the n characteristics of the board configuration that are considered to have influence on the relative merit of the configuration. Examples of these characteristics are piece advantages, mobility, etc. The coefficients C_i are constants that serve as the weighting factors indicating the relative importance of the corresponding characteristics X_i.

The evaluation function must be determined by the player as part of his playing strategy. Once an evaluation function is established, all the possible board configurations are evaluated using this function. The player then determines the best next move based on the numeric values assigned to these configurations.

The following discussion shows how an evaluation function is used to direct the search for good moves as a game tree is generated. The idea of establishing an evaluation function for tree search is a very general one and is equally applicable to other problem-solving tasks.

The Minimax Backward Search

Now that we have found a way to generate the game trees for looking ahead purposes and a method to determine the effectiveness of the board configurations generated, we must decide how to use this information to arrive at the optimal next move so that the player using this technique has the best chance of winning. There are many search strategies that have been developed to accomplish this. By far the most commonly used strategy in many problem-solving tasks is the *minimax procedure.* This procedure is described as follows.

Consider a game involving two players, A and B, who move in turn. Since each player is trying to win, player A would choose the move that leads to the node (board configuration) having the maximum numeric value. On the other hand, player B, who is also trying to win, would presumably choose the node with the minimum numeric value, since this is the one which is least advantageous to player A. This situation is shown in Fig. 11-27 in which one level of look-a-head is used to illustrate the minimax procedure. The numbers shown in the terminal squares and circles are assumed to be the numeric values assigned by a given evaluation function. In Fig. 11-27(a), the three board configurations that player A can select next are assumed to have the values 30, −5, and 20, respectively. Player A determines his best move by calculating the maximum function

$$\text{Max}(30, -5, 20) = 30$$

Thus, the best move for player A is from P_1 to $P_{2,1}$ (in symbols, $P_1 \rightarrow P_{2,1}$) and the configuration P_1 is assigned the value 30, the highest value that player A can achieve by looking ahead one future move. Similarly, in Fig. 11-27(b), player B calculates the minimum function

$$\text{Min}(20, -40, 15) = -40$$

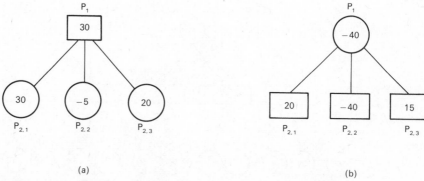

(a)   (b)

FIGURE 11-27 ■ The minimax strategy of one move lookahead. (a) Player A moves to node with maximum value. (b) Player B moves to node with minimum value.

and arrives at his best move $P_1 \rightarrow P_{2,2}$. The assigned value at P_1 for player B is therefore -40. In order to increase his chances to win, player A must look ahead two or more moves of the game tree. When this happens, it is not satisfactory for player A to choose the next move which leads to the terminal node with the highest value. This is because to reach this node would require the cooperation of the opponent (player B).

To overcome this difficulty, an analysis must be made proceeding backward from the terminal board configurations through the game tree of all possible moves that player A looks ahead. At each level of this backing up process, it is assumed that player A would always attempt to choose the move leading to the configuration of maximum value while player B acts to choose a configuration of minimum value (so as to minimize player A's chance of winning). This "minimax" back-up procedure gives the value of the board configuration one level above the configurations under consideration. Carrying this procedure back to the starting root configuration of the game tree results in the selection of a "best move" for player A.

Figure 11-28 shows how the minimax backup procedure is carried out. The resulting values (shown in squares and circles) associated with each move are obtained for a game tree of four levels. Given the numeric values for the

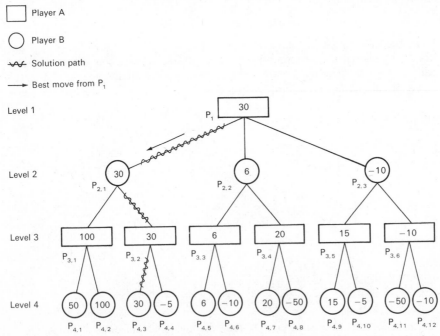

FIGURE 11-28 ■ A game tree showing the minimax backward search applied to player A looking ahead three moves.

terminal board configurations (level 4), the detailed calculations are shown below.

First backup

Assigned value at $P_{3,1} = Max(50,100) = 100$
Assigned value at $P_{3,2} = Max(30,-5) = 30$
Assigned value at $P_{3,3} = Max(6,-10) = 6$
Assigned value at $P_{3,4} = Max(20,-50) = 20$
Assigned value at $P_{3,5} = Max(15,-5) = 15$
Assigned value at $P_{3,6} = Max(-50,-10) = -10$

Second backup

Assigned value at $P_{2,1} = Min(100,30) = 30$
Assigned value at $P_{2,2} = Min(6,20) = 6$
Assigned value at $P_{2,3} = Min(15,-10) = -10$

Third backup

Assigned value at $P_1 = Max(30,6,-10) = 30$

The solution path—anticipated moves

$$P_1 \rightarrow P_{2,1} \rightarrow P_{3,2} \rightarrow P_{4,3}$$

The selected best next move by player A

$$P_1 \rightarrow P_{2,1}$$

A general flowchart summarizing the major steps of determining the best move for a player using the concepts of game tree, evaluation function, and minimax search is shown in Fig. 11-29.

An Example—The Game of Tic-Tac-Toe

Let us now consider a simple example using the game of tic-tac-toe to illustrate how the concepts of game trees, the evaluation function, and the minimax backup search are applied in a problem-solving task.

The rules of this game can be described as follows. Player A moves first by placing his marker X in one of the nine spaces on a three (row) by three (column) board. Next player B places his marker O in one of the eight spaces remaining. Players A and B continue to move alternately by placing their respective markers on the remaining spaces on the board. A player wins if he is the first to get three of his markers in a row—horizontally, vertically, or diagonally. The game is a draw if neither player wins after nine moves. Figure 11-30 shows two board configurations of the game.

Let the evaluation function E(P) be chosen as follows:

$$E(P) = X_1 - X_2 \text{ if P is not a winning configuration}$$

where X_1 is the total number of rows, columns, or diagonals that are open for

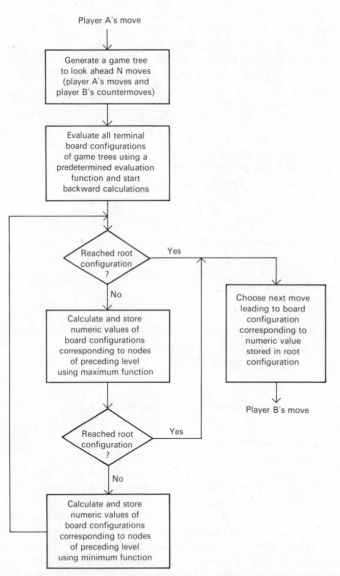

FIGURE 11-29 ■ General flowchart illustrating the minimax backward procedure to determine best move for player A.

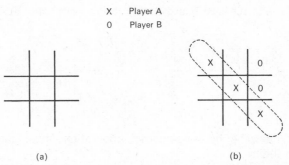

(a) (b)

FIGURE 11-30 ▉ The game of tic-tac-toe. (a) Starting configuration. (b) A winning configuration for player A after five moves.

player A, and X_2 is the total number of rows, columns, or diagonals that are open for player B.

$E(P) = \infty$ if P is a winning configuration for player A

$= -\infty$ if P is a winning configuration for player B

(∞ denotes a very large positive value)

Thus, for example, if P is the configuration

then $X_1 = 5$, $X_2 = 4$, and we have $E(P) = 5 - 4 = 1$. If the board configuration is

then $X_1 = 6$, $X_2 = 4$, and we have $E(P) = 6 - 4 = 2$. A comparison of these two numeric values indicates that the second configuration is more favorable if player A is to make the next move.

To determine the best next move for player A in a given situation, we can generate a game tree representing all the possible moves that player A looks ahead. For purposes of our discussion, we assume that player A always looks ahead two moves (his move and player B's counter move). Furthermore, in order to keep our discussion simple, we make use of the symmetry that exists in generating the successive board configurations. For example, the four configurations

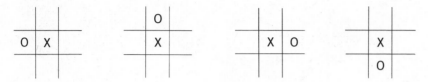

are all considered to be the same board configuration. Thus, in generating the successors of the node

only two rather than eight successors need to be generated, namely,

Now that we have decided how the game tree is generated at each point and how the various positions are evaluated, the next step is to examine the backup procedure for conducting the minimax search for the optimal move. In

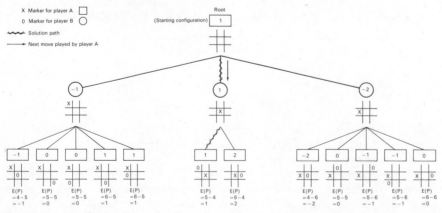

FIGURE 11-31 ■ Minimax backward search applied to tic-tac-toe to determine the initial move for player A.

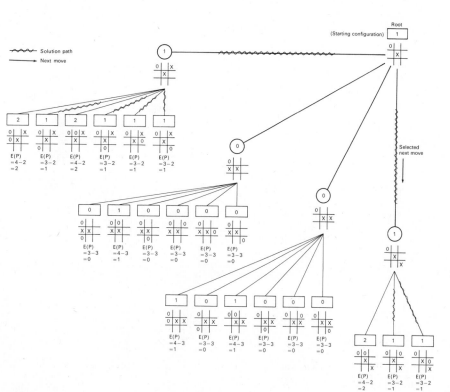

FIGURE 11-32 ■ Minimax backward search applied to tic-tac-toe after two moves.

Fig. 11-31 we have a game tree generated for player A to determine his best first move by looking ahead two moves. The values for the terminal nodes are calculated from the evaluation function defined above, while the assigned values of the nonterminal nodes are derived from the minimax backward procedure. Examining these values in Fig. 11-31, we see that the best next move for player A is to place his marker X in the center position.

After the first move is completed and player B has replied, a new game tree is generated by moving the root node to the position resulting from these two moves, and expanding the tree by again looking ahead two moves. Assume that player A makes his best move and player B replies with the move leading to

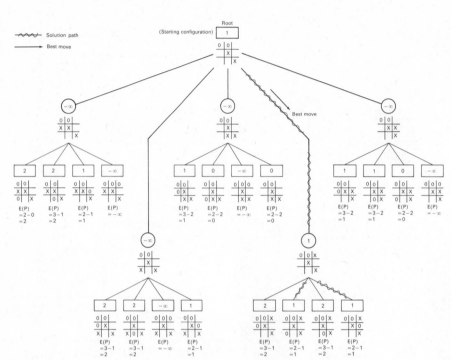

FIGURE 11-33 ∎ Minimax backward search applied to tic-tac-toe after four moves.

(the anticipated worst situation for player A). The details of the new game tree and its associated minimax search is shown in Fig. 11-32. In this figure, we see that there are two equally good moves that player A can make. Figure 11-33 shows the details of the game tree of player A after four moves. In this figure, we have assumed that each player has made two moves (player A selected two best moves but player B made a mistake and failed to select the best on his second move) leading to the new starting configuration:

From the above example, we see that the tree representation and minimax search methods can be easily applied to our advantage whenever the problem on hand requires not just a solution but an optimal or a near-optimal solution. If these methods are properly implemented on a computer, considerable amounts of saving in computer resources and programming effort may be achieved.

Exercises

1. For each of the following passages, show the graphical representation of its concordance tree and give the concordance list as printed out from the tree using the postorder traversal algorithm:

   (a) COMPUTER PROGRAMMING IS HALF ART AND HALF SCIENCE

   (b) GOVERNMENT OF THE PEOPLE, BY THE PEOPLE, AND FOR THE PEOPLE

2. A game tree is shown below. Numeric values given for the terminal nodes are calculated from a given evaluation function. Show the step-by-step minimax procedure and determine the best first move for player A.

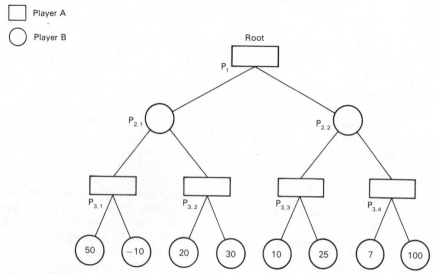

FIGURE E11-3

3. Show the complete minimax backward search applied to the game of tic-tac-toe to determine the next move for player A if the current starting configuration is

X player A (moves first)

O player B

Assume that the evaluation function is the same as that used in Figs. 11-31 through 11-33.

4. Show how the minimax search procedure is applied to the game of tic-tac-toe if a new evaluation function is used:

$$E(P) = X_1 + 5 X_2 + 25 X_3 \text{ if P is not a winning configuration}$$

where X_1 is the unblocked-one-in-a-row advantage for player A, X_2 is the unblocked-two-in-a-row advantage for player A, and X_3 is the unblocked-three-in-a-row advantage for player A.

$E(P) = \infty$ if P is a winning configuration for player A
$\quad\quad\;\; = -\infty$ if P is a winning configuration for player B

Example:

$$
\begin{array}{c|c|c}
 & & X \\
\hline
O & X & \\
\hline
O & &
\end{array}
\qquad
\begin{aligned}
X_1 &= 4 - 1 = 3 \\
X_2 &= 0 - 1 = -1 \\
X_3 &= 0 - 0 = 0 \\
E(P) &= 3 + 5(-1) + 25(0) = -2
\end{aligned}
$$

Determine, using a two-level search, the best move for player A.

5 ■ Summary

In this chapter we have presented some of the important concepts and techniques used in representing nonlinear data structures. Tree structures play a very important role in many information-processing tasks. The basic tree-structure processing techniques discussed here form the core of many of these information-processing programs.

The application areas discussed are only examples of the many computational tasks that make use of tree structures. Some of the more challenging tasks in the area of quality control, artificial intelligence, computational linguistics, operation research, etc., would be very difficult to carry out without using one or more tree structures to represent the data base on which the computations are performed. The references at the end of this chapter provide a number of examples of how tree structures can be used in the solution of complex problems.

References

Some of the applications of tree structures to complex problems are covered in [1], [4], [8], and [10]. The other references discuss some of the more advanced properties of tree structures and the operations that can be performed upon these structures. [7] is a particularly definitive work on this subject. PL/I has many language features that make it easy to develop programs involving trees. FORTRAN IV does not have this capability and special techniques must be used to develop the necessary subroutines to allow the use of trees. [3] gives a particularly thorough treatment of these FORTRAN programs.

1. Alt, F. L., and Rubinoff, M. eds. (1968) *Advanced in Computers,* Vol. 9, Academic Press, New York.

2. Berztiss, A. T. (1971) *Data Structures — Theory and Practice,* Academic Press, New York.

3. Brillinger, P. C., and Cohen, D. J. (1972) *Introduction To Data Structures and Non-Numeric Computation,* Prentice-Hall, Englewood Cliffs, N.J.

4. Feigenbaum, E. A., and Feldman, J., eds. (1963) *Computers and Thought,* McGraw-Hill, New York.

5. Fox, L. ed. (1966) *Advances in Programming and Non-Numerical Computation,* Pergamon Press, Elmsford, N.Y.

6. Hays, D. G. (1967) *Introduction to Computational Linguistics,* American Elsevier, New York.

7. Knuth, D. E. (1968) *The Art of Computer Programming, Vol. 1, Fundamental Algorithms,* Addison-Wesley, Reading, Mass.

8. Nilsson, N. J. (1971) *Problem-Solving Methods in Artificial Intelligence,* McGraw-Hill, New York.

9. Rosen, S., ed. (1967) *Programming Systems and Languages,* McGraw-Hill, New York.

10. Slagle, J. R. (1971) *Artificial Intelligence—The Heuristic Programming Approach,* McGraw-Hill, New York.

Home Problems

If possible, the algorithms developed to solve the following problems should be programmed and tested on a computer.

1. It is necessary to maintain a file of student names in alphabetic order. Each time a new student is admitted, a new name is inserted in the file. Similarly, a name is deleted each time a student graduates. Develop the flowchart of an algorithm which will perform this record-keeping task. Assume that all of the information is to be stored using a binary tree.

2. Three different data structures—an array, a linear linked list, or a binary tree—could be used to store the file of problem 1. Compare the advantages and disadvantages of using each structure for the task described in problem 1.
    A *nested binary tree structure* can be thought of as a binary tree structure in which one of the fields in each node points to the root node of another binary tree. (A graphical representation of a nested tree structure is given on p. 366.) For example, the nodes in the main tree might represent states and the nodes of the subtree would represent towns and cities in the state represented by the main tree node. The following four problems deal with nested tree structures:

3. Give the flowchart of an algorithm which can locate an item in a nested binary tree. Assume each item is indicated by 2 keys. The first key locates the main tree. The second key is used to locate the item in the subtree.

4. Give the flowchart of an algorithm which can:
    (a) insert a new main node in the main tree;
    (b) insert a new node in one of the subtrees.

5. A postorder traversal of a nested binary tree can be carried out in the following manner.

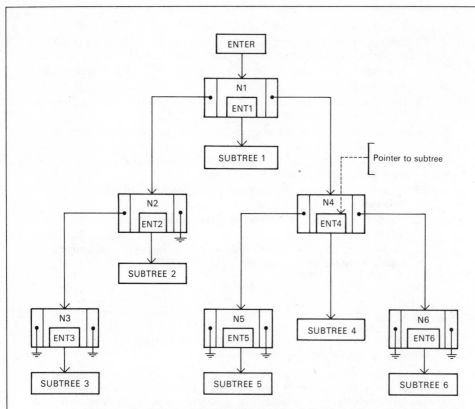

1. Traverse the nodes of the main tree on the left side of the main-tree parent node.
2. Visit the main-tree parent node. Include a postorder traversal of the subtree associated with the parent node as part of the visit.
3. Traverse the nodes of the main tree on the right side of the main-tree parent node.

Give the flowchart of an algorithm which carries out a postorder traversal of a nested binary tree.

6. Carry out home problem 7 of Chapter IX using a nested-binary-tree data structure to store the required information.

7. In Section III an algorithm and flowchart was presented for the postorder traversal of a tree. Another method of traversing a tree is called a *preorder traversal.* This traversal is accomplished by the repeated execution of the following steps:

1. Visit the parent node.
2. Traverse the nodes to the left side of the parent node.
3. Traverse the nodes to the right side of the parent node.

If the tree of Fig. 11-13 were traversed according to this set of rules, the nodes would be visited in the following order

N1   N2   N3   N4   N5   N6   N7

Develop a flowchart, similar to that of Fig. 11-14, which describes an algorithm to carry out the preorder traversal of a binary tree.

8. A binary tree is said to be well balanced if, for each node in the tree, the number of nodes linked left is approximately equal to the number linked right. For example, in the following figure the tree on the left is well balanced while the one on the right is not. Well-balanced trees require, on the average, less time to search for a given item than a poorly balanced tree.

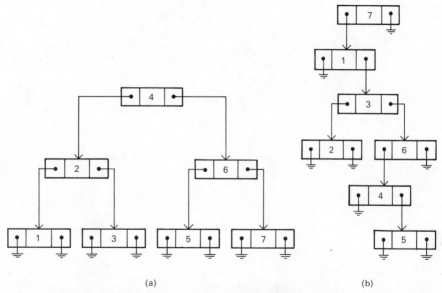

(a)   (b)

There are a number of algorithms that can be used to transform a poorly balanced tree into a well-balanced tree. One of the simplest is to find the "middle" item in the poorly balanced tree. Using this item as a root node, a new well-balanced tree can then be constructed. Develop the flowchart of an algorithm which will generate a well-balanced tree from a poorly balanced tree.

9. Develop the flowchart of a program which will play tic-tac-toe.

10. Develop the flowchart of an algorithm that will convert a general tree into a binary tree.

11. Give the flowchart of an algorithm which will merge two binary trees into a binary tree.

12

processing experimental information

1 ■ Introduction

In many areas of business and technology it is necessary to record and analyze information obtained by some type of measurement process. For example, the owner of a restaurant may wish to investigate how the number of customers in his restaurant varies with the time of day, or a chemist may wish to record the temperature variation of a mixture after a new chemical compound has been added. The result of these types of measurements is a large collection of numerical data that must be processed if the person carrying out the measurement is to gain any useful information. One of the basic ways in which this is accomplished is to try and find a mathematical function of some type that will "fit" or represent the measured information in a meaningful manner. The function chosen for this task is usually based on past experience or on the results of some type of theoretical analysis.

Any function selected to represent experimental data will contain one or more constants that can be selected to give the best fit of the function to the data. The values of these constants are determined from the data by using a formula that is developed by a general analytical investigation of the properties of the function being used to represent the data.

In this chapter we investigate some of the techniques that can be used to process data involved in a number of experimental investigations. The particular topics presented in this chapter were selected because of their general usefulness. Many of the advanced techniques for processing experimental data are discussed in the references at the end of this chapter.

2 ■ Curve Fitting

In algebra or calculus we define a mathematical function as being a relationship between a set of x-values (associated with the independent variable x) and a set of y-values (associated with the dependent variable y). Symbolically we describe this mathematical relationship by

$$y = f(x)$$

The function can also be displayed by a graph or curve depicting the set of pairs (x,y).

In some cases the function is represented in terms of a mathematical expression such as

$$y = x^2$$

which can easily be evaluated. If we are given the mathematical equation that describes the relationship between x and y, we can easily plot the curve corresponding to this relationship.

When dealing with experimental information we often face the opposite

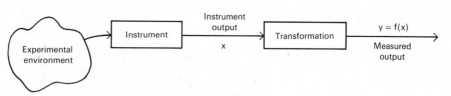

FIGURE 12-1 ■ A typical measurement situation.

problem. We are given a set of points (x,y) and we must find a function which generates a curve that fits these points in some manner.

Interpolation

In many experimental situations we use an instrument to measure some quantity. The output of the instrument must often be transformed, according to a particular relationship, to obtain the desired value for the measured quantity. This situation is illustrated in Fig. 12-1.

If the function f(x) can be represented by a mathematical expression, a computer can evaluate this expression for every possible value of x obtained from our instrument readings. There are many situations where the function f(x) is only available in graphical or tabular form. If we are to use a computer to compute a value y for every value x, we must convert f(x) into a form that can be stored in a computer. One way to handle this problem is to make a table of values listing x and y for a fixed number of points. If we must find y for a value of x not in the table, we must use interpolation to compute the value of y.

To illustrate this method of representing a function, assume that we have been given a function in graphical form, such as the one illustrated in Fig. 12-2, and we wish to store this graph in a computer.

All of the functions we are dealing with are assumed to be continuous. This means that for any value of x in the interval [a,b] there is a unique value for y = f(x) given by the graph. In addition any small change Δx in x produces only a small change Δy in y. The function shown in Fig. 12-2 is continuous in the interval [a,b].

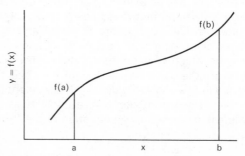

FIGURE 12-2 ■ Graphical representation of the relation y = f(x).

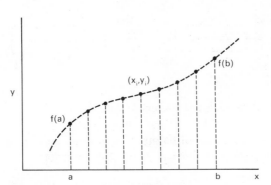

FIGURE 12-3 ■ Discrete representation of a continuous function.

If we are to store a continuous function in a computer, one method is to approximate the continuous function by a finite set of discrete pairs (x_i, y_i). Thus, instead of the continuous graph of Fig. 12-2 we have one with the appearance of Fig. 12-3. Each point in this graph corresponds to a pair (x_i, y_i). A graph such as this one consisting of a finite number of points is said to represent a *discrete* function. The process of deciding which values of x we want to use and then matching the proper y-values to these x-values is sometimes referred to as *analog-to-digital conversion*. The study of this conversion process will not be pursued here as it does not directly concern the computational aspect of problem solving on computers.

In the course of processing experimental data, an x-value may be encountered which does not correspond to any one of the stored values. We must then develop some way of filling in the gaps between the x-values. This "filling in" process is called *interpolation*. Whenever interpolation is called for, an error may be introduced in our computation.

Linear Interpolation

To illustrate this idea, let us focus our attention on a small portion of a curve f(x) that falls between the two adjacent data points x_1 and x_2. An enlarged view is shown in Fig. 12-4, where $P_1 = f(x_1)$ and $P_2 = f(x_2)$. Suppose that in the course of computing it is necessary to know the y-value corresponding to an x-value which is between x_1 and x_2. The simplest approach would be to approximate the curve with a straight line. This form of interpolation is called *straight-line or linear interpolation*. The straight line P(x) shown in Fig. 12-4 is used for the approximation of the curve f(x) between x_1 and x_2.

The straight line is described by an equation of the form

$$P(x) = a_0 + a_1 x$$

The coefficients a_0 and a_1 can easily be obtained by solving the following two equations

$$P(x_1) = f(x_1) = a_0 + a_1 x_1 = P_1$$
$$P(x_2) = f(x_2) = a_0 + a_1 x_2 = P_2$$

for a_0 and a_1. This is easily done and gives a value

$$a_1 = \frac{P_2 - P_1}{x_2 - x_1} \qquad a_0 = \frac{x_1 P_2 - x_2 P_1}{x_1 - x_2}$$

For example, assume that

$$x_1 = 1 \qquad x_2 = 2 \qquad P_1 = f(x_1) = 3 \qquad P_2 = f(x_2) = 4$$

Then

$$a_1 = 1 \qquad a_0 = 2$$

Thus,

$$P(x) = 2 + x$$

If $x = 1.5$, we have

$$y \cong P(1.5) = 2 + 1.5 = 3.5$$

as our estimate of $f(x)$ at the point $x = 1.5$.

The use of linear interpolation to estimate a value for y when x is in the interval $[x_1, x_2]$ results in an error. The size of the error depends upon the shape of the curve, the separation $x_2 - x_1$, and the location of x within the interval. The error as a function of x is

$$\text{ERROR } (x) = E(x) = f(x) - P(x)$$

For example, consider the case illustrated in Fig. 12-4. The error at $x = a$ is

$$E(a) = f(a) - P(a) > 0$$

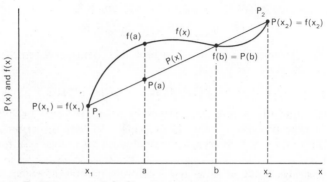

FIGURE 12-4 ■ Using a straight line $P(x)$, to approximate $f(x)$ between x_1 and x_2.

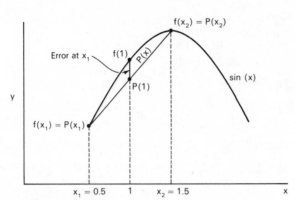

FIGURE 12-5 ■ Linear interpolation for sin(x) between x_1 and x_2.

and the error at $x = b$ is

$$E(b) = f(b) - P(b) = 0$$

since $f(b) = P(b)$.

It is usually very difficult to derive an analytical expression for the errors resulting from linear interpolation. The following example illustrates how the error is related to the location of x in the interval involved in the approximation.

Suppose that a section of the continuous function $f(x) = \sin(x)$ is represented by the values of two points at $x_1 = 0.5$ and $x_2 = 1.5$ (see Fig. 12-5) and we are given the value of $f(x_1) = f(0.5) = 0.479$ and $f(x_2) = f(1.5) = 0.997$. We use the method of linear interpolation to find the approximate value for $f(1)$ and then determine the error of this approximate value. Let us first obtain the equation for the straight line P(x) which approximates sin (x) between x_1 and x_2. Using the values for P_1 and P_2 gives

$$P(x) = 0.220 + 0.518x$$

The approximate value for $f(1)$ is given by P(1) which is

$$P(1) = 0.220 + 0.518 \times 1 = 0.738$$

The actual value $f(1)$ is known to be 0.841. Thus, the error due to our linear interpolation is

$$E(1) = f(1) - P(1) = 0.841 - 0.738 = 0.103$$

It should be noted that errors at points other than $x = 1$ may be different, as can be seen from the graph in Fig. 12-5. Table 12-1 lists the errors from several points between $x_1 = 0.5$ and $x_2 = 1.5$, including the point $x = 1$, for comparison purposes.

Errors always occur when we use a discrete number of points and linear interpolation to approximate a continuous function. The size of the error can

TABLE 12-1 ■ Interpolation error in approximating the value of sin(x)

x	f(x)	P(x)	Interpolation error E(x)
0.6	0.564	0.530	0.034
0.8	0.717	0.634	0.083
1.0	0.841	0.738	0.103
1.2	0.932	0.841	0.091
1.4	0.985	0.945	0.040

be reduced by taking the discrete values of the function closer together. Figures 12-6(a) to (c) illustrate how a function f(x) between the two points x_1 and x_2 can be represented by three different linear approximations. As the number of points used increases we can expect linear interpolation to become a better method for approximating the values of the function in the region between the given points. It is therefore very important that the spacing between points be carefully selected whenever a linear function is used to represent a continuous function.

Quadratic Interpolation

There are many other choices available to us if greater accuracy is essential in our computation and if we decide not to use linear interpolation. For example, instead of a straight line we could fit a polynomial of the form

$$P(x) = a_0 + a_1x + a_2x^2$$

between two points in the discrete representation of the continuous function. The resulting interpolation would then be called *quadratic interpolation*, since the interpolation curve is mathematically described by a second degree polynomial. Figure 12-7 illustrates this approach.

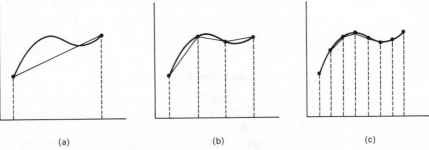

(a)   (b)   (c)

FIGURE 12-6 ■ A continuous function represented by various discrete functions. (a) Two points. (b) Four points. (c) Eight points.

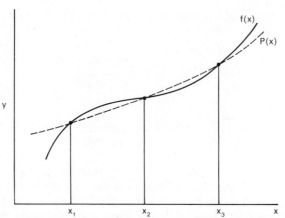

FIGURE 12-7 ■ Quadratic approximation of $f(x)$ between x_1 and x_3.

In this case the quadratic curve cannot be specified unless we have three points on the curve. Let them be

$$P_1 = P(x_1) = f(x_1)$$
$$P_2 = P(x_2) = f(x_2)$$
$$P_3 = P(x_3) = f(x_3)$$

With these three points it is possible to compute the three coefficients a_0, a_1, and a_2. This is done by solving the following set of equations for the desired coefficients

$$P_1 = a_0 + a_1 x_1 + a_2 x_1^2$$
$$P_2 = a_0 + a_1 x_2 + a_2 x_2^2$$
$$P_3 = a_0 + a_1 x_3 + a_2 x_3^2$$

This equation can be solved using the techniques presented in section four of this chapter.

The resulting quadratic polynomial $P(x)$ provides a better approximation to many curves than a linear polynomial. The price paid for the more accurate interpolation is an increase in the complexity of the computations involved. A compromise between accuracy and computational complexity is always a problem facing the computer user.

General Curve Fitting

In many technological applications measurements are made of one quantity as a second quantity is varied. The resulting measurements may be plotted in a graphical form such as that shown in Fig. 12-8.

The actual measured values of a variable will be subject to measurement error, and it is usually not possible to make measurements at every point of interest. For these reasons and from the need to be able to represent the

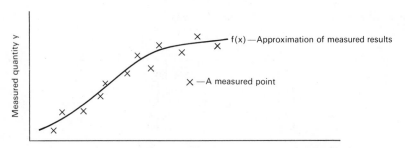

FIGURE 12-8 ■ Representation of a set of data points with a smooth curve.

experimental results in a compact manner, an experimenter often tries to fit his measurements to a smooth curve f(x) as illustrated in Fig. 12-8.

The form of the curve selected will, of course, depend to a considerable extent upon the type of measurements being made and the system under investigation. One standard function often used to represent a curve is a polynomial function of the form

$$f(x) = a_0 + a_1x + a_2x^2 + \cdots + a_ux^u$$

The shape of the resulting curve depends both upon the value of the coefficients a_i and the degree of the polynomial u. The larger the value of u the more difficult it becomes to compute the coefficients a_i and the more susceptible the calculations become to computation errors.

Least Squares Curve Fit

When we try to fit a curve to a set of data points it is not possible, and indeed not desirable, to have the curve pass through each point. What we would like to do is have the curve come as close as possible to all the data points. If we denote the set of data points as $\{(x_1,y_1), (x_2,y_2), \ldots, (x_v,y_v)\}$, where x_i is the value of the independent variable when the measurement y_i was made, then the distance of the ith data point from the curve f(x) is

$$d_i = y_i - f(x_i) = y_i - (a_0 + a_1x_i + a_2x_i^2 + \cdots + a_ux_i^u)$$

This distance represents the "error" between the value given by the curve and the measured value.

One of the common measures of the difference between the curve and the data is the sum of the squared errors. That is

$$C = \sum_{i=1}^{v} d_i^2 = \sum_{i=1}^{v} [y_i - f(x_i)]^2$$

If we are to minimize the total error we must select the coefficients a_0 through a_u in such a manner as to minimize C. A function which minimizes C is called a

TABLE 12-2 ■ Results of a set of measurements

x	y	x	y
1	1.72	6	4.05
2	2.65	7	5.11
3	2.58	8	5.10
4	3.61	9	6.17
5	3.59	10	6.51

least squares approximation. The differential calculus[†] can be used to find the conditions that must be satisfied. These calculations give us the following linear equations that can be solved for the values of the a_i coefficients. The equations are listed for $u = 1$, a linear fit, $u = 2$, a quadradic fit, and $u = 3$, a cubic fit. Higher order fits can be obtained by extending this approach. Note that in the following equations we are dealing with the summation over v data points. Thus we will use Σ to mean $\displaystyle\sum_{i=1}^{v}$.

Case 1. $u = 1$.   Linear fit, $f(x) = a_0 + a_1 x$.

$$a_0 v + a_1 \Sigma x_i = \Sigma y_i$$
$$a_0 \Sigma x_i + a_1 \Sigma x_i^2 = \Sigma x_i y_i$$

Case 2. $u = 2$.   Quadradic fit, $f(x) = a_0 + a_1 x + a_2 x^2$.

$$a_0 v + a_1 \Sigma x_i + a_2 \Sigma x_i^2 = \Sigma y_i$$
$$a_0 \Sigma x_i + a_1 \Sigma x_i^2 + a_2 \Sigma x_i^3 = \Sigma x_i y_i$$
$$a_0 \Sigma x_i^2 + a_1 \Sigma x_i^3 + a_2 \Sigma x_i^4 = \Sigma x_i^2 y_i$$

Case 3. $u = 3$.   Cubic fit, $f(x) = a_0 + a_1 x + a_2 x^2 + a_3 x^3$

$$a_0 v + a_1 \Sigma x_i + a_2 \Sigma x_i^2 + a_3 \Sigma x_i^3 = \Sigma y_i$$
$$a_0 \Sigma x_i + a_1 \Sigma x_i^2 + a_2 \Sigma x_i^3 + a_3 \Sigma x_i^4 = \Sigma x_i y_i$$
$$a_0 \Sigma x_i^2 + a_1 \Sigma x_i^3 + a_2 \Sigma x_i^4 + a_3 \Sigma x_i^5 = \Sigma x_i^2 y_i$$
$$a_0 \Sigma x_i^3 + a_1 \Sigma x_i^4 + a_2 \Sigma x_i^5 + a_3 \Sigma x_i^6 = \Sigma x_i^3 y_i$$

The equations for Case 1 can be solved to give

$$a_0 = \frac{\Sigma y_i \, \Sigma x_i^2 - \Sigma x_i y_i \, \Sigma x_i}{v \Sigma x_i^2 - (\Sigma x_i)^2}$$

$$a_1 = \frac{v \Sigma x_i y_i - \Sigma x_i \, \Sigma y_i}{v \Sigma x_i^2 - (\Sigma x_i)^2}$$

† The value of C will be minimum when all of the derivatives of the form $\dfrac{\partial C}{\partial a_i} = 0$. Carrying out this task and collecting terms gives the listed equations.

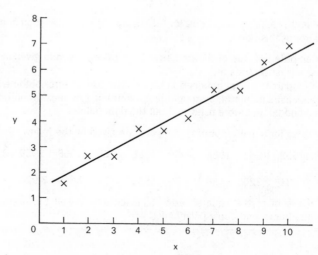

FIGURE 12-9 ■ Plot of measurements listed in Table 12-2.

The equations for the other cases can be solved by the techniques discussed in Section IV of this chapter.

As an example of how these equations are applied, assume that the measurements listed in Table 12-2 were made as part of an experiment.

Using this information gives (with $v = 10$)

$$\sum_{i=1}^{10} x_i = 55 \qquad \sum_{i=1}^{10} y_i = 41.09 \qquad \sum_{i=1}^{10} x_i^2 = 385 \qquad \sum_{i=1}^{10} x_i y_i = 268.85$$

$$a_0 = \frac{41.09 \times 385 - 268.85 \times 55}{10 \times 385 - 55^2} = 1.252$$

$$a_1 = \frac{10 \times 268.85 - 55 \times 41.09}{10 \times 385 - 55^2} = 0.51945$$

Figure 12-9 is a plot of the information contained in Table 12-2 and the curve that gives the least squares approximation to these measurements.

The computational errors present in trying to solve linear equations of the above form usually make it impractical to use polynomials of degree greater than six or seven. If polynomials of this degree are not satisfactory, other techniques must be used to represent experimental data.

Exercises

1. Let $f(x) = 5^x$. We have $f(0) = 1.00$ and $f(1) = 5.00$.
   (a) Determine the straight line that can be used to approximate $f(x)$ between $x = 0$ and $x = 1$.

(b) Find the approximate value for f(.5) using linear interpolation and determine the error at this point.

2. (a) Compute the sum of squared error C for the data points given in Table 12-2 using a least squares fit.

(b) Compare the error obtained in (a) with the sum of error obtained if, instead of the least squares fit, a straight line determined by the two end data points, (x_1, y_1) and (x_{10}, y_{10}), were used to fit all the data points.

3. The sales for a manufacturing company are given by the following data.

Year	1962	1963	1964	1965	1966	1967	1968	1969	1970	1971
Sales (×$100,000)	2,131	2,320	2,486	2,630	2,851	3,216	3,664	3,924	4,313	4,630

Using the sum of the squared error C, discuss how well this data is fit by a linear, quadradic, and cubic polynomial.

3 ∎ Statistical Data

Statistics deals with the problem of assembling, analyzing, and interpreting a collection of data. In a typical problem we observe a process that is made up of a collection of events. Each event is influenced by a large number of loosely related activities or actions. To describe the event we select a parameter or a set of parameters which we feel represent the important characteristics of the event. We then describe the process by measuring these parameters for each of the events that make up the process and then summarizing these measurements in a suitable manner.

For example, examinations are commonly used to measure how well a group of people understand a given body of knowledge. The process in this case is the group of people being examined and each person in the group represents an event. The measurement process consists of giving an examination covering the body of material of interest. Everyone taking the examination receives a grade. Hopefully, this grade represents the person's understanding of the material covered by the examination. If a large number of persons take the examination, the raw information represented by each individual score does not provide too much information about the general knowledge and understanding of the group taking the examination. Thus, a measure of the general group performance is necessary if we are to compare individual performance to overall group performance.

Histograms

If a large number of measurements are made concerning a particular process the results of these measurements could be reported in tabular form. Although all the information obtained by the measurement process is available in the table, it is very hard for a person trying to analyze the data to see the general form that the data takes. A better way of presenting this information is in a graphical form. *Histograms* are one such important graphical technique.

Let us assume that we have N data points $d_1, d_2, \ldots, d_N$ and that the maximum and minimum values of this set of data are d_{MAX} and d_{MIN}, respectively. To display the data in a meaningful manner we can divide the interval $d_{MAX} - d_{MIN}$ into K subintervals and count the number of data points that fall in each subinterval. We then plot a graph that indicates the value of these counts for each subinterval.

If we have N data points, then the following empirical formula may be used to determine the approximate number of intervals that we should use:

$$K = 1 + 3.3 \log_{10} N$$

For example, if we have 150 sample points then we have

$$K = 8.16 \cong 8$$

Thus, we divide the interval $d_{MAX} - d_{MIN}$ into eight subintervals.

As an example, assume that we have been given Table 12-3 containing the examination scores for a particular class. These scores can be grouped

TABLE 12-3 ■ Examination scores

Student number	Score	Student number	Score	Student number	Score	Student number	Score	Student number	Score	Student number	Score
1	34	26	65	51	63	76	66	101	51	126	70
2	43	27	75	52	80	77	45	102	83	127	59
3	51	28	47	53	51	78	80	103	92	128	71
4	53	29	63	54	74	79	85	104	63	129	65
5	60	30	52	55	96	80	54	105	84	130	48
6	71	31	82	56	37	81	79	106	70	131	87
7	62	32	62	57	83	82	80	107	44	132	73
8	80	33	85	58	64	83	64	108	68	133	58
9	67	34	81	59	76	84	75	109	64	134	78
10	52	35	36	60	69	85	72	110	85	135	62
11	70	36	84	61	57	86	56	111	57	136	88
12	59	37	62	62	60	87	61	112	75	137	45
13	79	38	95	63	75	88	78	113	86	138	77
14	59	39	53	64	63	89	70	114	59	139	66
15	71	40	68	65	87	90	47	115	74	140	54
16	67	41	73	66	68	91	88	116	69	141	89
17	82	42	80	67	43	92	78	117	49	142	69
18	52	43	43	68	74	93	98	118	70	143	90
19	87	44	70	69	75	94	65	119	60	144	61
20	67	45	51	70	58	95	90	120	75	145	73
21	90	46	73	71	77	96	69	121	63	146	85
22	60	47	61	72	66	97	46	122	44	147	76
23	81	48	79	73	80	98	76	123	72	148	53
24	72	49	54	74	70	99	52	124	53	149	88
25	68	50	92	75	66	100	70	125	43	150	71

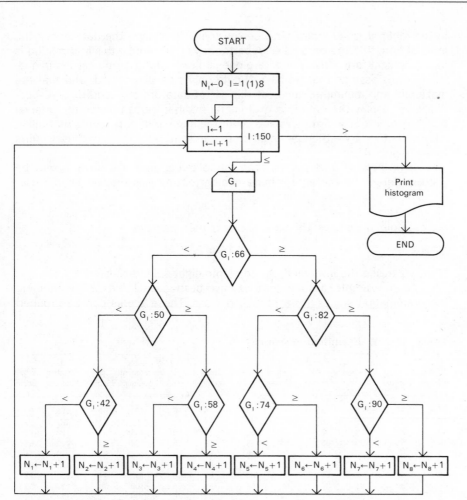

FIGURE 12-10 ■ Flowchart to compute histogram of test scores.

into eight classes. The algorithm that can be used to count the number of scores in each class is given by Fig. 12-10 and the resulting histogram produced by this program using the data of Table 12-3 is shown in Fig. 12-11.

A histogram gives a graphical indication of the characteristics of the data. It is often desirable to be able to summarize some of the general characteristics of the data by indicating such things as the average value of the data and the spread of the data. These two parameters are measured by giving the mean, m, and variance, σ^2 (or standard deviation, σ) of the data. These quantities are defined as

$$m = \frac{1}{N} \sum_{i=1}^{N} d_i \quad \text{(mean)}$$

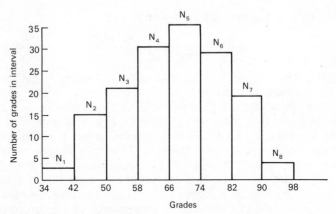

FIGURE 12-11 ■ A typical histogram.

and

$$\sigma^2 = \frac{1}{N-1} \sum_{i=1}^{N} (d_i - m)^2 \qquad \text{(variance)}$$

These two expressions are easily computed for tabular data.

Normal Curve

For many statistical processes it is possible to represent the general form of a histogram by a "bell" shaped curve which is called a *normal curve* or a *Gaussian curve.* The approximation of the histogram of Fig. 12-11 by such a curve is shown in Fig. 12-12.

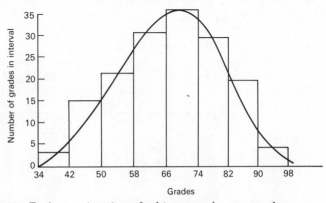

FIGURE 12-12 ■ Approximation of a histogram by a normal curve.

The normal curve is described by the function

$$p(x) = \frac{1}{\sqrt{2\pi}\sigma} \exp\left[-\frac{(x-m)^2}{2\sigma^2}\right]$$

Examining this function, we see that this curve is completely defined by the values of the coefficients m and σ.

Since we can always compute m and σ for any histogram we can always find a normal curve that tends to approximate the histogram. This approximation may be very good if the data is symmetric about m and has the same general shape as the normal curve. However, if the data does not satisfy these criteria, the normal curve will be a very poor approximation to the histogram. Because of this one should be very careful in assuming that a collection of data can be represented by a normal curve. A large number of false conclusions have been reported by researchers who have blindly assumed that their data could be represented by a normal curve without checking their data to see if this was a reasonable assumption.

A much more extensive discussion of the statistical methods that may be used to represent other distributions can be found in books on statistics and probability theory.

Linear Regression

In many situations we have an event which is described by two parameters. For example, we might measure the grade a student received on an examination and the amount of time the student spent studying for the examination. In this case our data would consist of pairs of measurements (x_i, y_i), where x_i is the examination grade and y_i is the number of hours spent studying. The purpose of this study would be to determine if there is any relationship between the time spent studying and the grade received. Assume that the

TABLE 12-4 ■ Measurement of examination grade and study time (x_i — grade, y_i — study time in minutes)

N	x_i	y_i	N	x_i	y_i	N	x_i	y_i
1	10	35	11	81	120	21	36	60
2	90	180	12	93	115	22	55	90
3	65	75	13	30	50	23	47	58
4	50	45	14	25	20	24	85	110
5	40	43	15	60	90	25	55	70
6	70	120	16	82	110	26	65	95
7	53	80	17	62	110	27	85	90
8	43	70	18	49	75	28	65	60
9	100	60	19	35	90	29	75	110
10	76	80	20	15	25	30	76	80

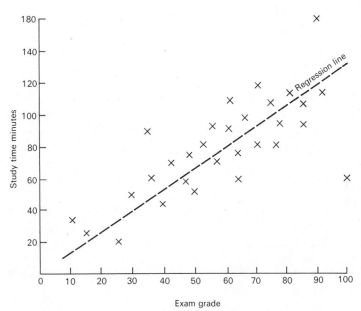

FIGURE 12-13 ■ Scatter diagram of examination grades and study time for 30 students.

measurements given by Table 12-4 are obtained from a typical class. One of the ways to represent this data is to plot a *scatter diagram*. This diagram consists of plotting each pair of points on a graph. Figure 12-13 is the resulting scatter diagram.

Examining this figure we see that the points tend to cluster around the dotted line. This type of clustering suggests that there is a relationship between x_i and y_i. One assumption would be that there exists a linear relationship of the form

$$y_i = a_0 + a_1 x_i$$

between these two measurements. If this is a reasonable assumption, we should be able to fit a curve to the measured points that is described by the equation

$$y = a_0 + a_1 x$$

Such a linear approximation is shown in Fig. 12-13, and it appears to be an acceptable representation of the relationship between the data points.

To find the coefficients a_0 and a_1 we can use the least squares curve-fitting technique discussed in the last section. This method of summarizing the relationship between the statistical data points is called *linear regression*.

It is always possible to compute a linear regression line for any statistically measured data. This does not mean that the measurements are related

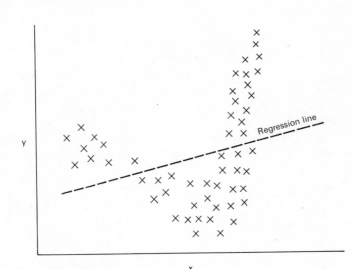

FIGURE 12-14 ■ Illustration of a scatter diagram that cannot be described by a linear regression line.

in a linear manner. For example, consider the scatter diagram shown in Figure 12-14. The linear regression line for this figure is plotted and it is easily seen that it does not give a true indication of the relationship of the measured values. One should be very careful to examine the scatter diagram associated with a measurement before it is assumed that the measurements can be summarized by a linear regression line.

Correlation and Other Measures

The characteristics of the data represented by a scatter diagram can also be described by parameters of the type used to describe histograms. In particular, we can consider x_i and y_i individually and compute the mean value of x.

$$m_x = \frac{1}{N} \sum_{i=1}^{N} x_i$$

the mean value of y

$$m_y = \frac{1}{N} \sum_{i=1}^{N} y_i$$

the variance of x

$$\sigma_x^2 = \frac{1}{N-1} \sum_{i=1}^{N} (x_i - m_x)^2$$

and the variance of y

$$\sigma_y{}^2 = \frac{1}{N-1} \sum_{i=1}^{N} (y_i - m_y)^2$$

The mean values of x and y indicate the average value of these two terms. The variance is a measure of the spread of the data about the mean. The larger the variance the larger the spread.

A linear regression line suggests that there is some type of linear relation between x_i and y_i. If such a linear relationship does exist, we say that there is a high degree of correlation between x_i and y_i. If there is no observable linear relationship, we say that the two terms x_i and y_i are not linearly correlated.

The degree of linear correlation between x_i and y_i is given by the *correlation coefficient,* defined as

$$C_{x,y} = \frac{\dfrac{1}{N-1} \sum_{i=1}^{N} (x_i - m_x)(y_i - m_y)}{\sqrt{\sigma_x{}^2 \sigma_y{}^2}}$$

This coefficient lies in the range $-1 \leqslant C_{x,y} \leqslant 1$. If $C_{x,y}$ is close to ± 1 there is a high degree of linear correlation between x_i and y_i. A value of $C_{x,y}$ near zero indicates that there is little or no linear correlation between the two terms. A positive value for $C_{x,y}$ indicates that y_i increases as x_i increases, and a negative value indicates that y_i decreases as x_i increases.

The correlation coefficient for the data given in Table 12-3 is calculated as follows:

$$m_x = 59.1 \qquad m_y = 80.53 \qquad \sigma_x{}^2 = 540.85 \qquad \sigma_y{}^2 = 1128.25$$

therefore,

$$C_{x,y} = 0.7188$$

which indicates that there is a strong relationship between study effort and the grade received on the examination.

The discussion in this section indicates how measurements can be processed using statistical techniques. It is quite easy to develop computer programs to carry out these calculations. However, one should not blindly apply these formulas without first understanding the characteristics of the processes which produced the data. In some cases more advanced statistical techniques must be used to fully represent the properties of a given situation.

Exercises

1. Draw a histogram for the following data. How well are these data approximated by a normal curve?

Data

3.5	2.8	3.4	3.2	3.7	3.6	3.3
3.9	3.2	3.5	3.8	3.6	3.5	3.6
3.7	3.7	3.6	3.4	3.8	3.5	3.4
3.5	3.4	3.7	3.5	3.3	3.4	3.2
2.7	3.1	3.6	3.2	3.5	3.2	3.4
3.1	3.6	3.5	3.3	3.7	3.2	3.0

2. For the following set of 20 paired data points:

N	x_i	y_i	N	x_i	y_i
1	0.5	20	11	5.5	55
2	1.0	15	12	6.0	50
3	1.5	35	13	6.5	65
4	2.0	30	14	7.0	60
5	2.5	30	15	7.5	55
6	3.0	45	16	8.0	70
7	3.5	55	17	8.5	80
8	4.0	40	18	9.0	75
9	4.5	50	19	9.5	70
10	5.0	45	20	10	85

(a) plot the scatter diagram, using x_i as the independent variable;
(b) determine the linear regression line;
(c) calculate the correlation coefficient $C_{x,y}$.

3. Develop an algorithm that will compute the mean and standard deviation of a set of N data points $d_1, d_2, \ldots , d_N$. Assume that the number N is unknown and that each data point is processed as it is received so that the algorithm is not limited by the available computer memory. Give the detailed flowchart.

4. Develop an algorithm that will compute the coefficients a_0 and a_1 of the best linear fit to a set of v data points $(x_1,y_1), (x_2,y_2), \ldots , (x_v,y_v)$. Assume that each data point is processed as it is received. Give the detailed flowchart.

4 ■ Solving Linear Equations

The discussion in the previous sections often ended with the requirement that we solve a set of linear equations of the form

$$a_{11}x_1 + a_{12}x_2 + \cdots + a_{1n}x_n = b_1$$
$$a_{21}x_1 + a_{22}x_2 + \cdots + a_{2n}x_n = b_2$$
$$\cdot \qquad \cdot \qquad \cdot$$
$$a_{n1}x_1 + a_{n2}x_2 + \cdots + a_{nn}x_n = b_n$$

for the values of x_1 through x_n. The standard method of solving these equations taught in high-school algebra courses is by the use of a technique numerical analysts call Gaussian elimination.

Gaussian Elimination Method

This method of solution is straightforward and, as we will soon see, easy to represent in an algorithmic manner. For large values of n, this method, as with all methods of solving linear equations, has several limiting features that we should be aware of before trying to apply it to the solution of a particular problem.

As a starting point consider the following simple case. Suppose we are given a set of equations

$$3x_1 + 4x_2 + x_3 = 8$$
$$(1/2)x_1 + 2x_2 + (1/10)x_3 = 1$$
$$10x_1 + x_2 + 5x_3 = 4$$

and we wish to find x_1, x_2, and x_3 that will satisfy the three equations simultaneously. The elimination method of solution proceeds by first multiplying the first equation by 1/3 to normalize the coefficient of x_1 to 1.

$$x_1 + (4/3)x_2 + (1/3)x_3 = 8/3$$
$$(1/2)x_1 + 2x_2 + (1/10)x_3 = 1$$
$$10x_1 + x_2 + 5x_3 = 4$$

Next the first equation, multiplied by $\frac{1}{2}$, is subtracted from the second equation:

$$x_1 + (4/3)x_2 + (1/3)x_3 = 8/3$$
$$0 + (4/3)x_2 - (1/15)x_3 = -1/3$$
$$10x_1 + x_2 + 5x_3 = 4$$

The first equation, multiplied by 10, is then subtracted from the third equation:

$$x_1 + (4/3)x_2 + (1/3)x_3 = 8/3$$
$$0 + (4/3)x_2 - (1/15)x_3 = -1/3$$
$$0 - (37/3)x_2 + (5/3)x_3 = -68/3$$

The second equation is then multiplied by 3/4 to normalize the coefficient of x_2:

$$x_1 + (4/3)x_2 + (1/3)x_3 = 8/3$$
$$0 + x_2 - (1/20)x_3 = -1/4$$
$$0 - (37/3)x_2 + (5/3)x_3 = -68/3$$

Finally, we multiply the second equation by $-37/3$ and subtract it from the third equation to give

$$x_1 + (4/3)x_2 + (1/3)x_3 = 8/3$$
$$0 + x_2 + (1/20)x_3 = -1/4$$
$$0 + 0 + (21/20)x_3 = -103/4$$

At this point we can obtain a value for x_3. This then allows us to work back and calculate x_2 and then finally x_1.

$$x_3 = -\frac{515}{21} = -24.523 \ldots$$

$$x_2 = -\frac{1}{4} + \frac{1}{20}x_3 = -\frac{31}{21} = -1.4761 \ldots$$

$$x_1 = \frac{8}{3} - \frac{4}{3}x_2 - \frac{1}{3}x_3 = \frac{807}{63} = 12.809$$

This last sequence of steps is referred to as the *back solution.*

In the above example all the calculations were carried out using fractions. Because of this, the answers are accurate since we do not have to worry about truncation errors. However, if we use a computer to carry out the calculations, we know that each time we encounter a number that must be truncated for use by the computer we introduce a source of error. Since even the simple example we considered involves a large number of multiplications, subtractions, and divisions, the effect of these truncation errors can become very significant when we work with n equations where n is much larger than 3.

Influence of Truncation Error

To illustrate the problems we may have with truncation error, assume that all calculations involve three-digit, floating-point arithmetic. Starting with the original equation

$$3.00x_1 + 4.00x_2 + x_3 = 8.00$$
$$.500x_1 + 2.00x_2 + .100x_3 = 1.00$$
$$10.0x_1 + x_2 + 5.00x_3 = 4.00$$

and going through the same sequence of operations gives:

(a) in normalizing the first equation and eliminating x_1 from second and third equations:

$$x_1 + 1.33x_2 + .333x_3 = 2.66$$
$$0 + 1.33x_2 - .066x_3 = -.330$$
$$0 - 12.3x_2 + 1.67x_3 = -22.6$$

(b) in normalizing the second equation and eliminating x_2 from the third equation:

$$x_1 + 1.33x_2 + .333x_3 = 2.66$$
$$0 + x_2 + .0496x_3 = -.248$$
$$0 + 0 + 1.06x_3 = -22.1$$

(c) in carrying out the back solution:

$$x_3 = -20.8$$
$$x_2 = -.248 - .0496x_3 = -1.27$$
$$x_1 = 2.66 - 1.33x_2 - .333x_3 = 11.2$$

As we can see, these results do not agree very well with the exact values previously obtained using exact fractions. The severity of these errors can be reduced if we used a greater precision for the numbers in our calculation. But there are situations where this approach will not provide the desired reduction in errors.

Singular and Near Singular Equations

A set of linear equations is said to be *singular* if one of the equations in the set is a weighted sum of other equations in the set. The following example illustrates this definition.

Assume that we have the three equations:

$$\text{Equation 1:} \quad x_1 + x_2 + 2x_3 = 5$$
$$\text{Equation 2:} \quad x_1 + 2x_2 + x_3 = 2$$
$$\text{Equation 3:} \quad x_1 + 4x_2 - x_3 = -4$$

But we note that

$$\text{Equation 3} = (-2)(\text{Equation 1}) + (3)(\text{Equation 2})$$

If we try to solve a set of linear equations which are singular, we run into difficulty. To see this we try to solve the above set of equations: (a) subtract the first equation from the second and third equation to give

$$x_1 + x_2 + 2x_3 = 5$$
$$0 + x_2 - x_3 = -3$$
$$0 + 3x_2 - 3x_3 = -9$$

(b) subtract three times the second equation from the third to give

$$x_1 + x_2 + 2x_3 = 5$$
$$0 + x_2 - x_3 = -3$$
$$0 + 0 + 0 = 0$$

We must stop at this point, since the third equation has disappeared. This means that we have only two independent equations and we need three independent equations to solve for three unknowns.

When working on a computer it is possible to run into great difficulty with a set of equations which are not singular but are very close to being singular. For example, the set of equations

$$x_1 + x_2 = 5$$
$$x_1 + 1.002x_2 = 4$$

are not singular and we can solve for x_1 and x_2: (a) subtracting the first equation from the second gives

$$0.002x_2 = -1$$

(b) carrying out the back solution gives

$$x_2 = \frac{-1}{.002} = -500$$

$$x_1 = 5 - x_2 = 505$$

Now let us see what happens if the coefficient of x_2 is represented as 1.0019 in a computer because of the error involved in decimal to binary conversion or due to the error introduced in the experimental measurement. Carrying out the same calculation gives

$$0.0019x_2 = -1$$
$$x_2 = -526.31$$
$$x_1 = 531.31$$

Which is a very large error in the value of x_1 and x_2. Thus, we see that very small errors can be magnified when we try to solve a set of equations which are nearly singular.

Any set of equations which are singular, or nearly singular, are particularly bothersome when trying to carry out a computer solution. A set of equations in which this situation occurs is called *ill-conditioned.* There is nothing we can do in this case except to be aware of the fact that the results obtained by solving these equations on a computer may be quite different from the true results that we would obtain from an error-free solution. There is no way to transform a set of ill-conditioned equations into a set of equations that are not ill-conditioned.

Order of Solution

There are some equations which are not ill-conditioned but which must be solved in proper order to minimize computational error. For example, consider the equations

Equation 1: $0.0003x_1 + 3.0000x_2 = 2.0001$
Equation 2: $1.0000x_1 + 1.0000x_2 = 1.0000$

These equations, when solved exactly, have the solution

$$x_1 = 1/3 \qquad x_2 = 2/3$$

However, let us solve these equations using 5-digit floating-point arithmetic. We will do it in two different ways.

Method 1

(a) Multiply the first equation by 1/0.0003 and subtract it from the second equation to give

$$0.0003x_1 + 3.0000x_2 = 2.0001$$
$$x_2 = 66666/9999 = .66666$$

(b) Solve for x_1

$$0.0003x_1 + 3.0000x_2 = 2.0001$$
$$x_1 = .40000$$

Method 2

(a) Interchange Equation 1 and Equation 2 to give

$$1.0000x_1 + 1.0000x_2 = 1.0000$$
$$0.0003x_1 + 3.0000x_2 = 2.0001$$

(b) Multiply the top equation by 0.0003 and subtract it from the bottom equation

$$1.0000x_1 + 1.0000x_2 = 1.0000$$
$$x_2 = 1.9998/2.9997 = .66666$$

(c) Solving for x_1

$$1.0000x_1 + 1.0000x_2 = 1.0000$$
$$x_1 = .33334$$

Examining these two methods of solving the same set of equations, we see that the second method gives a better result. The reason for this is that the coefficient for x_1 in the top equation was the largest possible value. When we multiplied by .0003 and subtracted, the influence of any accumulated computational error was reduced. In the first method we multiplied the top equation by

$$1/0.0003 = 3333.3$$

Thus, any computational error present was multiplied by the same amount.

To see the implication of this observation, assume that a general solution in a set of n linear equations has reached the point where we have

$$x_1 + a_{12}x_2 + a_{13}x_3 + \cdots + a_{1i}x_i + \cdots + a_{1n}x_n = b_1$$
$$0 + x_2 + a_{23}x_3 + \cdots + a_{2i}x_i + \cdots + a_{2n}x_n = b_2$$
$$0 + 0 + x_3 + \cdots + a_{3i}x_i + \cdots + a_{3n}x_n = b_3$$
$$\cdots$$

Equations i through n
$$\begin{cases} 0 + 0 + 0 + \cdots + a_{ii}x_i + \cdots + a_{in}x_n = b_i \\ \qquad\qquad\qquad \cdots \\ 0 + 0 + 0 + \cdots + a_{ki}x_i + \cdots + a_{kn}x_n = b_k \\ \qquad\qquad\qquad \cdots \\ 0 + 0 + 0 + \cdots + a_{ni}x_i + \cdots + a_{nn}x_n = b_n \end{cases}$$

To go on to the next stage we must multiply the ith row by $-a_{ki}/a_{ii}$ and subtract it from the kth row, for $k = i + 1, i + 2, ..., n$. If we wish to minimize the error, we should rearrange the equations so that the equation in the ith row has a coefficient a_{ii} which satisfies the condition

$$|a_{ii}| \geq |a_{ik}| \qquad k = i + 1, i + 2, \ldots, n$$

This reorganization of the order of the equations does not alter the theoretical solution of the equations but it does minimize the computational errors introduced.

With these observations, we now turn to the problem of developing a general algorithm which can be used to solve a set of linear equations.

The Computational Algorithm

When we deal with a set of linear equations such as

$$a_{11}x_1 + a_{12}x_2 + \cdots + a_{1n}x_n = b_1$$
$$a_{21}x_1 + a_{22}x_2 + \cdots + a_{2n}x_n = b_2$$
$$\vdots$$
$$a_{n1}x_1 + a_{n2}x_2 + \cdots + a_{nn}x_n = b_n$$

We can always represent these equations in the following matrix form

$$\begin{bmatrix} a_{11} & a_{12} & \cdots & a_{1n} \\ a_{21} & a_{22} & \cdots & a_{2n} \\ & & \cdots & \\ a_{n1} & a_{n2} & \cdots & a_{nn} \end{bmatrix} \begin{bmatrix} x_1 \\ x_2 \\ \vdots \\ x_n \end{bmatrix} = \begin{bmatrix} b_1 \\ b_2 \\ \vdots \\ b_n \end{bmatrix}$$

The coefficients a_{ij} are thus collected in a two-dimensional array $[a_{ij}]$ and the constants b_i are collected in a one-dimensional array $[b_i]$. It is quite easy to apply our elimination methods to these arrays. In particular, we see that the solution to the equations represented by this matrix form are not changed if:

(a) any two of the rows are interchanged

Example:

$$\begin{bmatrix} 1 & 3 & 5 \\ 2 & 1 & 0 \\ 3 & 2 & 4 \end{bmatrix} \begin{bmatrix} x_1 \\ x_2 \\ x_3 \end{bmatrix} = \begin{bmatrix} 1 \\ 4 \\ 6 \end{bmatrix}$$

and

$$\begin{bmatrix} 1 & 3 & 5 \\ 3 & 2 & 4 \\ 2 & 1 & 0 \end{bmatrix} \begin{bmatrix} x_1 \\ x_3 \\ x_2 \end{bmatrix} = \begin{bmatrix} 1 \\ 6 \\ 4 \end{bmatrix} \qquad \text{Row 2 and row 3 are interchanged}$$

will, when solved, give the same values for x_1, x_2, and x_3.

(b) any row is multiplied by a constant and added to any other row

Example:

$$\begin{bmatrix} 1 & 3 & 5 \\ 2 & 1 & 0 \\ 3 & 2 & 4 \end{bmatrix} \begin{bmatrix} x_1 \\ x_2 \\ x_3 \end{bmatrix} = \begin{bmatrix} 1 \\ 4 \\ 6 \end{bmatrix}$$

multiply the first row by -2 and add it to the second row to give

$$\begin{bmatrix} 1 & 3 & 5 \\ 0 & -5 & -10 \\ 3 & 2 & 4 \end{bmatrix} \begin{bmatrix} x_1 \\ x_2 \\ x_3 \end{bmatrix} = \begin{bmatrix} 1 \\ 2 \\ 6 \end{bmatrix}$$ ←Note the new values obtained by this operation

When solved, both matrix forms will give the same values for x_1, x_2, and x_3.

Note that in the two operations discussed above we are working simultaneously with both the $[a_{ij}]$ and the $[b_i]$ arrays.

Using these two operations, we carry out the elimination operations by reducing the matrix equation to the following form.

$$\begin{bmatrix} 1 & c_{12} & c_{13} & \cdots & c_{1n} \\ 0 & 1 & c_{23} & \cdots & c_{2n} \\ & & \cdots & & \\ 0 & 0 & 0 & \cdots & 1 \end{bmatrix} \begin{bmatrix} x_1 \\ x_2 \\ \cdot \\ \cdot \\ x_n \end{bmatrix} = \begin{bmatrix} d_1 \\ d_2 \\ \cdot \\ \cdot \\ d_n \end{bmatrix}$$

Once we get to this point, the solution becomes

$$x_n = d_n$$
$$x_{n-1} = d_{n-1} - c_{n-1,n} \, x_n$$
$$\cdots$$
$$x_1 = d_1 - c_{12}x_2 - c_{13}x_3 - \cdots - c_{1n}x_n$$

The way in which we find the $[c_{ij}]$ and $[d_i]$ arrays will be illustrated by the following example. (After we complete the example, a complete flowchart description of the algorithm will be given.) Assume that we wish to solve the following set of linear equations:

$$3x_1 + x_2 + 2x_3 = 10$$
$$-2x_1 + x_2 + 3x_3 = 7$$
$$4x_1 + 4x_2 - x_3 = 5$$

Writing this equation in matrix form gives

$$\begin{bmatrix} 3 & 1 & 2 \\ -2 & 1 & 3 \\ 4 & 4 & -1 \end{bmatrix} \begin{bmatrix} x_1 \\ x_2 \\ x_3 \end{bmatrix} = \begin{bmatrix} 10 \\ 7 \\ 5 \end{bmatrix}$$

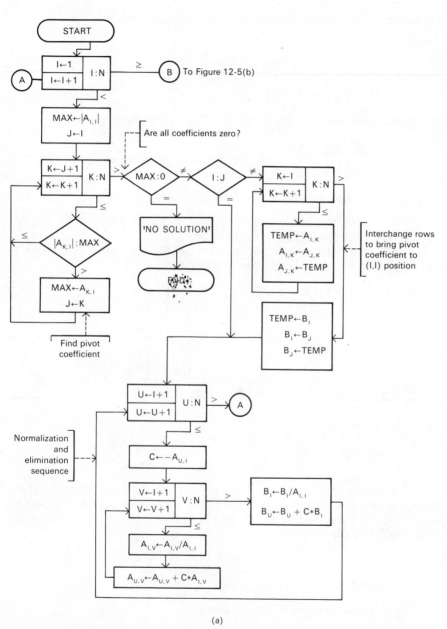

(a)

FIGURE 12-15 ▪ Flowchart for the Gaussian elimination method of solving linear equations. (a) Steps of elimination.

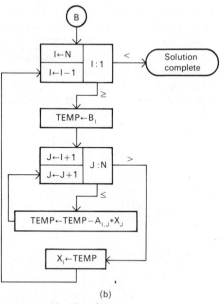

(b)

FIGURE 12-15 ■ (b) Steps of back solution.

The first task is to generate c_{11} by eliminating x_1 from the other equations. To do this, we search the first column to find the coefficient of x_1 with the largest magnitude. This coefficient is called the *pivot coefficient* of that column. In our example, the pivot coefficient is 4 and the third row which contains the coefficient is interchanged with the first row to give

These two
rows are
interchanged

$$\begin{bmatrix} 4 & 4 & -1 \\ -2 & 1 & 3 \\ 3 & 1 & 2 \end{bmatrix} \begin{bmatrix} x_1 \\ x_2 \\ x_3 \end{bmatrix} = \begin{bmatrix} 5 \\ 7 \\ 10 \end{bmatrix}$$

Now that the largest coefficient is in the (1,1) position, we proceed to normalize the first equation (i.e., to divide the first equation by a_{11} to make the coefficient of x_1 equal to 1) and to eliminate the coefficients of x_1 in the (2,1) and (3,1) positions. This is done by first dividing the first row by 4 and then subtracting the first row multiplied by -2 from the second row. Next the first row multiplied by 3 is subtracted from the third row. These two operations give

$$\begin{bmatrix} 1 & 1 & -\dfrac{1}{4} \\ 0 & 3 & \dfrac{5}{2} \\ 0 & -2 & \dfrac{11}{4} \end{bmatrix} \begin{bmatrix} x_1 \\ x_2 \\ x_3 \end{bmatrix} = \begin{bmatrix} \dfrac{5}{4} \\ \dfrac{19}{2} \\ \dfrac{25}{4} \end{bmatrix}$$

Next we look at the subarray indicated by the dotted line and try to introduce a zero into the (3,2) position. We do not have to concern ourselves with the first row. Thus we look for the pivot coefficient in the second column only for rows below the first. We see that 3 in the (2,2) position is the largest coefficient and thus it becomes the pivot coefficient. We do not have to interchange any rows. A zero is now placed in the (3,2) position by first normalizing the second row and then subtracting the second row multiplied by -2 to the third row. This gives

$$\begin{bmatrix} 1 & 1 & -\dfrac{1}{4} \\ 0 & 1 & \dfrac{5}{6} \\ 0 & 0 & \dfrac{53}{12} \end{bmatrix} \begin{bmatrix} x_1 \\ x_2 \\ x_3 \end{bmatrix} = \begin{bmatrix} \dfrac{5}{4} \\ \dfrac{19}{6} \\ \dfrac{151}{12} \end{bmatrix}$$

Finally, normalizing the last row gives

$$\begin{bmatrix} 1 & 1 & -\dfrac{1}{4} \\ 0 & 1 & \dfrac{5}{6} \\ 0 & 0 & 1 \end{bmatrix} \begin{bmatrix} x_1 \\ x_2 \\ x_3 \end{bmatrix} = \begin{bmatrix} \dfrac{5}{4} \\ \dfrac{19}{6} \\ \dfrac{151}{53} \end{bmatrix}$$

Using these results, we then solve the back equations to give

$$x_3 = 151/53$$
$$x_2 = 19/6 - (5/6)x_3 = 42/53$$
$$x_1 = 5/4 - x_2 + (1/4)x_3 = 62/53$$

This example has shown that the general algorithm has two major parts. The first task is to carry out the elimination steps and the second is to use the resulting matrix and work backward to find the value of the unknown variables. The complete flowchart for this algorithm is given in Fig. 12-15.

If we examine the flowchart for the algorithm, we can see why we may encounter problems because of truncation errors. A considerable portion of the operations involved in this algorithm involve multiplication and division. For large values of n, there are approximately $n^3/3$ such operations. As n grows, we can expect the size of the errors to grow until we reach a point that will substantially influence the results of the calculations. If the equations are not ill-conditioned, this algorithm can be expected to give satisfactory results for n less than 15 or 20, provided a reasonable precision is used for the numbers involved in the calculation. When the equations are ill-conditioned, we can have serious errors even for values of n as low as 2 or 3. If it becomes necessary to solve linear equations with 20 or more variables, it would be a wise precaution to use more advanced numerical analysis techniques than those discussed to minimize computational errors.

Exercises

1. Compute the *exact* values of x_1, x_2, x_3 using the Gaussian elimination method:

$$3x_1 + 2x_2 + x_3 = 20$$
$$5x_1 + x_2 + 2x_3 = 5$$
$$x_1 + 6x_2 + x_3 = 4$$

2. Repeat Exercise 1 but use three-digit, floating-point numbers.

3. For the equations

$$.0001x_1 + x_2 = 1$$
$$x_1 + x_2 = 2$$

(a) Find the value of x_1 and x_2 without interchanging the two equations. Use a three-digit, floating-point computation.
(b) Find the values of x_1 and x_2 by first interchanging the two equations. Use a three-digit floating-point computation.
(c) Compare the results in (a) and (b). Which calculation is more accurate?

---

5 ▌ Summary

This chapter has presented a number of the common techniques that are used to analyze and manipulate various types of data. The methods presented are the most common data-manipulation techniques and are suitable to handle many of the standard data-processing problems encountered in carrying out experimental measurements.

This discussion was meant to illustrate how a computer can be used in various data-processing applications. Therefore, only the basic processing methods are presented. These methods have many important applications and are used extensively in many fields. There are, however, many other important information-processing techniques that have not been discussed. The references at the end of this chapter cover these techniques and their application.

References

A general discussion of the statistical concepts discussed in this chapter are found in [3], [4], and [7]. The numerical analysis problems involved in processing different types of data are treated in [1], [2], and [5]. [6] presents a comprehensive survey of the standard statistical packaged programs which have been developed to carry out different data analysis tasks. Some of these programs are probably available in the local computer center.

1. Barrodale, I., Roberts, F. D. K., and Ehle, B. L. (1971) *Elementary Computer Applications in Science, Engineering, and Business,* John Wiley & Sons, New York.

2. Carnahan, B., Luther, H. A., and Wilkes, J. O. (1969) *Applied Numerical Methods,* John Wiley & Sons, New York.

3. Hogg, R., and Craig, A. (1970) *Introduction To Mathematical Statistics,* 3rd ed., MacMillan, New York.

4. Knuth, D. (1969) *The Art of Computer Programming, Vol. 2, Seminumerical Algorithms,* Addison-Wesley, Reading, Mass.

5. Ralston, A. (1965) *A First Course in Numerical Analysis,* McGraw-Hill, New York.

6. Schucany, W. R., Shannon, B. S., Jr., and Minton, P. D. (June 1972) "A Survey of Statistical Packages," *Computing Surveys,* Vol. 4, No. 2, pp. 65–79.

7. Sterling, T. D., and Pollack, S. V. (1968) *Introduction To Statistical Data Processing,* Prentice-Hall, Englewood Cliffs, N.J.

Home Problems

If possible, the algorithms developed to solve the following problems should be programmed and tested on a computer.

1. There are a number of pseudo-random-number generation algorithms available (for example, home problem 2, Chapter V). Develop a program that will plot a histogram of 1,000 numbers generated by a pseudo-random-number generator. How well does the distribution of these numbers correspond to the stated characteristics of the pseudo-random-number generator?

2. Let X_I, $I = 1, 2, \ldots, 1000$ be the numbers obtained from some pseudo-random-number generator. In many applications it is assumed that X_i and X_J are uncorrelated for $I \neq J$ (i.e., knowledge of the value of X_I gives us no information about the value of X_J; the correlation coefficient would be zero). Some pseudo-random-number generation algorithms have the unfortunate property that the numbers generated are not uncorrelated.

Assume that a pseudo-random-number generator produces the sequence

$$X_I, I = 1, 2, \ldots, 1000 + k$$

Define the sequence

$$Y_I = X_{I+k} \qquad I = 1, 2, \ldots, 1000$$

(a) Develop a flowchart of an algorithm which will compute the correlation coefficient $C_{x,y}$ for $k = 1, 2, \ldots, K_{max}$. A thousand samples (X_I, Y_I) should be used for this calculation.

(b) Use this algorithm to test one or more pseudo-random-number generators for correlation.

3. Let X_I, $I = 1, 2, \ldots, 5000$ be a sequence of uniformly distributed pseudo-random numbers. Define

$$V_K = X_{2K} + X_{2(K-1)}$$
$$W_K = X_{3K} + X_{3(K-1)} + X_{3(K-2)}$$
$$Y_K = X_{4K} = X_{4(K-1)} + X_{4(K-2)} + X_{4(K-3)}$$
$$Z_K = X_{5K} + X_{5(K-1)} + X_{5(K-2)} + X_{5(K-3)} + X_{5(K-4)}$$

(a) Compute and plot a histogram for each of the sequences V_K, W_K, Y_K, and Z_K produced for $K = 1, 2, \ldots, 1000$.

(b) Use the algorithm presented in problem 2 to compute the correlation coefficient for (V_K, V_{K+k}), (W_K, W_{K+k}), (Y_K, Y_{K+k}), (Z_K, Z_{K+k}), for $k = 1, 2, 3, 4, 5$.

4. In problem 3 all of the new random numbers (V_K, W_K, Y_K, X_K) are formed by adding groups of independent pseudo-random numbers (assuming that the numbers in the sequence X_I were uncorrelated). All of the terms in the sequence X_I appear in at most one group.

It has been suggested that the same type of random numbers could be generated by using the following equations.

$$V_K = X_K + X_{K-1} \qquad\qquad K = 2, 3, \ldots, 10001$$
$$W_K = X_K + X_{K-1} + X_{K-2} \qquad\qquad K = 3, 4, \ldots, 10002$$
$$Y_K = X_K + X_{K-1} + X_{K-2} + X_{K-3} \qquad\qquad K = 4, 5, \ldots, 10003$$
$$Z_K = X_K + X_{K-1} + X_{K-2} + X_{K-3} + X_{K-4} \qquad\qquad K = 5, 6, \ldots, 10004$$

where the X_I are uniformly distributed pseudo-random numbers.

(a) Compute 1000 values for V, W, Y, and Z. Plot a histogram for V, W, Y, and Z.

(b) Use the algorithm presented in problem 2 to compute the correlation coefficient for (V_K, V_{K+k}), (W_K, W_{K+k}), (Y_K, Y_{K+k}), and (Z_K, Z_{K+k}) for $k = 1, 2, 3, 4, 5, 6$.

(c) Discuss the meaning of the results obtained in part (b). In particular, is the above method a good technique for generating uncorrelated random numbers?

5. The following table gives the calibration curve for a special temperature measuring device. The output of the device is a voltage in the range 0 to 5.0 volts. The table is then used to obtain the temperature corresponding to this voltage.

Calibration curve for a special temperature measuring device

Output voltage (volts)	Temperature (°C)	Output voltage (volts)	Temperature (°C)	Output voltage (volts)	Temperature (°C)
.08854	0	.45938	45	1.7888	90
.10821	5	.54103	50	2.0503	95
.13150	10	.63514	55	2.3440	100
.15914	15	.74322	60	2.6729	105
.19182	20	.86687	65	3.0404	110
.23020	25	1.0078	70	3.4503	115
.27514	30	1.1683	75	3.9067	120
.32763	35	1.3504	80	4.4113	125
.38862	40	1.5563	85	4.9714	130

Develop a flowchart of an algorithm which will compute the temperature from the measured voltage value. What type of interpolation should be used to represent the value of the calibration curve between calibration points?

6. Sometimes it is necessary to fit data to a curve which is not describable by a polynomial. For example, we might have reason to believe that the results of a given experiment can be described by a function of the form

$$P(x) = Ae^{Mx+Nx^2}$$

where x is the independent variable and P(x) is the dependent variable. To compute A, M, and N, we note that $y(x) = \log_e P(x) = \log_e A + Mx + Nx^2$. Using this result, develop a flowchart of an algorithm that can be used to fit the data by first finding a least squares curve fit for y(x) and then using the result to define P(x).

7. Plot out on some graph the straight lines defined by the following equations

$$0.0003x_1 + 3.0000x_2 = 2.0001$$
$$1.0000x_1 + 1.0000x_2 = 1.0000$$

Use this graph to explain why we obtain different solutions to these equations depending upon the order in which we solve for x_1 and x_2.

8. A sequence of random numbers is said to have a *Normal distribution* if its histogram exhibits the behavior of a Normal curve. There are a number of algorithms available which will generate Normally distributed random numbers. One method makes use of N independent pseudo-random-number generators with uniform distribution over the interval [0,1]. Each Normal number Z is generated by adding N numbers X_i, i = 1, . . . , N, each X_i taken from an independent pseudo-random-number generation. Develop the flowchart of an algorithm which will produce Normal numbers using the above method. Discuss the effect of N on the outcome of the generator by choosing various values of N and examining the histograms constructed from at least 1000 Normal numbers.

9. Derive the equations given in Section II of this chapter that can be used to solve for the coefficients a_0 and a_1 to give the best linear fit for a set of v data points. Use either an algebraic method or a method from the differential calculus.

10. Given a set of N data points, the coefficients a_0 and a_1 for the best linear fit can be calculated by the equations given in Section II of this chapter in terms of the data points. The two coefficients can also easily be expressed in terms of the mean m and variance σ^2 of the N data points.
   (a) Derive the expressions of a_0 and a_1 in terms of m and σ^2.
   (b) Develop the flowchart of an algorithm which will compute a_0 and a_1 using the expressions derived in part (a). Assume that the number N is unknown and that each data point is processed as it is received so that the algorithm is not limited by the available memory space of a computer.

13

numerical methods
and algorithms

1 ■ Introduction

One of the original justifications for investing research money in the development of digital computers was the need to carry out massive numerical calculations which were impractical or too time consuming to do on a desk calculator. The computer, at this stage, was considered a high speed "number cruncher" with the ability of rapidly carrying out long and tedious calculations with a minimum of error. That computers have proven to be very effective for this type of computational task is attested to by the large amount of computer time expended each day upon routine data-processing and computational tasks.

After the novelty of the use of computers as calculators wore off, the mathematicians, engineers, and scientists associated with the development and use of the early computers soon realized that computers could be used as a powerful tool in analytical studies rather than simply as high-speed calculators. Richard W. Hamming, one of the early pioneers in the use of computers as a research and development tool, has vividly pointed out on a number of occasions that,

"The purpose of computing is insight not numbers."

By this statement, he indicates that it is not the numerical values that we obtain from many computations which are of importance but the relationship that these values bear to our understanding of a particular problem.

In the previous chapters we have explored some of the methods used to perform numerical calculations and we have investigated ways in which the computational errors introduced by a computer can be minimized. Our task in this chapter is to investigate some of the basic numerical analysis methods that have been developed to solve common numerical problems found in engineering and scientific work. This discussion is of an introductory nature and is intended to introduce the different classes of numerical methods that are useful in solving numerical problems. Many of the common numerical problems encountered in typical analytical studies can be handled with these techniques. The references listed at the end of this chapter expand upon the material presented in the following sections.

There is a wide range of numerical problems that can occur in carrying out scientific work. Each problem requires a specific method of solution. In some special cases it is possible to obtain an exact solution to the problem. The majority of real problems encountered in scientific work are, unfortunately, usually so complex that we must use numerical methods to obtain a particular answer rather than attempt a general analytical solution.

There are two basic techniques that are of particular importance in carrying out the numerical solution of problems. The solution to a large number of problems involves finding the value of one or more variables satisfying the set of mathematical equations that describe the system under investigation. Except for very special conditions, the only way to obtain the desired solution is to carry out a directed search of the possible values until the desired numerical values are found.

The second class of problems involve situations where we describe the quantity that must be calculated and the conditions that must be satisfied in such a way that the exact mathematical operations cannot be executed on a computer. A solution in this case can be found by using techniques which approximate the desired computation. The quality of the solution thus depends upon how close the approximation corresponds to the actual mathematical process being represented.

The accuracy of any numerical result obtained by a computer depends upon the particular numerical analysis technique being used to solve the problem and the magnitude of the computational errors introduced in the computation by the computer. Since the topic of computational errors has already been introduced in Chapter VIII, our main concern will be with the errors inherent in the particular techniques being considered. However, it should be realized that as the errors in the numerical techniques are reduced, the computational errors become more important and finally establish a lower limit to the accuracy of any calculation.

2 ▌ Numerical Solution of Equations by Iteration Techniques

In Chapter XII we developed an exact mathematical technique that may be used to solve linear equations of the form

$$a_1 x_1 + a_2 x_2 = c_1$$
$$b_1 x_1 + b_2 x_2 = c_2$$

for the values of x_1 and x_2 that satisfy these equations. Such a solution is called a *closed form solution* since there is an exact method to find the desired values of x_1 and x_2. The class of problems considered in this section either do not have a closed form solution, or the closed form solution is difficult to find or use. As a starting point, we assume that we are given one or more equations that describe the problem we are working on. Our task is then to search through a set of values associated with one or more variables to find the particular value or values that satisfy the equations.

To illustrate the types of problems that are of interest, assume that we have two functions $f_1(x)$ and $f_2(x)$ that have the form shown by the graphs in Fig. 13-1. Three questions that are often asked about such functions are:

1. What values of x satisfy the condition

$$f_1(x) = 0 \quad \text{(point A of Fig. 13-1)}$$

2. What values of x satisfy the condition

$$f_1(x) = \text{maximum value of } f_1(x) \quad \text{(point B of Fig. 13-1)}$$

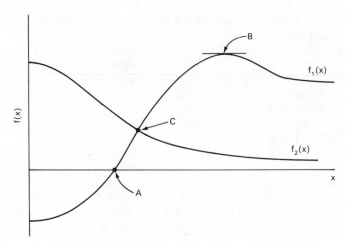

FIGURE 13-1 ▮ Typical problems associated with evaluating functions.

3. What values of x satisfy the condition

$$f_1(x) - f_2(x) = 0 \qquad \text{(point C of Fig. 13-1)}$$

(The third problem is essentially the same as the first, except that we are trying to determine where two curves intersect rather than trying to find where the curve intersects the x axis.)

Depending upon the way the functions are represented, and their form, it may be possible to give an algorithm which allows the direct solution of one or more of these problems. When no such algorithm exists, or when the anticipated computational errors introduced by using the algorithm are too large, we can often obtain a satisfactory solution to the problem by using a directed search technique.

In the directed search method, we first estimate an approximate value of x that we think may fall near to the value of x for which we are looking. We then evaluate f(x) and see if it satisfies the conditions of our problem. If it does, we report that value of x as the answer. If it does not, we then use the results of our calculation to estimate a new value of x which, hopefully, will be closer or equal to the value for which we are searching. This new value of x is then checked to see if it is correct. We repeat this iterative search process until we obtain a value of x that satisfies the conditions of our problem, or until we can determine that our method of solution is not working. The following discussion illustrates some of the common methods that have been developed to carry out problem solutions by this method.

Roots of an Equation

There are a wide range of mathematical problems that involve finding the values of x for which

$$f(x) = 0$$

where $f(x)$ is any function of x. The particular values of x which satisfy this condition are called the roots of the equation $f(x) = 0$. Under the most general conditions, the roots of an equation may be either real or complex numbers. For this discussion we limit our investigation to the problem of finding the real roots.

There are two broad classes of function that we may encounter. A function is said to be a *polynomial function* if it has the general form

$$f(x) = a_n x^n + a_{n-1} x^{n-1} + \cdots + a_1 x + a_0$$

In this case, the function may have n or fewer real roots. For values of $n \leq 4$ there are exact algorithms that can be used to find the roots of $f(x) = 0$. However, for polynomials with $n > 4$, we must use iterative methods to find the real roots.

Many of the functions that are encountered in numerical work are not polynomials. Some typical functions of this type are

$$f(x) = \sin(x) - .2$$
$$f(x) = \sin^2(x) + x^3 - 3\cos(x) + 10$$
$$f(x) = \frac{e^x - \sin(x)}{\cos(x^2 - 1)}$$

These functions may take on a variety of forms and may have zero, a finite number, or an infinite number of roots. The only restriction we place on the functions we consider is that they must be representable by a continuous curve in a reasonable interval around the roots of interest.

The Iterative Method of Solution

The general steps in finding a root of an equation using iterative techniques are indicated by the flowchart of Fig. 13-2. Examining this flowchart, we see that there are two major tasks that must be carried out and two questions that must be answered.

The first task, which is usually carried out by the computer user for simple problems but by the program in more complex cases, is to locate an interval $[x_1, x_2]$ that is known to contain a root. The way that this can be accomplished is illustrated in Fig. 13-3. Except for the very special case illustrated in Fig. 13-3(b), where the function is tangent to the x axis, we can locate the general position of a root by finding two values of x_1 and x_2 such that $f(x_1)$ and $f(x_2)$ have different signs. This situation is illustrated in Fig. 13-3(a). For the following discussion, we assume that no roots of the type shown in Fig. 13-3(b) are present. This problem will be considered a little later when we discuss the location of maximum and minimum points of a function.

Once we locate an interval that we know contains a root, we must then set up a method to search this interval for a value of x that makes $f(x)$ equal to zero within the precision desired. A large number of techniques have been

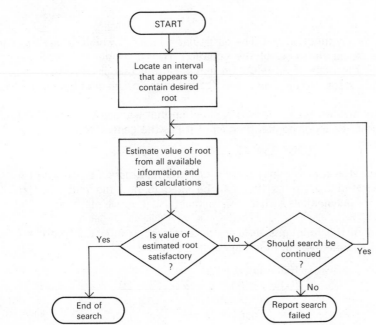

FIGURE 13-2 ■ General flowchart of iterative method for finding a root of an equation.

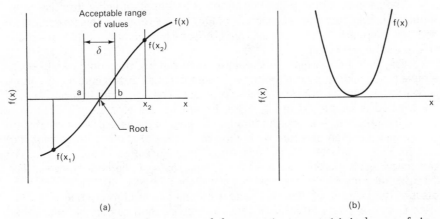

FIGURE 13-3 ■ Estimating an interval that contains a root. (a) A change of sign. (b) Special case.

developed to do this. Each time we carry out an estimation, we must see if the estimation gives us a satisfactory approximation to the desired root.

During the search process, computational errors and other reasons make it unlikely that we will find a value of x such that f(x) is exactly equal to zero. What we must do is locate an interval [a,b] contained in the original interval $[x_1,x_2]$ such that

1. $|b - a| < \delta$
2. the sign of f(x) changes in going from a to b
3. $f(x) \approx 0$ for all x in the interval [a,b]

We then know that the root is in the interval [a,b]. The value selected for the root depends upon the method of search used. In some cases, the root may be taken as a or b. At other times it might be (a + b)/2. In most cases, we have the situation that the interval [a,b] is very small and that f(x) is sufficiently close to zero for all x in the interval so that it is not too critical which value is selected for the root.

After every estimation of x is completed, we must check the estimated value to see if it is acceptable as a root. If it is satisfactory, we can terminate our search. Otherwise we must continue. For some of the estimation techniques, it is possible for the estimation process to diverge away from the value of the desired root rather than to converge towards it. If we did not account for this, there is the possibility that we might enter an infinite loop. For processes of this type, we must include a criterion that will tell us when to stop our search process. This criterion may be a simple limit on the number of iteration steps we can use in our search process or it may depend upon the values of certain parameters generated during the estimation process.

Now that we have a general outline of the search method, our next step is to look at one of the basic estimation techniques that can be used. We assume that the initial estimation of the interval in which we expect to find the root has already been carried out.

The Bisection Method of Root Location

The safest and most straightforward method for obtaining the root of an equation is the bisection method. This method will always give us an answer, to within an error ϵ, after a finite number of steps. The steps involved in the bisection method are illustrated graphically in Fig. 13-4.

Basically what we are trying to do is to systematically reduce the size of the interval that is known to contain the root until we reach an interval size δ that is small enough so that $\delta \leq 2\epsilon$. The root of f(x) = 0 is then taken to be the value of x that falls in the center of this final interval.

Assume that from an initial investigation we find that $f(x_1) < 0$ and $f(x_2) > 0$. This indicates that for some x

$$f(x) = 0 \qquad \text{where } x_1 \leq x \leq x_2$$

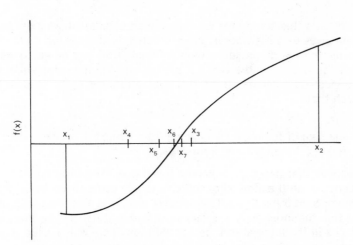

13-4 ■ Illustration of the bisection method of finding roots.

The interval $[x_1,x_2]$ is bisected and the function is evaluated at the midpoint x_3 where

$$x_3 = \frac{x_1 + x_2}{2}$$

This gives us two new intervals $[x_1,x_3]$ and $[x_3,x_2]$ each of which are half the size of the original interval. One of the intervals contains the desired root. To determine which one has the root we compare the sign of $f(x_3)$ to the sign of $f(x_1)$ and $f(x_2)$. The value of x_i, $i = 1, 2$, that gives $f(x_i)$ a different sign from $f(x_3)$ determines the interval selected. Examining Fig. 13-4, we see that $f(x_1)$ has a different sign than $f(x_3)$. Thus, the second interval selected for this example is $[x_1,x_3]$. This new interval is bisected, giving us x_4. The sign comparison process is repeated and for the function shown in Fig. 13-4, we find the third interval to be $[x_4,x_3]$. Continuing in this manner, we generate the increasingly smaller intervals $[x_5,x_3]$, $[x_6,x_3]$, $[x_6,x_7]$. If at this point we reach the situation where

$$|x_7 - x_6| = \delta \leqslant 2\epsilon$$

then the midpoint of this interval

$$x_M = \frac{x_6 + x_7}{2}$$

is selected as the approximate value of the desired root to within an error ϵ.

The algorithm to carry out the bisection method of root location appears to be straightforward. Our initial flowchart of the algorithm might look like the one shown in Fig. 13-5. In this flowchart we have carried out each step of the process as indicated in our discussion. The upper and lower bounds of the interval are adjusted after each bisection step. We test the value of the function at the new midpoint to see if it has the same sign as F(XL) or a different sign by multiplying the two values and seeing if the result is positive or negative. A positive result indicates that XM should become the new lower bound, while a negative result indicates that XM should become the new upper bound.

There is nothing wrong with this algorithm and it will work provided it is encoded properly in an appropriate language. The algorithm is not very efficient from a computer viewpoint because we carry out a larger number of computations than we actually need. Let us take a look at the algorithm to see how it might be revised to make it better suited for use on a computer.

We note that the evaluation of a function will probably be a very lengthy process. If we look at Fig. 13-4, we see that no matter how we change the value of the lower bound, the sign of the lower bound remains the same. Thus, the comparison of F(XM) can be replaced by comparing the sign of F(XM) to the known sign of F(XL). This comparison can be done by the multiplication process where F(XL) is replaced by a constant of Y = +1 or Y = −1, depending,

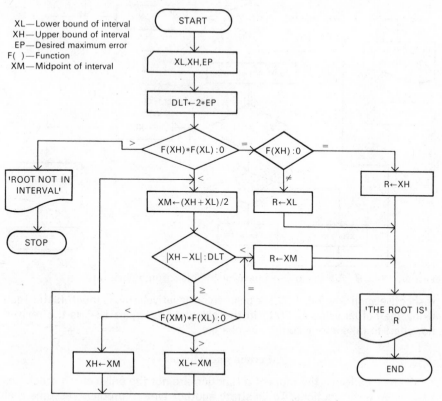

FIGURE 13-5 ■ Initial flowchart of the bisection algorithm.

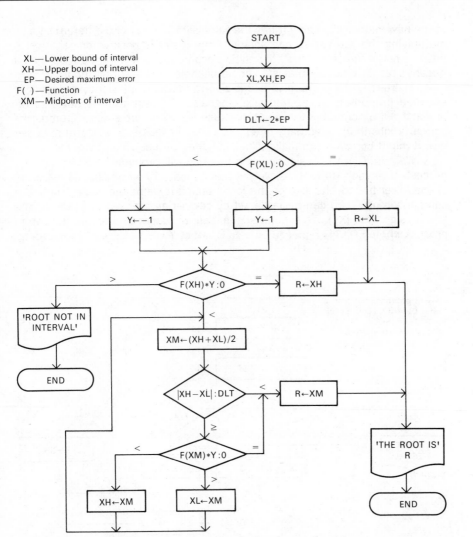

XL—Lower bound of interval
XH—Upper bound of interval
EP—Desired maximum error
F( )—Function
XM—Midpoint of interval

FIGURE 13-6 ■ A revised flowchart for the bisection algorithm.

respectively, on whether F(XL) is positive or negative. This is much faster than using the actual value of F(XL) in the calculation. Figure 13-6 is the revised flowchart to take into account this change.

Maxima and Minima

The location of the roots of a function are not the only search processes associated with functions. To illustrate another type of problem, assume that we have a manufacturing process where the cost of the process depends upon the value of some quantity x. Let this relationship be given by the equation

$$C = f(x)$$

where C is the cost associated with the process if x has a particular value. The problem of interest is to find a particular value of x, say x_{min}, so that

$$f(x_{min}) = C_{min}$$

where C_{min} is the lowest cost obtainable for all allowable values of x. Similar problems can be formulated where we look for a value of x that gives us a maximum rather than a minimum value for the function.

The need to "optimize" the operation of large-scale manufacturing and economic processes has led to the development of a large number of numerical methods that can be used to locate the maxima or minima of functions of one or more variables. Our discussion will illustrate one of the simplest of these search techniques, which can be used to locate the minimum of a function in a fixed interval.

The Basic Problem

Let us assume that we are given a function f(x), such as illustrated in Fig. 13-7, and that we wish to develop an algorithm to describe how we can locate the minimum value of the function in the interval $[x_1, x_2]$. The function of interest is assumed to have the following properties:

1. There is a single minimum in the interval $[x_1, x_2]$.
2. Moving from x_1 to x_2 the function decreases until it reaches its minimum value, then it continually increases until the point x_2 is reached.
3. The function is continuous without any abrupt discontinuities.

Making use of these restrictions, we develop a simple search technique to locate the minimum point of a function.

The Search Process

The basic searching process consists of developing a way to reduce the size of the interval in which we know the minimum to occur until we reach the

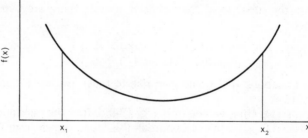

FIGURE 13-7 ■ A function with a minimum value in the interval $[x_1, x_2]$.

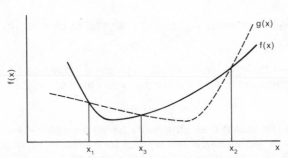

FIGURE 13-8 ■ Illustration of the fact that a single point inside the interval $[x_1, x_2]$ cannot help locate the minimum.

situation that the interval size is less than some preset value. The minimum point is then assumed to be at the center of this fixed interval. This search technique has a very strong similarity to the one used to locate the root of a function. There are, however, some important differences.

Assume that we wish to find the minimum of the function f(x) shown in Fig. 13-8 that is known to occur somewhere in the interval $[x_1, x_2]$. If we try to reduce this interval by looking at the value of the function at x_3, where x_3 is somewhere in the interval $[x_1, x_2]$, we are not able to decide if the minimum occurs in the interval $[x_1, x_3]$ or the interval $[x_3, x_2]$. In fact, we see that it is possible to have another function g(x) such that

$$g(x_1) = f(x_1)$$
$$g(x_2) = f(x_2)$$
$$g(x_3) = f(x_3)$$

but has a minimum in the interval opposite to the interval in which f(x) has a minimum. Thus, we need more information than can be obtained by looking at the function's value at a single point in the interval $[x_1, x_2]$.

To be able to reduce the size of the interval in which we must search for the minimum value, we must select two points inside of the original interval. Let these points be x_3 and x_4, where

$$x_1 < x_3 < x_4 < x_2$$

If we evaluate the function at the points x_3 and x_4, there are two conditions that may exist:

$$\text{Condition I:} \quad f(x_3) > f(x_4)$$
$$\text{Condition II:} \quad f(x_3) \leq f(x_4)$$

The possible situations that could give rise to these two conditions are illustrated in Fig. 13-9.

If Condition I is true, we see from Fig. 13-9(a) that the minimum must fall within the interval $[x_3, x_2]$, while if Condition II is true, we see from Fig. 13-9(b) that the minimum must fall within the interval $[x_1, x_4]$.

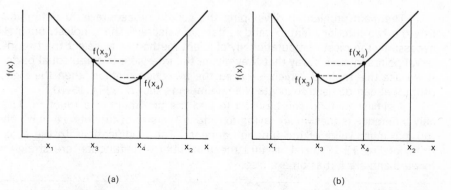

FIGURE 13-9 ■ Illustrating how two internal points in an interval can be used to reduce an interval. (a) Situation where $f(x_3) > f(x_4)$. (b) Situation where $f(x_3) \leq f(x_4)$.

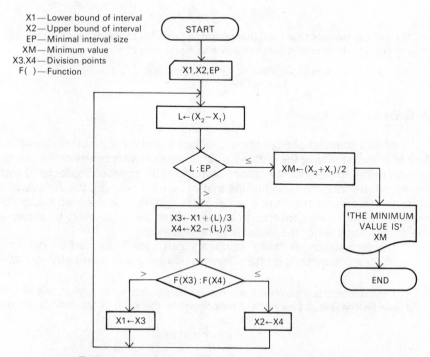

FIGURE 13-10 ■ Location of the minimum value of a function by trisection.

The main problem in developing the search procedure is to determine how the two interior points x_3 and x_4 can be selected. The simplest, but not necessarily the most computationally efficient method, is to select the two interval points in such a way that they divide the interval into three equal parts. If we use this method, which is called the *trisection method,* then the algorithm that can be used to locate the minimum is shown in Fig. 13-10.

A similar method can be used to find the maximum of a function. The only difference is that we are trying to reduce the size of the interval in which the maximum value of the function appears. The modifications to the algorithm of Fig. 13-10 to let us find the maximum of a function are straightforward and are left as an exercise.

Exercises

1. Using the bisection method, find the real roots of the equation

$$f(x) = e^{-x} - \sin(x) \qquad \epsilon = 0.001 \qquad 0 < x < 1$$

Use decimal float computation with a precision of three digits.

2. Using the trisection method, find the value of x that gives the minimum value of $f(x)$ in the interval $0 < x < 5$.

$$f(x) = 20 - 2x + x^3 \qquad \epsilon = 0.1$$

(a) Use decimal float computation with a precision of three digits.
(b) Use decimal float computation with a precision of six digits.

3. Give the trisection algorithm to find the maximum of a function.

---

3 ■ Computing Areas[†]

When a scientist or engineer encounters a particular problem, one of the first attempts at solving the problem often involves the formulation of a mathematical model to describe it in concrete terms. The equations associated with the model describe the relationships that must exist between the various variables that represent the system under investigation. These equations, which are often based upon concepts from the integral calculus, must be solved if the general behavior of the model is to be understood.

The formulation of these equations can usually be carried out in a straightforward manner. It is often difficult, however, to find an analytical solu-

---

[†] For students familiar with the integral calculus, the discussion of this section can be considered as a method for computing the value of the definite integral

$$R = \int_a^b f(x) \, dx$$

which can be interpreted as the crosshatched area shown in Fig. 13-11.

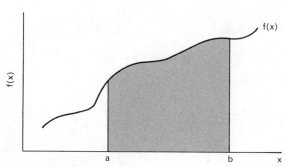

FIGURE 13-11 ■ Area under a curve.

tion to these equations and we must use numerical analysis techniques, based upon computing the area enclosed by a curve, to obtain an approximate numerical solution. In this section we investigate some of the simpler techniques that can be used to compute the area of complex figures.

The following discussion serves to introduce the reader to the general area of numerical analysis referred to as *numerical integration* or *numerical quadrature.* These techniques are discussed in greater detail in books on numerical analysis.

The basic problem considered in this section is to find a method to compute the approximate area that has a shape which is determined by one or more equations. For example, consider the shaded area in Fig. 13-11 defined by the function f(x) and the two boundary points a and b. To find this area, which we assume cannot be expressed by an analytical function, we approximate the unknown area by a collection of small, nonoverlapping figures. The desired value for the approximate area is then the sum of the areas of these small figures.

Standard Figures

There are three standard figures that are commonly used in the approximation process:

1. Rectangles
2. Trapezoids
3. Parabolic figures

These figures are illustrated in Fig. 13-12 along with the equations that describe their area. As we can see from these equations, we need an increasingly larger amount of information to describe each of these standard figures. It should also be noted that the equations for the area are perfectly general and can easily be modified for the case where the lower bound of the figure is not $x = 0$.

In order to approximate a complex area using a collection of these simple figures, we must divide the complex area into strips of width Δ and then fit a

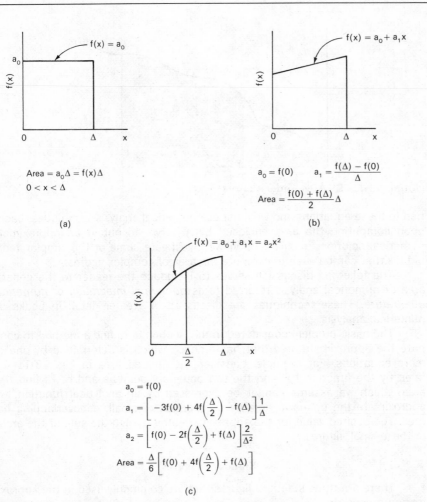

$$Area = a_0\Delta = f(x)\Delta$$
$$0 < x < \Delta$$

(a)

$$a_0 = f(0) \qquad a_1 = \frac{f(\Delta) - f(0)}{\Delta}$$
$$Area = \frac{f(0) + f(\Delta)}{2}\Delta$$

(b)

$$a_0 = f(0)$$
$$a_1 = \left[-3f(0) + 4f\left(\frac{\Delta}{2}\right) - f(\Delta) \right]\frac{1}{\Delta}$$
$$a_2 = \left[f(0) - 2f\left(\frac{\Delta}{2}\right) + f(\Delta) \right]\frac{2}{\Delta^2}$$
$$Area = \frac{\Delta}{6}\left[f(0) + 4f\left(\frac{\Delta}{2}\right) + f(\Delta) \right]$$

(c)

FIGURE 13-12 ■ Description and areas of simple figures used in area approximations. (a) Rectangle. (b) Trapezoid. (c) Parabolic figure.

simple figure to each of these strips. The approximate area is then obtained by summing the area calculated from the area formula associated with the given simple figure.

Rectangular Approximation

One of the simplest approximation techniques is to use rectangles to approximate the area enclosed by a curve. Figure 13-13 shows how this approximation is carried out. The crosshatched area is the approximate area computed.

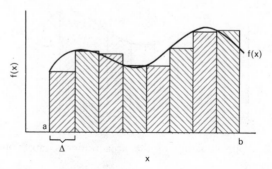

FIGURE 13-13 ■ Approximation of the area under a curve using rectangles.

As we see by examining Fig. 13-13, the approximation process is not exact. At some points the rectangles do not fully cover the strips that they are to approximate, and at other times the rectangles exceed the strips that they are to approximate. This error can be reduced by making the width, Δ, of the strips smaller.

The approximate area is easily calculated. Assume that the interval [a,b] is divided into N subintervals of length

$$\Delta = \frac{b-a}{N}$$

Then the area of all of the approximation rectangles is given by

$$AR = \sum_{i=1}^{N} f[a + (i-1)\Delta]\Delta$$

where the ith term in the summation corresponds to the area of the ith rectangle.

Trapezoidal Approximation

In most cases, the approximation of the area can be improved, for a given fixed value of Δ, if we use trapezoids to approximate the area of each strip. Figure 13-14 shows how the area of Fig. 13-13 may be approximated by trapezoids.

Again if we divide the interval [a,b] into N subintervals of length Δ, we can approximate the area as

$$AT = \Delta \left[\sum_{i=1}^{N} \frac{f[a + (i-1)\Delta] + f[a + i\Delta]}{2} \right] = \Delta \left[\frac{f(a) + f(b)}{2} + \sum_{i=1}^{N-1} f[a + i\Delta] \right]$$

where the ith term of the first summation corresponds to the area of the ith trapezoid in the approximation.

Examining the expression for AR, the rectangular approximation, and the expression for AT, we see that it is equally easy to compute both expressions.

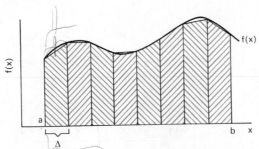

FIGURE 13-14 ■ Approximation of the area under a curve using trapezoids.

Since for a fixed Δ the area AT is usually a better approximation for the total area, we normally do not use rectangular approximations to estimate areas. The reason for this is that the trapezoids usually provide a better fit to the strips than do the rectangles.

Parabolic Approximation—Simpson's Rule

An even better approximation to an area can often be obtained if we use the parabolic figures of Fig. 13-12(c) to approximate the strips. In this case, we must know not only the value of the function at two sides of the strip but also the value in the middle. Figure 13-15 shows how parabolic figures may be used in the approximation process.

Examining the approximation in Fig. 13-15, we see that the parabolic area fits each strip better than the trapezoid. The price we pay for this better fit is that the computation of the area of each parabolic figure is more complex than that of the trapezoid. The approximate area is given by

$$AP = \frac{\Delta}{6}\left[\sum_{i=1}^{N} f[a + (i-1)\Delta] + 4\,f\left[a + \left(i - \frac{1}{2}\right)\Delta\right] + f[a + i\Delta]\right]$$

$$= \frac{\Delta}{6}\left[f(a) + f(b) + \sum_{i=1}^{N-1} 2\,f[a + i\Delta] + \sum_{i=1}^{N} 4\,f\left[a + \left(i - \frac{1}{2}\right)\Delta\right]\right]$$

where the ith term in the first summation corresponds to the area of the ith parabolic area in the approximation.

This expression usually gives the better approximation, for a fixed Δ, of the area being computed. This increased accuracy is obtained by using more values of the function in our calculation. Thus, if we compare the expression for AP to the expression for AT, the trapezoidal approximation, we see that we require more steps in the evaluation. This method of computing the area is called *Simpson's rule.*

Error Control

All of these techniques for approximating the area under a curve are not exact. The error in the approximation comes from two major sources: the

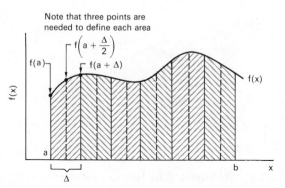

Note that three points are
needed to define each area

$f\left(a + \dfrac{\Delta}{2}\right)$

$f(a)$

$f(a + \Delta)$

$f(x)$

$f(x)$

a

b   x

Δ

FIGURE 13-15 ■ Approximation of the area under a curve using parabolic areas.

inability of the standard figure to cover each of the subdivisions of the area and computational errors of the type discussed in Chapter VIII. As we decrease the size of Δ, the approximation error decreases. At the same time, the number of computations also increases so that truncation and other computational errors become more important. Thus, we see that the number, N, of subintervals used in computing an area can be quite important. Unfortunately, it is difficult to choose the best value of N for a given problem.

One common method of implementing one of these area calculation formulas on a computer is to initially choose the number of subintervals N arbitrarily. The calculation is then carried out for N and 2N and the two values of area are compared. If they are sufficiently close to the same value, then the calculated value for the area is taken as the desired result. Otherwise, the process is repeated again with a new doubling of the number of intervals. This sequence of steps is repeated until comparable values for the area are obtained or until the value of Δ becomes so small that it becomes obvious that more powerful methods are needed to carry out the desired calculation.

Composite Figures

The techniques that we have just discussed can be extended to cover a large number of other area calculations. For example, suppose that we have the situation shown in Fig. 13-16 where we wish to find the shaded area enclosed by the two curves f(x) and g(x). To carry out this calculation we note that we must first determine the interval [a,b] by finding the points a and b, where a and b are defined by the condition

$$f(a) - g(a) = 0$$
$$f(b) - g(b) = 0$$

This step can be carried out using the methods of the previous section.

Examining Fig. 13-16, we see that in the interval [a,b] the curve defined

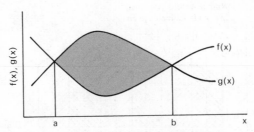

FIGURE 13-16 ■ Composite area defined by two functions.

by g(x) lies above the curve defined by f(x). Let us use the symbol

$$A(f(x), a, b, \Delta)$$

to denote the approximate area under a curve f(x) between the points a and b, with a given subinterval length Δ.
The desired area is

$$A = A(g(x), a, b, \Delta) - A(f(x), a, b, \Delta)$$

However, this can be reduced to

$$A = A(g(x) - f(x), a, b, \Delta)$$

To illustrate this type of calculation, assume that we wish to calculate the area indicated in Fig. 13-17. This area is obtained by computing the area enclosed by the function

$$d(x) = g(x) - f(x)$$
$$= 4 + x - \tfrac{1}{2}x^2$$

Thus

$$A = A(4 + x - \tfrac{1}{2}x^2, -2, 4, \Delta)$$

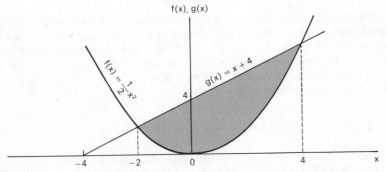

FIGURE 13-17 ■ A complex area.

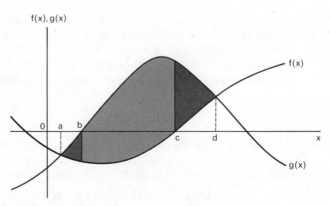

FIGURE 13-18 ■ An area between two curves

There is a problem if the figure of interest has one, or both, of the bounding curves that go below the x axis. For example, consider the figure shown in Fig. 13-18. As an initial approach, we locate the points a, b, c, and d which satisfy the conditions

$$f(a) - g(a) = 0 \qquad f(d) - g(d) = 0 \qquad g(b) = 0 \qquad f(c) = 0$$

Then we compute the total area as

$$A = (\text{Area from a to b}) + (\text{Area from b to c}) + (\text{Area from c to d})$$
$$= A_{a,b} + A_{b,c} + A_{c,d}$$

In this calculation we have assumed that the area can be divided into three subareas. The first, corresponding to the interval [a,b], is bounded by two curves that both lie below the x axis. The area of interest lies between f(x), which has a negative value in this region, and g(x), which also has a negative value. The area of interest is

$$A_{a,b} = A(-f(x), a, b, \Delta) - A(-g(x), a, b, \Delta)$$
$$= A(g(x) - f(x), a, b, \Delta)$$

Similar reasoning gives the area for the interval [b,c] and [c,d]. Thus,

$$A_{b,c} = A(g(x), b, c, \Delta) + A(-f(x), b, c, \Delta)$$
$$= A(g(x) - f(x), b, c, \Delta)$$

and

$$A_{c,d} = A(g(x) - f(x), c, d, \Delta)$$

This means that the total area is always given by the expression

$$A = A(g(x) - f(x), a, d, \Delta)$$

Thus, it is not necessary to worry about the individual subareas.

The problem of finding the area enclosed by one or more curves has many important applications. The subroutine libraries associated with the common programming languages have a number of programs that can find these areas under a number of different conditions. These subroutines are referred to as numerical integration subroutines or numerical quadrature subroutines.

Exercises

1. Let $f(x) = e^{-x}$. The area under the curve from $x = 0$ to $x = 1$ is $1 - e^{-1} = .63212$. Use $N = 10$ and compare the ability of the three approximation formulas to represent this area. If a computer is available, study how this error varies with N.

2. Do exercise 1, only now let $f(x) = x^2$. The exact area under the curve from $x = 0$ to $x = 1$ is $\frac{1}{3}$.

3. Find the area bounded by the functions

$$f(x) = x^2 \qquad g(x) = x \qquad h(x) = 2x$$

Hint: Draw the figure described by the curves before you try to carry out the calculation.

4 ■ Computing Paths that Are Defined by Mathematical Relationships†

There are many mathematical models that describe the behavior of some physical process by specifying the rate of change of one variable with respect to another. This rate of change is expressed in a functional form, and we must determine the actual value of the changing variable at any point by computing the complete past history of the values that the unknown variable has taken since the process was initiated.

Euler's Method

Assume that $f(x)$ is the variable that is changing as x is changed. We do not know $f(x)$. All we know is an expression $g(x)$ that describes the rate at which $f(x)$ changes with x. This rate of change is defined as

$$g(x) = \frac{\Delta f(x)}{\Delta x}$$

where $\Delta f(x)$ in the small change in $f(x)$ caused by the small change Δx in x.

† For students familiar with the differential calculus, the discussion of this section can be considered as a method for computing the value of the function $f(x)$ defined by an equation of the form

$$\frac{df(x)}{dx} = g(x)$$

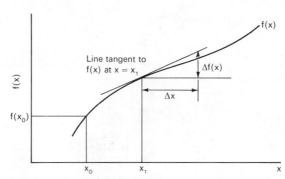

FIGURE 13-19 ■ Meaning of rate-of-change.

The function g(x) corresponds to the slope of a line that is tangent to the curve defined by f(x). This idea is illustrated in Fig. 13-19. As x varies, the slope of this tangent line varies. The above equation thus describes the local characteristics of the curve f(x) in terms of the slope of the tangent to the curve at a given point. To evaluate f(x), we must extend this local property to the whole region of interest. There are, of course, many curves that have the same slope. We are looking for the particular curve that in addition to having the behavior described by g(x) also passes through a given initial point $(x_0, f(x_0))$.

One simple way to compute f(x) is to start at $x = x_0$, where it is assumed that the initial value $f(x_0)$ is specified, and calculate the value of $f(x_0 + \Delta x)$ by using

$$f(x_0 + \Delta x) = f(x_0) + \Delta f(x) = f(x_0) + g(x_0)\, \Delta x$$

This then gives us a new value for f(x) at $x = x_0 + \Delta x$. Continuing in this manner, we obtain the general relationship

$$f[x_0 + (n + 1)\,\Delta x] = f(x_0 + n\, \Delta x) + g(x_0 + n\, \Delta x)\, \Delta x$$

Providing we made Δx small enough, we can easily calculate the path followed by f(x) by calculating $f(x + i\, \Delta x)$ for $i = 1, 2, \ldots$. This method, which is called *Euler's method,* can be carried out quite easily on a computer.

To illustrate this idea, let us assume that we are given the following equations:

$$g(x) = \frac{\Delta f(x)}{\Delta x} = \frac{10}{x^2} \qquad f(x_0) = 10 \qquad x_0 = 1$$

To calculate f(x) for values of x between 1 and 3, we must proceed in steps of Δx. The size that we select for Δx will influence the accuracy of our calculation. Table 13-1 lists the value of f(x) for representative values of x and for Δx equal to 0.1, 0.01, 0.001, and 0.0001. The true value of f(x) is also listed. Examining this table, we see that the accuracy of the calculation improves as Δx is

TABLE 13-1 ■ Computed values of f(x)

x	True value	Δx 0.1	0.01	0.001	0.0001
1.0	10	10	10	10	10
1.5	13.333	13.622	13.361	13.336	13.333
2.0	15.000	15.389	15.037	15.003	15.000
2.5	16.000	16.435	16.042	16.004	16.000
3.0	16.666	17.127	16.711	16.671	16.667

reduced in size. The largest value that Δx should be is approximately 0.01 while a value of 0.001 would be better. The difficulty is that as Δx becomes smaller the number of steps needed to perform the calculation increases.

For the above example, we see that we need 200 steps to compute f(x) for Δx = 0.01, 2,000 steps for Δx = 0.001 and 20,000 steps for Δx = 0.0001. Thus, each factor-of-10 decrease in Δx introduces a factor-of-10 increase in the computation time.

Errors

As we can see from the above example, the size of the increment Δx plays a very important role in determining the error between the true value and the computed value of f(x). This type of calculation is particularly sensitive to errors, since any error introduced in the calculation of $f(x_0 + n\Delta x)$ will be retained in the calculation of the following values of the function.

Advanced numerical analysis texts present many methods which may be used to reduce errors in the calculation of the solution function $f(x_0 + n\Delta x)$. For many applications where we are only interested in the general behavior of the solution function, it is often not necessary to use these advanced techniques if we make Δx small enough. Whenever the solution function requires a large number of points to cover the desired range of x, one should begin to question the values of $f(x_0 + n\Delta x)$ as the value of n Δx increases.

An Example

The following example illustrates the type of problems that may be solved by the method just discussed. Assume that we have a cylindrical water tank arranged as shown in Fig. 13-20. Water is flowing into the tank at the rate of $f_1(t)$ liters/second while water is being pumped out of the tank at the rate of

$$f_2(t) = \begin{cases} ky^2 & y > 0 \\ 0 & y \leq 0 \end{cases} \quad \text{liters/second}$$

where k is an appropriate constant and y is the current depth of the water in the tank.

At time $t = 0$, the height of the water is y_0. What we would like to do is calculate the height of the water at any time $t > 0$ if we are given the function $f_1(t)$. To solve this problem, we proceed in the following manner. First, we note that the total volume of water in the tank is

$$V = \pi R^2 y$$

where R is the radius of the tank. Thus,

$$y = \frac{V}{\pi R^2}$$

Now we note that the rate of increase in volume is

$$\frac{\Delta V}{\Delta t}$$

where ΔV is the change in volume in time Δt. But this rate of change is just the difference between the amount of water flowing into the tank minus the amount of water flowing out of the tank. Consequently, we have

$$\frac{\Delta V}{\Delta t} = f_1(t) - f_2(t)$$

From this, we see that the change ΔV can be approximated by

$$\Delta V = [f_1(t) - f_2(t)] \, \Delta t$$

provided Δt is made small enough so that the values of $f_1(t)$ and $f_2(t)$ do not appreciably change in the time increment Δt. However, a change in volume ΔV will produce a change

$$\Delta y = \frac{\Delta V}{\pi R^2}$$

in y. Thus, the rate of change of y with respect to a change in time is given by

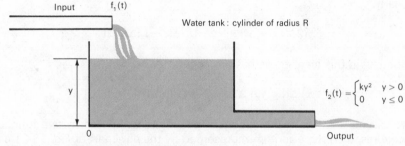

FIGURE 13-20 ■ Model of a water tank with water entering and leaving.

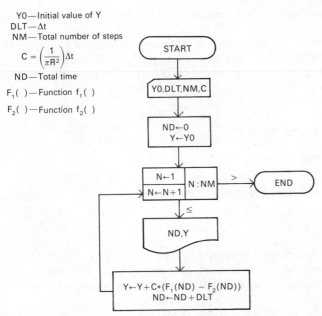

FIGURE 13-21 ■ Flowchart to compute height of liquid in tank shown in Fig. 13-20.

$$\frac{\Delta y}{\Delta t} = \frac{1}{\pi R^2}\frac{\Delta V}{\Delta t} = \frac{1}{\pi R^2}[f_1(t) - f_2(t)]$$

Now let us pick Δt small enough so that

$$f_1(t) \cong f_1(t + \Delta t) \qquad f_2(t) \cong f_2(t + \Delta t)$$

Then, if y_0 is the value of $y(t)$ at $t = 0$, the value $y(t + \Delta t)$ is

$$y(\Delta t) = y_0 + \Delta y = y_0 + \frac{1}{\pi R^2}[f_1(0) - f_2(0)]\,\Delta t$$

Similarly,

$$y(2\Delta t) = y(\Delta t) + \frac{1}{\pi R^2}[f_1(\Delta t) - f_2(\Delta t)]\,\Delta t$$

Continuing in this manner, we have in general

$$y[(n + 1)\,\Delta t] = y(n\,\Delta t) + \frac{1}{\pi R^2}[f_1(n\,\Delta t) - f_2(n\,\Delta t)]\,\Delta t$$

If we assume that the two functions f_1 and f_2 are computed by two function procedures, then the algorithm represented by the flowchart of Fig. 13-21 can be used to compute y as a function of t.

Exercise

1. The rate-of-change of a function f(t) is defined as

$$\frac{\Delta f(t)}{\Delta t} = e^{-t}$$

If at $t = 0$, $f(t) = 5$, compute and plot the values of f(t) for t in the interval $0 \leq t \leq 1$. Use the following values for Δt.

   (a) $\Delta t = 0.1$ (b) $\Delta t = 0.01$ (c) $\Delta t = 0.001$ (d) $\Delta t = 0.0001$

The true value for f(t) is given by $6 - e^{-t}$. Compare your computed results with the true values.

5 ■ Summary

Numerical techniques play a very important role in many types of problem solving. The numerical methods introduced in this chapter were selected to introduce the techniques used to solve numerical problems. Fortunately, it is not necessary for a computer user to become an expert in numerical analysis to use these methods. Most programming languages have an associated collection of scientific subroutines already programmed that may be used by a computer user to carry out many of the standard numerical analysis tasks. If the user is aware of the general properties of a subroutine, he may then use it in carrying out a problem solution without spending the time to actually program the underlying algorithm. The only caution that must be observed is to make sure that the subroutine is appropriate for the problem under consideration and that the error limits are acceptable.

The methods of solving numerical problems using numerical analysis techniques is a well-established branch of applied mathematics that has been strongly influenced by the availability of modern digital computers. The references listed at the end of this chapter provide an introduction to this important area. To pursue this subject further, however, requires a complete understanding of the integral and differential calculus.

References

A large number of books are available concerning numerical analysis and the use of computers to solve numerical problems. The ones listed below are a representative cross section of these.

1. Barrodale, I., Roberts, F. D. K., and Ehle, B. L. (1971) *Elementary Computer Applications in Science, Engineering, and Business,* John Wiley & Sons, New York.

2. Conte, S. D. and deBoor, C. (1972) *Elementary Numerical Analysis,* 2nd ed., McGraw-Hill, New York.

3. Hamming, R. W. (1973) *Numerical Methods for Scientists and Engineers,* 2nd ed., McGraw-Hill, New York.

4. Hamming, R. W. (1968) *Calculus and the Computer Revolution,* Houghton Mifflin, Boston, Mass.

5. Henrici, P. (1964) *Elements of Numerical Analysis,* John Wiley & Sons, New York.

6. Kuo, S. S. (1972) *Computer Applications of Numerical Methods,* Addison-Wesley, Reading, Mass.

7. McNeary, S. S. (1973) *Introduction to Computational Methods for Students of Calculus,* Prentice Hall, Englewood Cliffs, N.J.

8. Ralston, A. (1965) *A First Course in Numerical Analysis,* McGraw-Hill, New York.

9. Scheid, F. (1968) *Numerical Analysis,* McGraw-Hill, New York.

10. Smith, C. L., Pike, R. W., and Murrill, P. W. (1970) *Formulation and Optimization of Mathematical Models,* Intext, Dunmore, Pa.

11. Thomas, G. B., Jr. (1953) *Calculus and Analytic Geometry,* Addison-Wesley, Reading, Mass.

Home Problems

If possible, the algorithms developed to solve the following problems should be programmed and tested on a computer.

1. Most computer centers have a collection of scientific subroutines that can be used to carry out the tasks discussed in this chapter. Investigate the properties of these subroutines in terms of the accuracy of the calculation and possible limitations. Compare the results that you get from these subroutines to those from the methods discussed in this chapter.

2. In many scientific and engineering problems, we reach a point where two variables are related by a mathematical relation which must be satisfied for all values of the variables. For example, let ϕ and θ be the two angles which must satisfy the following relationship

$$R_1 \cos\theta - R_2 \cos\phi + R_3 - \cos(\theta - \phi) = 0$$

It is possible to plot a graph of ϕ vs. θ for $0 \le \theta \le \pi$ by substituting values for θ in the above expression and then solving for ϕ. Compute this graph if $R_1 = 1$, $R_2 = 2$, $R_3 = 1.25$.

3. Assume that the following function of two variables is given

$$S = [x - \sin(x + y)]^2 + [y - \cos(x - y)]$$

Develop the flowchart of an algorithm which can be used to search for the values of x and y which minimizes the value of S.

4. There are many methods available for finding the roots of an equation. One method, the bisection method, was discussed in Section II of this chapter. Another method, called the Newton–Raphson method, determines the root of an equation $f(x) = 0$ by successive approximation. First an initial guess of the root x_0

is made. A sequence of approximate roots is then generated according to the following relationship

$$x_{n+1} = x_n - \frac{f(x_n)}{f'(x_n)} \quad \text{for } n = 0, 1, 2, \ldots$$

where $f'(x_n)$ corresponds to the slope $\Delta f(x_n)/\Delta x_n$ of the function $f(x)$ at the value x_n [$f'(x_n)$ is also known as the derivative of $f(x)$ at x_n in differential calculus]. The calculation of the root is repeated until two successive approximate roots are found sufficiently close, i.e.,

$$|x_{n+1} - x_n| < \delta \quad \text{(the error limit)}$$

Develop a flowchart of the Newton–Raphson algorithm to calculate the root of an equation and compare this algorithm to the bisection method.

5. One method of improving the calculation of the approximate area under a curve is as follows. Initially, the number of subintervals N is arbitrarily chosen. The calculation of area is then carried out for N and 2N, and the values of the two calculations are compared. If they are sufficiently close, say within an error limit δ, the calculated area is taken as the desired result. Otherwise, the calculation is repeated with a new doubling of the number of subintervals. Develop the flowchart of an algorithm which will calculate the area using the above improved method for:
   (a) Rectangular approximation
   (b) Trapezoidal approximation
   (c) Simpson's Rule approximation

6. The area under the curve sin(x) from $x = 0$ to $x = \pi/2$ is known to be 1. Compute this area using both the trapezoidal rule and Simpson's Rule.
   (a) Find the value of Δ which produces a smallest error in each case.
   (b) Estimate the number of arithmetic operations needed to find the area at the minimum error point for each method.
   (c) How does the precision attribute of the identifiers used in this calculation influence the error?

7. Repeat problem 6 but compute the area under the curve e^{-x} from $x = 0$ to $x = \infty$. This area is known to be 1.

8. Develop the flowchart of an algorithm that can be used to compute the area indicated in the following figure:

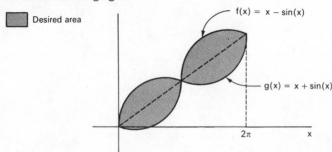

Generalize this computation for the case where f(x) and g(x) are arbitrary functions which cross over in two or more points.

9. In many experimental situations, a curve is defined by a collection of measured pairs of values $[f(x_i), x_i]$, $i = 1, 2, \ldots, N$. For some cases the distance between adjacent values of x_i is the same, while for other cases it can vary. Develop an algorithm that will compute the approximate area under the curve f(x) between x_1 and x_N when the distances between adjacent values of x_i are not equal.

10. A projectile is fired into a very dense fluid. The motion of the projectile is governed by the following physical laws:

$$\frac{\Delta V}{\Delta t} = -k\, V^2$$

$$\frac{\Delta X}{\Delta t} = V$$

where V is the velocity of the projectile, X is the distance the projectile has traveled after entering the liquid, V_0 is the initial velocity of projectile at the instant it entered the liquid, and $X_0 = 0$ is the initial position of the projectile when it entered the liquid.

Develop a flowchart of an algorithm that can be used to compute X as a function of t.

11. Assume that the water tank problem illustrated in Fig. 13-20 has the following parameters (note that 1 liter = 1000 cm³):

$$R = 2/\sqrt{\pi} \qquad k = 1.615 \qquad f_1(t) = (1 + \sin\omega t) \qquad y_0 = 1\ mt$$

Assume that the height of the tank is 3 mt. If the water completely fills the tank, there is an overflow which turns off the input flow of water. Compute y(t) vs. t for $\omega = 0.01, 0.1, 1, 10$. Will the tank overflow for any of these values of ω?

appendix I

decimal to
binary conversion

This appendix summarizes the two algorithms that are commonly used for converting decimal numbers to their corresponding binary numbers. These two algorithms taken together are known as the *multiplication/division* method. This method requires that the decimal number to be converted be separated into two parts: the integer part and the fractional part. In the conversion process we first convert the decimal integer to its corresponding binary form and then we convert the decimal fraction to its corresponding binary form. These conversions are carried out separately using the two algorithms described below.

First we note that any decimal number N_{10} can be written

$$N_{10} = d_{m-1}d_{m-2} \cdots d_0 \cdot d_{-1}d_{-2} \cdots d_{-n}$$
$$= <\text{Integer Part}>_{10} \cdot <\text{Fractional Part}>_{10}$$
$$= I_{10} \cdot F_{10}$$

We wish to convert N_{10} to its equivalent binary number N_2 which can be written

$$N_2 = b_{u-1}b_{u-2} \cdots b_0 \cdot b_{-1}b_{-2} \cdots b_{-v}$$
$$= <\text{Integer Part}>_2 \cdot <\text{Fractional Part}>_2$$
$$= I_2 \cdot F_2$$

Conversion of Integers (Division Algorithm)

Consider the conversion of the integer part of the decimal number $I_{10} = d_{m-1}d_{m-2} \cdots d_0$ to its binary equivalent $I_2 = b_{u-1}b_{u-2} \cdots b_0$. To accomplish this conversion, we note that I_{10} can be written in terms of the binary digits in I_2.

$$I_{10} = b_{u-1}(2^{u-1}) + b_{u-2}(2^{u-2}) + \cdots + b_1(2) + b_0$$

If we divide I_{10} by 2, we obtain an integer quotient Q_1 and a remainder b_0. This allows us to write

$$I_{10} = 2Q_1 + b_0$$

where $Q_1 = b_{u-1}(2^{u-2}) + b_{u-2}(2^{u-3}) + \cdots + b_1$. Note that the first binary digit, b_0, that is extracted from this process is the remainder (0 or 1) resulting from the first division operation. To extract the next binary digit, we divide the quotient Q_1 by 2 and obtain a new quotient Q_2 and a new remainder b_1. Thus we have

$$Q_1 = 2Q_2 + b_1$$

where $Q_2 = b_{u-1}(2^{u-3}) + b_{u-2}(2^{u-4}) + \cdots + b_3(2) + b_2$. We see that the second binary digit, b_1, can be extracted from the above by taking the remainder of the second division operation. Continuing this division process, we will reach a state, say the nth division, such that the quotient Q_n becomes zero. The successive remainder terms generated by this process are then read off as the digits of the binary integer I_2 corresponding to the decimal integer I_{10}. Figure

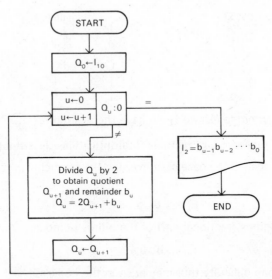

FIGURE I-1 ■ A flowchart for the division algorithm

I-1 gives a flowchart of this division algorithm for converting decimal integers to their equivalent binary integers.

Example

To illustrate the division algorithm, let $I_{10} = 53$. The detailed calculation is shown in the following table.

Iteration step u	Current quotient Q_u	Division operation $Q_u = 2\,Q_{u+1} + b_u$	Next quotient Q_{u+1}	Remainder b_u
0	53	$53 = 2(26) + 1$	26	1
1	26	$26 = 2(13) + 0$	13	0
2	13	$13 = 2(6) + 1$	6	1
3	6	$6 = 2(3) + 0$	3	0
4	3	$3 = 2(1) + 1$	1	1
5	1	$1 = 2(0) + 1$	0	1
6	0	END OF DIVISION	–	–

The corresponding binary integer is $I_2 = b_5 b_4 b_3 b_2 b_1 b_0 = 110101$. This number can be easily read off from *bottom to top* of the remainder column b_u.

The above process can also be carried out by hand in the following form:

```
2|53                              ⌐ Remainders
2|26  ← Quotients    b₀ = 1
2|13                 b₁ = 0
2|6                  b₂ = 1
2|3                  b₃ = 0
2|1                  b₄ = 1
 0                   b₅ = 1
```

Reading from *bottom to top* we again have the desired result.

Conversion of Fractions (Multiplication Algorithm)

We now consider the case of converting the fractional part of the decimal number

$$F_{10} = . \, d_{-1} d_{-2} \cdots d_{-n}$$

to the corresponding fractional part of the binary number

$$F_2 = . \, b_{-1} b_{-2} \cdots b_{-v}$$

There is one difficulty that may arise in the conversion of fractions. It is possible that a decimal fraction with a finite number of digits (i.e., n finite) must be expressed in terms of a binary fraction with an infinite number of digits. When this occurs, we must terminate the binary fraction with an arbitrarily selected maximum number of digits, say v_{max}, so that

$$F_2 = . \, b_{-1} b_{-2} \cdots b_{-v_{max}}$$

is a close approximation but not exact representation of F_{10}.

To describe the conversion process, we first write the general expression for F_{10} in terms of binary digits

$$F_{10} = b_{-1}(2^{-1}) + b_{-2}(2^{-2}) + \cdots + b_{-v}(2^{-v}) + \cdots$$

Our task is to determine the binary digits $b_{-1}, b_{-2}, \ldots, b_{-v}$, for some value $v \leq v_{max}$ which would give the equivalent binary number either exactly or with the desired accuracy. This can be achieved by multiplying F_{10} by 2 in the above equation. This gives

$$2F_{10} = b_{-1} + b_{-2}(2^{-1}) + \cdots + b_{-v}(2^{-v+1}) + \cdots = b_{-1} + C_1$$

where C_1 is the fractional part of $2F_{10}$ ($C_1 < 1$) and b_{-1} is either 1 or 0 (1 if $2F_{10}$ is greater than or equal to 1 and 0 otherwise). Note that b_{-1} is the first extracted binary digit in F_2. Next we multiply C_1 by 2 to obtain

$$2C_1 = b_{-2} + b_{-3}(2^{-1}) + \cdots + b_{-v}(2^{-v+2}) + \cdots = b_{-2} + C_2$$

where $C_2 < 1$ and b_{-2} is either 1 or 0, giving the second extracted binary digit in F_2. Continuing this multiplication process, we obtain the general formula

$$2C_{v-1} = b_{-v} + C_v$$

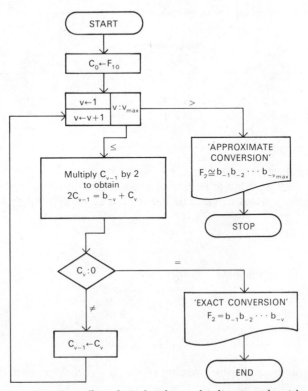

FIGURE I-2 ■ A flowchart for the multiplication algorithm.

If $C_v = 0$ for some value of v, then the binary digits $b_{-1}b_{-2} \cdots b_{-v}$ constitute the exact binary fraction F_2 corresponding to F_{10}. Otherwise we terminate the multiplication process at a prespecified value v_{max}. The last binary digit is determined by

$$2C_{v_{max}-1} = b_{-v_{max}} + C_{v_{max}}$$

The resulting binary fraction $F_2 = b_{-1}b_{-2} \cdots b_{-v_{max}}$ is an approximation of the original decimal fraction F_{10}. This approximation contains an error $\epsilon_{v_{max}}$ which is bounded by

$$\epsilon_{v_{max}} \leq 2^{-v_{max}} C_{v_{max}}$$

A flowchart of the multiplication algorithm for converting the decimal fractions to their equivalent binary fractions is shown in Figure I-2. Two examples illustrating the two situations of fractional conversion are given below.

Example (Exact Conversion)

Let $F_{10} = .375$. The detailed calculation is shown in the following table:

Iteration step v	C_v	Multiplication operation $2C_{v-1} = b_{-v} + C_v$	C_{v-1}	Binary digit b_{-v}
0	.375	–	–	–
1	.75	$2(.375) = 0 + .75$	.375	0
2	.5	$2(.75) = 1 + .5$	.75	1
3	0	$2(.5) = 1 + 0$	.5	1

The corresponding binary fraction is $F_2 = . \; b_{-1}b_{-2}b_{-3} = .011$. This number can easily be read off from *top to bottom* of the b_{-v} column in the table.

The above process can also be carried out by hand in the following form:

$$
\begin{array}{r}
.375 \\
\times \quad 2 \\
\hline
\boxed{0}.750 \leftarrow c_v \\
\times \quad 2 \\
\hline
\boxed{1}. \; 50 \\
\times \quad 2 \\
\hline
\boxed{1}. \quad 0
\end{array}
$$

coefficients $\boxed{b_{-v}}$

$F_2 = .011$ is again obtained by reading off the b_{-v}'s from top to bottom.

Example (Approximate Conversion)

Let $F_{10} = .1$. The detailed calculation is shown in the following table:

Iteration step v	Multiplication operation $2C_{v-1} = b_{-v} + C_v$
1	$2(.1) = 0 + .2$
2	$2(.2) = 0 + .4$
3	$2(.4) = 0 + .8$
4	$2(.8) = 1 + .6$
5	$2(.6) = 1 + .2$
6	$2(.2) = 0 + .4$
7	$2(.4) = 0 + .8$
8	$2(.8) = 1 + .6$
9	$2(.6) = 1 + .2$
10	$2(.2) = 0 + .4$

$$F_2 \approx .0001100110 \text{ if } v_{max} = 10$$

$$F_2 \approx .00011 \text{ if } v_{max} = 5$$

$$\epsilon_{10} \leq 2^{-10}(.4) = \frac{1}{2560}$$

$$\epsilon_5 \leq 2^{-5}(.2) = \frac{1}{160}$$

appendix II

binary codes for character representation

Standard binary codes have been developed to represent alphanumeric and special characters within a computer. The code length that is most commonly used for the representation of one character contains eight bits per character.[†] For an eight-bit binary code, we can create $2^8 = 256$ different binary patterns of 1's and 0's, representing a maximum of 256 distinct characters. The following table gives a subset of characters and their representations in two standard eight-bit binary codes that are in common use today.[‡]

	Character	EBCDIC representation	ASCII representation
	Blank	0100 0000	0000 0000
.	Period, decimal point	0100 1011	1010 1110
<	Less than	0100 1100	1011 1100
(	Left parenthesis	0100 1101	1010 1000
+	Plus sign	0100 1110	1010 1011
|	Logical OR	0100 1111	
&	Ampersand	0101 0000	1010 0110
$	Dollar sign	0101 1011	1010 0100
*	Asterisk, multiplication	0101 1100	1010 1010
)	Right parenthesis	0101 1101	1010 1001
;	Semicolon	0101 1110	1011 1011
¬	Logical NOT	0101 1111	
—	Minus, hyphen	0110 0000	1010 1101
/	Slash, division	0110 0001	1010 1111
,	Comma	0110 1011	1010 1101
%	Percent	0110 1100	1010 0101
_	Underscore	0110 1101	
>	Greater than	0110 1110	1011 1110
?	Question mark	0110 1111	1011 1111
:	Colon	0111 1010	1011 1010
#	Number sign	0111 1011	1010 0011
@	At sign	0111 1100	1100 0000
'	Prime, apostrophe	0111 1101	1010 0111
=	Equal sign	0111 1110	1011 1101
"	Quotation mark	0111 1111	1010 0010

† Standard 6-bit binary codes have also been developed, but they are used to a lesser extent in modern large-scale computers.

‡ EBCDIC—Extended Binary Coded Decimal Interchange Code
ASCII—American Standard Code for Information Interchange

Character	EBCDIC representation	ASCII representation
A	1100 0001	1100 0001
B	1100 0010	1100 0010
C	1100 0011	1100 0011
D	1100 0100	1100 0100
E	1100 0101	1100 0101
F	1100 0110	1100 0110
G	1100 0111	1100 0111
H	1100 1000	1100 1000
I	1100 1001	1100 1001
J	1101 0001	1100 1010
K	1101 0010	1100 1011
L	1101 0011	1100 1100
M	1101 0100	1100 1101
N	1101 0101	1100 1110
O	1101 0110	1100 1111
P	1101 0111	1101 0000
Q	1101 1000	1101 0001
R	1101 1001	1101 0010
S	1110 0010	1101 0011
T	1110 0011	1101 0100
U	1110 0100	1101 0101
V	1110 0101	1101 0110
W	1110 0110	1101 0111
X	1110 0111	1101 1000
Y	1110 1000	1101 1001
Z	1110 1001	1101 1010

Character	EBCDIC representation	ASCII representation
0	1111 0000	1011 0000
1	1111 0001	1011 0001
2	1111 0010	1011 0010
3	1111 0011	1011 0011
4	1111 0100	1011 0100
5	1111 0101	1011 0101
6	1111 0110	1011 0110
7	1111 0111	1011 0111
8	1111 1000	1011 1000
9	1111 1001	1011 1001

appendix III

answers to
selected exercises

■ Chapter 2

Section II

1. $Y = (U + V)^2$.

2. (a)

Instruction List	Remarks
1. COPY U to 1	
2. COPY X to 2	
3. CLEAR	
4. ADD 2	
5. MULTIPLY 2	
6. COPY ACCUMULATOR TO 3	X^2 stored in 3 of record list
7. MULTIPLY 2	X^3 in accumulator
8. ADD 3	$X^2 + X^3$ in accumulator
9. ADD 2	$X + X^2 + X^3$ in accumulator
10. ADD 1	$1 + X + X^2 + X^3$ in accumulator
11. COPY ACCUMULATOR TO 4	
12. OUTPUT 4 TO Y	
13. END OF COMPUTATION	

(b) History of calculation for $X = 1.2$

Last instruction executed		3	6	7	8	9	10	12
Accumulator		0	1.44	1.728	3.168	4.368	5.368	5.368
Record list	1	1	1	1	1	1	1	1
	2	1.2	1.2	1.2	1.2	1.2	1.2	1.2
	3		1.44	1.44	1.44	1.44	1.44	1.44
	4							5.368
SLIP Y								5.368

3. ADD { }
   MULTIPLY { }
   COPY ACCUMULATOR TO { }
   CLEAR

Section III

1. (a) -7.375 (b) 29   (c) 211.25   (d) -4.75
2. (a) .31415E1   (b) .47526E4   (c) $-.77852E3$ (d) $-.16475E-4$
3. (a) ±9999 (b) ±999.99 (c) ±32767
4. (a) $99999999 = 10^9 - 1$
   (b) $2^{32} - 1 = 4, 294, 967, 295$

Section IV

1. (a) $1,500   (b) $906   (c) Save $594
    (d) Saving = $150,000 − 90,006 = $59,994
2. (a) NO   (b) YES

■ Chapter 3

Section II

1. (a) Constant, numeric.
    (b) Constant, character.
    (c) Constant, character.
    (d) Variable, either.
    (e) Variable, either.
    (f) Neither−space between two identifiers PAY and AMOUNT.

Section III

		A + B	A − B	A * B	A/B	A ** B
1.	(a)	14.5	10.5	25.0	6.25	156.25
	(b)	.57E2	.53E2	.11E3	.275E2	.3025E4
	(c)	.118E3	.122E3	−.24E3	−.6E2	.69444E−4

		A ‖ B	B ‖ A
2.			
	(a)	'MY␣NAME␣IS␣JOHN␣'	'IS␣JOHN␣MY␣NAME␣'
	(b)	'A␣COMPUTER␣PROGRAM␣'	'PROGRAM␣A␣COMPUTER␣'
	(c)	'PEOPLE'	'PEOPLE'
	(d)	'␣'	'␣'

		¬A	¬B	A ∧ B	A ∨ B
3.					
	(a)	0	1	0	1
	(b)	0	0	1	1
	(c)	1	1	0	0

(1 indicates TRUE, 0 indicates FALSE)

Section IV

1. (a) $(((A ** B)/C) − (D * (E ** F)))$
    (b) $((((A * B) > (C * D)) < E) ∧ ((F‖G) = H))$
    (c) $(((¬B) ∧ (A > C)) ∧ (E ⩽ (F ** G)))$
2. (a) 4   (b) 1   (c) 30
3. (a) 'BIGDEAL'   (b) 1
4. TEN contains the number 5 and FIVE contains the number 10.

■ **Chapter 4**

Section II

1.

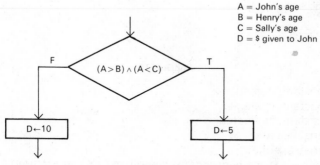

A = John's age
B = Henry's age
C = Sally's age
D = $ given to John

FIGURE III-1

2.

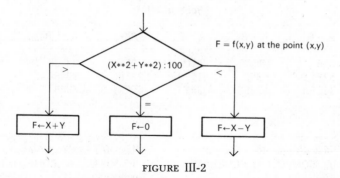

F = f(x,y) at the point (x,y)

FIGURE III-2

Section III

1.   (a)

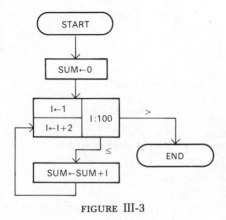

FIGURE III-3

(b) Same as (a) except that the counter service symbol should be replaced by

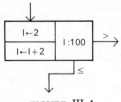

FIGURE III-4

(c) Same as (a) except that the counter service symbol should be replaced by

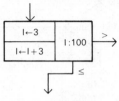

FIGURE III-5

2. (a) Fifty times.
    (b) A character sequence of 50 A's followed by 50 B's.

3.

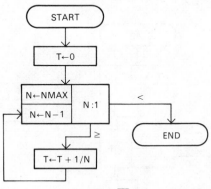

FIGURE III-6

4.

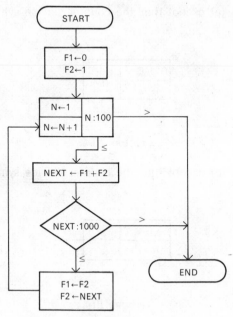

FIGURE III-7

Section IV

1.

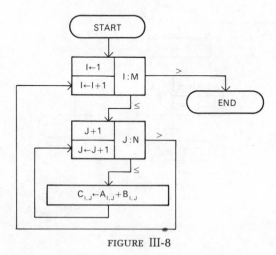

FIGURE III-8

2.

Statement	Number of times executed
1	5
2	5(10) = 50
3	5

3. (a) The N numbers of each row are summed and the largest sum is found and stored in MAX. RSUM is a temporary location to store the sum of each row.

(b) Each row sum would not be calculated correctly, as the location RSUM would contain the accumulated sums from each row if not initialized before the sum operation (inner loop) takes place each time.

Section V

1.

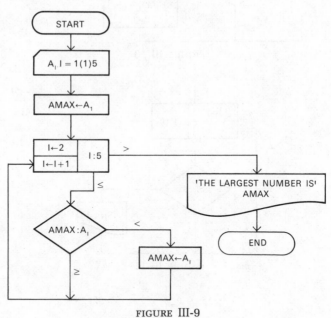

FIGURE III-9

Section VI

1. (a)

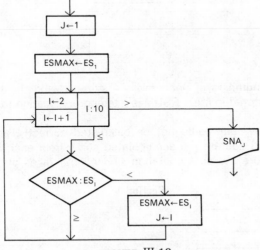

FIGURE III-10

(b)

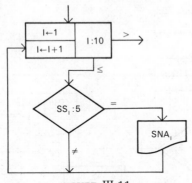

FIGURE III-11

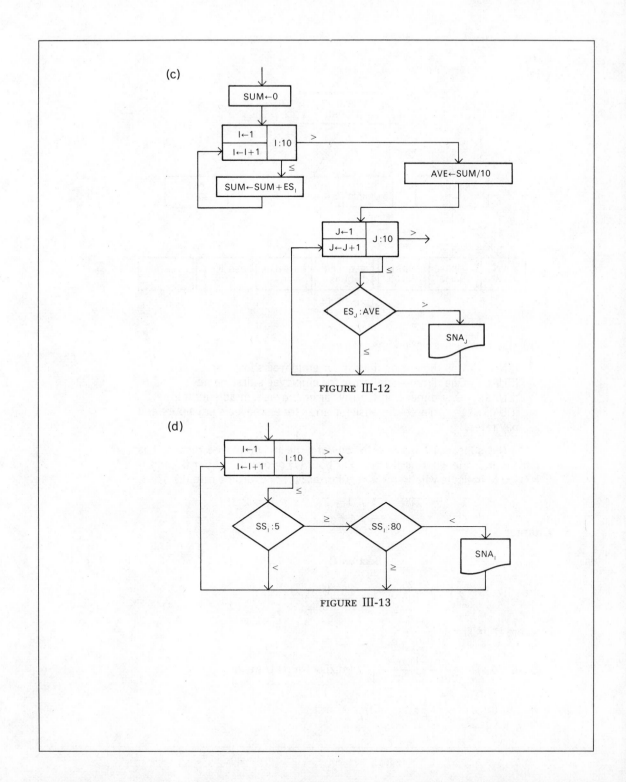

FIGURE III-12

FIGURE III-13

2.   (a)

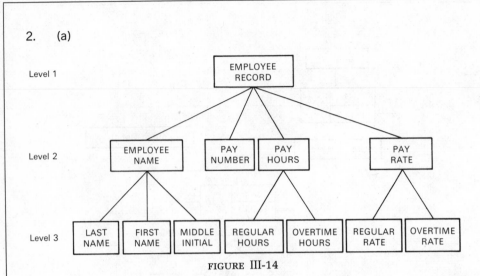

FIGURE III-14

(b) Use four arrays defined as follows:

$[ENAL_I]$ — One-dimensional array for employee's last name;
$[ENAF_I]$ — One-dimensional array for employee's first name;
$[ENAM_I]$ — One-dimensional array for employee's middle initial;
$[COMPAY_{I,J,K}]$ — Three-dimensional array for employee's pay hours and pay rates.

The subscript I is used to indicate the Ith employee record. J is used to indicate whether it is regular hour (1) or overtime hour (2) and K is used to indicate whether it is regular rate (1) or overtime rate (2). Thus,

$$1 \leq I \leq 100 \qquad 1 \leq J \leq 2 \qquad 1 \leq K \leq 2$$

▮ Chapter 5

Section II

1. $$\cos(x) \cong 1 + \sum_{m=1}^{N} (-1)^m \frac{x^{2m}}{(2m)!} = 1 + \sum_{m=1}^{N} U(m,x)$$

where $$U(m,x) = \frac{(-1)^m x^{2m}}{(2m)!}$$

$$U(m+1,x) = \frac{(-1) x^2}{(2m+2)(2m+1)} U(m,x) = f(m,x)\, U(m,x)$$

where $$f(m,x) = \frac{(-1) x^2}{(2m+2)(2m+1)}$$

The flowchart of the algorithm to compute cos(x) is essentially the same as that shown in Fig. 5-5 with the following changes:

(1) ALL SIN variables are changed to COS;
(2) COS is initialized to be 1;
(3) The assignment for the computation of F is replaced by

$$F \leftarrow C/((2*M+2)*(2*M+1))$$

2.   (a) $U(m,x) = \dfrac{x^m}{m!}$

$U(m+1,x) = \dfrac{x^{m+1}}{(m+1)!} = \dfrac{x}{(m+1)} U(m,x) = f(x)\, U(m,x)$

where $f(x) = \dfrac{x}{m+1}$

(b)

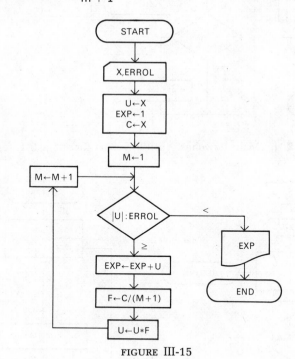

FIGURE III-15

Section III

1.

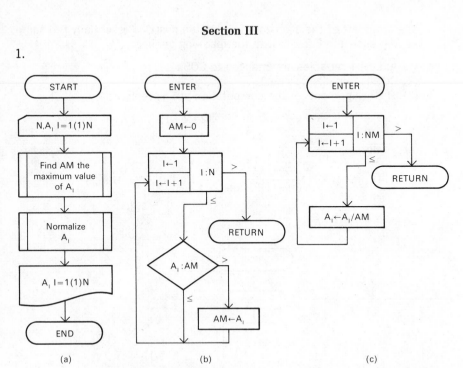

(a)   (b)   (c)

FIGURE III-16 ▮ (a) Main flowchart. (b) Flowchart for subtask 1. (c) Flowchart for subtask 2.

2.

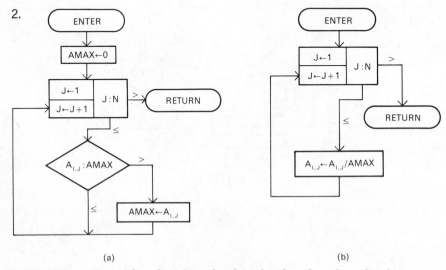

(a)   (b)

FIGURE III-17 ▮ (a) Flowchart for subtask 1. (b) Flowchart for subtask 2.

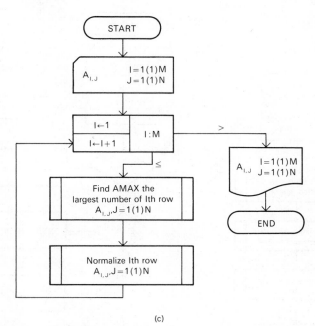

(c)

FIGURE III-17 ■ (c) Main flowchart.

3. Subtask 1—Count the number of times each vowel appears in the character string.

Subtask 2—Determine the vowel that occurs most often in the string by finding the largest of the five counts and its associated character.

Subtask 3—Determine the vowel that occurs least often in the string by finding the smallest of the five counts and its associated character.

Main task—Input the string of N characters, execute the subtasks, and print out the results obtained from each subtask.

For convenience, the following numeric code is used.

Vowel	A	E	I	O	U
Code	1	2	3	4	5

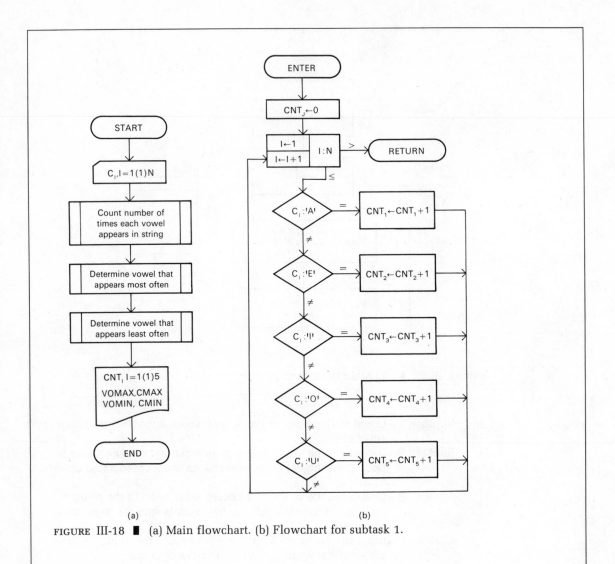

(a)   (b)

FIGURE III-18 ∎ (a) Main flowchart. (b) Flowchart for subtask 1.

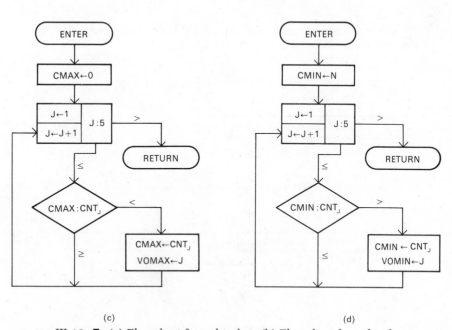

(c)   (d)

FIGURE III-18 ■ (a) Flowchart for subtask 2. (b) Flowchart for subtask 3.

■ Chapter 6

Section III

1. (a) The flowchart computes two averages: the average of the maximum values and the average of the minimum values from the N pairs of numbers (x,y).

    (b)

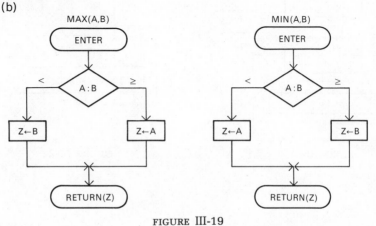

FIGURE III-19

(c) Use the function procedure MAX(A,B). Then the computation within the loop of the main flowchart is changed to

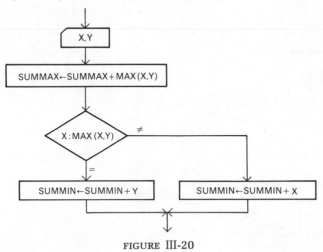

FIGURE III-20

2.   (a)

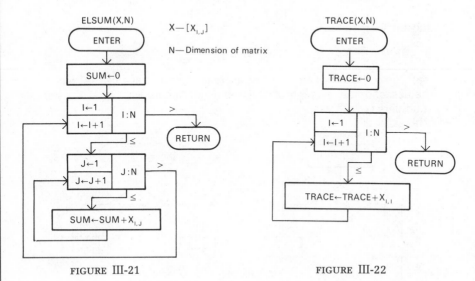

X—$[X_{I,J}]$

N—Dimension of matrix

FIGURE III-21   FIGURE III-22

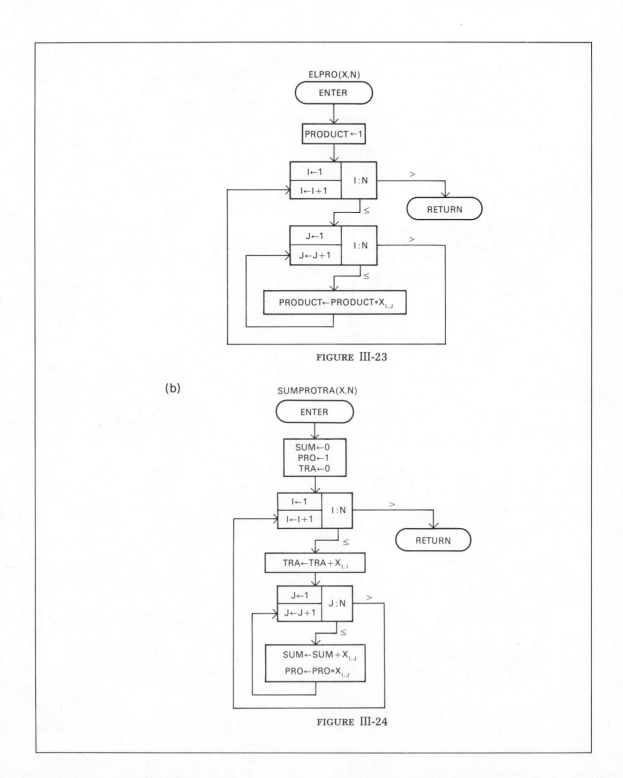

FIGURE III-23

(b)

FIGURE III-24

3. (a) Five arguments are needed; three are used to pass the coefficients
    and two are used to store the two roots computed in the subroutine.
    (b) Assume SQRT(X) is a function procedure developed elsewhere. This
    exercise shows the use of a subprocedure within a subprocedure.

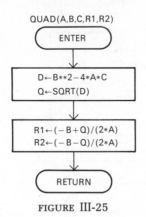

FIGURE III-25

(c)

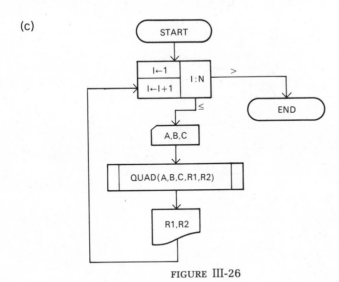

FIGURE III-26

4.

(a) QUAD(A, B, C, ROOT1, ROOT2)   (b)

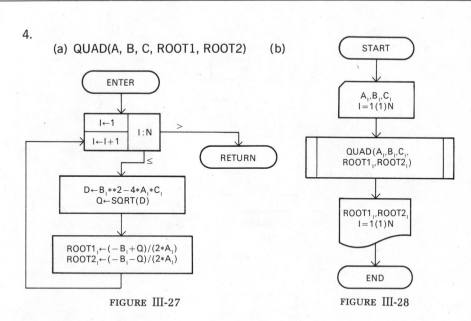

FIGURE III-27

FIGURE III-28

∎ Chapter 7

Section II

1. Total time required
    = (Time to Input numbers) + (Time to perform additions)
      + (Time to perform tests) + (Time to output the sum)
    (a) Total Time = 4MN + 3MN + 4 = 10MN + 4 units
    (b) Total Time = 8MN + MN + MN + 8 = 10MN + 8 units
2. (b) Total time required = (Time to input characters) + (Time to perform tests)
    + (Time to increment the counter) + (Time to output the count I)
    = 10(I+1) + 10(I+1) + 3 I + 10 = 23I + 30 units

Section III

1. (a) U←SIN(TH)
        V←COS(TH)
        XP←X∗U+Y∗V
        YP←X∗V−Y∗U

    (b)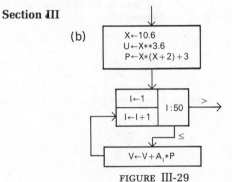

FIGURE III-29

2.

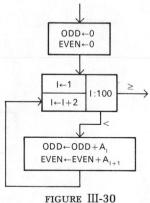

FIGURE III-30

Section IV

2.

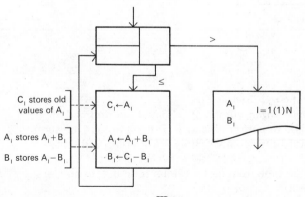

FIGURE III-31

One temporary array must be used to store one of the two arrays before their values are changed. A sequence of statements like

$$A_I \leftarrow A_I + B_I$$

$$B_I \leftarrow A_I - B_I$$

in the loop would not work because the values of A_I in the second statement have been modified after the execution of the first statement.

■ **Chapter 8**

Section II

1.

		Range	Resolution
	(a)	±999.99	.01
	(b)	±.99999	.00001
	(c)	±99999	1

2.

		Truncation error	Rounding error
	(a)	.0002	.0002
	(b)	.0008	−.0002
	(c)	.00099E−2	.00001E−2
	(d)	.00024E6	.00024E6

3.　(a) Overflow in X.
　　(b) Underflow occurs after the operation A ∗ B.
　　(c) Underflow in X.

4.　$0.4_{10} \cong .011001 = \frac{1}{4} + \frac{1}{8} + \frac{1}{64} = \frac{25}{64}$

Actual error $= \frac{4}{10} - \frac{25}{64} = \frac{3}{320} = .009375$

Section III

1.　(a) 6.65　(b) 5.07　(c) 44.6　(d) 13.8
　　(e) 7.18　(f) 1.18　(g) 46.2　(h) 9.70
　　All but (a) are in error.

2.　(a) Computed sum = .999; actual sum = 1.00.
　　(b) Computed sum = 3.31; actual sum = 3.33.
　　(c) 90.9 after 300 additions. Only .3 is added to the partial sum after the thirty-first addition until the required 300 additions have been made.
　　(d) After 331 additions, there is overflow into the hundreds digit. The sum becomes 100 and adding .333 is the same as adding 000.

3.　$\epsilon_X = X - \overline{X} < .01; \epsilon_Y = Y - \overline{Y} < .01$
　　For addition　$(X + Y) - (\overline{X} + \overline{Y}) = (X + Y) - 8.71 = \epsilon_X + \epsilon_Y = .02.$
　　Maximum error = .02.
　　The actual sum could be as large as 8.73.
　　For multiplication $XY - \overline{X}\overline{Y} = \epsilon_X\epsilon_Y + \epsilon_X\overline{Y} + \epsilon_Y\overline{X}.$
　　The actual product could be as large as 17.98, accurate to two decimal places.

4.　22.3 or .223E2

Section IV

1. Left to right evaluation $= 198$ (more accurate).
   Right to left evaluation $= 197$.
2. Computed values: left to right evaluation $= .994$.
   right to left evaluation $= .998$.
   Actual sum $= .999$ accurate to three decimal places
3. (a) Overflow   (b) -20
4. (a) 10.5   (b) 11
5. For a six-digit computation
   (a) $(A + B) + C = 9.51000$
   (b) $A + (B + C) = 9.51000$
   (a) and (b) have identical results
   For a three-digit computation
   (a) 9.51   (b) 10.0
6. (a) $x_1^2 = 11,800$

   $x_2^2 = 11,400 \qquad 5\left(\sum\limits_{i=1}^{5} x_i\right) = 275,000$

   $x_3^2 = 11,000$

   $x_4^2 = 10,600 \qquad \left(\sum\limits_{i=1}^{5} x_i\right)^2 = (525)^2 = 27,500$

   $\underline{x_5^2 = 10,200} \qquad \text{Sigma} = \sqrt{275000 - 275000} = 0$

   $\sum\limits_{i=1}^{5} x_i^2 = 55,000$

   (b) Increase precision of computation from 3 to a higher digit could avoid error. Let a precision of 6 be used.
   Then

   $$\sum\limits_{i=1}^{5} x_i^2 = 55165$$

   and Sigma $= \sqrt{5(55165) - 275000} = \sqrt{825}$

Section V

1. (a) Four terms $\cos(1) = .540$
   (b) Five terms $\cos(2) = -.416$

■ Chapter 9

Section II

1. (a)

I	Unsorted array A_I	1	2	3	4	5	6	7	8	9	10
1	9	9	6	6	3	3	3	3	3	3	3
2	6	6	9	3	6	6	5	5	5	5	5
3	3		3	9	9	5	6	6	6	6	6
4	5				5	9	9	9	9	9	2
5	10							10	10	2	9
6	2								2	10	10
7	7										
8	4										

(Step number columns 1–10. ↙ indicates the two elements being compared; curly brace points to the two elements to be exchanged.)

11	12	13	14	15	16	17	18	19	20	21	Sorted array 22
3	3	2	2	2	2	2	2	2	2	2	2
5	2	3	3	3	3	3	3	3	3	3	3
2	5	5	5	5	5	5	5	5	5	4	4
6	6	6	6	6	6	6	6	6	4	5	5
9	9	9	9	7	7	7	7	4	6	6	6
10	10	10	7	9	9	9	4	7	7	7	7
		7	10	10	10	4	9	9	9	9	9
					4	10	10	10	10	10	10

(Step number columns 11–22.)

↙, indicates the two elements being compared; ⌇, points to the two elements to be exchanged.

    (b) Number of comparisons = 21.
        Number of exchanges = 17.
        Number of data movements = 2 (number of exchanges = 34).
        (Note: each exchange involves two data movements.)

2.   (a)

I	Unsorted array A_I	Step number 1	2	3	4	5	6	7	8	9	10
1	9	▸⑨	6	▸⑥	3	3	▸3	3	3	3	3
2	6	▸⑥	▸9	⑨	6	▸6	⑥	5	5	5	5
3	3			▸3 ▸③	▸9	9	⑨	6	7	6	▸6
4	5				▸5	▸5	▸⑤	▸9	9	▸9	9
5	10							▸10	▸10	10	10
6	2								▸2	▸2	▸2
7	7										
8	4										

Step number 11	12	13	14	15	16	17	18	19	20	21	Sorted array 22
3	▸③	2	2	2	2	2	2	2	2	2	2
▸5	5	3	3	3	3	3	3	3	3	▸3	3
6	6	5	5	5	5	5	5	5	▸5	⑤	4
9	9	6	6	▸6	6	6	6	▸6	6	6	5
10	⑩	9	▸9	9	7	7	▸7	7	7	7	6
▸2	▸②	▸10	10	⑨	9	▸9	9	9	9	9	7
		▸7	▸7	⑩ ▸⑦	▸10	10	10	10	10	⑩	9
					▸4	▸4	▸4	▸4	▸4	▸④	10

▸, indicates the two elements being compared; ⟩, points to the two groups of elements to be moved.

(b) Number of comparisons $= 21$
Number of data movements $= 2 + 3 + 3 + 6 + 3 + 6 = 23$

3.

I	Unsorted array A_I	Step number 1	2	3	4	5	6	7	8	9	10
1	9	⤢ 9	9	9	2	2	2	2	2	2	2
2	6	6	6	6	⤢ 6	6	6	6 ⤡	3	3	3
3	3	3	3	3	3	3	3	⤢ 3 ⤡	⤢ 6	4	4
4	5	5	5	5	5	5	⤢ 5	5	5	5	5
5	10	10	10	10	10	⤢ 10	10	10	10	10	10
6	2	2	2	⤢ 2 ⤡	9	9	9	9	9	9	9
7	7	7	⤢ 7	7	7	7	7	7	7	7	7
8	4	⤢ ④	⤢ ④	⤢ ④	⤢ ④	⤢ ④	⤢ ④	⤢ ④	⤢ ④	6	6

11	12	13	14	15	16	17	18	19	20	21	22	23
2												2
3												3
4												4
⤢ 5	5	5	5	5	⤢ 5	5						5
10	⤢ 10	10	10	⤢ 10	10	6						6
9	9	9	⤢ 9	9	9	9	⤢ 9	9	9	9	⤢ 9 ⤡	7
7	7	⤢ 7	7	7	7	7	7	⤢ 7	⤢ 7	7	⤢ ⑦ ⤡	9
⤢ ⑥	⤢ ⑥	⤢ ⑥	⤢ ⑥	⤢ ⑥	⤢ ⑥	10	⤢ ⑩	⤢ ⑩	⤢ ⑩	10		10

○, estimate of median element; ⤢, indicates comparison; ⤡, indicates exchange.

Section III

1. (a) According to the algorithm given in this Chapter, only one of the duplicate keys will be found unless a special search provision is included in the algorithm.
    (b) 4.75 (Note that there are only eight distinct keys)
    (c)

Keys	A2	B1	B5	C3	D4	MS	P3	P9
Number of comparisons	4	3	2	3	1	3	2	3

Average number of comparisons $= 21/8 = 2.625$.

2.   (a) Average number of comparisons

$$= \frac{1}{100} [1 \times 5 + 2 \times 10 + 3 \times 5 + 4 \times 25 + 5 \times 20 + 6 \times 5 + 7 \times 10 +$$
$$8 \times 10 + 9 \times 5 + 10 \times 5] = 5.15$$

(b) A better arrangement is according to the descending order of percentage of requests.

I	1	2	3	4	5	6	7	8	9	10
A_I	A_4	A_5	A_2	A_7	A_8	A_1	A_3	A_6	A_9	A_{10}
%	25	20	10	10	10	5	5	5	5	5

Average number of comparisons = 3.85.

3.   Flowchart of modified sequential search

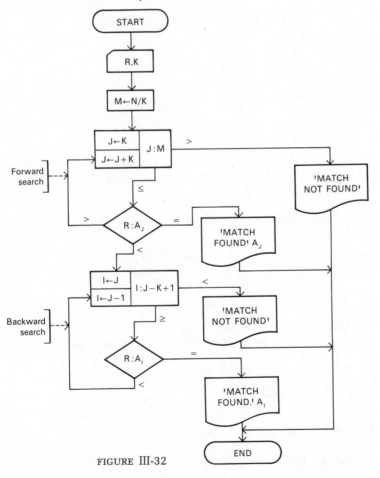

FIGURE III-32

(a) K   (b) N/K   (c) 1

4. | (a) | (b) | (c) | (d) |
    |---|---|---|---|
    | 1 | 7 | 7 | 71 |
    | 1291 | 1129 | 121 | 91 |
    | 16 | 21 | 26 | 16 |
    | 56 | 25 | 26 | 56 |

Method (d) is the best for the set of keys given.

■ Chapter 10

Section II

1. (a) Top element = 'MARY'
       Bottom element = 'JOHN'
    (b) Top element = 'MARK'
       Bottom element = 'JOHN'
2. (a) Top element = 'MARY'
       Bottom element = 'JOHN'
    (b) Top element = 'MARY'
       Bottom element = 'SUSAN'
3. (b) $[A_I]$ — storing values of I which correspond to contents of both stacks S1 and S2.

Set 1				Set 2	
A_I		I		A_I	
S1 {3	Bottom of S1	1	Bottom of S1	1)	
4		2		3) S1	
6	Top of S1	3		4)	
S2 {5	Top of S2	4	Top of S1	5)	
2		5	Top of S2	6) S2	
1	Bottom of S2	6	Bottom of S2	2)	
	Three elements in each stack for data set 1		Four elements in S1 and two elements in S2 for data set 2		

4. (a) The queue will overflow as soon as PT > N. The queue becomes empty as long as the number of elements taken from the queue (less than or equal to N) is exactly the number of elements entered.
    (b) For a queue with foldover, overflow occurs only if the difference between the number of elements added to the queue and that taken from the queue exceeds N. For a queue without foldover, overflow occurs as soon as the number of elements added to the queue exceeds N.

Section III

1.   (a) 'ART'   (b) 'COOPER'   (c) 88   (d) 2   (e) 'TERRY'
2.

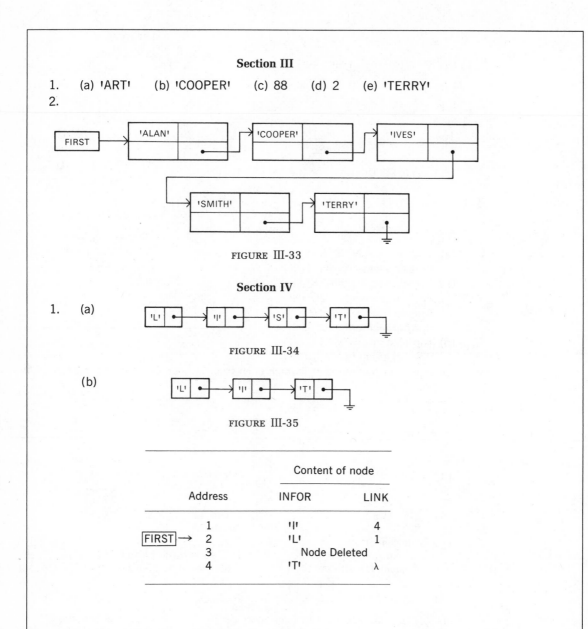

FIGURE III-33

Section IV

1.   (a)

FIGURE III-34

(b)

FIGURE III-35

	Address	Content of node	
		INFOR	LINK
	1	'I'	4
FIRST →	2	'L'	1
	3	Node Deleted	
	4	'T'	λ

2.

		Content of node		
	Address	INFOR	LINKP	LINKN
	1	'I'	2	3
FIRST →	2	'L'	λ	1
	3	'S'	1	4
	4	'T'	3	λ

3.   (a) POP operation—assume that the node to be popped up will not be kept on a free list.

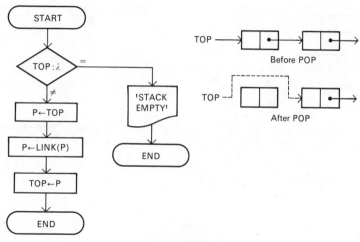

FIGURE III-36

(b) PUSH operation—assume no limitation on the size of the stack and the node to be pushed down is pointed to by a pointer variable P.

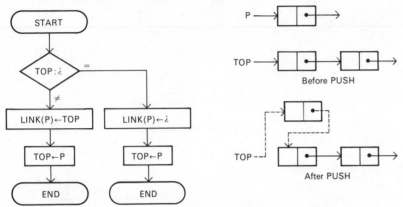

FIGURE III-37

4. In order to realize a queue efficiently, the input to the queue should be at the end of the singly linked list and the exit from the queue should be at the head of the list.

5. (a) Deletion—assume that the Kth node is to be deleted and the deleted node is not kept on a free list.

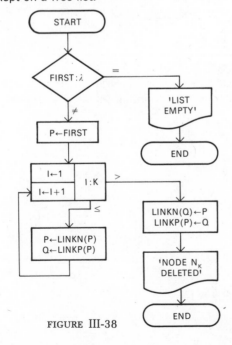

FIGURE III-38

(b) Insertion—assume that the new node, pointed to by FREE, is to be inserted between the two nodes N_K and $N_{K\pm}$.

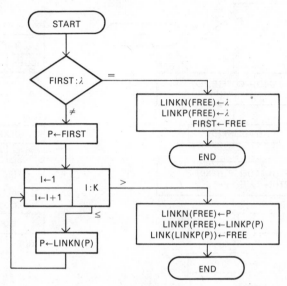

FIGURE III-39

Section V

1.

Address	INFOR	(a)		(b)		(c)		(d)	
		LINKP	LINKN	LINKP	LINKN	LINKP	LINKN	LINKP	LINKN
1	'HALL'	8	10	8	10	8	10	8	10
2	'CARTER'	4	9	4	9	λ	9	4	9
3	MOORE	5	7	λ	6	λ	6	λ	6
4	ALBERT ALDER	λ	2	λ	2	λ	3	λ	2
5	'LEWIS'	10	3	10	7	10	7	10	7
6	GRANT	λ	20	λ	20	λ	20	λ	20
7	'TERRY'	3	λ	5	λ	5	λ	5	λ
8	'FRANK'	9	1	9	1	9	1	9	1
9	'ERICK'	2	8	2	8	2	8	2	8
10	'JAMES'	1	5	1	5	1	5	1	5

FREE 3   FIRST 4

———— Name deleted or changed to

▨ Pointer changed

FIGURE III-40

4.

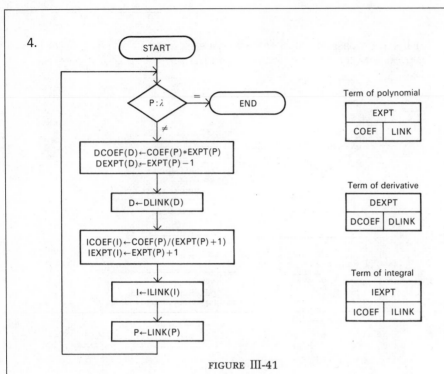

FIGURE III-41

P—pointer variable initially pointing to first term of polynomial.
D—pointer variable initially pointing to first term of derivative.
I—pointer variable initially pointing to first term of integral.

5. (a) 40,000 (b) $2[4(200) + (200 + 200)] = 2,400$

6.   (a) $[A_{I,J}]$

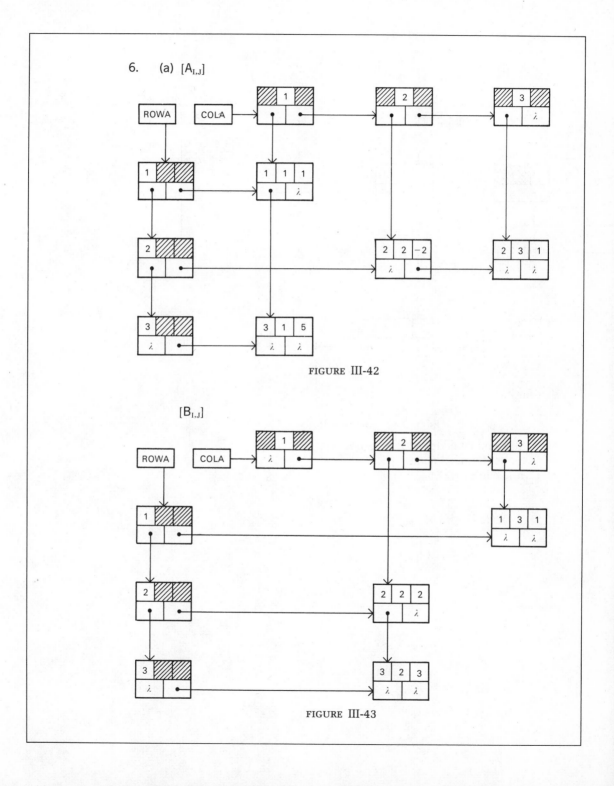

FIGURE III-42

$[B_{I,J}]$

FIGURE III-43

(b) $[B_{I,J}]$

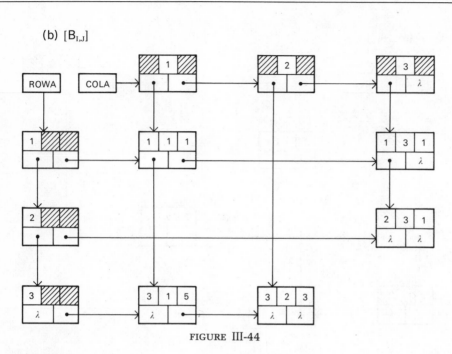

FIGURE III-44

▋ Chapter 11

Section II

1.   (a) Terminal nodes = G, H, I, J, F
         Nonterminal nodes = B, C, D, E
      (b) Node B: {D,E}
          Node C: {F}
          Node D: {G}
          Node E: {H,I,J}

(c)

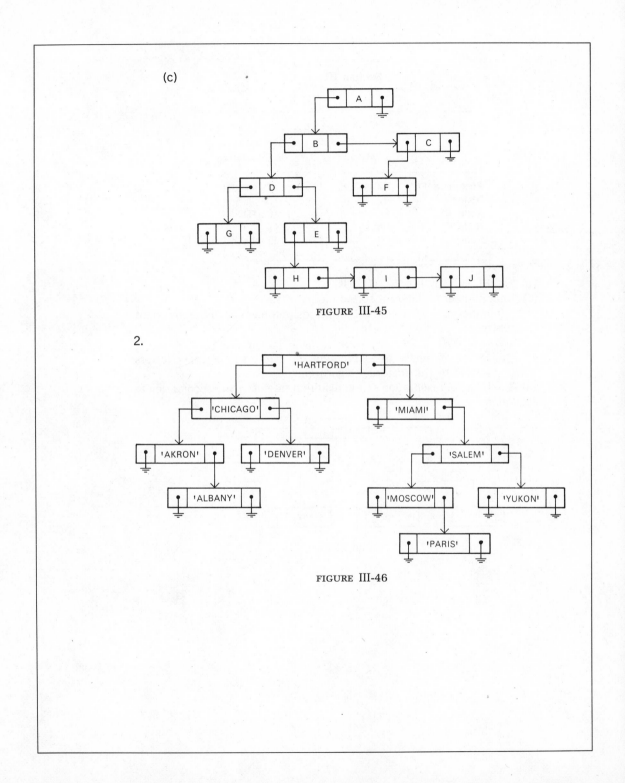

FIGURE III-45

2.

FIGURE III-46

Section III

1.   (a)

	Nodes in	
	Left subtree	Right subtree
Root node 'P'	'M', 'C', 'O', 'E'	'R', 'U', 'T'
Node 'M'	'C', 'E'	'O'
Node 'R'	Empty	'U', 'T'
Node 'C'	Empty	'T'
Node 'U'	'T'	Empty

(b) 'C', 'E', 'M', 'O', 'P', 'R', 'T', 'U'

(c) Total number of different sorted binary trees
   = (number of different left subtrees)(number of different right subtrees)
   = (14)(5) = 70

   All different binary trees produce the same sequence of letters when traversed by the postorder algorithm.

2.   (a) Graphical representation of the resulting tree after the second delete operation:

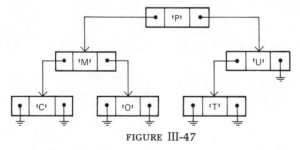

FIGURE III-47

Graphical representation of tree after all five operations are completed:

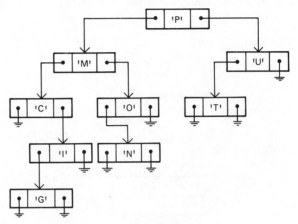

FIGURE III-48

(b) 'C', 'G', 'I', 'M', 'N', 'O', 'P', 'T', 'U'

Section IV

1. (a) Concordance Tree

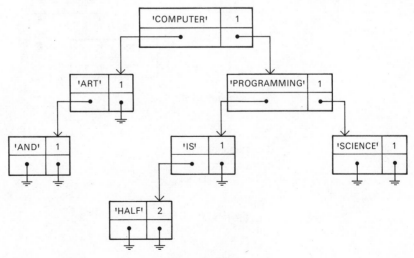

FIGURE III-49

Concordance list

AND	1
ART	1
COMUTER	1
HALF	2
IS	1
PROGRAMMING	1
SCIENCE	1

(b) Concordance Tree

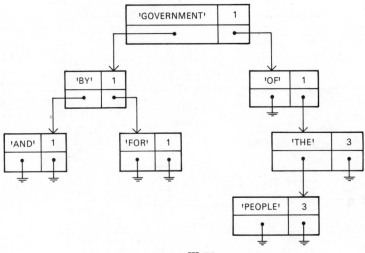

FIGURE III-50

Concordance list

AND	1
BY	1
FOR	1
GOVERNMENT	1
OF	1
PEOPLE	3
THE	3

2. $P_{3,1} = 50$, $P_{3,2} = 30$, $P_{3,3} = 25$, $P_{3,4} = 100$,
     $P_{2,1} = 30$, $P_{2,2} = 25$,
     $P_1 = 30$.
     Best move for player A is $P_1 \rightarrow P_{2,1}$.

4.

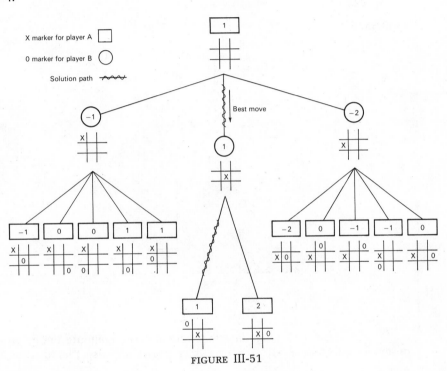

FIGURE III-51

▮ Chapter 12

Section II

1.   (a) Equation of straight line: $P(x) = a_0 + a_1x$. a_0 and a_1 are determined by requiring the two points $(0,1)$ and $(1,5)$ to satisfy the equation. Thus,
     $$1 = a_0 + a_1(0) \qquad 5 = a_0 + a_1(1)$$
     Solving the two equations simultaneously gives $a_0 = 1$ and $a_1 = 4$.
     (b) Approximate value for $f(.5)$ is $P(.5) = 3$
         Exact value for $f(.5) = 2.236 \ldots$
         Error $(.05) = 0.763 \ldots$

2.   (a) $C = 0.6388$
     (b) Equation of straight line $y = a_0 + a_1x$ passing through (x_1, y_1) and

(x_{10}, y_{10}). a_0 and a_1 are determined by solving

$$y_1 = a_0 + a_1 x_1 \qquad y_{10} = a_0 + a_1 x_{10}$$

$$a_1 = \frac{y_1 - y_{10}}{x_1 - x_{10}} = 0.5322 \qquad a_0 = \frac{x_1 y_{10} - y_1 x_{10}}{x_1 - x_{10}} = 1.187$$

$$C = 0.6576$$

Section III

1.

$$K = 1 + 3.3 \log_{10}(42)$$
$$\cong 6 \text{ intervals}$$
$$d_{min} = 2.7$$
$$d_{max} = 3.8$$

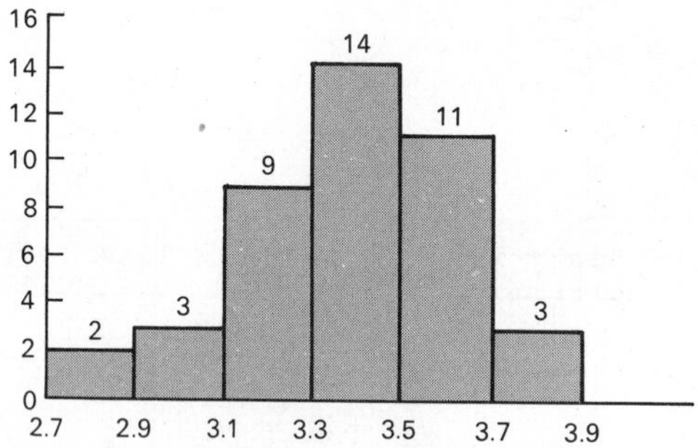

FIGURE   III-52

To compare the histogram with a normal curve, compute the mean m and standard deviation σ of the data points and use the function
$$P(x) = \frac{1}{\sqrt{2\pi}\, \sigma} \exp\left(-\frac{(x-m)^2}{2\sigma^2}\right).$$

$$m = 3.42 \qquad \sigma = .260$$

2. (b) $\sum_i x_i = 105 \qquad \sum_i x_i^2 = 717.5 \qquad \sum_i y_i = 1030 \qquad \sum_i x_i y_i = 6437.5$

$a_0 = 18.97 \qquad a_1 = 6.195$

(c) $m_x = 5.25 \qquad m_y = 51.5 \qquad \sigma_x^2 = 8.75 \qquad \sigma_y^2 = 379.21$

$C_{xy} = 0.9411$

3. Rewrite σ^2 so that the term $(d_i - m)^2$ can be separated to allow processing d_i without first computing m. This can be accomplished by expanding $(d_i - m)^2$ and collecting terms.

$$\sigma^2 = \frac{1}{N-1} \sum_{i=1}^{N} (d_i - m)^2 = \frac{N}{N-1} \left[\frac{1}{N} \left(\sum_{i=1}^{N} d_i^2 \right) - m^2 \right]$$

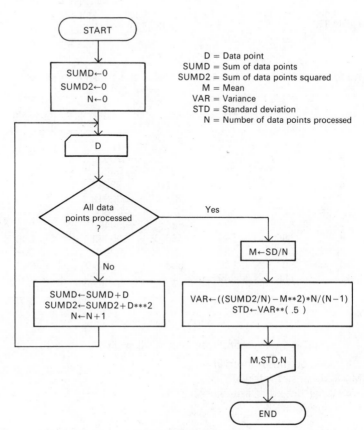

FIGURE III-53

Section IV

1. $x_1 = 94/5 = 18.8$, $x_2 = 27/5 = 5.40$, $x_3 = -236/5 = -47.2$
2. $x_1 = 18.7$, $x_2 = 5.25$, $x_3 = -47.0$
3. (a) After elimination of x_1, we have

$$\begin{bmatrix} .0001 & 1 \\ 0 & -9990 \end{bmatrix}\begin{bmatrix} x_1 \\ x_2 \end{bmatrix} = \begin{bmatrix} 1 \\ -9990 \end{bmatrix}$$

$x_2 = 1$ and $x_0 = 0$
(b) After interchanging of equations and elimination of x_1, we have

$$\begin{bmatrix} 1 & 1 \\ 0 & .9990 \end{bmatrix}\begin{bmatrix} x_1 \\ x_2 \end{bmatrix} = \begin{bmatrix} 2 \\ .9990 \end{bmatrix}$$

$x_2 = 1$ and $x_1 = 1$ (more accurate)

■ **Chapter 13**

Section II

1. The following table is used to summarize the solution process.

Step	XL	XH	XM	F(XM)	|XH − XL|
1	0	1	.5	.127	1
2	.5	1	.75	−.209	.5
3	.5	.75	.625	−.0498	.25
4	.5	.625	.562	+.0371	.125
5	.562	.625	.593	−.00618	.063
6	.562	.593	.577	+.0160	.031
7	.577	.593	.585	+.00490	.016
8	.585	.593	.589	−.000647	.008
9	.585	.589	.587	+.00212	.004
10	.587	.589	.588	+.000739	.002
11	.588	.589	−	−	.001

$$|XH - XL| = .001 < 2\epsilon$$
$$.588 < \text{Root} < .589 \quad \text{or Root} = (XL + XH)/2 = .5885$$

XL—Lower bound of interval
XM—Midpoint of interval
XH—Upper bound of interval
F( )—Function

2. (a)

Step	X1	X2	X3	X4	F(X3)	F(X4)
1	0	5	1.66	3.33	19.4	24.3
2	0	3.33	1.11	2.22	19.0	20.4
3	0	2.22	.740	1.48	19.0	19.2
4	0	1.48	.497	.988	19.2	19.0
5	.494	1.48	.822	1.15	19.0	19.0
6	.494	1.15	.712	.832	19.0	19.0

Due to truncation errors in the computed values of F(X3) and F(X4) after six steps, the next interval [X1, X2] = [.494, .832] will not contain the true minimum (true minimum occurs at x = 1). Thus, further computations will not produce the correct answer.

(b)

Step	X1	X2	X3	X4	F(X3)	F(X4)
1	0	5	1.66667	3.33333	19.4444	24.4444
2	0	3.33333	1.11111	2.22222	19.0123	20.4938
3	0	2.22222	.74074	1.48148	19.0672	19.2318
4	.493827	1.48148	.823045	1.15220	19.0313	19.0231
5	.823045	1.48148	1.04252	1.262	19.0018	19.0686
6	.823045	1.262	.969361	1.11568	19.0009	19.0133
7	.823045	1.11568	.920591	1.01814	19.0063	19.0003
8	.920591	1.11568	.985621	1.05065	19.0002	19.0025
9	.920591	1.05065	.963944	1.0073	19.0013	19.0000
10	.963844	1.05065	—	—	—	—

$$0.963944 < X_{min} < 1.05065, \text{ or } X_{min} \cong \frac{1}{2}(.963944 + 1.05065) = 1.00729$$

3.   Make two changes to the flowchart in Fig. 8-10.

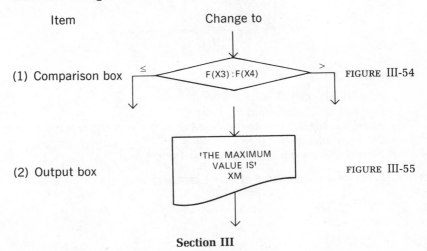

Item	Change to	
(1) Comparison box	$\leq$ F(X3):F(X4) $>$	FIGURE III-54
(2) Output box	'THE MAXIMUM VALUE IS' XM	FIGURE III-55

Section III

1.

Number of intervals N	Rectangular approximation AR	Trapezoidal approximation AT	Parabolic approximation AP
10	.664253	.632647	.667181
50	.638458	.632137	.639128
100	.635280	.632120	.635621

2.

N	AR	AT	AP
10	.285000	.335000	.383333
50	.323399	.333399	.343333
100	.328348	.333348	.333331

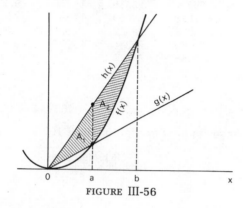

FIGURE III-56

Area $= A_1 + A_2$
$A_1 = A(h(x) - g(x), 0, a, \Delta)$
$A_2 = A(h(x) - f(x), a, b, \Delta)$
where a is the solution to the equation $h(x) = g(x)$ and b is the solution to the equation $h(x) = f(x)$.
Solving the two equations gives $a = 1$ and $b = 2$.

Exact area $=$ Exact area of $A_1 +$ Exact area of A_2
$$= \frac{1}{2} + \frac{1}{3} = \frac{5}{6}$$

Section IV

1.   Computed values of f(t)

t	True value	Δt		
		0.1	0.01	0.001
0	5	5	5	5
0.2	5.18127	5.17236	5.18036	5.18108
0.4	5.32968	5.31347	5.32802	5.32932
0.6	5.45119	5.42900	5.44891	5.45069
0.8	5.55067	5.52359	5.54788	5.55001
1.0	5.63212	5.60104	5.62892	5.63132

index